Some Bodies
The Eucharist and Its Implications

Some Bodies

The Eucharist and Its Implications

Jonathan Bishop

MERCER UNIVERSITY PRESS
Macon, Georgia
•1992•

ISBN 0-86554-401-8

Some Bodies.
The Eucharist and Its Implications.
Copyright ©1993
Mercer University Press, Macon, Georgia 31207 USA
All rights reserved
Printed in the United States of America

The paper used in this publication meets the minimum requirements
of American National Standard for Information Sciences—
Permanence of Paper for Printed Library Materials, ANSI Z39.48

Library of Congress Cataloging-in-Publication Data
Bishop, Jonathan.
Some bodies : the Eucharist and its implications / Jonathan Bishop.
xvi+244pp. 6x9in. (15x23cm.).
Includes bibliographical references.
ISBN 0-86554-401-8 (alk. paper).
1. Lord's Supper. 2. Last Supper.
3. Body, Human—Religious aspects—Christianity.
I. Title.
BV825.2.B554 1992
234'.163—dc20   93-3986
                                                          CIP

Contents

Preface vii

Acknowledgments xv

Abbreviations xvi

Chapter 1
    Eucharistic 1

Chapter 2
    Individual 53

Chapter 3
    Erotic 89

Chapter 4
    Metaphoric 111

Chapter 5
    Communal 149

Chapter 6
    Cosmic 197

*Let us give thanks to the Father
for having made you worthy
to share the lot of the saints
in light.*

*He rescued us
from the power of darkness
and brought us
into the kingdom of his beloved Son.
Through him we have redemption
the forgiveness of our sins.*

*He is the image of the invisible God,
the firstborn of all creatures.
In him everything in heaven and on earth was created,
things visible and invisible;*

*All were created through him;
all were created for him.
He is before all else that is.
In him everything continues in being.*

*It is he who is head of the body, the church!
he who is the beginning,
the firstborn of the dead,
so that primacy may be his in everything.*

*It pleased God to make absolute fullness reside in him
and, by means of him, to reconcile everything in his person,
both on earth and in the heavens,
making peace through the blood of his cross.*

—Colossians 1:12-20
International Committee on English in the Liturgy, 1975

Preface

I need not inform any probable reader of this book that the body has become an occasion for a fair amount of contemporary discussion in more than one context. Prompted to begin with, one imagines, by the feminist revival, this focus for too many collections, conferences, and special issues has attracted support from a variety of other cultural concerns and academic preoccupations. The need for and doubts respecting current forms of solidarity that attract or repel; anxieties attending the sense of isolation and insubstantiality so typical of our transient society; a common distrust for and fascination by this or that erotic hope or fear might all be counted in as contributory. Beneath the more obvious motives, public or personal, one would also need to add a shared fear for the health of the planet as a whole. And in academic or other presumably sophisticated milieux the terror of absence so repeatedly disclosed by this or that skeptical strategy, imaginative or critical or simply fashionable, has not unnaturally stimulated memories and hopes of what some degree of bodiliness, immediate or remote, might yet offer for identity and purpose in life, art, or the accessible future.

The difficulty has regularly been to understand anew what the or any body might in fact amount to; where this should be located with respect to whatever was so evidently *not* bodily; and what about this or that version might or had better not be trusted in. Bryan Turner's comprehensive endeavors at a "sociology of the body" could be taken as one of several representative attempts to situate the claims of bodiliness in the terms provided by an available discipline. He would not, I am sure, be the last to end or begin in what might seem a typical uncertainty: "The body is at once the most solid, the most elusive, illusory, concrete, metaphysical, ever-present, and ever-distant thing—a site, an instrument, an environment, a singularity and a multiplicity."[1] And he—one would have to remember as one estimates the resonance of such a summary—is concerned only with what I shall be calling the natural or individual body as this confronts the social order. If other kinds and conflicts are counted in, the puzzle could only complicate.

That other modes of bodiliness beside the "biological"—if the term is still permitted—need to be distinguished is accordingly one purpose of this argument. The prevalent disposition to reaffirm the natural body should not obscure the erotic

---

[1] Bryan S. Turner, *The Body and Society: Explorations in Social Theory* (Oxford: Blackwell, 1984) 8.

or imaginative investments that this is bound to attract, either of which might better therefore be separated out for independent attention. Nor would it be possible to exclude the social or even cosmic overtones from any serious preoccupation with the motif. Aesthetic and communal bodies have both found themselves subject to violent criticism, practical or theoretical, in this century; so much the more reason, one may feel in response, to offer these species sufficient room for independent consideration. There should then be opportunities to clarify the interrelationships among the modes of bodiliness and perhaps as well the limits of any claims founded on one or another of them. *To be in touch,* as we most properly put it, or *to make contact with* the truth of the matter (or entertain the alternative fictions) is in virtually any context to find ourselves within or near some body, whether we consent or protest. If so, it could never seem irrelevant to reexplore one or another aspect or effect of so inescapable a condition.

This study might then be distinguished in the first place as allowing deliberate scope for the several kinds of body. But it would still more obviously stand out among most other recent inquiries by putting first not the natural or even the symbolic but what by explicit contrast would need to rank as the eschatological instance. To begin with what I shall intermittently be calling the eucharistic body would not only presume at least an implicit declaration of faith but must also make a continuing difference to the way in which any subsequent discussion deals with the other species of bodiliness.

The reasons for such a choice need not be identified as exclusively religious. It should not take long before any inquiry into the "problematic" of the body would find itself within the range of the possibility in question—if only as an idol to be overthrown or interpreted away. Jesus' determination at the Last Supper (assuming, as the world has in effect agreed to do, its essential historicity) has in practice, deliberate or unconscious, provided a model for the place and value of bodiliness in all the other contexts therein presupposed or invoked. To appreciate what could have been or may yet be intended by this frankly apocalyptic moment is accordingly crucial (in at least a double sense) to evaluating subsequent ideas of the "corporate" life, in or out of declared ecclesial communities, as well as whatever might be presupposed by the idea of art (or the symbolic generally) in our culture. In too many ways our sense also of the individual or natural body has found itself influenced by, even if not some direct metamorphosis of, the "supernatural" in one or another of its variants—of which the eucharistic action would appear an otherwise unidentifiable source.

The initial and in due course general thesis of this book could in consequence begin as an answer to the question that has regularly troubled more than one professional student of the immediate problem. In the opening sentence of his own preface to a review of recent scholarship on Jesus and the Kingdom of God, G. R. Beasley-Murray observes that "the twentieth century has been marked from its outset, and is likely so to continue to its close, by an uncertainty as to who Jesus was."[2] Helmut Koester begins a section of the second volume of his equally up-to-date introduction to the New Testament with a similar remark: "It is difficult to find categories by which the ministry of Jesus can be correctly described."[3] Ernst Haenchen, a still better-known commentator on one of these texts, finds himself puzzled "that the Christian faith is dated from Easter forward and that it is yet indivisibly connected with the preacher from Galilee who was crucified in Jerusalem."[4] The eschatological body is the latent answer to the question all but patent in these sufficiently indicative and certainly respectable complaints. But if *the* body is the answer, then the key event in which this is indeed disclosed would have to be the moment in which Jesus not merely said whatever he had to say or did what he took it upon himself to do but communicated the very identity that had brought these about. What we somewhat patronizingly call the Last Supper would then become not only a penultimate but the climactic deed for this particular agent, the action in terms of which all the others, past or future, attributable or projected, would need to be weighed—the completion, one could therefore say, of an obviously exceptional career.

The task following any such demonstration would be to connect what is proposed as the central case with modernity. The Eucharist must in principle already be—and has in practice often enough actually been—at the center of any specifically Christian idea of community, marriage, or the value of life, not to mention (for the first generation at least) the creation, the Parousia, and the relation to the Jews. Any of these issues that became troublesome had accordingly to be resolved after some fashion that could be felt to rhyme with whatever took place within the typical celebration—or be realized in proportion as for the time being at least irreducible. But what is formally required within "Christianity" would also have to prove rediscoverable outside it if the option in question is to seem plausible. The modern, like the Gentile *oikoumenē* once upon a time, would need to be weighed not just as a programmatic opposite but as an anticipation or echo of the central event—and therefore an opportunity for continuous reinterpretation.

The review of the several contexts that follow a reformulation of the principal instance must attend accordingly to the more obvious modes of what a Paulinist could call the "body of Adam" as opposed to the "body of Christ." The individual body naturally comes first, followed by the erotic and then the symbolic. Each of these offers opportunities for elaboration but, on the scale of the whole, they amount to successive parentheses on the way to the communal body, the chances for which

---

[2] G. R. Beasley-Murray, *Jesus and the Kingdom of God* (Grand Rapids: Eerdmans, 1986).
[3] Helmut Koester, *History and Literature of Early Christianity,* vol. 2 of *Introduction to the New Testament* (Philadelphia: Fortress; New York: de Gruyter, 1982) 77.
[4] Ernst Haenchen, *A Commentary on the Gospel of John, Chapters 7–21,* trans. Robert W. Funk, ed. Robert W. Funk and Ulrich Busse, Hermeneia (Philadelphia: Fortress, 1984) 139.

must stand out as imperative from any perspective that has already committed itself to the primary instance. The argument is brought to a close with an excursus on the cosmic possibility, these days already a popular topic, but in any case also called for as a conclusion by the beginning chosen.

The last two options also provide openings to question the scope of the two principal "anti-bodies" of this age: textuality and objectivity. The first of these may most appropriately be addressed in terms of the biblical examples. *The* "book," after all, remains an obvious test case for such latter-day oppositions as voice and text, society and community, identity and relation, or the literal and the symbolic. The relevant biblical instance will also appear in connection with the cosmic possibility. But here the alternative or Greek (and therefore modern) strategy must also be addressed, and what will be called the cognitive paradigm situated with respect to the corresponding mode of the body. In all these instances, it will be presumed as well as argued, the fact of our starting point is bound to offer a constant opportunity to rediscover within what could otherwise seem at best a transcendable moment some latent manifestations of what could still be identified as the eschatological possibility. If the body of Christ *is* at all, we need not be altogether surprised if the several Adamic bodies "are" too, after some appropriately parabolic fashion.

All this makes for an unwieldy undertaking, which has had to be worked out within painfully specifiable limits, generic and individual. The task assumed has had to be carried out not by a systematic theologian—on the grounds of which speciality I have been warned I am trespassing—nor even by a formally recognized scholar of either the biblical or philosophical issues addressed, but simply one more practitioner within the humanities. Hence to begin with, perhaps, the reliance on personal anecdote at what is hoped will not seem oppressive intervals, wishing thereby not to advance but avoid egotism. The accidents of professional practice have still more obviously supplied some of the literary instances advanced. But here too I have often been reminded of other cases that might demonstrate even better one or another aspect of the case: Ovid, for instance, or Goethe. The movement from the experiential to the verbal body should emerge from the instances offered well enough to demonstrate the trajectory any argument of the kind proposed would need to trace.

Throughout I have also been made aware of the historical differences between what is sometimes called a "classic" study of this or that author or topic and the more recent and usually denser labor of the contemporary academy. This distinction has as often reminded me of my own membership in a professional cohort now irresistibly identifiable as previous to that which is currently still ascendant. Such a predicament cannot seem argumentatively irrelevant either: temporality is one more aspect of the larger question addressed as well as another personal limit. But there could also be a "theoretical" advantage, in both the current and ancient senses of that term. For I hope among other expectations to carry one of the more formidable intentions explicit in most recent "critiques" to what could in Kierkegaardian language be identified as the second power. "Deconstruction" is by now virtually a popular metaphor, but its serious function (if that too remains an applicable trope) has repeatedly been to anatomize the specious body wherever this might be found, leaving "the text" behind as what remains to be taken as real, whether this is literal or social. When I propose as the next step on any critical agenda an ideal reduction if not quite elimination of this equivocal nonentity, I need not claim that to adventure as much as seems invited anyway will be completed altogether on my own. I would rather suggest in fact that this always potential result has as a matter of fact already been accomplished in another style, which is part of what *eschatological* would have to mean.

Meanwhile a parenthetic or embolic style of argument means that any local question is addressed only at whatever length seems minimally necessary for the immediate case. So the sequence as a whole may appear alternately to leap ahead or dawdle in and out of the notes, if not quite to digress altogether. I hope better-instructed readers will be able to amplify or resist as they go, supplying whatever seems missing out of their own resources. The several authorities whose views may be roughly summarized in a paragraph or referred to even more slightingly in a footnote should also be understood throughout as representing styles or methods of approach to their respective topics. I need not pretend to be making an exhaustive report on any of the "fields" so irregularly trespassed upon. There is always more to learn; other moments to appreciate if not include; additional information to seek out and respond to. So one necessarily breaks off rather than properly finishes.

To admit limits, though, would not mean abandoning ambition, which in this case includes a wish to reflect some light on a variety of topics connected with the principal theme. But the first intention is simply to affirm the radicality of the motif as such. *The* body, or *a* body, or *some* body is always what there is to discover: that I inhabit one, to begin with; that I am not alone in this respect, a moment or two after; that what grows around me is of one gender rather than the other, somewhat later. The symbolic or communal or cosmic variants are apt to stem from comparatively adult intuitions, if we allow ourselves to trust any of these at all, though families and gravity are elementary facts of life, and representation is already indispensable to play. Meanwhile too the continuing difference between *a* and *the* body, or the initial and the terminal, must remain an ambiguity even when it does not become a problem.

To remember representation brings me to another proposition I wish to underline. The body is what may be discovered; and what we find the body up to, proximate or ultimate, is reproducing itself. That the body reproduces itself could seem a banality rather than a mystery, but even the bare formulation should help justify subsequent efforts to appreciate how many distinguishable sorts of replication should be understood as included. Clearly *reproduction* could have almost as many synonyms as contexts within which something like the event in question might be encountered. *Representation,* however prominent of late, is only one among these. *Repetition,* the very principle of "textuality" of any kind, is very evidently another. *Recovery* and *rehearsal* would add two obvious dimensions of temporality. *Rhythm* must be counted in as soon as language too becomes bodily. The "m" series—memory, mimicry, and mimesis—would nickname large regions of potentially relevant inquiry. And among these *anamnesis* is already the term of order within the liturgical context with which we begin.

The double claim that the body is there to be discovered, and discovered most completely as reproducing itself, amounts to an admission that what is sought in this (as in other projects of the kind) is one more approach to what in the cosmological context can frankly be called a theory of *everything*. A slightly more modest and perhaps more exact metaphor is supplied from the computer world, which often seeks a "very wide instruction word" that can be made to set off several processes at once. A sufficiently traditional single term that has occupied this role in the past, ancient or recent, is *Being*, with or without capital letters or quotation marks; and *ousia* or *substantia* or *Sein,* unapologetic or "under erasure," will indeed appear at intervals in the course of this argument. To be sure, any such possibility has itself been repeatedly denied. The well-known feminist critic Toril Moi, for instance, puts what has become a conventional wisdom with respect to these matters as neatly as anyone. There is in language, she agrees with the relevant authority, "no final element, no fundamental unit, no *transcendental signified* that is meaningful in itself and thus escapes the ceaseless interplay of linguistic deferral and difference. The free play of signifiers will never yield a final, unified meaning that in turn might ground and explain all the others." For Moi, any "metaphysical essentialism" that would claim such a meaning must derive from patriarchy, which is to say, from "the phallus."[5] With this addition she shifts her antecedent from Derrida to Lacan; but would not the latter, an outsider to both these allegiances might be entitled to observe, advance (or betray) yet another version of the master word indeed that the former has so notoriously rendered dubious? We have many names for the Name, including those that dare appear only in the negative. But the body, our first instance would suggest of itself, is perhaps the most formidable of these, even or especially for those who must refuse either the possibility in general or this type of them all in particular.

In confronting such "discourse" one would wish not merely to offer some nostalgic reconstruction of what has in fact been duly disassembled. What does seem possible though, indeed invited, is a resituation of the elements in question, so that what is obviously *not* the body, whether explicitly linguistic or not, might also fall into place as a reduction or an ascesis, positive or negative, collective or critical, contemporary or antique, in advance though not necessarily in prevention of—however frequently in apparent contradiction to—the inevitably eschatological presence of whatever may be announced by the chosen word. And if the *logos* in question has already been identified with the *sōma,* then even a critical repetition

---

[5]Toril Moi, *Sexual/Textual Politics: Feminist Literary Theory* (London: Methuen, 1985) 9n.

of "body" should retain its usefulness as a name for the unnamable along with all the others.

In any case, movements still more recent than the one that initiated the critique just glanced at could remind us that others as well have begun to seek out if not alternatives to at least supplements for and so perhaps advances upon what can seem to have become all too repeatable a strategy. Any likely reader of this project will already be aware of so many of these efforts as have sought to reground the linguistic in the social, not to say the historical or even the ethical. Such shifts of opinion and method, and therefore of expectation and concern, might indicate a degree of recovery from whatever has proved merely automatic about the "orthodox" varieties of commentary in and out of literature as an institution. Such a reader is obviously apt to have found him or herself too within the academy, that Solomon's portico of our day, where opinion, whether constrained or free, is apt to be as chaotic as it is overdetermined. So I need not anticipate more than a rough overlap of experience or acquaintanceship, though a certain curiosity is obviously presumed. We are all, it has been easy to confess, equipped and limited in unpredictable ways. What I do expect is some recognition of what has clearly become a common need. As Odo Casel once observed of the "mystery" he would later be credited with reviving a stronger sense of in its liturgical form, "Everything we say of it will fall short of the mark; but just because it is ineffable, there is always occasion for saying something about it."[6] The thought must have encouraged others before me.

On my desk rests a pale stone, which others who have traveled to the place where it was found should have no difficulty recognizing, if only by color, as a memorial of Jerusalem. It is my piece of the rock, which I picked up, some years ago, from a path under the walls of the Old City. It has been used often to weigh down one or another pile of such sheets of paper as this book has been made up of as it was assembled from scattered notes into a consecutive text. Perhaps it might stand rather better than most of the words these final sheets are now imprinted with for the subject I have all the time been pursuing—or which has been after me. There is always, it is fair to suggest in advance and perhaps assert in conclusion as well, no more than one thing to say—if only this could get said.

But a stone is probably too inanimate a figure to supply metaphoric closure, even for a preface. Let me compensate for its too-obvious objectivity with another image, which might seem merely self-indulgent. As I labored over one more version of a chapter in this apparently endless project, a bizarre accident occurred: climbing the stairs to my office, I stumbled and fell upon my hand against a step in such a

---

[6]Odo Casel, *The Mystery of Christian Worship* (Westminster MD: Newman, 1962) 7. The movement beginning with this Benedictine monk at Maria Laach in the early twenties has since borne ambiguous fruit in Catholic and other practice. But we can still realize what he hoped for.

way that one of the set of keys I had got out was braced upright. Its tip punctured the flesh between palm and thumb, opening a coarse hole. I could scarcely believe such an event had occurred: how could a key become so firmly propped, or its blunt end penetrate instead of slipping? But so it did, forcing a gap beneath a layer of flesh. The flow of blood seemed sufficient to cleanse the wound and quickly stopped once the flap was pushed back, so I calculated I need not seek first aid or walk home early. My hand, though, felt the shock and could not be written with for some time.

The next morning as I lay in bed, a sentence formed in my mind. "The door to the body is open." It seemed an answer to the question posed so awkwardly by this minor accident. I did not need a "key" to unlock even my own body in its gradual decline, if this event was one more piece of evidence to that effect, or any other body either. The door to the body was open. I already was that door, I could also think; or more generally, any natural body, my own or some other, was a door to the body indeed—like the Eucharist, with which this book begins or the idea of the One, with which it ends—and so in proportion even the book itself, for its author and perhaps some other as well. The door to the body is open. That is what I wished were true; but perhaps it was true anyway, and I need not have worried, however often I stumbled, physically or otherwise. One may pass through at any time.

Acknowledgments

Let me offer separate thanks here to some who have tried to make up for one or another deficiency or limit of this project. Sheldon Flory, an old friend in these as in so many matters, has most usefully reviewed two important chapters. John and Julia Gatta have offered helpful responses to the initial thesis. Coraleen Rooney has indefatigably repeated all these words, over and over, with a good-humored tenacity I much admire. Craig Noll and Susan Carini have helped prepare the text for publication. And others have contributed more casually as the gist of the argument advanced has been presented on this or that occasion.

Jonathan Bishop
Ithaca, New York

Abbreviations

AAR	*Journal of the American Academy of Religion*
AAS	*Acta apostolicae sedis*
BibRev	*Bible Review*
BSac	*Bibliotheca Sacra*
BTB	*Biblical Theology Bulletin*
CBQ	*Catholic Biblical Quarterly*
ITQ	*Irish Theological Quarterly*
JBL	*Journal of Biblical Literature*
LS	*Louvain Studies*
NovT	*Novum Testamentum*
NTS	*New Testament Studies*
PG	J. Migne, *Patrologia graeca*
PL	J. Migne, *Patrologia latina*

Chapter 1

Eucharistic

So Joshua took all of the land, according to all that the Lord had said to Moses; and Joshua gave it as an inheritance to Israel according to their divisions, by their tribes, and the land had peace from war. —Joshua 11:23

Structural

"This is my body," says someone. And presently the same person says, or almost says, "This is my blood." What is going on? The action in question has been repeated as the heart of Christian worship since the beginning, a cause of edification and scandal, joy and violence, celebration and denial. And through all this considerable time it has provided, more or less consciously, a model in terms of which a variety of other activities, imaginative or political, have been understood. So it could never seem out of place to think through once again what might be happening, either on the original or any subsequent occasion, and to follow out some of the implications for other matters, near or far.

A convenient point at which to start would be not the content but the form of the action.[1] A proposition is offered that declares an identity: in the first place between the person speaking and a pair of elements referred to by the demonstrative pronouns—a loaf of bread and a cup of wine. This set of foods, solid and liquid, everyday and holiday, is asserted to be, for the purpose at hand, coincident with a

---

[1] My focus on the structure of the act determines which authorities have contributed most to the argument that follows. Among the traditional figures Paul counts for more than Aquinas, as will shortly become evident. The two persistent modern influences here have been Joachim Jeremias, *The Eucharistic Words of Jesus* (New York: Scribner's, 1966) and John A. T. Robinson, *The Body: A Study in Pauline Theology,* Studies in Biblical Theology 5 (London: SCM Press, 1952), though specific elements of both would require adjustment in the light of more recent scholarship. It has also been a pleasure to reread Gregory Dix's classic *Shape of the Liturgy* (Westminster: Dacre, 1945) and to work through Xavier Léon-Dufour's sensitive and thorough *Le Partage du Pain Eucharistique* (Paris: Seuil, 1982), now translated as *Sharing the Eucharistic Bread* (New York: Paulist, 1986). Jerome Kodell's *Eucharist in the New Testament* (Wilmington: Glazier, 1988) provides a convenient review of recent German and American scholarship. The revival of what is now called "Jesus Research" has unfortunately contributed little to any resolution of the problem addressed.

previous set from a different context, the "body" and "blood" of the person speaking. "Body and blood," though, might sound discordant as a rendering of this contrast. A more likely pair of opposites in English, at least, would be flesh and blood, a duality that has equivalents both in Greek (*sarx kai haima*), and Hebrew (*basar v' dam*). Among the New Testament authors, John does in fact employ the word *sarx* rather than *sōma* ("body") in a verse (John 6:51) that evidently alludes to the action in question. It accordingly would be tempting to agree immediately with Joachim Jeremias, the father of modern scholarship on this topic, that the Hebrew (or Aramaic) equivalent of "flesh" may well have been the original expression employed, for which the apparently less scandalous "body" would have become an early substitute. In that case we would be able to reserve *sōma* for the whole made up by the combination of flesh and blood together, as Paul in fact already encourages us to do and as Bultmann and Robinson, among the moderns, have influentially argued.

To be sure, scholarly objections have been raised more recently, most notably by Robert H. Gundry, who argues that *sōma* retains too much of its primary sense of concrete physicality to serve easily as an equivalent for "identity" or "person" and so for any ideal whole.[2] Gundry, though, concentrates on the "physical," that is, the individual instance, where "body" and "flesh" are indeed likely to coincide. The ritual or erotic or imaginative or communal varieties of *sōma* seem to him merely metaphoric. Paul is clearly less narrowly focused. His letters to the Corinthians presume an eschatological *sōma* that might be composed of several different kinds of *sarx*: bread and wine, to start with, but also the male and female bodies of a married pair, or the members of an ecclesial community, together with their houses and equipment. So he is obliged to press whatever may have been the potential of the term within his culture to intimate the whole as opposed to a part as far as he can. In this way he begins the process that Jeremias and Bultmann and Robinson are carrying on—and against which Gundry is reacting.

This scholarly controversy exposes the absence of a completely unobjectionable term for the whole in any context—including, to begin with, the agent of this action. There is no one word that will quite do in any of the relevant languages. We can use *body* in English only with qualifications, of which Gundry's philological objections will not be the last. The term resists, for instance, including whatever we also mean by soul or person. Yet the event in question clearly does not leave that ele-

---

[2]Already we are drawn aside to an apparently technical problem; they are hard to avoid. The history of the contest between "body" and "flesh" in modern scholarship is summarized by Robert H. Gundry in his Σῶμα *in Biblical Theology with Emphasis on Pauline Anthropology,* SNTSMS 29 (Cambridge: Cambridge University Press, 1976) 3-8. Léon-Dufour reviews the problem in his *Le Partage du Pain,* 139-43; and Joseph A. Fitzmyer, in his *Gospel according to Luke 10-24,* AB 28A (Garden City NY: Doubleday, 1985) 1399, counters Gundry with some uses of *sōma* that mean "self" not only in the New Testament but also in other Greek texts.

ment out, even if what it might consist of in this case remains problematic. The semantic deficiency, though, however intriguing in its own right—Why don't we have such a word?—need not interfere with a fair appreciation of the action we are concerned with. For the polarity of flesh and blood, or even "body" and blood, will evidently serve of itself to evoke the whole, whether or not a sufficient name for this can be found. At each stage the deed in question enacts what in terms of Greek rhetoric would be called a *merismos,* or that which combines opposites, *ta enantia,* so as to communicate an entirety otherwise inexpressible. Such redefinitions by polarity also occur in biblical Hebrew.[3] In this way difference, "incorporated" within the structure of the symbol, evaporates between the sign and its meaning. Form becomes content, and representation, re-presentation. This advantage too seems intended.

Whether we should understand the predicate of the first proposition as "body" or "flesh" is one problem that interrupts as we attend to the form of the action. A second uncertainty hovers over the corresponding element in the second proposition. Two versions in the written sources, 1 Corinthians and Luke, employ circumlocutions that seem to register a degree of embarrassment at the simplicity of an outright identification. They offer instead a more elaborate formulation that links "this cup" with "the new covenant in my blood." But Mark, and Matthew after him (though with additions of his own), repeat what once again it seems easiest to propose as original because at once most direct and coincident with formal expectation: "This is my blood." Let me accordingly offer a matching pair of propositions, amounting in English to "This is my flesh" and "This is my blood," as best reproducing the intention presupposed by the structure of the action as that may now be recovered in ritual, imagination, or hypothesis.[4]

Such a pair of parallel formulae would evidently echo the traditional pattern of Hebrew poetry. And it would accord well with the shape of a Passover meal.[5] In

---

[3]A. M. Honeyman, *"Merismos* in Biblical Literature," JBL 71 (1952): 11-18. The role of polarity has been familiar since G. E. R. Lloyd's classic *Polarity and Analogy* (Cambridge: Cambridge University Press, 1971).

[4]The argument here follows Jeremias. Objections have since been raised to the conclusion that the simplest formulations would have obtained on the original occasion. In his *Supper of the Lord* (Philadelphia: Fortress, 1985), John Reumann offers a recent review of these, mentioning Roth, Bornkamm, Aulen, and Braun. It has been one of the oddities of the scholarly tradition to assume that a formal parallelism between the bread and wine words would be the product of liturgical development rather than original pronouncement. It seems easier to suppose that the additions, substitutions, and grammatical irregularities in the texts are the result of ecclesial efforts to assimilate the memorial, covenantal, and sacrificial motifs that had come to seem essential than to attribute any of these to the founder. Who would be more likely to value simplicity at such a moment, the church or Jesus?

[5]The authorities continue of more than one mind as to whether the supper was or was not a seder. Gordon Bahr's "Seder of Passover and the Eucharistic Words," NovT 12 (1970):

that ceremony, bread is broken and distributed at the beginning of the meal to the accompaniment of the appropriate blessing. A cup of wine is similarly blessed and passed at the conclusion. The ritual of the day also supplies a precedent that the former if not the latter element in what thus becomes a pair is explicitly interpreted. This would supply an immediate model for the parabolic extrapolation upon which Jesus embarks, very much in his usual style. In a Semitic language the propositions offered would take shape still more abruptly than in Greek, Latin, or English as a demonstrative pronoun verblessly juxtaposed to a noun equipped with a possessive suffix. But in any language the effect is the same: one pair of contrasting units, flesh and blood, is affirmed as identical for the purpose at hand with another pair, bread and wine. So far at least—it seems fair to conclude—so good.

The next step would be to understand how the person announcing these propositions would intend the contrast they begin by presuming. For an ordinary human being there is no problem. Flesh and blood are simply equivalent to body and soul, flesh and bones, *sarx* and either *psychē, nous,* or *esō anthrōpos*—each pair amounting to a dual formula for the whole individual. And Jesus is, to begin with, an ordinary man. By dividing himself into his own flesh and blood in this limited sense, he would seem to be proposing himself in advance as a sacrifice, which physically effects just such a division between these "halves" of the victim. And if the Last Supper was indeed a Passover, the *un*remarked presence of the lamb on the table might have served to confirm such an understanding of the difference presumed, for that creature had already suffered a ritual separation of flesh from blood. If human flesh and human blood together compose the whole identity of the person speaking, then by directing his disciples to consume the bread and the wine with which these contrasting elements of himself had been successively identified, Jesus would have been inviting them to participate in a prophetic interpretation of the suffering he anticipated for the morrow. He would, that is, have been asking them to join him in a sacrifice for sin, either as fellow victims—if matters fell out so—or as beneficiaries of the action thereby accomplished. Such an understanding of the scope and significance of the initial contrast, and therefore of the intention behind the redefinition itself, would presume that Jesus had already accepted and meant to apply a sacrificial understanding of his death that was presently to become normative in the community.

But Jesus would also have to be understood as understanding himself not just as an ordinary man but as extraordinary, an individual endowed by the Spirit of God for a unique task. The role of victim is essentially negative, and special rather by selection than by character. But his conduct through what we can learn of the ministry would clearly show that Jesus believed himself exceptionally authorized to manifest and distribute the power of the one he is represented as calling *Abba*. The

---

181-202, can represent the "festive meal" alternative, which has since become popular. As with other issues, I assume, with Jeremias, the simpler case.

titles employed within the community after the fact to distinguish this aspect of his identity might not all have seemed acceptable to him without ironic qualification—with the possible exception of "Son of Man." But that he presumed himself uniquely distinguished from other human beings as the chosen representative of God seems undeniable.[6]

In that case, the contrast presupposed by the double proposition would need to be read in an expanded sense as well, so as to embrace what would thereby become the all-important remainder of the identity presumed. The ordinary human being, including both "body" and "soul," would then have to be ranked together as amounting to the flesh of another and broader version of the initial polarity, so as to free the blood to represent not just the vitality or interiority of one more creature but the Spirit of the Lord indeed. As usual in biblical poetry, sequence enacts hierarchy: that which comes after either intensifies or goes beyond whatever has come before—in the case now proposed, absolutely.[7] By predefining himself as divided into flesh and blood in this unlimited sense, Jesus would then be redefining himself by way of the propositions offered not only as a sacrifice (for that meaning might very well continue as included) but as a gift. And the Passover lamb, not just as ritually slaughtered but also as roasted and served for all to consume, could then serve to reinforce this second version of the difference as well as the first.

The bread at the beginning of the meal would also underscore this difference, as soon as we realize that the sense given it within the traditional Passover interpretation as the bread of *affliction,* which without change suits the sacrificial understanding, would in this further interpretation become instead a taste of the world to come. In that case the Passover celebrated just after the Jordan was crossed under the first Joshua, when the manna ceased and the corn of the land was first eaten, might serve as a suitable scriptural antecedent (Josh. 5:10-12). The command to drink at the close of the meal would serve this purpose still more emphatically. For only if the blood does indeed reproduce the Spirit could it have become right to consume it. The blood of a sacrifice, after all, should only be poured out at the foot of the altar. To drink *that* would be an abomination.

The paired propositions would still amount to a reconstitution of the initiating identity—understood now in an enlarged sense as a new configuration of equivalent elements. As the man Jesus of Nazareth is to the Spirit of God, we would then be able to say, so flesh is to blood; and therefore this bread must be to this wine. The translation throughout would still be complete and without remainder, according to

---

[6] Any diagnosis of Jesus' intention can profit from the recent explosion of interest in what used to be called the "historical Jesus." My argument here presumes a reading of such authorities as Beasley-Murray, Borg, Charlesworth, Flack, Fredericksen, Freyne, Harvey, Hengel, Horsley, Meier, Meyer, Perrin, Sanders, and Vermes.

[7] James Kugel and Robert Alter, two recent authorities on the genre, would agree on this much, though not with each other. The controversy is reviewed by John Gammie, "Alter vs. Kugel—Taking the Heat in Struggle over Biblical Poetry," *BibRev* 5/1 (Feb. 1989): 26-33.

the usual rule for polarities. The appointed set of symbols would accordingly continue to embody the whole of the larger identity presumed. Nothing would be held back or left out. For what is transmitted in any such double proposition is not just the content of the signs, however this may be understood, but the contrastive pattern itself—which, as we have observed, would guarantee the integrity of everything entrusted to it.

We now arrive at the third "moment" in the communicative process that begins with Jesus and moves on to the bread and the wine. The double message, or step two, is only briefly in existence. For the bread and the wine are almost immediately consumed by those to whom they are offered. If the identifications proposed are understood in the second or expanded sense just outlined, the recipients would then be obliged to realize themselves too as changed in proportion. Their own identities, or rather their shared identity as a community, would as a result be redefined as completely as the food and drink. Now they too would need to understand themselves as consisting not just of so much "flesh"—which would have to include whatever they had hitherto supposed themselves to be, either as so many individuals or as a set of disciples—but also as incorporating besides a new and extraordinary "blood," the very Spirit of the same God who had, they already believed, in some extraordinary fashion empowered their leader. To eat the bread would in that case be to acknowledge themselves from then on as the eschatological successors of the man addressing them—but on the new scale of a community instead of as an individual. And to drink the wine would be to receive the same authorization they had come to recognize and depend on in him—in order to continue his work for what remained of the future. By "taking in" the message as a whole, then, its recipients would in effect become a new version of the one who transmitted it to them, another mode of the identity in question as absolutely different as the medium was from either him or them, yet at the same time as absolutely the same. For if he could be the bread and the wine, they could become him in proportion. The first metamorphosis would entail the second—provided the initial identity is understood in the larger as well as the narrower sense of what we could then most properly call the body of Christ indeed.

To understand the action in so inclusive a way though is to enter a zone of theological as well as scholarly controversy. Must what has since come to be called the "Church," or the community that is implied by a reception of the elements understood in this larger (and so most thoroughly sacramental) sense, indeed be the "body of Christ" without qualification? Would not such an interpretation dangerously overprivilege her members—or even impugn the celestial authority of her risen master? Throughout the tradition there have occasionally been advances toward such a radical understanding of the action. But these have as regularly been followed by qualifications and retreats even among the strongest champions of the familiar Pauline expression. The issue is evidently of some importance. How high an identity does the community have a right to claim? It could seem as if the inheritance with which she may in fact have been endowed in this testamentary action were rather too much for the actual heirs, who have therefore been inclined to withdraw, usually without quite knowing it, into less overwhelming notions of their common identity.

The safest and most persistent way out offered by the tradition has been a retreat to a strictly sacrificial understanding of the original contrast. This option has been made easier by the narrative accounts of the Last Supper, where such an interpretation is already built into the language assigned to Jesus. An expiatory understanding of what thereby becomes "the passion" rapidly became normative for the traditions concerned, which would naturally enough have presumed that Jesus must have intended to anticipate just such a definition of his death on the previous night. The phrases employed in the versions of the rite repeating the supper from which the authors of the several narratives would have drawn their terminology accordingly rehearse a sacrificial understanding of what must have been going on. In Mark this is secured by adding the phrase "which is poured out for many" to the wine word, which has also acquired a covenantal reference (Mark 14:24). In Matthew a further phrase, "for forgiveness of sins," additionally specifies an expiatory intention (Matt. 26:28). In Luke the bread word too acquires the phrase "which is given for you" (Luke 22:19). These narrative renderings, in turn accepted by the Church at large, would have reinforced the influence of their liturgical sources and so confirmed a propitiatory understanding of the continuing ritual as well as of the founding event.

The earliest and perhaps most determinative single verse in the New Testament for a sacrificial interpretation is probably 1 Corinthians 11:26, which reminds the delinquent members of that community that as often as they eat the bread and drink the cup, "they proclaim the Lord's death until he comes." This instruction appears to support the idea that sharing in the food and wine amounts to a participation in the human body and blood as offered up. If so, we might understand Paul as having supplied a key formula to which all the others in Scripture and later doctrine might be reduced. But in fact the rhetorical context of this reminder would also allow for a reading that would in effect presume the latent presence of an additional phrase, as so often in a Pauline argument. He is rebuking the congregation for their selfishness and disorder, which prevents them from recognizing the true supper of the Lord in the midst of their own separate meals. They do not sufficiently respect what is presupposed by the privilege they enjoy, a sacrifice that should always provide the model for their personal conduct. As often as you eat and drink, Paul would then be saying, you implicitly take for granted the death of the Lord—as well as explicitly enjoy the fruits of his resurrection, upon which you too easily and casually depend. So behave accordingly: the End is still ahead.

That the primary meaning of communion for Paul was rather positive than negative would be confirmed by a passage earlier in the same letter where the contrast is not between respectful and rude conduct within the congregation but between the Church as a whole and those who share in idolatrous worship. "The cup of blessing which we bless, is it not a sharing in the blood of Christ? The bread which we break, is it not a sharing in the body of Christ? Because there is one loaf of bread, we are though many one body, for all partake of the one loaf" (1 Cor. 10:16-17). The community is the product of communion, that is, and both must be positive because both are created by the Spirit of God and not some demon. The cross is for Paul a moral prerequisite for an authentic enjoyment of the privileges of the resurrection among all Christians, as it once was for their Lord. But it is not as such among these. That would be bad, not good news.

But these considerations did not arise as the sacrificial interpretation took hold. As this view became normative, it inevitably produced the idea that at the supper Jesus must have been "offering" his body and blood (in the limited sense thereby assumed) to the Father rather than delivering these (in the expanded sense) to his companions. The judgment not unnaturally followed that what Jesus transmitted to his followers was not his full identity but simply his intention to perform a sacrifice, so his disciples might in turn repeat the action he initiated. The supposition that the eucharistic action was essentially cultic would have determined that the officer presiding would in due course become a "priest" and the table on which the food and drink rested an "altar." What else does a priest do, after all, but perform sacrifices? The ritual reproduction of the original event would thus have become not just a replacement for analogous pagan ceremonies but a successor to the temple cult. The *dis*advantages of defining an eschatological action in priestly and therefore essentially this-worldly terms need not have been felt.[8]

A key source for this development is the Letter to the Hebrews, which, from the already traditional doctrine that Jesus was an expiatory sacrifice, extrapolates the conclusion that he must also be the ultimate high priest as well as the victim. The references are multiple, and the moral consequences for this author's addressees insistent. Hebrews 6:19-20 and 7:3 in particular imply in addition that Jesus' priesthood should be understood as "forever," after the model of Melchizedek, and 7:24-25 affirms that he is continuously interceding in heaven on behalf of all believers. Hebrews 8:2-3 situates this constant sacrifice in a celestial "tent," though later references at 10:12 and 12:2 repeat the older idea that Jesus is sitting on a throne awaiting the moment of return, which is at least imaginatively in some conflict with the priestly conception. We are able to participate in this heavenly and therefore unceasing sacrifice, the author claims, by our own "sacrifice of praise" and good works (13:15-16).

When the problem of the real presence came to the fore, this conception of an eternal heavenly sacrifice proved useful, for it provided a means to resolve the implicit contradiction between the idea that each Eucharist was a reenactment of the passion, which by then seemed indispensable, and the equally important belief that the body present in the species must be that of the risen Jesus. If the sacrifice was perpetually continued before the Father in heaven by the resurrected Son, it would

---

[8]The development of a "priesthood" practicing a new cult is reviewed in Bernard Cooke, *Ministry to Word and Sacrament* (Philadelphia: Fortress, 1976) 537-47.

be possible to understand his exalted humanity as descending upon earthly altars without the embarrassment of supposing, as popular legend occasionally did, that the flesh and blood of a crucified man were somehow concealed behind the bread and wine, through which disguise they might now and then manifest themselves. The subtler difficulty that this solution involved assigning what must remain the all-too-human act of sacrifice to the divine side of the relation was not, as far as I know, felt as itself in need of explanation.

If the rite, then, is understood as reenacting both the original *and* an eternal sacrifice, and this rite is directed, as such an action would have to be, to God rather than to the congregation, it follows that participation must take the form of sharing in the offering by supplying the elements and by faith, that is, by a vicarious identification with what the priest is doing. In that case, communion is in no danger of becoming an appropriation for the current human context of the power of God indeed. It remains an individual adherence to the ongoing sacrificial intention. The properly sacramental potential of the action would then be realized not directly in the consumption of the species but in the "graces" each participant might expect to receive in proportion to the disposition shown. If the action repeated is an expiatory sacrifice, the chief of these benefits would be forgiveness of sin, other things being equal. An individual moral participation in the End, then, would still remain possible—only one element, to be sure, in what might otherwise amount to a larger whole, but obviously not nothing, and enough, apparently, to satisfy most inquirers.

There are to be sure some interesting moments in the Fathers where the argument occasionally approaches what I have been calling a more thoroughly sacramental view of the action. Hilary of Poitiers says of the "Word become Flesh" that he has "mingled his fleshly nature with his divine nature to be communicated to us in the Sacrament" (PL 10.246). Cyril of Jerusalem observes that "in the figure of bread the body is given to you, and in the figure of wine, the blood is given to you, so that, having received of the body and blood of Christ, you may become one body and one blood (*sussōmos kai sunaimos*) with him" (*Cat. Myst.* 4, PG 33.1099). In his *Great Catechism,* Gregory of Nyssa affirms that he "shares himself with every believer . . . in order to bring it about that, by communion with the Immortal, man may share in incorruption" (37.12). Pope Leo, somewhat later, affirms that "partaking of the body and blood of the Lord does nothing less than transform us into what we eat" (*Sermo* 63, PL 54.357). A similar sentence appears in Leo's *Epistolae* (59, PL 54.868). The idea appears as well in a more rhetorically charged form in more than one context of Augustine. *Sermo* 27 (PL 38.389) invites his hearers to become what they receive: *simus quod accipimus.* This invitation is repeated in *Sermo* 227 (PL 38.1099) as *si bene accepitis, vos estis quod accepistis,* and still more firmly in *Sermo* 272 (PL 38.1247) as *estote quod videtis, et accipite quod estis.* There are also references in *In Psalmis* 122 (PL 37.1630) and *Sermo* 133 (PL 38.742). Augustine's commentary on John contains a rehearsal of his eucharistic doctrine in *Tractate* 26.12-20 (PL 35.1611). Section 26.13 in particular includes two striking sentences: *Novunt fideles corpus Christi, si corpus Christi esse non negligant. Fiant corpus Christi, si volunt vivere de Spiritu Christi.*[9] But in his *City of God* Augustine firmly repeats a sacrificial understanding of the action (book 10, chapters 4-6 and 20). In this respect too Augustine is sufficiently typical of the authorities who precede him.[10]

The medieval thinkers, preoccupied with the problem of the real presence, rather assumed than reargued the sacrificial character of the rite, though traces of the alternative understanding may still be detected.[11] The devotional extravagances recently catalogued by Caroline Bynum and others evidently presume such an interpretation of the central rite.[12] This presumption was in due course thrown into relief by the Reformation, which began in a refusal of just such a conception of what was going on—a denial that not unnaturally produced contrary reaffirmations of the traditional case on the Catholic side. But the rejections or qualifications of the idea that the mass should be understood as a reenactment of the original sacrifice were rather negations of the inherited interpretation than alternatives to it. For Luther, the eucharistic action became a communion in or promise of faith, in his view the essential factor. For Zwingli, it was a sign that saving faith had already been bestowed, and therefore a thanksgiving for what had once and for all been achieved on the cross. The English reformers understood the rite as intended to

---

[9] I found the quotations from Hilary and Gregory in James O'Connor's *Hidden Manna* (San Francisco: Ignatius, 1988), otherwise a firm defense of the sacrificial interpretation. A translation of sermon 272 and the Johannine material may be found in Daniel Sheerin's *Eucharist* (Wilmington: Glazier, 1986) 94-96 and 218-24 respectively. Augustine's chief focus is evidently on the unity of the ecclesial body, which the Eucharist effects—a very Pauline concern, and fully consistent with the interpretation proposed. An interesting article by Cor Traets, "The Eucharist and Christian Community: Some Pauline and Augustinian Evidence," LS 12 (1987): 152-71, seems to offer support for the reading offered from a sufficiently professional perspective.

[10] Robert J. Daly's thorough *Christian Sacrifice: The Judaeo-Christian Background before Origen* (Washington: Catholic University Press, 1978) reviews the practice and theory of sacrifice from the Scriptures through the pseudoepigraphists, Qumran, the New Testament, and the Fathers down to Origen. Daly agrees that the later authorities concur in defining the Eucharist as sacrificial—though as a theologian himself he would prefer to emphasize the "spiritual" side of this action. Willy Rordorf has also edited a collection of the relevant patristic texts in *The Eucharist of the Early Christians* (New York: Pueblo, 1978). Together with those that appear in Sheerin or O'Connor (n. 9 above), these would confirm a suspicion that the sacrificial interpretation tends to be followed conventionally if emphatically.

[11] Gary Macy argues in *The Theologies of the Eucharist in the Early Scholastic Period* (Oxford: Clarendon, 1964) 106-32, that one "ecclesiastical" party at least was ready to understand the Church as the product of the Eucharist, or the *res* of that *sacramentum*.

[12] *Holy Feast and Holy Fast* (Berkeley: University of California Press, 1987) is perhaps the fullest version of Bynum's influential case. The central place of the Eucharist in medieval culture is more elaborately reviewed in Miri Rubin, *Corpus Christi* (Cambridge: Cambridge University Press, 1991).

strengthen the same faith. All agreed, though in varying degrees, that the Eucharist could only be a sign essentially distinct from its historical antecedent rather than a reproduction or, as the Catholic understanding had it, an "application" of the moral advantage obtained by the original to recipients in other times and places.[13]

With the larger possibility in view, one might feel that what both sides failed to understand even of the matters over which they struggled, not to mention what they unavoidably neglected, could seem more important than any of the gains or losses achieved or suffered at the time. It might, for instance, be possible to see the Reformers' emphasis on "justification by faith" as the individual or psychic equivalent of what the Catholic party understood to be taking place in a collective and therefore cultic mode instead of as its religious opposite. More important, the emphasis on the sacrificial interpretation, whether refused as a "work" or reaffirmed as literally crucial, made it impossible even to entertain what a modern, Protestant or Catholic, would identify as the eschatological dimension of the event. In the absence of this, the rite could not help but continue as an unconscious repetition of what would still officially have been thought of as its prefigurement, the temple cult. And this assumption in turn would have reinforced an understanding of the Church as primarily if not quite essentially an institution established to repeat what had once occurred in this world and would therefore need to be indefinitely repeated within the same limits. David Power's convenient little book on the Tridentine doctrine of sacrifice shows—without meaning to—how an exclusive attachment to the sacrificial sense of the Eucharist would have tended of itself to bring about the very conditions complained of by the Reformers: an overprivileged priesthood, a mechanization of the ritual process, the privatization of function and language, and a disposition to understand the opus as an automatically meritorious action. For all these results would add up to a temple rebuilt by hands indeed.[14]

An interiorization of the same process in terms of the faith of the individual would not as such come nearer to the eschatological character of the event. But if that dimension is counted back in, as it now seems easier to do, one would once again be in a position to entertain the possibility that the privilege so named might hold not just for the founding individual or even the elements but for the recipient

---

[13]The best account I have found of these controversies is still Francis Clark's classic *Eucharistic Sacrifice and the Reformation*, 2nd ed. (Oxford: Blackwell, 1967). His not-unbiased rendering of the views of several reforming parties may be found on pp. 103-12. The relevant reassertions of the sacrificial understanding in the Council documents may now be conveniently found in Michael O'Carroll's encyclopedic *Corpus Christi* (Wilmington: Glazier, 1988). But even Trent, one may discover there, was willing to call the Eucharist a "symbol" of the communal body (203).

[14]David Power, *The Sacrifices We Offer: The Tridentine Dogma and Its Reinterpretation* (New York: Crossroad, 1987). Though Power withdraws somewhat from the sacrificial interpretation in his own conclusion, he has no alternative to offer in its place, perhaps because the limits of the topic do not oblige him to return to what Jesus may have intended.

community as well. And that community would then not have to suffer schism within its (we should now definitely say her) proper mode of being, however divided "it" might in fact become on this side of the barrier. The opportunity, though, to entertain such a thought could revive only with a fresh appreciation of the initial situation, which in turn required the emergence of biblical scholarship. The results of that activity, I have sometimes thought, might accordingly count as the true *patrilogia* of the modern Church—which is to be found, alas, in at least as many volumes.[15]

One almost incidental by-product of the revived eschatological awareness from which it has since become impossible not to profit would be the chance to resolve what seemed at the Reformation an insoluble semiotic problem. In what sense ought one to think of the Eucharist as a "remembrance"? Is it a reenactment in the strong sense of such language, or barely a reminder? If one reverts, as it has also become easier to do, to the Passover context of the initial event, and measures what that ceremony recalled and recalls by the same standard that—we are now better prepared to understand—would have governed all of Jesus' behavior, it becomes easier to appreciate that whatever one does religiously is sure to reproduce whatever experience still serves to define one's position in what might then be called the eschatological scenario. If the Exodus represents that point, one re-presents the Exodus; if what Jesus did, then so much of his action as may in its turn be reenacted. In every context we repeat the degree of being to which we have arrived, as if to remind ourselves how far we have got. If it is reasonable to reproduce the liberation from Egypt, it cannot a fortiori be wrong to celebrate what a believer can by analogy understand as entry into the promised land indeed.[16]

---

[15] A standard reference for the eschatological possibility is Geoffrey Wainwright's *Eucharist and Eschatology* (New York: Oxford University Press, 1981), which strongly affirms that the Eucharist should be understood primarily as a meal anticipating the End. This claim sounds useful, but in fact Wainwright omits—indeed shrinks from—the ecclesiological implications of his own argument. The typically modern emphasis on eschatology as such goes back of course to Albert Schweitzer.

[16] It seems unclear to what extent the Passover model might itself contribute to a sacrificial interpretation of the supper. In his *Christian Sacrifice,* Daly reads the contemporary evidence as suggesting that it would, chiefly by way of current associations to the sacrifice of Isaac and to circumcision (177-86, 190-95, 196-207). All sacrifices at the time, he observes, had attracted some degree of expiatory meaning. Judah Benzion Segal, though, argues in his classic *The Hebrew Passover from the Earliest Times to A.D. 70,* London Oriental Series 12 (London/New York: Oxford University Press, 1963), that this sacrifice would have had no such significance, if only because even after the festival was centralized at Jerusalem, the lamb was killed by a layman, not a priest. The rite, after all, predates not just the temple but the cult in general as otherwise defined (106). And even in terms of that system in its developed form, the Passover was a *zevah,* since the flesh is returned to the offerers to be consumed, and within this category a *todah,* or act not of atonement but of thanksgiving. In any case, the sacrificial act is preliminary to a festive meal, which would have provided the focus

A review of some prominent modern authorities could though remind a contemporary student of the continuing influence of the sacrificial interpretation, in spite of the opportunity offered by a new awareness of eschatology. It is not surprising that the traditional interpretation has persisted among Catholic scholars. La Taille, Vonier, and Masure, three older authorities who continue to influence discussion, all firmly support the inherited doctrine.[17] But more recent inquirers also have on the whole maintained the same understanding. For J. M. Powers, for instance, "The Eucharistic presence of Christ is . . . a sacrificial presence."[18] Léon-Dufour continues to articulate this interpretation in his own nuanced style.[19] Bernard Cooke's encyclopedic summary on the ministry accepts the doctrine as a matter of course, though in a later popular book he shows some evidence of discontent with it in the circles whose views he represents.[20] The liturgist Leo Hay, for instance, approaches the alternative possibility in his own book on the subject, but so casually it is difficult to decide how seriously.[21] Among the theologians Rudolf Schnackenburg does indeed include one paragraph explicating 1 Corinthians 10:16-17 in such a way as to accept that "a profound relation exists between the body of Christ in the eucharist and the Body of Christ represented by the congregation."[22] This suggestion sounds promising, but typically Schnackenburg does not develop the hint, preferring to continue with Colossians and Ephesians, where an ecclesial identity is elaborated in apparent independence of the eucharistic model. Walter Kasper's leading article in a recent issue of *Communio* devoted to the subject preserves the traditional emphasis while summing up recent German discussion, though with at least a glance at the testamentary aspect of the event, as when he speaks of the Eucharist as a "bequeathing of himself by Jesus" so that he might "remain with, and be present to, his own."[23] Two younger theorists already alluded to, Robert J. Daly and David

---

then as it has since. As the "pretext" for what Jesus did, then, the ritual does not clearly reinforce a sacrificial interpretation of his action, though it need not conflict with such a reading.

[17]M. de La Taille, *The Mystery of Faith* (London: Sheed and Ward, 1940); A. Vonier, *A Key to the Doctrine of the Eucharist* (London: Burns and Oates, 1925); and E. Masure, *The Sacrifice of the Mystical Body* (London: Burns and Oates, 1954) are accessible translations of the principal texts.

[18]J. M. Powers, *Eucharistic Theology* (New York: Herder, 1967) 70.

[19]Léon-Dufour, *Partage du Pain,* 327-28 and 337-39. One might add Nicolas Lash, *His Presence in the World* (London: Sheed and Ward, 1968), and Luis Bermejo, *Body Broken and Blood Shed* (Anand, Gujarat (India): Gujarat Sahita Prehash, 1986).

[20]Cooke, *Ministry to Word and Sacraments,* 636-38, and *Sacraments and Sacramentality* (Mystic CT: Twenty-Third Publications, 1983) 104-109.

[21]Leo Hay, *Eucharist: A Thanksgiving Celebration* (Wilmington: Glazier, 1989) 124, 129, 132.

[22]Rudolf Schnackenburg, *The Church in the New Testament* (London: Burns and Oates, 1965) 170.

[23]Walter Kasper, "Unity and Multiplicity of Aspects in the Eucharist," *Communio*

Power, are inclined to withdraw into ethical or "metaphoric" reinterpretations respectively of sacrifice as such, whether in the crucifixion or the Eucharist.[24] But these, like other liberal doubts, seem rather a weakening of the traditional position than an alternative to it. Meanwhile *Mysterium fidei,* the papal encyclical of 1965, not unexpectedly repeats the canonical understanding against what was then seen as the threat posed by recent Dutch criticism of the doctrine of transubstantiation.[25]

One might have supposed that the modern revival of interest in Pauline theology in particular might also have provided an opening for a less exclusive vision of the eucharistic action. For that expansion has necessarily brought into the foreground a need to comprehend how the several modes of the "body of Christ" should be thought of as related. Anglican scholars were in the lead on this topos—most prominently John A. T. Robinson, whose classic monograph makes an explicit point of affirming an essential identity between the individual body at the supper or on the cross, the resurrected body, and the Church. The specifically eucharistic mode of this would then become, as it were, the copula between the individual and the community. And when Robinson arrives at the Eucharist, he formulates very nearly the argument I have been advancing: the identifications at the supper, he affirms, mean that "Jesus is making over to His followers 'till He come' His actual self, His life and personality. Insofar then as the Christian community feeds on this body and blood, it *becomes* the very life and personality of the risen Christ."[26] To be sure, the terminology here is psychological rather than theological. And Robinson begins his next paragraph with a question, "But does it?"—though not so much to raise a doubt as to look for other influences on Paul's doctrine, particularly the resurrection vision. But the essential case is at least proposed.

Other Anglican authorities of the same generation, though, remained much more traditional in their approach. E. L. Mascall, for instance, explicitly "high church" in his sympathies, is correspondingly cautious. A summary paragraph in his *Christ, the Christian, and the Church* concludes by repeating that the Eucharist repeats the sacrifice, so that in the ritual, "Christ offers us."[27] A chapter reviewing some of the

---

(Summer 1985): 115-38. Robert J. Daly's summary "The Eucharist and Redemption . . . ," *BTB* 11 (1981): 21-25, had already discovered with apparent relief that post-Jeremian German scholarship as represented by Betz, Schurmann, and Pesch was still willing to attribute a sacrificial intention to Jesus at the supper.

[24] Robert J. Daly, *The Origins of the Christian Doctrine of Sacrifice* (Philadelphia: Fortress, 1978), the popular version of his larger book (*Christian Sacrifice*), and David N. Power, "Words That Crack: The Uses of 'Sacrifice' in Eucharistic Discourse," *Worship* 53 (1979): 386-404. Power's article is more critical than his book on Trent.

[25] The most convenient reference in English is *The Papal Encyclicals, 1958–1981,* ed. Claudia Carlen, vol. 5 of the series (Raleigh: McGrath, 1981) 165-77.

[26] Robinson, *Body,* 57.

[27] E. L. Mascall, *Christ, the Christian, and the Church* (London: Longmans, 1946) 161-62.

then-recent versions of the sacrificial interpretation in the first edition of his *Corpus Christi* continues to take this for granted—though in such a way as to expose some of the difficulties that attend it. A second edition of his influential book expanded this single chapter into three, the better to celebrate what seemed a new agreement that the Eucharist is indeed the original sacrifice made sacramentally present.[28] C. F. D. Moule, a self-declared Evangelical, also found himself prepared to accept the idea of a eucharistic sacrifice in a brief but subtle study of the atonement.[29] His later book on Christology resists the idea that the community should be thought of as the "corporate" Christ, though he admits the Pauline evidence is compelling. And he positively rejects the possibility that the Eucharist could be the reason for this idea.[30] L. S. Thornton, the earliest and most conservative member of the group, had long since defined the "mystical body" as a sharing in the sacrifice.[31] Against this or other variants of the disposition to assimilate the several modes of the body stands Ernest Best, Mascall's Low Church analogue, for whom the differences among these are more important than the identity maintained by Robinson.[32] Meanwhile, on the exegetical side, A. J. B. Higgins had already drawn on German scholarship, especially Jeremias, to reaffirm the older Protestant principle that the Eucharist must "represent" rather than be assimilated to the sacrifice of the cross—which would still leave the traditional interpretation in place to just that extent.[33]

Meanwhile too, Lucien Cerfaux, to revert to the Catholic line, positively denies that *sōma* should be understood as referring to the Church except in a metaphoric sense safely separated from its individual and ritual meanings. For Cerfaux the community is no more than the "radiation" of the risen body, which should be conceived of as individual still.[34] It is all right for Christians to think of themselves as "mystically" identified with the body of Christ, but only so far as this means with his person—which is once again to say, his identity as victim. Like so many others, Cerfaux does not want the living Church to become Christ. But it is typical too that

---

[28] E. L. Mascall, *Corpus Christi* (London: Longmans, 1953). The 2nd ed. (1965) also responds to Vatican II and to Clark, *Eucharistic Sacrifice*.

[29] C. F. D. Moule, *The Sacrifice of Christ* (Philadelphia: Fortress, 1964) 30-45.

[30] C. F. D. Moule, *The Origin of Christology* (Cambridge: University Press, 1977) 87. Moule reviews the post-Robinson discussion of the different modes of the body on pp. 47-96.

[31] L. S. Thornton, *The Common Life in the Body of Christ* (London: Dacre, 1942). *Eucharistic Theology Then and Now,* ed. Ronald E. Clements (London: SPCK, 1968), a collection of Anglican essays, can stand as another monument of the impulse to unite all parties on the basis of the sacrificial interpretation.

[32] Ernest Best, *One Body in Christ* (London: SPCK, 1955).

[33] A. J. B. Higgins, *The Lord's Supper in the New Testament* (London: SCM Press, 1952) 52-54.

[34] Lucien Cerfaux, *The Church in the Theology of St. Paul* (New York: Herder, 1959) 328.

he cannot stop worrying the possibility repeatedly, unable to remain content with any single reformulation of the traditional view.[35] L. Bouyer, reviewing the ecclesiological scene more recently, comes still nearer a positive rendering of the eucharistic origin of the Church in a few pages, without though quite allowing himself to formulate the possibility in so many words. It is, we can fairly say, a continuing and even embarrassing predicament.[36]

If theologians of Catholic sympathies or allegiance have been more comfortable reaffirming the sacrificial understanding (and are certainly uncomfortable with any alternative), some Protestant authorities at least have served to keep the question open. To be sure, Jeremias, whose classic reconstruction of the supper I began by rehearsing, himself adopts the sacrificial interpretation both there and in his *Theology of the New Testament*.[37] So does Bornkamm in a chapter on the relation of the supper to the Church in Paul, and Hengel in his study of the atonement.[38] So also, with special vigor, does Markus Barth in his more recent *Rediscovering the Lord's Supper*.[39] Bultmann had already frankly identified the Eucharist as a sacramental communion in the whole body of Christ.[40] He rather spoils this unexpected affirmation, though, by proposing, in a way that used to be more fashionable, that we should understand the privilege in question as reproducing a Hellenistic mystery, and so as an unfortunate ecclesial development rather than the original intention. Käsemann's commentary on Romans is similarly more at home tracing possible Stoic or Semitic influences on Paul's version of the "theologoumenon" of the body

---

[35] Ibid., 266-83, 343-45, 365-83, 395-97.

[36] Louis Bouyer, *The Church of God: Body of Christ, and Temple of the Spirit* (Chicago: Franciscan Herald, 1982) 294-98. It seems significant that neither of the two most-prominent recent American theologians within the Catholic tradition have found it necessary to address the issue either positively or negatively. See David Tracy, *The Analogical Imagination* (New York: Seabury, 1981), and Elisabeth Schüssler Fiorenza, *Foundational Theology: Jesus and the Church* (New York: Crossroad, 1984). One would have hoped that the latter in particular might have wished to confront this sufficiently "foundational" question.

[37] Jeremias, Eucharistic Words, 222; idem, Theology of the New Testament, vol. 1, The Proclamation of Jesus (London: SCM, 1971) 290-91.

[38] Günther Bornkamm, "Lord's Supper and Church in Paul," in *Early Christian Experience* (London: SCM Press, 1969) 123-60. Unfortunately his better-known *Jesus of Nazareth* (New York: Harper, 1960) is of no use on this question. Martin Hengel's *Atonement: The Origins of the Doctrine in the New Testament* (Philadelphia: Fortress, 1981) helps fill out the elements in Hellenistic as well as Jewish culture that would have made a sacrificial understanding plausible. But Hengel too attributes the initiative to Jesus at the supper (72-73).

[39] Markus Barth, Rediscovering the Lord's Supper (Atlanta: John Knox, 1988) esp. 18 and 20-21. One might add as another Protestant authority Harmut Gese, whose "Origin of the Lord's Supper," in his collected Essays on Biblical Theology (Minneapolis: Augsburg, 1981) 117-40, supports the todah hypothesis.

[40] Rudolf Bultmann, *Theology of the New Testament*, vol. 1 (New York: Scribner's, 1951; London: SCM Press, 1952) 146-52.

than with more central "obscurities surrounding the whole question."[41] An essay on Paul's conception of the Supper, though, would seem to place Käsemann firmly on the side of those who agree that it must be the resurrected and not the mortal body one is joined to in the rite, which would at least permit if not enforce a sacramental understanding of what is going on.[42] Willi Marxsen straightforwardly denies bodiliness to any phase of the action except the last in his influential *The Lord's Supper as a Christological Problem*. The traditional "sacralization" of the "material" elements he is still inclined to attribute to Hellenistic infiltration, and even the ordinarily unchallenged assumption that whatever was done, Jesus must be understood to have done it, is for him a retrojection from subsequent interpretation. This approach would solve the problem by leaving two-thirds of it out.[43]

Meanwhile, at the more practical level of the current ecumenical discussion, the sacrificial understanding continues to predominate, as it has from the beginning.[44] Max Thurian, for instance, monk of Taizé, intends his recent *Mystery of the Eucharist* as a contribution to theological unity and so assembles evidence to show that all explanations of the event, Catholic or Protestant, Eastern or Western, ought in the end to prove "compatible." To that end he repeats the sacrificial doctrine without embarrassment: "The Eucharist is the cross present in the Church." But when he comes to the real presence, which he also wishes to defend, he finds himself using more inclusive language, apparently without feeling any latent contradiction: "Under the outward signs of bread and wine, the profound reality is the whole being of Christ, who comes to us to feed us and transform our very being."[45]

Behind all the Protestant authorities stands not just Bultmann but Karl Barth—whose views retain a certain ambiguity. In the relevant portions of *Church Dogmatics* Barth rejects any identity between the initiator of the action and its

---

[41]Ernst Käsemann, *Commentary on Romans* (Grand Rapids: Eerdmans, 1980) 336-39.

[42]Ernst Käsemann, "The Pauline Doctrine of the Lord's Supper," in his *Essays on New Testament Themes* (London: SCM Press, 1964) 114.

[43]Willi Marxsen, *The Lord's Supper as a Christological Problem* (Philadelphia: Fortress, 1970) 33.

[44]The modern beginnings and (now) middle of this ongoing process are traced from a Lutheran perspective in Gustaf Aulén, *Eucharist and Sacrifice* (Philadelphia: Muhlenberg, 1958), and John Reumann, *The Supper of the Lord* (Philadelphia: Fortress, 1985). Behind both of these is G. Brilioth, *Eucharistic Faith and Practice: Evangelical and Catholic* (London: SPCK, 1953), which could stand as a Swedish parallel to Gregory Dix's better-known liturgical history (see n. 1 above). The text against which skeptics on all sides have been measuring their views of late has been *Baptism, Eucharist, and Ministry,* Faith and Order paper no. 111 (Geneva: World Council of Churches, 1982), the so-called "Lima" document. This too repeats the sacrificial interpretation, but so cautiously as to mean nothing in particular to anyone.

[45]Max Thurian, *The Mystery of the Eucharist: An Ecumenical Approach* (Grand Rapids: Eerdmans, 1984). The two sentences quoted are on pp. 21 and 31 respectively.

recipients, preferring to stick with the language of Colossians: Christ is the "head," and therefore the community is no more than the flesh, of the *totus Christus*.[46] "Christ is the community," he warns, but "there can be no reversing this important statement. The community is not Christ."[47] At the same time it is possible to locate in Barth a version of the complementary truth impressive enough to prove quotable by more than one subsequent authority: *Das Sein Jesu Christi ist das Sein der Kirche*.[48] Barth's "Christocentric" bias, as C. O'Grady—in whose summary article I found this formula repeated—points out, could have led him to slight the liturgical and ecclesiological applications of Paul's body language.[49] But Barth's insistence on the trajectory of the action could, if followed without inhibition, invite inferences of which he might have been suspicious taken by themselves. Anders Nygren, for instance, a major name within the Barthian line, does in fact allow himself to take the next step; he is even willing to say outright that "the Church is Christ as he is present among and meets us on earth after his resurrection."[50] One would still want to agree with the Barthian warning that the community would remain the predicate for which the individual is the subject of the relevant sentence. But that is indeed precisely what the action would seem to be "saying," in a language either beneath or beyond any Scripture—and therefore even that of Barth's master, Paul, who had found himself a writer too, after all.

There is no reason meanwhile to doubt that it has been and still could be entirely plausible to see what in that case becomes "the passion" as an atoning sacrifice for the sins of Israel—including whoever else is enabled to accept it as such. Nor need we suppose that such an understanding of his death could not have determined some part of Jesus' own attitude toward events as they unfolded, even before the moment of crisis. Isaiah 53 was already there for him to remember as well as his followers—perhaps even at the Supper itself.[51] The adoption of the

---

[46] Karl Barth, *Church Dogmatics* (Edinburgh: T. & T. Clark, 1936–1961) 4:59-60.

[47] Barth was objecting specifically to a sentence in the encyclical *Mystici corporis* that seemed to affirm the opposite: "Ecclesia . . . ipsa quasi altera Christi persona existat" (AAS 35 [1943]: 218).

[48] Barth, *Church Dogmatics* 4/2:655.

[49] C. O'Grady, "The Church the Body of Christ in the Theology of Karl Barth and in Catholic Theology," *ITQ* 35 (1968): 3-21.

[50] Anders Nygren, *Christ and His Church* (Philadelphia: Westminster, 1956) 97; his discussion of the Eucharist is on 107 and 122-23.

[51] George R. Beasley-Murray proposes as much in his *Jesus and the Kingdom of God* (Grand Rapids: Eerdmans, 1986) 268-71. This book incidently can serve as another summary of the post-Jeremian discussion in Germany. The second volume of Donald Goergen's *Theology of Jesus* (Wilmington: Glazier, 1986–1988) 39-68, reviews the modern examination of the "servant" identity. Geza Vermes had already reminded Christian readers that behind Isaiah 53 lies a traditional association of the Passover with the *akedah*, or sacrifice of Isaac, which might accordingly have been at least as influential. See his *Scripture and Tradition*

interpretation offered therein and its appearance in the earliest versions of "the gospel" would certainly suggest dominical authority for so immediate and universal a conviction. It need not follow, though, that we would have to see the eucharistic action, past or present, as no more than a vehicle for the application of what the doctrine of the atonement serves to explain. Jesus did not, after all, approach Jerusalem for the last time in order to celebrate Yom Kippur but Passover. We need not elevate what might more fairly be considered a subordinate though necessary presupposition of the communication into its central intention—which would displace what the form of the event might suggest was in fact primary to the metaphoric margins.

To propose as much would not be to deny that Jesus may well have meant to include a preunderstanding of his anticipated suffering within the scope of the action initiated. The separation between the bread word and the wine word, and so the body and blood, may indeed have been intended to bear precisely the sacrificial association assigned to it down through the tradition, as one half, as it were, of the somatic pun being proposed. That too would have been very much in his style, since he appears never to have done or said anything without at least a double meaning. The possibility that this significance should be thought of rather as presupposed than as positively affirmed would seem though to be supported by a purely semiotic feature of the gesture that does not ordinarily attract the attention it deserves. For Jesus must in any case be understood as abandoning his individual selfhood, whatever that might consist of, in order that the elements chosen might indeed suffice to include the whole of the relevant identity. As the action moves from moment to moment, each previous state of affairs is necessarily used up so the next may obtain. This linguistic immolation occurs as the body of the individual becomes its symbolic equivalents, the bread and the wine. But it also occurs a second time when these are in their turn consumed: when the symbol is "interpreted" by becoming its interpreters. We do not usually think of the elements as having to "die" for us as we consume them, but it would be as reasonable to do so as to overburden the inevitable semantic gap between the first and second moments of the action.

Whatever else the sacrificial doctrine has done, whether in its primary form as an interpretation of the crucifixion, or its secondary mode as a reading either of the Last Supper or of the Eucharist as this can be repeated within the Church, it has certainly thrown an extravagant emphasis on the close of Jesus' life, as if his death were all he had to accomplish, and a symbolic anticipation or memorial of this conclusion would therefore suffice to concentrate whatever he was and meant. The result has been to limit the intention of this eschatological agent not just to one half of a possible final action but to a single context within which this could be presumed to take effect, as if his whole purpose were only to become a scapegoat

---

in Judaism (Leiden: E. J. Brill, 1961) 193-227.

for the sins of random individuals.[52] Such a focus presumes an inconveniently "low" Christology, which in turn limits the spiritual benefits that could be understood to have been released by the offering in question. Forgiveness is the traditional type of these, though by now not the only instance. It is still presupposed in such a formulation as the well-known remark of Bultmann that Jesus "rose into the kerygma." More recent versions seem evacuated of even this much spiritual content. To pass along an assurance that the "cause" of the individual does in fact go on, for example, as Marxsen and more recently Thomas Sheehan repeat, would reduce the resurrection to no more than authorization for an idealism of some kind, "humanistic" or heavy-breathing.[53]

But if the "high" Christology of the eventual confessions is essentially correct—if Jesus, that is, must indeed be understood as a representation of the presence of God and not merely as a victim on behalf of others—it need not surprise us that how he represents that representativeness would communicate precisely this apocalyptic identity. A high Christology should accordingly entail an equally high ecclesiology. In that case the resurrection need not amount only to a reconciliation of other individuals with God on a one-to-one basis or the disclosure of a possible goal for humanity at large but the constant possibility of an actual community as distinctive as the individual himself ever was—for he would now have become precisely that.

When the tradition agreed to accept the narrative Gospels, it agreed that Jesus must be rather more than a victim who *was* sacrificed once upon a time. What he did and said while still free to act as he pleased must also, it was tacitly acknowledged, be understood as expressive of his ultimate identity. By shifting the initiation of this backward, first to the baptism, then to the conception, and finally to the

---

[52]The word *scapegoat,* if not my argument so far, will remind some readers of the theory of sacrifice advanced by René Girard, which has acquired a degree of notoriety among biblical scholars as well as literary critics. For him sacrifice is a species of "sacred" violence against a scapegoat by which a collective fortifies itself against the threat of anarchy. Girard's readings of Scripture suggest that he has confused sacrifice proper, or that which is to be done within the relation to God, with the ban (*herem*), by which what is not to be done is put away. This confusion considerably reduces the interpretive usefulness of his scheme, which though could itself be read as one more symptom of the sacrificial inheritance it is intended to master. The principal sources now include Girard's own *Scapegoat* (Baltimore: Johns Hopkins University Press, 1986) and *Things Hidden Since the Foundation of the World* (Stanford: Stanford University Press, 1987). The two principal examinations of the relevance of Gerard's theory to biblical matters are Robert North's "Violence and the Bible; the Girard Connection," *CBQ* 47 (January 1985): 1-27, and Raymond Schwager, *Must There Be Scapegoats?* (San Francisco: Harper, 1987).

[53]Thomas Sheehan refers back to both Bultmann and Marxsen in his self-consciously scandalous but in fact somewhat old-fashioned *First Coming: How the Kingdom of God Became Christianity* (New York: Random House, 1986).

moment of creation, these narratives, and therefore the Church that accepted them, consented to regard the period of the ministry as revealing a Jesus who already disposed of just those powers that would after his death determine the appearances and the presence of the Spirit within the community. *This* Jesus would have to count as "resurrected," that is, well before the resurrection. He would therefore have to be understood as present at the supper too, as well as the carnal victim—altogether ready, that is, to complete on behalf of the Lord the summary commandment that heads the repetition of the Decalogue in the central chapter of Leviticus: you shall be holy (*kedoshim t'hiyu*), for I am holy (*ki kadosh ani*) (Lev. 19:2). But for such a gesture to make sense, the agent of it would already need to understand himself as incorporating (we can properly say) an absolute authority, which in fact does not seem to have been questioned within the inheritance reflected by the narratives, however ironic or cautious the stories also show their protagonist to have been about the titles this identity might entail.

In that case we are once again free to outline the structure of the action in question in thoroughly positive terms. We might see this accordingly as centered upon a line in the shape of an arrow passing, we could imagine, from left to right. This axis would represent the trajectory of the body as a whole—if that term may indeed be employed to name what is in fact not literally nameable. We may then picture three shorter lines drawn vertically at intervals across this horizontal. The first of these, we began by supposing, would be labeled "blood" at the top and "flesh" at the bottom. This pair would then amount to the first interpretation proposed, though within the action it is taken for granted rather than becoming the matter of a separate proposition. We have argued besides that in this way Jesus as what a modern could call the eschatological agent would have implicitly defined himself as consisting not only of so much human "flesh," physical or psychic, as there would already happen to be but also of an equal quantity of divine "blood." For it is that which would make him the Son of the Father indeed. The second vertical line may in the same manner be labelled "wine" at the top and "bread" at the bottom. The propositions explicitly offered would then identify the first set with the second without omission or remainder. And the third set could then, still without diminishment, be named "Spirit" and "community" in accordance with the same rule. This scheme would serve to outline what might then be imagined as the skeleton at least of the body indeed. It would provide what we might call an anatomy of what would seem to have been going on then and since, into which other interpretations might be fitted as required—including, as we have seen, the sacrificial. For such an outline would provide a norm by means of which to measure the real function as well as the plausibility of any of these, as occasion might require.

We might incidentally, for instance, appreciate better why it became appropriate for the assembly to celebrate the Eucharist on Sunday from the beginning. (If the sacrificial intention had indeed been primary, we might expect Friday would have been preferred.) We could also understand why the resurrection experiences, and what would later be retold as a distinct moment of inspiration by the Spirit, would in fact have served to constitute a new version of the relevant community which could experience just that identity as including not only the forgiveness of individual members but also the right and power to continue the public task its leader had begun upon: to announce and demonstrate, that is, the presence of God's future. If the sacrificial understanding had in fact dominated at the supper, Jesus would have been inviting the twelve (or at least the eleven) to join him in his death. This they most certainly did not do. But there is in any case no suggestion that he meant them to. If they had, the movement they shared would have been over then and there—which could scarcely have been anybody's intention.

It is easier to suppose what is already implied by the structure we have outlined: that Jesus, knowing that he was to die at the midpoint in what otherwise would have become the normal lifetime of an individual, devised a strategy that would permit the community which would inherit from him to live out what was left of "this generation" in the only mode now possible for the identity in question. By physically incorporating what thus becomes their inheritance, the nucleus of an eschatological assembly would be taking over the "messianic" enterprise from him—if that is the proper name for the intention he had begun by embodying. The disciples already represented the whole of an ideal Israel, as their appointed number sufficiently indicates. It is even possible to imagine that Jesus may have remembered the blessings of the twelve tribes by Jacob in Genesis 49, or the repetition of this terminal gesture by Moses in Deuteronomy 33. In any case it is clear that the representative individual could not on this occasion be succeeded by some *other* individual, as had hitherto been the rule for royal or prophetic figures. Jesus had no son—one of the more obvious negative features of his career. Nor did he have any single successor, as Elijah had in Elisha—in spite of Peter's claims at the time or since. But he did have several potential "siblings." To them accordingly he may be understood as handing over the identity he was in any event forced to relinquish as a singular human being. This mode of being should not, after all, be allowed to lapse, we must suppose him to have believed, for otherwise he would have been a liar to proclaim the presence of the Kingdom—and God would have proved a cheat.[54]

We might also make better sense of the convenantal dimension of the action, concerning which a formula appears in all four of the New Testament accounts. If the event inaugurates a new version of the relation in which Israel had stood from the beginning, God would have to continue to be what he had begun to show himself in the behavior of the appointed individual: an unlimited, concrete, merciful presence. This novelty the tradition would in due course refer to as grace, and match

---

[54]It is revealing that Robert Kress, who reviews the modern discussion of *The Church: Communion, Sacrament, Communication* (New York: Paulist, 1985), does not make any reference to the eucharistic action as he takes up the old question, Did Jesus found a Church? (36-59). But if the view proposed is adopted, we need not look elsewhere for an answer.

it with the complementary demand required under such a form of the relation, or "faith." The consent of faith is already in principle a reduction of the subject, whether of the originator or any of his followers. That is the truth of sacrifice, which is indeed the last thing that could possibly be done on this side of the relation either in its old or its new version. In Jewish terms, the most any human being is capable of is a *kiddush ha shem* of one kind or another, through which, as the Christian repetition of the idea has it, the "Name" is "hallowed." But if faith must for that reason always count as a negative, grace is as constantly exhibited as positive. Jesus not only exemplifies our prayer, that is, but answers it. In fact he answers it before it is formulated, as he forgives sinners even before they have had time to repent. The gift anticipates the faith that must receive it. And this generosity the properly sacramental character of the action would continually manifest, for what gift could possibly be greater than the very being of the one who thereby proposes a version of the relation within which just this privilege may in fact be shared? We might accordingly find both meanings of the Greek term regularly employed most applicable to the matter at hand: the action is indeed at one and the same time the reproduction of a covenant and a "testament," or transmission of an inheritance by the testator to his heirs. *Diatheke* will cover both.[55]

In that case it could also be fair to conclude that the action shows Jesus making what we might familiarly call the best of a bad situation, though in no derogatory sense, and that without abandoning his proper style: which is to say, by means of an acted parable. Like the other parables, this incorporates other than eschatological meanings, as if to show that the simplest features even of our most mortal life are susceptible to recuperation as revelations of the reign of God indeed. But such elementary elements, together with any presumed or supplementary meanings, are still under the sway of the eschatological intention, which evidently dominates whatever he may be understood to do or say, and therefore offers our best criterion for deciding which instances of either may reasonably be assigned to him. As sacrifice, we may say, the sins of many are indeed representatively expiated by the chosen individual. Their identification with him then becomes the moral content of their faith. As sacrament the spiritual privilege of the same individual is contrastingly transferred to the many who will ever receive it, including those who may not in the least deserve or understand what has been given them. That response, after all, is also predicted by the reactions described in the stories. The movement is thus from the many to the one on one side, and from the one to the many on the other. Such a reversal from sin (first actual, then ritual) to blessing (first ritual, then actual) would parallel the corresponding shifts from passion to resurrection or human to divine, and so most generally from negative to positive.

---

[55]A recent discussion of the covenantal aspect of the Eucharist appears in Reumann, *The Supper of The Lord,* 34-41. This review though does not consider the testamentary character of the action.

The sacrificial and sacramental dimensions of the action would then correspond as well to the semantic distinction between the literal and the metaphoric. The words of institution, we might say, are spoken from the same point of origin as the words of creation in Genesis. But they are spoken within the order of signs rather than the order of existence. That is the difference between the Father and the Son. But if the Son of the Father has in fact been revealed, then signification must be as blessed as being; and if signification, then the human order that corresponds to and is produced by it—which is to say, the eventual community. We are luckier than we knew. The action as a whole would then be a play on words of just the kind we might expect from an artist in that kind, but an artist, we can remember, after the Spirit rather than the flesh. In a play on words, two meanings cohere. Parables of any species can be several sided, as this is, but never decomposed. For the body imports integrity to any context within which it may be found. And there need in principle be no limit to these settings, if what is going on should indeed offer the type of all possible action. All we need do is apply whatever we have come to understand.

Accidental

Once we have caught up with this much at least of what is going on, we are ready to resituate some other corollary matters, minor or major. One of the former that might seem bothersome is the historical gap between the Last Supper and the rite as this may now be repeated in a latter-day congregation. These are indeed sufficiently different—but not, as it turns out, with respect to the purpose at hand, as the very change in the balance of realities that raises the question will show of itself. The act, we have found, breaks apart into three moments: Jesus, the bread and wine, and the community, which is to say, the author, the symbol, and the recipients. As these phases of the communicative situation came together at the supper, the first two were real and the last represented, for the disciples as they then reclined around the table were not yet the full community as this was presently to come into being, while Jesus was still no more and no less than simply himself. When the act is repeated within any congregation, though, the first moment must be represented, while the second and third are real. So the actual and imagined phases change places, while the intermediate sign remains the same. It is accordingly the bread and the wine that are experienced in either context as carrying the burden of the bodiliness affirmed. But this role is thoroughly transitive. What counts in the end is still the shift from the individual to the community, or from what has been real to what might yet become so. The change in the ontological balance from the original to its reproductions is not a diminishment of the act, then, but one more illustration of its central intention.

The mediating elements, though, have been experienced through the several generations that have in fact revolved as a chief focus for the meaning of the event. And the employment of the word *body* for the bread alone was to make this half of the symbolic pair an occasion for what came to seem a major problem respecting the action as a whole. An initial abstraction of the present moment from the temporal trajectory from past to future was reinforced by a second abstraction of one pole from the contrast that had begun by serving to generate a symbolic whole. Together these removals produced what could then present itself as a metaphysical problem respecting the status of an ambiguous object. How could this bread also *be* the body of Christ? And once the question had acquired a philosophical shape, it was inevitable too that modes of explanation that had already been worked out to deal with the universe of cognition in general would be drawn upon to interpret the Eucharist as well, for this would then seem an exception to be reduced as soon as might be to the intellectual norm. If the preliminary steps away from the action as a whole are *not* taken, it might seem more likely that reality in general should show itself susceptible to reinterpretation by way of the Eucharist than the other way around. But that is not how it worked out.

The key term in Aquinas's explanation of the eucharistic transformation, to take the obvious major instance, is of course *substance*. "Substance" as he understands it may be defined most generally as that which really exists in and as itself. It is accordingly the first category of being in the scheme of The Philosopher whom he is repeating; the others are merely "accidents," which in principle cannot exist on their own. Substances are outside our own bodies and must therefore be grasped by way of the senses, but they are understood by the intellect, which arrives at a judgment that whatever-it-is does in fact exist. So substance becomes the object of an ostensive definition, or the matter of any discourse, or that which may be dignified by a distinct noun.

What happens in the first half of the second stage of the eucharistic action is according to Thomas a change of the *substance* of the bread into the *substance* of the body of Christ. That this is what "transubstantiation" means is clearer in his *Summa Contra Gentiles* (4.63.4, 64.4, 66.9) than in the *Summa Theologica* (3a.73-83). If the substance of anything is whatever it *is,* it follows that the substance of the body of Christ too must be an object of knowledge—though in this case only for angels (ST 3a.76.7). On earth faith is required for human beings to realize that one substance has been replaced by another. In other words, faith on earth is an incomplete version of what would already be knowledge in heaven, not a mode of relation beyond the scope of knowledge as such. This strategy replaces a communicative situation with a cognitive uncertainty, which "reserves the sacrament" intellectually instead of liturgically—as the Church had in fact begun to do in Thomas's day. So it Hellenizes a Hebraic event, we might also observe; but more significantly, it secularizes or profanes a spiritual action. An exchange of one substance for another, which is to say of one kind of *object* for another, would in effect convert Jesus (or the priest after him) into a physical experimenter at best and a sleight-of-hand man at worst—someone engaged in replacing one thing in this world with another thing that would also appear to us in this world if only our instruments, as we might put it, were capable of registering the change. But something of the sort is the inevitable effect of shifting the action from a relational to a constitutive context. In the former we would hear the accent on the first word of the formula: "*This* is my body (for our purposes now)." In the second the accent falls on the last word, "This is my *body* (in spite of appearances)." A transitive situation has thus been replaced by a static problem, the solution to which not unexpectedly produces secondary problems of its own.

One of these difficulties is the question of "subsistent accidents." If the accidents of bread remain after the substance has been replaced by another substance of a different kind, how could they "subsist" in the absence of their usual support? Do they become quasi-substances in their own right? Or does one of the accidents suffice to back up the others? In Thomas's case, the second alternative is adopted as a solution: quantity survives the removal of its proper substance well enough to support the other accidents. If so, the appearances of bread can still be consistent with the reality of the body of Christ—or rather, the *substance* of the body of Christ.[56] One may feel this "solution" is something of a stopgap, the need for which betrays a more general weakness in the argument as a whole. The local embarrassment derives more generally from the fact that transubstantiation explains not too much but too little. It accounts for the change in the substance of the entity concerned while leaving the accidents to the senses to deal with as best they can. In a more inclusive view the action would be understood as bringing about an entire change, as we have seen, "body" and soul alike, or flesh and Spirit—in which case a more holistic explanation would still be required, and with that a sufficiently all-embracing term. "Transfinalization" or "transignification" will not quite achieve what is needed either, though these substitutes for Thomas's language have both been offered and condemned, and each would still have its potential hermeneutical use. *Metousiosis,* the irresistibly ambiguous Greek word, might seem preferable to all the other candidates—if anyone could be persuaded to adopt it.[57]

Whatever its limits as an explanatory terminology, Thomas's idea of substance would still be easier to rescue for an account of the event that wished to stay closer to the metamorphoses of the body than some later developments of that Aristotelian concept. With his help one could at least think of substance as something more

---

[56] I found a convenient review of the subsistent-accident question in R. G. Fontaigne, *Subsistent Accident in the Philosophy of Saint Thomas and His Predecessors* (Washington: Catholic University of America Press, 1950). If a dissertation presented to Catholic University in 1950 could not solve this problem, it is hard to imagine what might.

[57] A summary of the modern Dutch discussion, from which the extra-Aquinan terms quoted derive, may be conveniently found in J. M. Powers, *Eucharistic Theology* (New York: Herder & Herder, 1967). Edward Schillebeeckx, *The Eucharist* (New York: Sheed and Ward, 1968), represents a (comparatively conservative) review by a participant. The major name here is Franz J. Leenhardt, the Reformed theologian whose "Ceci est mon Corps" of 1955 initiated the controversy. This work is available in English in *Essays on the Lord's Supper,* ed. Oscar Cullmann and Franz J. Leenhardt (Atlanta: John Knox, 1958).

specific than a sort of underlying or extended stuff, like sand in a wilderness or ore dug from a mine. That notion would derive from later permutations of the idea through Descartes and Locke—not to mention Marx or even Heidegger. In Thomas, substance is still close to the principle of individuation, or the practical reason for the relative autonomy of any single thing. To say of anything that it was or had a substance would in his terms be to recognize in it something of that integrity and independence we attribute to bodies in general. Substantiality might accordingly be classed as one of the notes of bodiliness as well as a property abstracted from bodies. The doctrine employing the term could then be read as affirming that the bread, or (if we correct a previous partiality) the bread and the wine together, would indeed compose a body and that this combination would therefore have to be taken as amounting to *another* body for the purposes at hand—which might in its turn be understood as consisting of another substance. In that case, the word could be treated as the name within a certain universe of discourse for what indicates the presence of a body. "Transubstantiation" would then specify a reproduction of the body after the manner of a certain metaphysics, which is to say, as far as the actual *conversio* might prove knowable by way of the Aristotelian categories. One would prefer some such solution, for then the doctrine could become one more act of homage and not just an inappropriate reduction.[58]

Ontological uncertainty is one problem that may arise, whether because of a shift in the place of representation from one end of the action to the other or because of a doubt respecting the referentiality of the intermediate symbol. More impressive in the long run than either, I suspect, is the import of what takes place for our sense of both time and gender. These advance into the foreground as soon as we realize the action as a last will and testament, or quite literally a *diathēkē,* as the Septuagint and thereafter the New Testament texts call a covenant. Jesus is bequeathing his "property"—which is to say whatever is indeed proper to him—to his heirs, as Moses and the first Joshua had done in their day, or Isaac and Jacob before or the Davidic kings after them. The major prophets too had once conveyed their oracles to their disciples, who in due course arranged and redacted them to compose the texts we now read. But the inheritance in this case is eschatological, not patriarchal. The transfer is therefore not from father to son or "sons," and so from one generation to the next, but from an elder brother to his siblings of *both* sexes within a single because ultimate generation. The early Church at first assumed that the remainder of the seventy years Jesus might have lived would make up the

---

[58]The difficulties that followed at the time from substituting "substance" for "body," and so metaphysics for mystery, is traced in G. Martelet, *The Risen Christ and the Eucharistic World* (New York: Seabury, 1976) 133-37. One might recall in connection with this issue that Trent too speaks of the conversion in question as appropriately "called" transubstantiation, which has seemed to leave room for alternative explanations. See O'Carroll, *Corpus Christi,* 204 and 205.

rest of what was therefore called "this," meaning the last, generation. That did not happen—in the flesh. In the flesh there have in fact been many generations since, and there may yet be many more. But in the Spirit, each of these must still be counted as identical for the purpose in question with the first. Temporality as such is revealed as mediate rather than ultimate. Our repeated experience of generational change will serve to exhibit but does not determine the form in which the new version of the relation demonstrates itself.

This is a major change from the state of affairs maintained within the older dispensation, where the right to participate is passed down from father to son—and must therefore be limited in principle as well as practice to a succession of male descendants. The eschatological Israel is not, Jesus would then be showing, dependent on this mode of transmission. The action converts all those who share in it into coheirs with him of what he had already received from the Father, who is therefore the only "patriarch" that counts in the end. In this version of the relation, the inheritance is passed on laterally rather than vertically. All members of the relevant community, then or since, are in effect contemporaries in the Spirit. Jesus has thus provided ahead of time, ours as well as his, a way to transcend a mere recapitulation of the past in the present, which is otherwise the best we can do in or out of the religious relation. He gives us at least the beginning of a future (as absolute as it is constant) that coincides with his own immediate identity. That condition is in fact the "nearness" of the Kingdom. In the action he initiates, this identity becomes our own present too. An otherwise unexperienceable dimension of time is thus begun upon whenever the corresponding rite is celebrated. In this way the Church repeats her own origin over and over, reopening on each occasion just that mode of temporality which in fact is proper to her, day after Day. For the communal mode of the body has always existed at just this moment: about, as we might also put it, to be born again at last. The Kingdom has not yet "come," we know all too well, but it is as "near" still as it ever was for him. At the close of his life, that is, Jesus repeats the apocalyptic instant in which he first assumed his spiritual identity. What the Father did for him in what we are able retrospectively to reimagine as the baptism or the conception or the "procession," depending upon which narrative we presuppose, is what he is accomplishing in this action for the sake of a community that is thereafter utterly free to assume the same eschatological task: to *be* an embodiment of the absolute future in human form, lest that possibility cease to be credited. The Church, we might say accordingly, is now in her version of the "ministerial" phase of his existence. The corresponding "passion" and "resurrection" are evidently still ahead.[59]

---

[59]It has been part of the conventional wisdom for some time that Jesus intended to announce the Kingdom of God by making so much of the absolute future as must be meant by that term indicatively present. A useful review of the scholarly tradition may be found in Robert W. Funk, *Parables and Presence: Forms of the New Testament Tradition* (Philadel-

And the change of scale involves a temporal difference even for a state of being that as such transcends time. Up until the moment when the transfer of identity takes place, the eschatological privilege has been exercised on the scale of the individual alone. There is only one of him, nor has there ever been anyone else of just the same kind, before or since. As an individual, exceptional or not, he was in the nature of this mode of being limited to a comparatively brief period and a few places in what has turned out to be no more than one part of the world—however central in its own or any one else's estimation. The corresponding community, though, has in the nature of that mode of existence been able to manifest herself at any time or place—and may accordingly go on doing so, for as long as there shall ever be times or places. The eschatological Israel is therefore free to live through one half of a single generation—or all of as many generations as there may yet be. That makes no difference in the Spirit. For what would have once held true for the representative group originally assembled would continue possible for any subsequent gathering within the scope of the persisting intention. A repetition of the founding gesture on subsequent occasions would do no more than spell out an obvious implication of the initiating event: that others would in due course come to share in and pass along the benefit transmitted, including the temporal privilege—if only on the condition proposed, which would in the first place be to realize at least this much of what in fact was going on.

To feel a change in the species of temporality that accompanies the action is also, as our pronouns have already announced, to reflect upon the event as a shift in gender. Jesus is a man—as an individual. That is how he can be the "son" both of an earthly and the heavenly king. His gender enables him to convert the patriarchal relation, like the rest of the world it begets, into a parable of the ultimate state of affairs. What is literally male, whether familial or Davidic, is thereby metamorphosed into an image of the Spirit, through which any feature of this age must be reinterpreted as binding in the age to come only metaphorically. Nor is anything more representatively masculine, one may fairly concede, than his willingness to disappear body and "soul" into the polarity formed by the symbols chosen. For in any age it is typically the male who is most unqualifiedly placed at the service of a social intention. The female is by tradition and biology alike invited to reserve her individual body for the sake, precisely, of the next generation. The male can afford to use himself up—or be used up. Jesus is at least a sacrifice, we have agreed, and firstborn sons are ripe for that in any age, though the god in question is more often an idol than the Lord indeed.

---

phia: Fortress, 1982) 69-75. Bruce Chilton has edited a collection of essays on the topic, entitled *The Kingdom of God in the Tradition of Jesus* (Philadelphia: Fortress, 1984). Beasley-Murray, *Jesus and the Kingdom of God,* also includes a summary of recent German work on the Kingdom (258-73). It seems to the point we have been following that none of the authors collected by Chilton mentions the Eucharist.

But if the first moment of the action is decidedly male, and the surrender of that to form the second moment scarcely less so, the consumption of the latter to produce the third reveals a result that would have to be just as evidently female, though no longer in the mode of a single individual. For the body of any community is bound to take on this gender, as soon as we are able to realize that a body is present at all. The Church cannot be an "it," except as one more institution in this world, which would obviously *not* be the ultimate Israel produced by the action in question. That would have to be a woman, in any language. It would not therefore be altogether frivolous, though it could seem tasteless, to observe that the resurrection amounts to a sex-change operation. The body of Christ on the scale of the individual is male. The *same* body on the scale of the community is female. The Eucharist, we could then say, is the rib of the new Adam.

This aspect of the metamorphosis has of course been realized, though not perhaps as completely as it might. We still regularly call the resultant community the "body of Christ," for instance, as if by virtue of the title this were still somehow masculine, like the individual before the change. And such an attribution would be supported by the resurrection appearances and the story of the ascension, which also present the individual all over again in the mode of vision, as well as by so much of the language to follow as makes the risen Jesus into the "head" of the subsequent body, as if he were still one of its members, though the highest in rank, from whom a correspondingly masculine hierarchy of subordinate authorities might be derived. The development within the tradition of the figure of Mary, on the other hand, with the corresponding dogmas and devotions, might seem at least a partial expression of a deeper intuition that any communal mode of the body would need to be realized as feminine.[60] But these renderings still maintain a certain alienation from their own import, which is registered in the implied presence throughout of a son or a husband or simply of an addressee for the words put in her mouth. This displacement reinforces the subordinate place of the figure she makes even as it exaggerates, as if to compensate, the deference invited. So her statues, for instance, remain portraits of an aestheticized or sentimentalized great goddess, and to that extent a compromise with a half-assimilated paganism, original or feral, rather than a full confirmation of the eschatological privilege. But if Mary is in fact not merely a fictional or popular image only, much less an exploded superstition or inherited embarrassment, but in fact a reproduction at a certain mythical distance of the principle of the whole, then her apparently "supplementary" position could itself be

---

[60]The history of traditional Marianism is copiously if uncritically surveyed in Hilda Graef's *Mary: A History of Doctrine* (London: Sheed and Ward, 1985). Marina Warner's influential *Alone of All Her Sex: The Myth and the Cult of the Virgin Mary* (New York: Knopf, 1976) has retold this story from the corresponding post-Catholic, feminist perspective. The identification of Mary with the Church, already implied by Rev. 12, became explicit with Ambrose. It has recently been reaffirmed by such defenders of her traditional role as von Balthasar and John Paul II.

interpreted as evidence for what still remains Jewish or Roman or simply profane and therefore at once worldly and masculine in the Church's idea of what ought better to be thought of as *herself* indeed. If the body of Christ is now indeed feminine, the apparently obsolete extravagances of Marian doctrine and practice might better be thought through again than marginalized or patronized.[61]

It might even be possible too, though obviously not soon, for those now associated with the otherwise very opposite movement stimulated by the recent revival of feminist theology to interpret their own struggle to recast the tradition, textual or social, as yet another displacement from the long-incomplete task of appropriating the identity provided the community as a whole. Neither a traditionalist sect nor any progressive caucus could as such represent this community in full ("Church" had better be reserved for that whole, present or absent), but either or both might serve to manifest what remains to be acknowledged and therefore, sooner or later, incorporated. A symptom, physical or cultural, is not a solution, but at least it calls attention to a deficiency. Obviously neither party would care to see itself in any such indeterminate position. We would all rather be interpreters than in need of interpretation.[62]

If, though, the initial transmission may be read as implying among its other concomitants a change of gender for the eschatological identity in question, other alterations might follow. We could, for instance, apply the dogmas associated with Mary as an individual to the community she would then enfigure without qualification. Is it not, after all, the final Israel which could either be immaculately conceived or assumed into heaven? And if that much were clearer than now seems possible, it might even be the familiar image of the risen Jesus that could come to seem "mythological" in the pejorative sense instead of the figure of Mary. We might be confident too that such currently contested issues as the liturgical role of

---

[61]Renzo del Fante, ed., *Our Lady Speaks to Her Beloved Priests* (Milan: Marian Movement of Priests, 1982) might stand as one of many specimens of the Marian subculture, with its "cenacles," "interior locutions," and "special revelations," not to mention apparitions, recognized or irregular. The cryptic prophecies mixed with demands for an unqualified consecration, the emphasis on purity and allegiance to the pope, and dark anticipations of a "calvary" ahead severally represent the paranoid style of a cult rather than a movement. John Paul II, *Mary: God's Yes to Man* (San Francisco: Ignatius, 1988) represents by contrast a sober and thoroughly authorized version of the possibility. It includes useful references to the link between Mary and the Church: 50, 52, 93-94, 102, 135-39, and 146-47.

[62]Daly, Reuther, and Fiorenza are already familiar names in and out of the movement in question. Others might easily be listed, serious or popular. Among the former I would rank Schneiders, Trible, McFague, Englesman, and Heine; among the latter, and therefore better known at large, Pagels, Boff, and Haddon. The feminists should be distinguished from what might be called the "femalists," who frankly call for a revival of the goddess indeed. Gimbutas, Christ, Weber, Griffen, and "Starhawk" could specify this neo-Romantic option. The issue will recur as we proceed.

women in the community would seem easier to resolve. To begin with, at least, a believing woman would already be enabled in the light of such an appropriation to realize herself as already an instance of the whole even on the scale of the individual in a way not open to the male, who has as it were been preempted for good by his elder brother. And we might even come to be more content than has recently seemed possible with the idea that the image of God had better remain masculine—for we would then know that nobody else absolutely is.[63]

Evangelical

But the most important corollary had better not even be called by any such diminishing title. This consequence would be the import of the action for that often-abused expression "the gospel." We could appreciate better what might properly be meant by this term if we attend to the grammar of the principal instances. And these should be thought of as beginning not with Christianity but in the Old Testament moments of self-declaration. In Exodus 3, the type of them all, the Lord reveals to Moses that his Name is "I am who I am," *ehyeh asher ehyeh.* The tense of the verb is imperfect, which accordingly bears a future sense. So I AM means "I will be," an affirmation that immediately attracts a prepositional phrase to complete it. The Lord's future presence "with thee" is the way in which his Name will be spelled out, as it were, starting with Moses before Pharoah. That promise of future assistance and support is the identity of the true God of Israel, as far as its citizens need realize this. The formula is accordingly repeated or alluded to at intervals thereafter both before and after the central Mosaic moment, either to introduce episodes of special revelation or authenticate passages of instruction. *Ani* or *anōchi* YHWH, "I am the LORD," is one version; *ani hu,* "I am he," is a prophetic variant. Such declarations of identity in as near the first person as possible thus become the core of the kerygma, as it will later be called, or that which is to be revealed: the presence, that is, of the revealer. The Word that authorizes all the other words is always essentially the Name, which cannot do otherwise than disclose the very presence it announces in the act of being spoken.

In the third person, which must be used by any human being speaking to another human being *about* this divine identity, the Name becomes what appears in

---

[63]That the Father of Jesus should still remain masculine is itself a contested issue. Leonard Boff has recently attempted to bring together modern feminism with traditional "femininity," dogma and myth, Scripture and liberation theology, to produce (by way of a possible hypostatic union with the Holy Spirit) a redefinition of Mary as already *The Maternal Face of God* (San Francisco: Harper, 1987). The result, as one might expect, is more rhetoric than theology, perhaps because the traditional analogy between Mary and the community does not attract him personally. I would guess that an appropriate development of this metaphor would make any current extravagance, fanatical or modish, equally unnecessary.

writing as the tetragrammaton, which would accordingly have to be translated as "he will be (with you)." It is this objective form that is explicitly referred to as "the Name" through the rest of Scripture, including especially the Psalms. It is therefore this version that forms the core of the priestly blessing, as in Numbers 6:24-27: "Let him bless thee, the LORD, and keep thee. . . . " The explanatory directive adds (v. 27), "So they shall set (*samu*) my Name (*shemi*) on the sons of Israel, and I will bless them." To bless is to call the Name out over the heads of the people, so as to invoke on their behalf the assistance of the One to whom it refers. So holy did this privilege come to seem that in later times at least only the high priest was allowed to pronounce even the third-person form of the Name aloud in public, and then only on Yom Kippur. In ordinary use it remained necessary to substitute "the Lord" for the syllables of the tetragrammaton when it occurred in the text. So we read rather a name for the Name than the thing itself; as in still-later times, the bare abstraction *Ha Shem,* that is, "the Name," was in turn substituted for the previous substitution.[64] There will be more to say in a later chapter about the difference between the third- and first-person forms of the Name in connection with the communal mode of the body.

All we need remark now is that what we have come to call "the gospel," or the Word as that may be proclaimed, is still essentially identical with the Name, or that which makes present the presence of God. The form of the fundamental declaration varies with the species of discourse employed as well as the occasion or speaker. In the prophetic mode, for instance, the action promised might appear as impersonal and the verb in a future tense that does *not* apply in the present: salvation, it would then be said, *will* indeed *be,* but not yet, and we do not know how or by whom. The New Testament authors find themselves looking back on rather than ahead to the beginning of the time of salvation. They accordingly adopt the historic mode, in which this much of the future has already become the past, and the action hoped for has therefore acquired an identifiable agent. *He was* can then provide an implicit master sentence for their elaborations.

This tense and person is accordingly the way in which what we would identify as the gospel in the familiar sense is formulated in the letters of Paul as well as in the narratives of Acts. In such a dense summary as Romans 3:21-26, for instance, where Paul concentrates a version at once thoroughly traditional and acutely personal of the message he intends to develop throughout the remainder of that epistle, he takes for granted that one complex sentence will suffice to rehearse the major features of a past event involving an individual chosen by God with whom his addressees have already come to terms. Other reminders and allusions implicitly sharing the same grammar may be found elsewhere in the letters where Paul is

---

[64]The history of the Name is conveniently reviewed in F. Gavin's classic *Jewish Antecedents of the Christian Sacraments* (New York: Ktav, 1969) esp. 59-63. Gavin appears to be a source for the idea of the Eucharist as a blessing, which appears later in Dix and Bouyer.

indeed "preaching the gospel" as opposed to drawing out its implications for the ethical life. The same formula in the third person and the past tense would also generate those sermons in Acts where Luke is reproducing the style of the earliest proclamations. The longer narratives of the synoptics and presently of John could then be read as elaborations on the scale of whole books of this fundamental *he was*, with other verbs and predicates to specify as required. None of these narrative versions, it needs to be remembered, is able to transcend the condition thereby presumed: that the revelation must be realized imaginatively as distanced in time and person. The modern "quests" for the historical Jesus, we may observe, continue to be governed by the same condition, with the additional disadvantage that the pastness of the past in question, not to mention the character of the person concerned, has in the nature of the case become even more remote. Equally derivative, we would also have to realize, must be any formulation of the revelation in terms of a putative *he said*. Here Matthew is the primary instance, with his disposition to predefine "the gospel" as one speech complex after another, like the Sermon on the Mount or the Apostolic Discourse.

Within the evangelical mode strictly so called, though, the tense of the fundamental proposition becomes present once again, though still in the third person. The corresponding formula then reads *he is*! This would be the gospel as immediate proclamation or oral testimony. Into this category would go the several Christological titles when they are used as acts of faith, together with the various "proofs" offered of the resurrection in terms of current cure or wonder. That the one chosen not only *was* but still *is*, and therefore *will* continue to *be*, then becomes the burden of the message. In the corresponding responsive mode, a confession is addressed to the person proclaimed in the form of prayer: which is to say, as *thou art*. With either of these forms we obviously come closer to the heart of the matter than with the historical tense and the third person. But only a truly apocalyptic grammar could reveal the whole truth at stake in what would then become once again the first person and the present or future tense of the verb in the same style as the earliest revelation: *I am*. The gospel, to become altogether itself, would have to be declared by the subject of it in his own person, here and now.[65]

The tradition quickly assumed from its own appreciation of this necessity the right to speak out prophetically "in Jesus' name"; that is, to employ the *egō eimi*

---

[65]If the gospel is most inwardly the *I am* as spoken from the other side of the relation, one would have a way of defining the various *anti*gospels of modernity in terms of the same grammar. Objectivity, for instance, the principal idol of our world, could be summed up as the hegemony of an impersonal *it is*. The prevalence of the exceptional individual in the flesh as opposed to the Spirit could be expressed by a contrary *I am*, as illustrated by a variety of instances in thought, politics, and especially art since Descartes at least. The "anti-Christ" is multiple in our world, and includes many of those figures we most properly admire. The roar of the crowd would then amount to an equally carnal *we are*. But a study of these permutations would require a book in itself.

formula for the publication of supplementary declarations in the Spirit as required by circumstances. We find this ecclesial permission at once encouraged and resisted by Paul, who found himself obliged to recognize the gift in himself and others even as he sought to limit its exercise.[66] In Mark, who seems to have appreciated very well what the formula implies, the *egō eimi* coincides with what scholarship has come to call the "messianic secret." This is narratively revealed when Jesus claims his full identity before the high priest at the trial. In answer to the key question, "Are you the Christ, son of the Blessed One?" he answers, *egō eimi,* "I am," and follows this with a prophecy of the future shape of the identity thereby announced (Mark 14:62). But for Mark, prophecy within the Church after the fact is evidently to be discouraged. It is only *pseudochristoi* who can be expected to employ the formula of themselves (Mark 13:21).

John is the evangelist who best understands how the motif of the Name may be employed to provide not just a climax for exceptional units but a structure for an entire composition. His narrative and discourses alike are formed to throw into relief a core proposition that typically surfaces at the end of important episodes as a sentence of which the subject and verb is always *egō eimi* and the predicate whatever serves in context as a vehicle for the central self-revelation. The Jesus of this history says of himself that "I am" successively the Christ, the bread of life, the living water, the light of the world, the good shepherd, the resurrection, the way, truth, and life, and the true vine. There are also less-explicit self-identifications with the wine in the Cana story and the temple in the polemic with "the Jews" that follows. Each instance of the key sentence thus constitutes a parable, in which the ineffable identity is manifested in some phenomenon drawn from the practice and tradition of this world. It is fair to conclude (though this would take a longer argument to support) that the famous formula of the Johannine prologue, "And the Word was made flesh," *kai hō logos sarx egenetō,* is advanced as an introductory summary of the propositions offered in the narrative to follow. For if the *egō eimi* or Name is indeed the true *logos* or Word of God, then all the contexts within which this identity may reveal itself are cumulatively the "flesh" that embodies it. What has happened in Jesus, John understands, is that the Name of God has indeed been "spelled out" in our world. To provide the *I am* (which in Exodus must repeat itself in a circle of pure subjectivity) with a set of predicates is thus to discover a gram-

---

[66]The possibility of identifying Jesus' identity with that revealed in the Name may have begun in an early rereading of Ps. 110:1, "The Lord said to my Lord," which Peter quotes in Acts 2:34. This usage in turn might have prompted the declaration of faith repeated in 1 Cor. 12:3 and Rom. 10:9, "Jesus is Lord!" which also occurs in John 20:28 as Thomas's confession. Barnabas Lindars conveniently connects these verses in his *Gospel of John* (Grand Rapids: Eerdmans, 1987) 176-77. Goergen (*Theology of Jesus* 2:174-79) brings the relevant discussion of the titles *mar, kurios,* and *adonai* up to date. Once the third-person version of the Name had been accepted as appropriate, the first could not have been far behind—to start with among prophets, then for narrators.

matical equivalent for the new version of the constant gospel that the fact of Jesus imparts.[67]

John's narrative notoriously omits an account of the establishment of the Eucharist, substituting instead the washing of the feet, which dramatizes the sacrificial half of the action, and a last discourse, which provides a verbal equivalent to the sacramental intention. His specific allusions—if they are his—to the rite are to be found in chapter 6, at some distance from their obvious context.[68] Yet the prayer of Jesus to the Father at the close of the final discourse can serve as an admirable meditation on the meaning of the omitted action. In this so-called high-priestly prayer Jesus speaks of his need to give the disciples what had been given to him. This is variously named: eternal life, your Name, your word, the words. Jesus asks that his followers, who will have to remain in the world, may receive from the Father what he has received and repeatedly given to them, so that they too may be one. One, word, truth, glory, love—the language moves in and around the major words in the elusive Johannine style, as if to keep active within the thought proposed all the elements that make it up: the unity of the Father and the Son, the existence and needs of the community to follow, the gifts provided him or them.

A key verse is John 17:11b: "Holy Father, keep them in your Name through which you have given to me, that they may be one as we." This is a difficult sentence to translate, for the *hō dedōkas moi* clause is inconveniently situated, and the dative pronoun especially has proved troublesome from the beginning, as alternatives in the versions show. If the English above is a possible, if grammatically clumsy, rendering of the sense intended, then the Jesus of this speech is saying that as the Father gave the Son his own Name, so by way of that Name it has

---

[67]Raymond Brown's splendid Anchor Bible commentary, *The Gospel according to John*, 2 vols., AB 29 and 29A (Garden City NY: Doubleday, 1965, 1970) 2:754-56, includes a brief survey of the Name problem, together with a quotation from the gnostic *Gospel of Truth*: "The name of the Father is the Son." Discussion of the *egō eimi* in general is summarized in Philip Harner, *The "I am" in the Fourth Gospel* (Philadelphia: Fortress, 1970) and G. H. Parke-Taylor, *Yahweh: The Divine Name in the Bible* (Waterloo, Ontario: Wilfred Laurier University Press, 1975) 73-78. Thomas H. Tobin's scholarly "Prologue of John and Hellenistic Jewish Speculation," *CBQ* 52 (1990): 252-69, and Werner Kelber's acutely post-Derridian "In the Beginning Was the Word: The Apotheosis and Narrative Displacement of the Logos," *AAR* 58 (1990): 69-98, represent more recent attention to the *logos* problem, neither of which in fact associates the Word with the Name. Warren Carter, "The Prologue and John's Gospel: Function, Symbol, and the Definitive Word," *NTS* 39 (1990): 35-58, offers several ways in which the prologue might be connected with the narrative, but not the one proposed here.

[68]John 6:51-58, where the eucharistic allusions cluster, has been an occasion for contention among the commentators. Some (Barrett, Brown, Schnackenberg) are willing to read these verses as belonging to the principal author of the gospel. Others (Bultmann, Marxsen, Haenchen) prefer to assign them to a redactor. But a putative "I am the flesh and blood," and therefore "the bread" and the wine, would be consistent with the underlying grammar of the narrative as a whole.

become possible for the Son to establish the unity of the community in that Name. The idea is repeated in the next verse. "When I was with them, I kept them in your Name . . . " and the same *hō dedōkas moi* clause succeeds—"through which you have given to me"—though this time a *hina* does not follow, but instead a break in the movement of the sentence: "and I guarded, and none out of them was lost, except for the son of destruction, so that [here another *hina* does appear] the scripture might be fulfilled" (17:12). The whole thought might be paraphrased as follows: "When I was with them, I kept them in your Name, through which you have given to me that they may be one, and I guarded this unity so well that none of them was lost except the son of destruction, who was bound to be."

The word *one* especially would thus become a virtual synonym for the Name itself. The unity of the community is then a revelation to its members of their participation in the Name, which allows them to remain in the same mode of being with their founder and his Father. We are very close here to a *you are* that would correspond to the *I am*—in which case the final discourse would become a climactic repetition of the fundamental Johannine sentence, which would propose not merely one more in a sequence of predicates for a singular version of the divine identity but a new and plural version of the subject. The proposition would then amount to a tautology: what *I am, you will be*. But in fact, as we have just seen, this does not quite happen. The language hovers about such a declaration without altogether arriving there. There remains for John a slight but significant difference between the privileges of the individual and those with which the community is here being endowed. "I am the vine," says Jesus, and you are the "branches." It is a characteristic image for subordination. And even after the "other" Paraclete has arrived, he will tell the disciples only what his predecessor has already said (John 14:16, 26).

There could be more than one explanation for this reserve. But one is simply literary. It is Jesus who speaks. John's narrative, like that of the other evangelists, must in the nature of the genre adopted limit itself to what the individual can be re-imagined as having done and said in what from the writer's and reader's point of view has become the past. A *you are* is therefore conceivable, even if it does not quite take place; a *we are,* the plural version that would most fully correspond to the singular original, would have to be spoken by the community in the present of the readers—and there is no room for that to occur within the narrative that is being read.

But what cannot be expressed as content continues as a necessary presupposition of the form. For only if the community has indeed understood herself (could John have tolerated the feminine pronoun?) to have inherited a full measure of the founder's identity would it be possible for one of the members to assume the right to formulate such revelatory words at all. John writes *as* Jesus—for the sake of his own readers. The truth that cannot quite be declared then functions as a condition for the teasing approximations that do in fact appear. For if we can now hear the risen Christ speaking to us in these words, over the heads, as it were, of the characters in the story, this can only be because the author is already addressing his congregation in the same Spirit that has authorized them; and we, from a further distance in space and time, can identify ourselves as in the same Spirit still members of what remains in principle yet another instance of the same community. This is the rhetorical reason for the uncanny force of these discourses. The *egō eimi* is all but patent in their content. The corresponding *hemeis esmen,* or *we are,* is necessarily latent in their form.

The discourses of John's gospel, then, and the last of these especially, can be read as an equivalent in the mode of written prophecy to the bodily action with which we have been concerned. It is therefore appropriate that John should situate his climactic discourse at the point in the narrative that corresponds to a rehearsal of the ritual transmission he has deliberately left out. Let me conclude with an episode later in John's narrative that is not usually evoked in connection either with the Name or with the Eucharist. This is 19:25-27, where Jesus while still hanging alive upon the cross makes provision for his mother and "the disciple whom he loved." Here too the grammar is interesting. Jesus offers a double proposition to the persons addressed. Each proposition offers a redefinition in the declarative present tense. "Woman, this is your son" is followed by "This is your mother." The action is virtually liturgical as well as literally testamentary. In it the family obligations of the parties concerned are redefined. A reception of the implied command entails a new relationship between the two persons addressed, who thereby acquire a new identity toward each other. In all these ways the double declaration resembles the words of institution. It is easy to infer besides that each person bears a symbolic meaning: the disciple is a figure for the tradition within which this text is composed, and so of the author himself, and Jesus' mother correspondingly represents the community that sustains this tradition and supplies John's audience. The declaration as a whole both looks forward to and constitutes a version of the Church. Should we distinguish as well between the woman, who is addressed first, as an equivalent of the "bread" and the man as the "wine" of this redefinition? Presumably that would be forcing the parallel. But as a whole the episode might help clarify not just an aspect of John's own eucharistic thinking but part, I suspect, of the meaning of the event itself. For John is a good interpreter of what he had received, even when he does not mention all of it in so many words.

John understands Jesus; but Jesus does more than John. What John does, or almost does, can occur in language alone. He is a Christian prophet, the only one of that kind among the narrative Evangelists; but he is still a member of the relevant community, not its founder. The prophet understands, we have been arguing, that the Word is the Name, and therefore that an articulation of the Name is the special task of the chosen individual. He knows too that this self-manifestation is at the heart of what we call "the gospel," and that the predicates in terms of which the master sentence is completed must always refer to some element in the sarkic life of those addressed. The *logoi* of the *logos* are whatever realities already have meaning for the audience presumed.

What John cannot do is pass beyond words. But Jesus has already done this by the time John writes. We may suppose that Jesus would indeed have shared with his second-generation disciple a similar consciousness of the Name as this appears especially in what we now call Second Isaiah. That is, after all, a text both of them could read: the *egō eimi* of the Septuagint appears in Hebrew, we have already noticed, as *ani hu,* with the same reference to a first-person revelation. The eucharistic action, we have also argued, would already presume that the agent of it had arrived at a self-identification equivalent to that which is expressed by the Name as it is dramatized in John's narrative. The "blood" of the identity presupposed would then be a vehicle for the presence affirmed, as the "flesh" would be analogous to one or another of the Johannine predicates—which in Jesus' case would all be implicit in his own individual existence as a human being.

The Name is thus as good a clue as we have to the central identity of the person who initiates the action with which we have been concerned, an action that, we have also been claiming, sums up all the other actions. For only the Name can be "spoken" in the first person, explicitly or implicitly, in one language or another, and therefore fully appropriated. The other titles must be applied from without in the third person. Christ, Son of David, Son of Man, even Son of God, are therefore all indirect, parables of the presence but not yet the presence itself. They are predicate nominatives, as it were, but not yet the subject proper. Jesus may accordingly be understood as the one who understood himself as authorized to "say" the Name of himself, and with the same intention already registered in the story of the revelation to Moses. Later on in Exodus, as the specific commandments of the Book of the Covenant are about to conclude in a series of warnings, the Lord is reported as saying, pay attention to my "messenger," for "my Name is in him"—most literally, in his insides, *sh'mi b'qirbo* (Exod. 23:21). That seems a fair description not only of Moses, who must be referred to in this context, but even more scandalously of Jesus. And did not the same Moses change the first Joshua's name from Hoshea, according to Numbers 13:16, so that his successor too might bear the Name most literally within his own into the promised land? Or the prepositional relation may be reversed. Psalms 118:26, "Blessed is he who comes in the Name of the Lord," is quoted in the story of the entry into Jerusalem in all four of the narrative gospels. The Name may be "in" Jesus, then, or Jesus may be "in" the Name. In either case, the Name is most seriously who he is. For his own "proper" name would in effect only translate this identity once again. *Yeshua,* or "Yah saves," comes true precisely as the divine presence, which *is* the action referred to.

And the Name indicates purpose as well as identity. That purpose, either in the history of the nation or the ministry of the individual, is always in the long run beneficent. In the short run God may have to be with his people in the mode of being against them, as instruction or punishment. In the End he is sure to be with them in the mode of support, validation, victory, salvation. And clearly Jesus acts as the agent for this side of the divine purpose. So he demonstrates the positive meaning of the Name in his own person—which is also to say, in the body, which is therefore to say, in the bodies of others. That is what *his* work consists of. Jesus is the Name embodied.

When the time comes to pass on this identity, he must do so in the third person, for he accepts the conditions of signification. The two demonstrative pronouns employed announce a public state of affairs. But if the same double proposition is recast in the first person, it would read as "I am (divided between) this bread and this wine." When these are consumed, therefore, a complementary "you are" emerges on the farther side. What *I am,* that is, has been converted by way of this double locution into what *you will be.* And once the communication is accepted, the "you" of address converts into a "we" of appropriation. To receive the Name is to become as much of this as can ever be made flesh all over again for a second—or rather a third—time. It is to declare the identity of God once again as the core of any good news in yet one more language as Israel made good at last. The individual, or at least *this* individual, the individual of individuals, is by virtue of the very identity that defines him bound to bring about the very community that will repeat him, ad infinitum. No wonder then that the last verse of Matthew should, as a conclusion to the commissioning of the disciples in his climactic resurrection appearance on the mountain in Galilee, promise in so many words that "I will be with you," *egō meth' humōn eimi,* until the winding up of the ages (Matt. 28:20). What else should the resurrection amount to, in any properly evangelical vocabulary?

But the idiom in which this miracle is most directly accomplished is *not* verbal. If it had been, the result could have become no more at best than a prophetic or imaginative anticipation of itself, as in the sayings or stories of the narrative gospels. Even the so-called words of institution are strictly speaking less indispensable than pedagogical. They are rubrics or stage directions that serve to frame the exchange of one mode of the body for another. The central metamorphosis in fact goes forward in an uninterrupted silence as inaudible as the conception—as invisible, indeed, as the resurrection. In the unspoken and unspeakable language of the body, the action announces that the Kingdom of God is indeed upon us, *like this.* The End is shown to be as "near" as the next gesture one makes, or breath one draws, or thing one touches, or person one hears speaking to somebody else down the corridor. We are invited to consider the extent and meaning of all our relations before language has begun—or just after it has fallen silent for good. For in the body alone can all things be just what they "say," and a word coincide at once with its origin and its import.

The term *basar,* after all, is a pun. It means either "tidings," especially good news, or flesh. In the eucharistic action the flesh *is* the news. The body of Christ is therefore the whole of the gospel already, without omission or displacement: the kerygma indeed. What could be better news, after all, than to discover at last who *we* truly *are*? As with the singular, the plural version would allow for a variety of predicates. In the case of the individual as retrospectively imagined by the fourth evangelist, these become a sequence of parabolic nouns: water, light, shepherd, and the rest. In the case of the community, I suspect the equivalent would be a set of participles. *We are* some representative group of people in the process of doing this or that cryptic, beneficent, but always concrete thing that will indeed exhibit the presence of God—to those who have eyes to see. And whatever is done in this style will count as fully analogous to what he did once upon a time. For all behavior of the kind rhymes.

The Eucharist may then be understood as conveying the full gospel without deficit or projection either in time or figure. The past may belong to me in imagination, but in reality the future belongs to God. So any individual body, including my own, is already in principle over and done with, except insofar as I may be able to convert it into some semipermanent fiction that I call my self. But *the* body into which I am inducted by this action is always just about to take place. The Eucharist is the fulfillment of the promise made in the Name, the firstfruits of the land that would otherwise be missing from under our feet, the one absolutely unqualified positive, which is therefore on the far side of all the familiar negatives. In the act of receiving, the community can therefore awaken as who there is to be for sure. For to comprehend the message is to become what it proclaims.

To know who this one is, Hans Frei has observed, is to be placed in his presence.[69] His identity *is* his presence. It is a stunning observation. But Frei himself has trouble explaining how this epiphany could still be true by way of the evidence provided in the narrative gospels. For these, though they do indeed display an identity, cannot as such prove it present beyond the text from which it has to be imagined—except as prophecy. But in the Eucharist it is always possible to realize the full meaning of the proposition that the identity of Jesus is indeed one with his presence. That action *is* how this can be proved true over and over.

The Eucharist is therefore our real "new testament." No additional text is finally necessary either as supplement or replacement for those already in existence. What is most deeply required, after all, is not another Scripture, useful as this or that instance may be, but what all these, old or new, can at best prophesy: the fulfilment of textuality as such. For what else could the meaning of any writing amount to if not the body? So the Eucharist can function as the covenant "document" of the final son of David, the equivalent within an eschatological version of the relation to the stones once secured within the ark, or their successor, the scroll of the Torah. Nothing else could possibly do as well. The "historical Jesus" in any of his variants (including the one we have had to presuppose here) is at best a hypothesis built up out of evidence read from outside the relation proposed. The other sayings and parables, however true they ring, come down by way of the traditions as these have been reconstructed by the evangelists, who again as so many possible individuals are *not* our contemporaries but historical figures in their own uncertain right. Now and again a reader of the *Old* Testament will come across some passage that seems to bring him or her closer to what he or she can then understand as the mind of

---

[69]Hans W. Frei, *The Identity of Jesus Christ* (Philadelphia: Fortress, 1975).

Jesus than anything that can be read out of the later texts.

But these intuitions, though a fair equivalent to what the first generation discovered as it "searched the Scriptures," can supply no more than lateral support for any completely satisfactory Christology. The gift of prophecy is, we also know, rare at best and ambiguous even if recognized at all. And the authority asserted by the several versions of the institution can seem dubious in origin as well as contested in scope. It is in fact doubtful if, since the Twelve disintegrated, we have ever had a model of ecclesiastical government that could claim dominical authority without qualification. The "descendants" of Peter alone have survived, like Judah among the tribes. What we *do* have, in spite of all, is the eucharistic action, and that from the beginning until now. *This,* we may fairly say, is how the agent of it could indeed rebuild the temple without hands. This testament is therefore how he could refound the nation without waging war against the Romans. And this is how, most important for the future, he could manifest the resurrection in advance of any of the experiences we ordinarily denote by that term. In the action initiated at the supper, then, we can find concentrated in a typically concrete, parabolic, and generous gesture the whole of the relevant teaching and performance. We might as well make the most of it.

The very indispensability of the action, to be sure, can also help us to appreciate the value of whatever else has come down. It will assist a reading of the surviving texts rather better, I suspect, than these can help interpret the origin or meaning of the rite. The resurrection appearances, for instance, are readable in the light of the Eucharist as parables of what is in fact accomplished in this action—midrashim, as it were, on the principal event. They represent the risen Lord by way of a set of visions experienced by certain individuals at one time and a few places. But the action already re-presents the same Lord in the mode of ritual: a species of demonstration that can be repeated at any time and place. The rite is accordingly the real "proof" of what we mean by the resurrection, the fullness of which it conveys to us in the body, which is to say, as our bodies. One could hardly do better than that.[70]

I am reminded in particular of the story in John of the appearance at which Jesus repeats the word *peace* to his disciples in their locked room. He says this twice on the first occasion of the kind, and a third time for Thomas's sake. *Eirēnē* translates *shalōm,* we know, another singular word that simultaneously reveals and

---

[70] I accordingly find appealing the proposal by James Mackey in his *Modern Theology* (New York: Oxford University Press, 1987) that the resurrection appearances should be understood as figurations of what is accomplished in the Eucharist (78-83). One might conclude too that the psychologization of the resurrection by such as Edward Schillebeeckx in his influential *Jesus: An Experiment in Christology* (New York: Seabury, 1979) or more recently by Sheehan in his overinfluenced *First Coming* would correspond in embarrassment, if not elaboration, to the equivalent physicalization in the narratives. But if we take the hint supplied, we would already have Jesus' own preinterpretation of the matter.

conveys the completion of all things in God, a word, that is, of blessing, or the Name in one more vocabulary. But the meaning of all these words is already embodied in the body indeed. No wonder, then, that several of the appearances reflect eucharistic practice in one way or another. In that fashion they can allude to the principle that explains them all.

But we could also go back to reread the other forms of self-presentation that appear in the stories of the ministry with a similar sense of recovering an aspect of their purpose that may not have been so evident before. The *abba* relationship we have already mentioned: that Jesus was accustomed to refer to God by this most intimate of familial terms has often seemed more securely original than almost any other feature of the narratives. But the "Lord's prayer" shows that precisely this relationship can be thought of as conveyable to others. The direction to say *"our Father"* passes on the same value that is transmitted in the Eucharist. And other aspects of Jesus' activity can also take on a new significance. We may observe, for instance, that the cures, apparently the least "advanced" form of ministry, are all very much of the body—including the exorcisms, which restore the victims to the psychic equivalent of physical health. These anecdotes show a Jesus who consents to transmit his power in such a way as to re-create the bodies of those he encounters—whether or not they deserve it or become disciples in any formal sense. Such generosity shares the trajectory as well as the idiom of the ritual transfer. In each case, as still more obviously in the feeding miracles, Jesus is represented as giving himself away. He does *not* hold on to or assert what distinguishes him as an individual. This communicative disposition is so deeply embedded in the plot of the several episodes that it must, we can fairly conclude, echo the original practice. And it is almost as clearly not the skill of some wandering healer from Galilee that accomplishes these apparently random benefactions, as Mark at least shows the crowd as supposing (and some scholars have argued since), but the divine *exousia* passing through him for the sake of others—so as in fact to demonstrate itself. This transitiveness or radiation is, we have already observed, the very essence of the *I am*. The Name is the givenness in any gift, which can be maintained as such only by being passed on. The community, like the individual, would therefore exist most properly in giving herself away.

The parables, which have frequently seemed the very type of the original teaching, exhibit the same character in the mode of imaginative discourse. Here too bodiliness obtains—in the form of some image, commonly most concrete, local, and familiar, that in context becomes the "flesh" of a meaning that must be sought for within the scope of a promise now at last becoming unpredictably true. The parable of the Sower, for instance, which Mark situates as the parable of all parables, already reads as an anticipation of the eucharistic transmission. Jesus is revealed in this narrative within a narrative as casting himself out as seed upon the earth, where this action can be counted on to produce a great harvest in the End, whether or not the ground on which it falls is propitious. And the form of any parable, with its combination of the enigmatic and the popular, repeats the same combination of transcendence and transitiveness. Jesus takes no means to ensure the preservation of his teaching. Most especially he writes nothing down—an omission as formidable, and as suggestive, as his failure to beget a son. He takes the chance that his words will or will not be recalled accurately or otherwise in the memories of his hearers. No other artist has ever risked quite that much. The texts of those who have succeeded him would then function as aides-mémoires for them, not publications for him. This is sowing the seed indeed.

The note of self-abandonment that may be detected in the form or content of all the media of the ministry may be imagined from a certain distance at least as presupposing an exceptionally unqualified patience with the actual results. These are already registered within the narratives as comparatively feeble if not hostile, an effect that has obviously continued ever since, in spite of local "successes." For the third phase of the eucharistic metamorphosis, unlike the first and the second, has never yet been entirely filled out. The communal body has had to be exemplified—authentically, we may concede, but also all too often pathetically or even paradoxically—by whatever assembly of individuals happened to be on the scene. The ways in which the eschatological identity thereby received might ever be manifested in practice must, in the nature of the case proposed, remain unspecified within the rite. A sign cannot predict the particulars of its own interpretation, though it may indicate by its structure the standard in terms of which an adequate fulfillment might be measured. The usual disposition has been to do as little as possible—except repeat the rite itself.

So the Church is perpetually recommencing, like the sprouts of the chestnut, only to die back again without, one may feel, ever achieving a mature growth. This incompletion need not have been unanticipated; what was for Jesus a Last Supper is meant, we may gather, as only a first breakfast for us. But it can seem disappointing all the same, in the light of the possibility so repeatedly revealed, which goes on proposing a body that would incorporate not just the city or the nation, or even all the peoples of all the nations, but the cosmos itself. We may go on behaving as if this were still the intention, and for the moment at which the rite is celebrated, or in some unusual set of circumstances, it can seem almost true for the time being. But in ordinary fact an unqualified appropriation of the message is too often aborted, for the most part without anybody noticing. The Israel of God does *not* come into full existence. The seed goes on being sown, as in the parable, and there it lies, as far as too many of us can tell. But if an unconditional transmission has indeed been the intention from the beginning and in every context, we should probably not be altogether surprised or scandalized. (If Jesus called Simon, of all people, "Rock," we may guess how sturdy and obvious a temple he foresaw without apparent distress.) The body, we might tentatively conclude, has been made accessible. It is not guaranteed but simply offered—not imposed, then, or invented, but rendered perpetually possible. The transfer has been accomplished in principle and a sufficiently representative practice. The rest can be left to us, and has been.

Didactic

As we have just seen, it is possible to read John's gospel as reproducing the structure of the body in the form of a proposition that begins with the Name in the first person and ends with an expressive predicate of one kind or another. This proposition, "spelled out," generates John's history of Jesus. But the actuality of the body remains implicit in John, who omits the Last Supper and alludes to the Eucharist only indirectly in a few earlier verses. For an equivalently explicit appreciation of the body as this is provided in the Eucharist and may therefore be rediscovered in one or another context of the eschatological life, we would need to revert to Paul—the first as opposed to one of the later witnesses—and follow what in his case is an argumentative rather than a narrative version of the essential message. The principal evidence would be supplied by the first letter to the Corinthians.

This communication presents a modern reader with an initial difficulty: the first four chapters apparently have nothing to do with the topic. They are devoted instead to the problem of distinguishing the wisdom of God and its corresponding folly from the wisdom of men, which has its own notion of what counts as foolishness. This double contrast becomes one more way of articulating what Paul would formally recognize as "the gospel" which complements the more elaborate presentation in terms of justice to be found in Galatians and Romans. But it does not seem at first sight to bear on the question of the body, which certainly dominates the remaining chapters of this letter. These take up, one after the other, a variety of contexts within which the body of Christ may indeed be shared or lost, together with the corresponding ethical directives, negative and positive.[71]

The first of these contexts is new as far as we are concerned, since it does *not* appear within the eucharistic action. The whole body of Christ, Paul observes, should be understood as exemplified quite as fully on the scale of the couple as on the scale of the community as a whole. This idea is not original with him. His argument at once presupposes, elaborates, and reapplies a "word of the Lord," which is also reproduced in Mark 10:1-12 and the parallel discussions of marriage in the other synoptics. Man and wife compose a single spiritual body, Paul accordingly repeats, of which the flesh includes not only their individual male and female bodies but those of their children as well (7:14). The power of the Spirit within this dual version of the body suffices in fact to hallow even an unbelieving spouse, Paul goes on to affirm, provided the other partner already belongs to the

---

[71]My survey of 1 Corinthians presupposes an acquaintance with the standard commentaries, including those of Barrett, Black, Conzelmann, Orr and Walter, Fee, and Talbert. Since I will not be arguing with these or most other Pauline authorities I omit specific references. The form of my analysis owes more in any case to repeated teachings of this primary text.

community. Fornication, though, like incest and homosexuality (and a fortiori adultery), would count as sexual apostasy. *Porneia* in all its versions is the worship of a strange god—in this case Aphrodite. For here as in other contexts there is, according to Paul, a sinful body of Adam as well as the gracious body of Christ. Marital intercourse, though, is in his view not merely licit for Christians but holy. In fact it amounts to a celebration of the rite that corresponds in this context to the Eucharist within the community at large. Paul personally prefers celibacy, which permits uninterrupted service to the Church as a whole, and says what he can to encourage that option. But his application of the dominical redefinition of marriage which has been passed on to him strongly confirms the potentially eschatological character of sexual union. The apostle has only to draw the relevant conclusions for a different set of social circumstances. The effect can seem startling: Paul has found a way, as traditional in principle as it is practical in detail, to bring the realm of sexuality back within the import of the model supplied by the Eucharist. Thus he recovers erotic bodiliness too as a mode of the solution as well as part of the problem for any subsequent inquirer into either topic.

The second context presupposing the body as a determining motif is food. Here the spiritual norm can afford to be the Eucharist directly. Paul therefore defends the dignity of the rite against trivializing complacency (1 Cor. 10:16; 11:29) and disorder (11:21-22, 27-34) alike. Within the perspective supplied by this standard, it is possible for Paul to reread the experience of the Israelites in the desert with the manna and the water from the rock as exhibiting the same privilege in terms of the promise (*epangelia*) that the Eucharist has now supplied in terms of its fulfillment (*euangelion*). That generation abused its form of the gift; let this still-more-privileged generation beware. With such parallel instances of an entirely hallowed consumption in mind, it also becomes possible to determine that every other sort of eating must now be legitimate in principle, whether or not it would be permitted by the Law or even involved meat already offered to idols. Here too sin is all too likely—most seriously, in the form of a consumption of such meat *as* offered to another god, which for the person concerned would amount to communion with a demon (8:7; 10:20-22). The same error could also be committed as it were vicariously if food from such an offering were eaten in circumstances that would scandalize a weaker member of the community (8:10-13). The complacency of those who might think themselves assured of eventual salvation only because they had once shared in the Eucharist would represent a third mistake, for such an attitude would betray a magical idea of the rite amounting to unconscious blasphemy.

Throughout these applications Paul's principle remains at once elementary and thoroughly eucharistic: you are what you eat.[72] The members of the communal body

---

[72] Not "you eat what you are." It is easy to agree with most of Jerome Murphy-O'Connor's double article entitled "Eucharist and Community in First Corinthians," *Worship* 50 (1976): 370-85; 51 (1977): 56-69, but not the suggestion that in Paul's view the efficacy

are free to incorporate anything edible besides the Eucharist on the very basis of the Eucharist—but only in an unqualified faith. Outside of that some modes of consumption are sure to involve the risk of antichristic identifications, as sharing in the flesh of a prostitute is bound to do within the erotic context. So be watchful, Paul concludes—which is to say, let your faith be clarified in proportion to the benefit enjoyed.

The reference to an apostle's right to support from his congregation would fit neatly as a corollary to the topic of food. A missionary is indeed entitled, he affirms, to "food and drink" (1 Cor. 9:4) for himself and a wife too if he has one by divine ordinance, both Mosaic (9:9) and dominical (9:14). Such a stipend would thus be sacramental for him, as it is a sacrifice in faith for those who provide it. But Paul personally has not made use of this right, lest he seem to exploit his congregations. He has refrained from sharing the body in this way, as he has forsworn marriage forever, and occasionally suspends his right to eat idol meat when that might cause scandal. He remains "celibate" in all these respects so as to preserve his role as a founder of communities free from even the appearance of involvement in an exchange economy, which would fatally compromise its true character as transmitter of a divine gift.

As in the Eucharist itself, community follows upon food. The third context through which the motif of the body is traced is accordingly provided by the current behavior of the Corinthian congregation. A variety of special topics are fitted under this general head, such as the collection for Jerusalem or the discussion of what to do about quarrels within the assembly that would otherwise go to law outside it. The questions that arise in connection with food and sex themselves require resolution in terms of their effect on community morale. One especially prominent issue of this kind is the matter of gender hierarchy, on which Paul has strong but apparently conflicting and somewhat less than securely based opinions. There is no inherited word of the Lord to determine what access women should have to those leadership roles within the community that presume endowment with one or another of the "higher" gifts. Nor has there been, apparently, any special revelation on the topic, though contemporary custom evidently allowed women to function as prophets, if not as apostles or (perhaps) as teachers. Paul at first appears to accept this practice (11:5, 13) and then abruptly (if the passage is authentic, as it is more difficult but also more honest to assume) decides against countenancing it (14:33b-36). Let women keep silence in public. For this judgment he then and there (if this *is* him) claims prophetic authority (14:37). But it is not hard to discern in such an assertion another instance of the same tendency to confuse pneumatic authority with the psychic hubris of which he has so freely accused his Corinthian opponents elsewhere in the letter. For his previous reasons for affirming male dominance in

---

of the rite depends upon the reality of the communal body that celebrates it. The apostle could never have been quite so pleased with the spiritual condition of his addressees.

or out of the family unit are admittedly sarkic, whether they appeal to Moses (11:7), nature (11:14-15), or "the traditions of men" within the Church (11:16). So we are not obliged to agree with him on this point—and it is fairer to object openly than look for reasons to assign the most embarrassing passage to a later author.

A better argument against Paul's position could simply revert to his own conception of the body in the communal mode. For any definition of this that would exclude some category of its potential members in advance from participation in the higher gifts would amount to a denial of the resurrection to precisely that extent. It would prevent the wholeness of the whole body from being realized as the Spirit might determine rather than the customs of society. In this case it would condemn half the race to a merely silent participation in the body as so much subordinate flesh either in the dual or the ecclesial form. Women would not be free to act as individuals in the Spirit, which would deny them precisely that liberty of mind, will, and speech Paul insists is essential to the character of the believer. They would instead remain "Gentiles" forever—which would also be inconsistent with Paul's conviction that the eschatological community is in principle universal. The regulation proposed would therefore amount to a second version of the same Law he had already realized was in fact abrogated in every other respect. In more than one way, then, Paul may be seen to contradict his own gospel on this point—and therefore becomes subject to contradiction in his turn, as he reports Peter to have been on another memorable occasion (Gal. 2:11-14).

With Paul's views on other aspects of the communal body there is less to find fault with. For spiritual gifts in general, for instance, as opposed to those who may exercise them, the outline offered is fully consistent with the structure we would expect to find for any version of the eschatological body: its flesh should consist of whatever entities, natural or human, the Spirit is free to compose into a whole. The organic metaphor presumed throughout is explicitly elaborated in what had long since become a traditional style (1 Cor. 12:12-26). Any body already implies a ranking of its "members," which justifies the distinction between the "higher" and the "lower" gifts alluded to. The apostleship, prophecy, and teaching—that is, the gifts Paul himself exercises—deserve more honor than miracles, healing, and tongues. Love is the greatest gift of all because *agapē* is in effect the blood of the communal body, circulating through all its members to give them life as parts of the whole. It is therefore the presence or absence of love that distinguishes any of these gifts, but especially and in proportion the higher, from the same resources employed as occasions for "boasting" in the flesh alone. For this reason too, love is eternal, though its manifestations must be temporal, adult as opposed to childish, direct rather than reflected. The key difference between the higher and the lower gifts, typified by prophecy and tongues respectively, is the presence or absence of articulate discourse, by means of which alone the community can in fact be organized. It is always the Word that constitutes the body, as we might expect.

Paul's review of the final resurrection in 1 Corinthians 15 may be read as dealing with the future of the same communal body. If the privileges now enjoyed count as "firstfruits," these must entail a corresponding harvest. In the present it is no more than just possible even to imagine this final stage, when the combination of Spirit and flesh that makes up the gracious body will be succeeded by a glorious body that must be spiritual through and through. Such a somatic ultimacy would no longer therefore be the body of Christ but the body of God—which by definition is still unthinkable, for how can God have or be a body? To be sure, the question does not arise in quite this form; instead Paul supplies a pair of images. The more original and difficult of these is a set of ratios. All bodies emanate a characteristic aura that betrays a disposition to pass beyond their inherent limits. The hair of a woman, Paul has already observed in another connection, is the "glory" of her body, as she is in turn the glory of man, and man the glory of God (11:7, 15). We might guess accordingly that a flower, say, would be the "glory" of a plant, and its scent the "glory" of a flower. But the glories of celestial bodies are more impressive than those of terrestrial bodies in proportion to their greater dignity. So the body of the sun gives forth a characteristic glory as its proper kind of light, and the moon the sort of light that belongs to it, and the stars the same. It would follow that the glory of the communal body would simply be the glory of God indeed—which is to say, the Spirit unmediated, when the natural bodies out of which the body of Christ is now made will be entirely converted into the energy, as we might now put it, that corresponds to their mass.

The several analogies here take some teasing out, and Paul himself is evidently dissatisfied with the complications of his own comparison, since before it has been properly unpacked he has already abandoned it in favor of the more familiar and traditional image of seed and harvest. In both analogies, though, what is striking is his refusal to abandon the body motif even when this has reached the limits of its comprehensibility. The body, we may conclude, is forever as well as for today: what begins does not lapse but continues from now until the End.

We began our review of 1 Corinthians by observing that the first four chapters appear to have no thematic connection with the remaining twelve, most of which are obviously concerned with one or another mode of the body indeed. What has the gospel according to wisdom, as Paul elaborates this in the first "half" of his letter, got to do with the doctrine of the body, as that is pursued from context to context through the rest of it? In the eyes of men, we could guess Paul would reply, nothing: human wisdom, after all, especially in its Hellenistic variants, had always been impelled by a determination to escape from or at least dominate the body. But the wisdom of God does not repudiate or look down on the flesh. On the contrary, this wisdom is revealed only through what happens in and to the body. The cross exhibits as much on the scale of the individual, as if to prove the universality of death. The resurrection discloses what may in faith be recognized as the *same* body, but now on the scale of the community as a continuing demonstration of eternal life. If so, we might put the two parts of the letter together in the form of a generalization that would take in both sides of the argument as a single proposition. The wisdom of God, we could then propose, *is* the body of Christ—in whatever form that appears.[73]

The wisdom of God is the body of Christ: once such a formulation for the deep structure of 1 Corinthians as a whole has been arrived at, we are also in a position to realize the parallel between the version of the gospel elaborated in this letter and the apparently quite different doctrine spelled out in Galatians and Romans. In those letters the issue is justice, not wisdom. The corresponding formulation thereby becomes a redefinition of the justice of God as opposed to human justice. The central proposition lies closer to the surface of the Pauline argument in this context: the justice of God, he is there affirming, is now identical with the mercy of God—*not* with his wrath, unrelenting as this must be still against every form of evil. For Jesus has absorbed that wrath on behalf of all those who will accept his suffering as sufficient punishment for their own sins. In the case of these individuals—and them only—then, the mercy of God has indeed been released to become the whole of his justice.

The justice of God is the mercy of God, and the wisdom of God is the body of Christ. Between them these formulations would exhaust the principal values respectively of Jews and Greeks. Paul did not need to develop a third or fourth proposition in terms of some other divine attribute. His missionary occasions did not require it. But we are free to suppose that any equivalent reformulation of the essential proclamation might also need to redefine some attribute of God in terms of a value as crucial to the culture in which the declaration was being made as the gospel *kata dikaiosunēn* (according to righteousness) was for the Jews and the gospel *kata sophian* (according to wisdom) was for the Greeks.

What might be the corresponding value for our own culture? One could suppose, knowledge or consciousness, for is not cognition our master faculty, by way of which modernity has in every context been determined? But Paul would surely reply that *gnōsis* cannot penetrate beyond the limits of this world. *Presence* might serve better. It is certainly a traditional attribute of God—and one notoriously experienced as absent in modern circumstances. The presence of whoever might *be* present could then amount to whatever consciousness would in the End have to become conscious of—if this were ever to be revealed, and the mind could in fact open itself to it. In which case a version of the message might be tentatively formulated in terms of a proposition for which the subject would be the presence

---

[73]That Paul believes Christ to be the wisdom of God has been affirmed and denied in a long book and a cranky article: André Feuillet, *Le Christ sagesse de Dieu* (Paris: Lecoffre, 1966), and A. van Roon, "The Relation between Christ and the Wisdom of God according to Paul," *NovT* 16 (1974): 207-39. Both, though, presume that "wisdom" should be definable in terms of the inherited sapiential texts, which limits the case made or contested to the level where exegesis applies. But if the order of the proposition in question is reversed and the body counted back in, we would seem closer at once to Paul's sequence of topics and his underlying argument.

of God, altogether unqualified, that is, by any absence, as the presences "of men" are obliged to be. What then would be the corresponding predicate? With the help of Paul, an answer already seems to declare itself: the presence of God, like his wisdom, would once again have to be the body indeed. The presence of God is the body of Christ, we could accordingly affirm. But the presence of God, we have already seen, is in fact what is communicated by the Name. And would not the Name count as the most intimate "attribute" of God indeed, closer to him even than his justice or his wisdom? The Name of God, we can always repeat, is the body of Christ. Such a formulation would return us to the proposition we have detected as supplying a grammar for the gospel according to John—and incidentally enable us to reconcile these otherwise very different representatives of the earliest tradition.

It would also bring us back to the Eucharist, which for us as for Paul (and even for John) would necessarily provide the constant type in terms of which to understand all the other recapitulations of the body. The familiar hypothesis that the body motif in Paul would not only be illustrated by but derived from this rite would then seem the merest common sense. How else indeed could body language have become so prevalent in the earliest Church, especially as the authorized way in which the community might recognize its own identity? We need not suppose that Paul invented the communal any more than the marital application, though their elaborations are of course his work. Body language, we may additionally presume, would not otherwise have come naturally to a man in whom can be found so little of the priest and so much of the Pharisee. Nor, as we have also noticed, is he altogether free from the contemporary "philosophical" bias against the body and all its works. The flesh as such was no friend of his! So the dominance of the motif in 1 Corinthians and elsewhere would of itself testify to the force of the original example within the tradition at large. Jesus had unexpectedly employed just this "idiom" for the most central of purposes; it must therefore be legitimate across the board for all his disciples.

So the Eucharist is central for Paul too, almost in spite of himself. And to return to his example, especially in the letter we have just recapitulated, is to realize anew the inescapability of the project it illustrates: to seek out applications for the principle disclosed in the principal action, context by context, contingency by contingency, as occasion offers. For the eucharistic action itself predicts just such an elaboration of the gesture made as it flings its seed outward, as it were, into the rest of the world—including so much of this as might take the form of propositions, evangelic or explanatory. The remainder of this study must accordingly attempt a more modest but inevitably more contemporary version of the same task. For to realize the body in the metamorphoses of the original action and its ritual repetitions is to become that much more aware of bodies of every kind: natural or individual, erotic and symbolic, communal or cosmic, and therefore by a necessary contrast that much more conscious of all those competing powers that in one way or another destroy, deny, displace, frame, or divide the bodiliness that still pulses through them all. The body interprets bodies, and bodies the body, by a familiar rule of hermeneutics. So attention to this motif cannot help but draw along with it other elements that also occur within or near the eucharistic action: language, art, temporality, the person, texts, and institutions. Let me accordingly arrange a few of these in what I hope will seem a plausible sequence through the remainder of this book. No one argument, we have repeatedly seen, can possibly include all that might be said. But a representative selection, as Paul also shows, is just possible, and worth trying to put together.

Chapter 2

Individual

If you do know that here is one hand, *we'll grant you all the rest.*
— Ludwig Wittgetstein, *On Certainty,* the first sentence.

Primal

What counts as a body? Sometimes it seems easy to tell. As my car turns down a steep street, two children begin to run along the sidewalk beside my cautious descent—not because of me, but on their own. Our progress is for a brief while coincident, and I can admire the vigor and confidence of their precipitous career. The older girl (she is perhaps six) is a few steps ahead of her brother, and especially attracts my eye as her young body leaps down the slope, each stride jarring on the irregular rectangles of the old sidewalk, her bright hair flying loose in the sunlight, arms pumping to preserve a constantly challenged but always spontaneously recovered equilibrium. She is running flat out down a steep hill, which frightens me; suppose she fell? But I am the one who feels the danger. She is at ease in herself, and so is her younger brother pattering behind. Neither of them is in the least afraid to do what they need not think about to bring off quite perfectly. Why are they running, then? For the fun of it, I am sure. I drive on beyond them with a renewed sense of just that vitality that a middle-aged man no longer experiences in his own person, though we still remember the sensation. To be sure, I am in my car, which is evidently a body of another kind—bilaterally symmetrical, with a front and a back, and internal organs, including myself as nucleus or soul. What other notes do such occasions reveal?

The question seems easy to answer in this case. These kids were reveling in their freedom. Vitality and autonomy are evidently indications of bodiliness. Substantiality would be another: both children were flesh and blood, I could plainly see, though I did not catch or hold them (that comes with grandfatherhood). I did hear the impact of their soles upon the hard surfaces they were *not* tripping on. Ideas, fictions, memories, dreams, and wishes are by comparison disembodied or spectral—as this girl and boy have since become for me as I write about and a reader must imagine them. But they were there once.

Matter of itself, though, is *not* bodily. Those sidewalks were not bodies, though perhaps the houses alongside were, in their way, like my car. But sidewalks or houses or cars have got to be put together. Bodies occur more or less on their own.

We do not need to make them up. They are *autopoetic,* as the biologists put it. Coherence would be another note: a body is made up of parts, like hair and legs, but interrelated, so as to compose a whole. Solidity and coherence are matched too by boundedness: I am in the presence of a body when I can tell the difference between what belongs to it and what does not, what moves and what is moved through. Motility is certainly another indicator: if anything moves, we are inclined to credit it with bodiliness until proved wrong. For motion is the chief evidence of life, and life of intentionality: all bodies seem properly alive and purposeful even if not, as in this case, also intelligent or personal. And life, like motion, implies an involvement with time. A body moves through the trajectory appropriate to it, whether a moment in some afternoon or a lifetime. All lifetimes, indeed, would be the same in principle, however long they might take on the clock or calendar. Bodies begin and end, sooner or later, even theirs, including mine.

For bodies to live and die in time presumes too that they exist within an "appropriate" environment. Bodies are always somewhere, from which they may be distinguished but upon which they are also dependent. So each of us experiences his or her own body as an exception to a rule that in due course will return us to the rest of what we are not yet a part of. Human beings know this gap between ourselves and the rest of the world as the space within which are disposed the products of culture. Words clot there, intersecting in loose skeins charged with points of ambiguous reference, like galaxies. The difference between myself as figure and everything else as ground hardens into a "membrane" that defines me. Language draws that line.

But it may do so from more than one point. My hair and nails are dead to me even now. And my exhausted air or urine or excrement I am positively eager to get rid of, though these too were once part of me. Even members that may have seemed intrinsic can become uninteresting. I once had a testicle removed, for cancer, and even before its abstraction, that minor globe had come to feel alien, an unnatural hardness to be rid of—a stone, no longer flesh. We redraw our boundary inside such things even while our skin still contains them. But our shoes, offices, and implements become extensions of our selves: this pencil point is now my hand metonymically refined. Inside and outside seem obvious only to someone else, who may very well be mistaken.

Propriety, like autonomy or coherence or boundedness or motility, would seem one more way to specify centricity, a principal note indeed, distinguishing whatever we are disposed to call a body from other things that do not seem so entitled. We are inclined to locate a "soul" of some sort in every body, even if, as in the case of a planet or plant, we may have to imagine this ourselves. Meanwhile it can be gratifying to an uninstructed curiosity to discover the several levels at which this feature might in fact be found. An atom, for instance, already seems the smallest "thing" there could be: but would not an atom too be a body of sorts, with its energetic nucleus of protons and neutrons and its successive circumferences more or less filled with electrons? If an atom is "smashed," what is left over are only magnetic charges of this or that kind. Evidently these would not count as bodies, though in quantity they might supply the radiance of one. From a "quantum perspective," as the phrase goes, there are no bodies: chaos is perfectly normal. Molecules too, at the next level up, are no more than aggregates of atoms held together by electronic exchanges. They are certainly substantial—are substance, in the modern sense of that term—but with no centers. Combined in repeating patterns, they accumulate as the stuff that surrounds and supports us but which without motion cannot seem to have any life of its own. DNA, the very long molecule that directs the production of all living bodies, simple or complex, might seem an exception. But it too "replicates" rather than reproduces by what has therefore come to be described as a linguistic or mechanical process, in which "information" "encoded" in the necessary sequences is "transcribed" as if from a "template" to trigger the manufacture of proteins, like a machine working off a "tape."[1] That is not how bodies behave.

Bodiliness appears for sure again at the level of the cell. The more primitive prokaryotes do without a nucleus, though already coherent and bounded and alive. In the more complex eukaryotes a nucleus does obtain, surrounded by its own membrane and containing a special combination of parts, including the chromosomes, themselves harboring the indispensable DNA. Cells metabolize on their own; they also reproduce sexually or by division or both, for all cells, though made up of and maintained by molecular interaction, must as such arise out of other cells. To be sure, there are still ambiguous cases at this level too. Are viruses "alive," and therefore bodies too? The authorities seem unsure. An individual virion consists of a molecule of DNA or RNA with a protein coat that can move about very much like a living creature. But it does not metabolize, and requires a host cell to reproduce; in fact the host cell does the work, manufacturing additional specimens of the invader. The nucleic acid of the virus only supplies "instructions." Such characteristics have suggested that viruses may resemble "prebionts," or forms once intermediate between nonliving and living things, like the chloroplasts and mitochondia now included as "organelles" within cellular bodies. Or they may simply be independent nuclear fragments or even what were once whole cells now functioning symbiotically. Would such ambiguous entities exist nearer the molecular or the cellular level?

---

[1] I owe my sense of the possible levels of bodiliness to an appreciative if ignorant reading of the well-known textbook by a late colleague, William Keeton's *Biological Science* (New York: Norton, 1980). The words in quotation marks at the end of the paragraph are his. Other information his book has supplied is scattered through this chapter. Renato Dulbecco's *Design of Life* (New Haven: Yale University Press, 1987) provides a convenient update. I have also been intrigued by the history of cellular evolution offered by Lynn Margulis and Dorion Dagan in their popular *Microcosmos* (New York: Summit, 1986), though hesitant to rely on this for sheer matters of fact. Margulis's thesis that eukaryotic cells are symbiotic prokaryotes is argued on a textbook scale in her earlier *Symbiosis in Cell Evolution* (San Francisco: W. H. Freeman, 1981).

If such cases could be reduced or assimilated, it might be possible to suppose that what we are willing to identify as a body seems to occur at intervals in what would then amount to a dialectical progress up the several levels of being, with an intervening stage of nonbodily existence before and after each. Particles would be to atoms, one might then be able to say, as molecules to cells, or tissues to multicellular organisms. In that case one could go on to understand the social assemblies of plants or animals as an equivalent at the next level up from the individual body of the combination of organs within it. Colonies or patches or tribes or nations would then, like molecules, be aggregates rather than bodies proper, though that would be what all these might be understood as striving to become. If so, a community that would in fact deserve identification as a body rhyming with the individual organism or the cell or perhaps the atom would indeed have to be *super*natural, for it has not yet occurred in a form that could be examined by any ordinary science. Such a continuation of the dialectic would then supply an evolutionary version of the eschatological intention, and approach the action we began with, as it were, from below.

Only on the basis of some such reproduction of moments through a succession of levels could I affirm with the theologian Benedict Ashley, who has done his scientific homework more thoroughly than I, that bodies are indeed the "primary, natural" units of being, whether on the scale of atoms or cells or organisms or a true equivalent on the scale of community.[2] And if a key to the more convincing moments seems always to be centricity, it would be worth articulating an understanding of this note that might apply across the several contexts. The simplest would pick up and apply the motif of reproduction. Then one could think of the core of any body as a replication of the larger difference between the body as a whole and its environment. An atom has a nucleus, and so do at least the more complex types of cell. In what appears an analogous way I am myself—in the first place, because I was born, but then as the subject of such experience as seems proper to me in a reproduction of the difference by which I once began to discover myself as alive within but also separate from the world. The soul, if one may still call it that, would then become comprehensible as a body to the second degree, or body within a body, though made up of "psychic" rather than physical elements. Such a rendering of the case would offer a three-dimensional model of what we could otherwise know only in two dimensions and therefore as an inexplicable hierarchy of ghostly mind and mechanical matter.

In that case too it might not be unreasonable to see this "subject" as at the same time the first human work of art. A baby would begin upon such an inward reproduction of its animal existence by the third week at least, when its parents

---

[2]Benedict Ashley, *Theologies of the Body: Humanist and Christian* (Braintree MA: Pope John Center, 1985). I can salute this enthusiastic project as an enterprise more or less parallel to my own.

catch the first smile. One may learn from a splendid book by Daniel Stern how studies in child development (and he is also a psychoanalyst) would appear to confirm the actual early existence of what he calls a "core self" as something "separate, cohesive, bounded," and even "physical," which provides babies with "a sense of their own agency, affectivity, and continuity in time."[3] Such a self would need to be conceived as the product of a responsive process, as my body is already a product of its interaction with the environment. The self is "intersubjective" from the beginning. "The newborn," Stern points out, "sees things best at a distance of about ten inches—the usual distance from a mother's eyes to the eyes of an infant positioned at the breast."[4] From then on whoever I am continues as the story of how I have come to be in relation to other persons like and unlike myself. So I go on rhythmically reincorporating myself as a psyche, as I continue incorporating myself as so much flesh. Given the "molecules" out of which it must be made, we may have trouble locating the self and begin to doubt its existence, or interpret it as the product of a social reality which would itself have to be understood in nonbodily terms.[5] But in that case we would be applying the wrong model. If I experience myself as myself with the same confidence as I realize the rest of my body, and for what amount to the same reasons, then this imagined and imagining nucleus would seem at least as secure as the rest of me—which is not nothing, after all, even if not quite everything that might be hoped for yet.

Obviously we may quarrel over what name to give this center, or how to specify its parts, for like an atomic or cellular nucleus, it is evidently not simple. The possibility of reproduction, once begun, might of course continue, the "ego" becoming for the rest of the psyche what the psyche is to the body. So in the Bible the "heart" or "life" is a repetition of the "flesh," as the "eye," or the "apple" of the eye, would become the center of these centers. It might take more than one renewal of the process before we were ready to identify with the result. But that difficulty

---

[3] Daniel Stern, *The Interpersonal World of the Infant* (New York: Basic, 1985). It would be gratifying to think that this book might come to influence not only clinical practice or research in child development but epistemology and "theory" generally. I have accordingly found it more useful than such recent philosophical analyses as Kathleen Wilkes, *Real People* (Oxford: Clarendon, 1988); Charles Taylor, *Sources of the Self* (Cambridge: Harvard University Press, 1989); or Jonathan Glover, *I* (London: Penguin, 1988), though the latter's trust in "self-creation" could be read as compatible with the rougher proposal offered here. In back of Stern is John Bowlby's massive *Attachment and Loss* (New York: Basic, 1969) and the object-relations school generally.

[4] Stern, *Interpersonal World,* 236.

[5] Much contemporary discussion has pressed this thesis. Rom Harre's *Personal Being* (Cambridge: Harvard University Press, 1985), for instance, advances a severely conceptual and therefore utterly asomatic account of the self. I was pleased to discover that Tertullian once affirmed the corporeality of the soul in his *De anima,* Ante-Nicene Christian Library (Edinburgh: T. & T. Clark, 1870) 15: 410-541.

would only reflect the necessarily imaginative character of what takes place at any stage.

No matter how often repeated, reproduction would begin and end in the body, which continues to supply a norm. No wonder, then, that the face has always seemed important as evidence of a soul. Animals do not have faces, quite, though they often look as if they almost did, and our wishes will make up the difference. The face is the body reproduced not just inwardly but outwardly as well. Our bodies are typically clothed, but the face is left naked, though we know it may sometimes be a mask. We see faces as a whole too, like bodies, which we recognize even when we do not recall the name. The face is so much of my soul as somebody else can see, a physical limit for what is otherwise immaterial. There is accordingly more to the face than the body apart from this much of itself can readily show. The face is the body as person, the body altogether reimagined. So the face is our principal proof of presence: one is present to some other only when one's face is turned toward him or her, who may be realized as a person too in proportion. For there are no persons without relation, and so none without a face, or rather, as this necessity implies, two faces face-to-face, making, as we also say, eye contact. That is how bodies meet.[6]

The face reproduces the body in visible and therefore social terms. My voice is my self as speech, as my name is a repetition of the same subject in terms of what others call me, which is, therefore, how I "introduce myself." "Property," as the word implies, would also reproduce the person as well as provide an environment for the body presupposed: my "things" represent me. A work of art too counts as property, and a name is signed to it, by hand if a painting, in print if a book, which is already a replication of still another kind. If someone asks me to sign my name, I do so on the title page, as if I had handwritten the whole. All these modes owe their "authority" or "authenticity" to their origin not just in one or another comparatively sophisticated repetition but in the body behind them all. That is the ground or source for what re-presents itself as if it were already a thing in itself. We need not be overcredulous, then, about the several modes of the human subject—or overskeptical either.[7]

---

[6]The indispensability of relation to our moral experience has been maintained through a sequence of modern witnesses, including Buber, MacMurray, and more recently Levinas and perhaps Bakhtin. My account of the face and voice owes a particular debt to Emmanuel Levinas's *Totality and Infinity* (The Hague: Nijhoff, 1979), though he does not track these phenomena back to the body.

[7]My references to centricity and presence, as well as to person and voice, will already have reminded my reader of Jacques Derrida, whose deconstructive readings of just these possibilities have had so powerful an influence on recent thinking in several fields. The problem of the text in particular will surface for explicit attention in a later chapter. For the time being, I need only repeat what has already been implied: the body, natural or supernatural, is too often what Derrida is "always already" leaving out.

A face repeats the person to the eye, as the voice repeats it to the ear. These rematerializations are the psyche's homage to the flesh of a body it is already reenacting. And the voice too may be reproduced in writing, another and very nonbodily species of matter. So we may recognize a tone: how Bellow tells a tale, perhaps, or how McCarthy makes a judgment. In proportion even a text can thus become a vehicle for the person, whom we would recognize without attribution—or so we claim. To read can then be like listening to a voice over the telephone, or picking a face out from a crowd. The moment of recognition is an acknowledgment that we are to that extent in the presence of another and so must exist at the same level ourselves. He or she stands before my soul as other bodies impinge on my body. But since persons are of the same species, their relation to me need not be merely repellent or consumptive on either side (though either can happen too) but antagonistic or affectionate, the primary possibilities with members of one's own kind.

For persons, like bodies, produce each other. Identity presumes relation, though this is often easy to forget. The sheer fact is the foundation of morality: to acknowledge the other as quite as actual as myself, as indeed prompting any reciprocal appropriation of myself, is the very practice of justice, not to mention manners. But this obligation can be ethical only because it is already ontological. It is a reproduction on the social and therefore the psychic level of the repeated revelation through which a body finds itself existing in a world that already includes at least one other body at any given moment. Duality and so plurality is then a repetition not of singularity, as the example of mathematics might suggest, but of the pair. We are coupled from the beginning: sun and plant, predator and prey, lover and beloved, reader and writer.

The truth that identity presupposes relation has come to seem almost normative with respect to persons. But if persons are reproductions of the corresponding bodies, then relation holds for human beings because it is already true for other creatures as well—or anything else that takes the form of a body. I had to feel that the pigeon which for a couple of sad days crouched in the outside corner of the window of this borrowed office amounted to another body on the same principle as my own, though the elements were different. A pigeon has translucent whitish scales over the ankles of its pink feet, like pantalets. They are unnoticeable except up close. And its eyes blink too, though with an odd motion of the lids. We are each of us distinct, united, alive, and so responsive in our respective ways to whatever else is going on in and about us, including each other. It was almost as clear that the elm sprouts which shaded the pigeon as it huddled next to the window could be traced back to a buried trunk and roots that together made up a body of still another kind, to which I could not quite attribute consciousness, though to become aware of it at all seemed almost to bring this about.

Other distinguishable things can sometimes seem on the way to becoming bodies as well: the old typewriter, for instance, on which I am now tapping out letters to form these words, jiggling gently at each noisy stroke; or the chair on which it rests, and the desk beside my elbow, so densely green, or the other pieces of furniture in this strange room; not to mention all the books, any one of which might be brought down from its place and read through, page by thin page. That at least would awaken some degree of consciousness. Could I even call the sunlight that reflects off each of the typewriter keys and stuns the floor beneath with a brightness vaguely passed through by shifting shadows from those elm leaves bodily too? I think not, though the sun itself, somewhere aloft and beyond this basement, is certainly a body, as Paul long ago observed. And light is an emanation from a body, like shadows from a branch, or murmurs from a pigeon, or pages from an author. We live as bodies in a world of bodies, or of things moving toward that condition, or perhaps away from it. The body is the memory and the promise of being, both what we take for granted and what we desire, myself and the other, apart or together.

This reciprocity is easier to realize and to elaborate in imagination when the body from which one begins can in fact be taken for granted: when it is whole and healthy, that is, and free to concern itself about other bodies. A defective body, whether by disease or injury, is in proportion turned inward. The world and its possible contents then disappear, to be replaced by concern for the self. When the singular body moves in upon itself as if that were another, a variety of morbid phenomena occurs: ulcers, tinnitus, or masturbation would all manifest a reflexivity that in certain cultural emergencies could even acquire a specious value. One clue that such reversals of attention are indeed abnormal lies in the fact that what is focused upon in such cases, painful or narcissistic, is always a part and not the whole even of oneself. The whole of oneself, on the contrary, can be fully experienced only by *not* paying attention, by remaining free precisely to address something else. It can become difficult for someone so entrapped to remember that beyond his or her own boundaries the world still takes shape as wholes too. The universe as well can come to seem another chaos of fragments, an aggregate of fictions in a void.

But the shape of living bodies already suggests that we are not at such a loss in some formless wilderness. The epistemological implications of our ordinary members are not, one suspects, taken seriously enough by philosophers. We are, for instance, equipped with two eyes, which presumes that the world contains distinguishable entities in three dimensions. We see *things* at least, that is, not objects or "sense data"; and things, we have already observed, are on the way to becoming bodies, for even when they do not move, they must stand out as figures from some ground in order to be visible at all.[8] An opposable thumb similarly

---

[8] The late David Marr developed this necessity from a rigorously "information-processing" perspective in his *Vision* (San Francisco: W. H. Freeman, 1982). I had hoped that James Gibson's "ecological optics" might confirm the approach from another direction, but his explanation, with its "layout" of "surfaces" providing "affordances" for this or that kind of behavior seems to preclude the full appearance of other bodies. His clearest book is *The Ecological Approach to Visual Perception* (Boston: Houghton Mifflin, 1979). The various issues are addressed from the point of view of professional philosophy in *Naturalizing*

presumes that the world contains a fair number of graspable entities approximately the size of an orange or the thickness of a branch. The fact that we have two hands implies there are other things heavy enough to lift and carry with both at once; and two arms, that still others may be fought off or embraced. Our feet and legs presuppose not only a surface to walk on but that doing so amounts to grasping not just some separate thing but the planet as a whole. We take hold of the earth with every stride. It is the largest body we can actually reach. And the shape of the mouth, throat, and intestines similarly presume that however large the other creatures we eat may begin as, they can be reduced to bite-sized chunks. All these modes of apprehension indicate that being in general becomes accessible to us as so many distinct creatures on one scale or another, each with its proper coherence and solidity. The world is not just gas or dust, then, or a universal solid, or some other unrealizable stuff. There should be room accordingly for a Kantian somatics to fill out what we might fairly call an animal a priori.

A variety of explorers since Kant have endeavored to supply just such an alternative to what has otherwise prevailed as the scientific and therefore disembodied and disembodying vision of the day. In comparatively modern times such names as Bergson or Whitehead might still evoke recollections of this or that species of "organicism." The Romantic impulse has produced many reproductions of itself. Phenomenology, for instance, as this school developed through more than one generation, could exhibit some memorable if no longer influential instances along one of the possible lines of descent. The name of Merleau-Ponty would still be recognizable as a type of this effort to recover the centrality of the body as a necessary ground for all our experiencing, intellectual as well as practical. His massive *Phenomenology of Perception* explores the condition of "being in the world" in the form of a body that must preexist any subsequent objectification on the one hand or ideal subjectification on the other. "Phenomena" are already meaningful; to recover them, one after another, is to experience the "advent of being" in those entities toward which we find ourselves directed. The body we exist as is a "prejudice" we might as well take advantage of; that by virtue of which there can indeed be objects for us, and therefore situations, and so a world. Not unexpectedly, such an account privileges those moments of incipience or "intention" wherein one desires or anticipates whatever has not yet become fully actual. The schemata of conventional epistemology is thus replaced by a concern with address or style or habit.[9]

Epistemology, ed. Hilary Kornblith (Cambridge: MIT Press, 1985).

[9]Maurice Merleau-Ponty, *Phenomenology of Perception,* trans. Colin Smith (London: Routledge; New York: Humanities Press, 1962). My paraphrase is influenced by the language of this standard translation. Merleau-Ponty's enterprise is continued in *The Visible and the Invisible* (Evanston: Northwestern University Press, 1968) and various other posthumous publications and commentaries. Drew Leder's useful *Absent Body* (Chicago: University of

To be sure Merleau-Ponty, like others who have shared this enterprise, remains somewhat overburdened still by the very experimental psychology he hoped to undermine. This struggle protracts his inquiry and the associated efforts to redefine sexuality and time or space or language. And it may help account too for what is gradually, as one follows his earnest if prolix elaborations, disclosed as a limit of the condition he hopes to release from its objective bonds. Perception is still realized, one discovers, as the activity of a single subject. This subject is indeed reintroduced to itself as a body rather than just the mind alone, but the focus of its attentions, though this may emerge as a thing rather than a pure object, does not quite grow all the way up into another body. Most of his examples are correspondingly visual rather than, say, alimentary, much less erotic or combative. The result can accordingly be reread from a current distance as a most thorough and it is fair to say decent recovery of the Cartesian (and for him Husserlian) *cogito* as incarnate rather than ideal, which nonetheless retains the assumption that subjectivity is to be found on one side only of the relevant polarity. Merleau-Ponty rediscovers the body as self, but not yet the body as other too. Centrality is reaffirmed, that is, at the expense of relation.

Other authorities within rather different intellectual genealogies have been inclined toward what can be identified from a common distance as the same limitation. Karl Menninger's *The Vital Balance,* for instance, which could also be read in retrospect as a monument to a moment that has passed in the history of what in his case is American psychiatry, announces the situation of the typical individual as "organismic," which sounds promising as theory if not quite as terminology. The "ego," in his account, moves through experiences of "disequilibrium" or "disorganizations" toward or away from a proper "integration" as it adapts to inner and outer pressures. Such an account of our psychic condition does appear to presuppose an idea of the person as the body repeated, which would continue to make primal sense. But the model assumed is homeostasis, or the interaction of a singular organism with its environment, which as such would still preclude the possibility of relation, and so any duality or plurality of bodies. On the basis of such a presumption any relation to the body or "ego" of another tends to precipitate as "aggression" (the common note, according to Menninger, of all varieties of "dysfunction"), and therefore as evidence of impaired selfhood rather than the recognition of another.[10] This would seem a theoretical if not also a therapeutic omission.

Both Merleau-Ponty and Menninger are bound to seem old-fashioned in this postmodern era, when in and out of science or philosophy the hegemony of objecti-

---

Chicago Press, 1990) shows that the tradition has not lapsed.

[10] Karl Menninger and Paul Pruyser, *The Vital Balance* (New York: Viking, 1963). I am relieved to discover that Walter Ong has more recently recuperated "adversativeness" as normal on sociobiological as well as cultural grounds in his *Fighting for Life* (Ithaca NY: Cornell University Press, 1981).

vism, molecular or linguistic, can seem almost unchallenged. But counterimpulses may still be detected in various contexts: child development, as the book by Daniel Stern would evidence, or the emergence of such a speciality (if indeed it is more than a fad) as "evolutionary epistemology," which, if one may judge from a representative collection of essays, is also looking for a way to translate the problems of knowledge downward from a cognitive method to what is there thought of as a biological style.[11] Science itself, it is claimed, "evolves" in the same fashion as the unconscious adjustments of less philosophically sophisticated organisms—by blind variation, that is, and selective retention. Its leading variety should therefore be biology rather than physics: Darwin is the ideal ancestor, not Descartes or Kant. This strategy would reinterpret consciousness as such by way of the homeostatic model, which (though it would indeed restore the mind to the body, or the body to the mind) still fails to do justice to the way in which the rest of the world takes shape in or out of theory. And other recent approaches in psychology or "cognitive science" seem susceptible to the same objection. Centrality is still apt to be reaffirmed at the expense of otherness.[12]

It can seem odd that a romantic or biologistic overidentification with the singular body should persist so strongly, even allowing for the various inheritances, intellectual and historical, that might repeat themselves in this continuing bias. There are, one would have supposed, a sufficient number of contrary instances in anyone's daily life: for instance, the familiar experience of seeing something from a distance about which one is uncertain. As one approaches, perhaps entertaining tentative names for whatever-it-is, the moment arrives when all of a sudden one sees what it really consists of, and says to oneself, well, that was not a garter snake after all but an exposed root, not a springer spaniel but a birch stump, not an ash but a locust tree. From within a disembodied perspective, these experiences are puzzling to explain, since both the false and what turns out to be the true judgments seem equivalent instances of conceptualization with nothing to choose between them. But it is fair to claim that everyone knows the difference between *wondering if,* whether idly or in terror, and *being sure that.* This difference would appear to depend on the security which follows from a discovery that not just some but all the relevant evidence coheres to determine the truth of the matter. What one finds out for sure is always a *whole* of some kind, which is to say, some *body,* and a body that necessarily belongs not to the self but to the other. Incarnation is not solitary but dual, and if dual, potentially plural. A body presumes bodies: we are not alone, in this or any

---

[11]*Evolutionary Epistemology, Theory of Rationality, and the Sociology of Knowledge,* ed. Gerald Radnitsky and W. W. Bartlet (LaSalle IL: Open Court, 1987).

[12]I have in mind here Seymour Fisher, *Development and Structure of the Body Image,* 2 vols. (Hillsdale NJ: Erlbaum, 1986), an immense compendium of research on the problem announced, and George Lakoff's more original, if deceptively titled, *Women, Fire, and Dangerous Things: What Categories Reveal about the Mind* (Chicago: University of Chicago Press, 1987), which will come up again in connection with metaphor.

other world.

And to admit the alterity of some other body as already presupposed by any appropriation of my own is at the same time to raise the possibility not just of another and so an indefinite number of individual bodies but of *the* or some ultimate body. Centricity on its own is always in some danger of circling back into solipsism, practical or intellectual; but duality already begins to imply infinitude. I come to the side door of my building and look down the long corridor to the opposite entrance. The lines formed where walls and ceiling or floor meet converge toward an ideal vanishing point. The effect is reinforced by old-fashioned oak trim around the classroom doors and their transoms, which contrasts agreeably with the pale walls. Where do such lines, at once physical and imaginary, come together? Upon a terminal point—*the* body, I could think, as such. The various parts of this building that catch my attention are not yet bodies but aggregates shaped: cellulose sawn and stained, dust compacted, fluent substances long since jelled. But the whole these have already been arranged to make up does seem a body of a kind: does it not have "wings" and a "front," if not quite a face? That entity at least may be taken as a figure for what I cannot see at the end of a hallway. But why need I complain of this ultimate invisibility? There are doors and windows and floors; and if I turn to climb the stairs, such a thought as their combination has provided.

Allegorical

But such anticipations, it may be complained, are at best intuitions or extrapolations—and from a dubious base. Do they not assume too easily that bodies, mine or another, not only exist but also can be appropriated or acknowledged without difficulty? This may not seem all that obvious, even with the partial help of phenomenology. How can one really know a body, after all, in what is still bound to seem the orthodox or objective sense, and to what extent? One of the appealing features of Jonathan Miller's *The Body in Question,* a book that helped prompt this inquiry, is the explanation offered there for the way in which our collective knowledge of the body has developed. Medical science has constituted itself, he observes, "by the accurate identification of the sort of thing our body is." And this has been achieved, Miller believes, through an application of certain metaphors drawn from devices already invented to deal with the external world. "It is impossible to imagine how anyone could have made sense of the heart before we knew what a pump was." As machines became more complex, they provided increasingly sophisticated models in terms of which to understand equivalently difficult aspects of the body's behavior. The invention of a governing device for the self-regulation of steam engines, for instance, led in due course to the idea of homeostasis. "Before the invention of automatic gun-turrets, there was no model to explain the finesse of voluntary muscular movement." And an understanding of the nerves and brain similarly presupposed the invention of the computer.[13]

As a contribution to the history of medical epistemology, this account seems brilliantly plausible, and its very clarity as an explanation for explanation might also help to specify the limits of the kind of knowledge in question. For a body that could be understood as Miller understands that understanding would have to be the body as object—which is to say, no longer *my* body or *yours* or those of the many-layered trees now gently stirring outside my proper window this hazy summer morning but the body-in-general as idea or set of facts and functions. Of this conceptual structure any singular body—and actual bodies are always individual—would become only an illustration or clinical example. To attend school and in due course to "practice" medicine, as Miller once did, would then be to learn how to translate from the particular instances one was confronted with up to the relevant idea and down again. That is what we call a profession.

To be sure, Miller does offer some suggestions concerning the "problem" of the subjective, or felt, body. This inner "body-image" is, he concedes, rather more actual to the inhabitant than what one learns in a lecture or can demonstrate on an autopsy table or even see in a mirror. But from the perspective his argument has adopted, this body is not some inward reproduction of the whole but a cartoonlike figure with large hands and mouth and a limited repertory of information: it can tell left from right, for instance, and up from down. It is admittedly "the image through which you recognize your physical existence in the world," and so that without which you could not be "yourself"—in short, almost a version of what we have just been calling, in another language, the soul. But this "image," though of course "valorized" (as usual, a pejorative word) by the subject of it, has from a scientific point of view serious deficiencies. The information it provides is really no more reliable than the evidence accumulated by other people's eyes and touch. It provides no proof that anyone or anything is actually there. Nor can it convey what is going on in those regions of bodily existence that are governed by unconscious processes. It leaves most of our "insides" quite blank. To really know these, we must look into some other body—by way of models drawn from the progress of technology. So Miller returns confidently to the perspective from which he began. He is writing in this book as a doctor and a philosopher, not as an artist—though in another context he can be one of those too.[14]

---

[13] Jonathan Miller, *The Body in Question* (New York: Random House, 1978) 9-10.

[14] Miller, *Body,* 15. Other authorities are somewhat less reductive. A story in Oliver Sach's *The Man Who Mistook His Wife for a Hat* (New York: Harper, 1987) about a woman who had lost the sense of "proprioperception" suggests that this delivers if not a protoself, at least the "inside" of the *sarx* as realized by the *psychē* (43-54). Paul Schilder's older but still impressive *Image and Appearance of the Human Body* (New York: International Universities Press, 1950) provides a more confident as well as elaborate picture of the "body-image," or "postural model," from a psychoanalytic point of view that takes gestaltist as well as neurological considerations into account. His subjective body is also composed in relation

Our private experiences of medical practice would tend to confirm the validity as well as the limits of Miller's explanation. Dentistry, for instance, seems to presuppose mining or quarrying as well as casting. On the occasions of its exercise the subject of it must withdraw from a body others have taken over—for one's own good, of course. Lying in the elaborate chair, eyes shut or blinking against bright lights and peering faces, the jaw numbed, the mouth open and clumsily crowded with a suction tube, alien fingers (now cased in rubber), and a drill, the bones of the skull reverberate as the head of the instrument sinks all too easily inward. For the time being I must indeed allow myself to be reduced to so much hard and soft matter, for only these aspects of my body will fit into the universe visible from the point of view adopted. The dentist is correspondingly abstracted and concentrated to enact just that quantity of attention and skill which the procedure requires. We are both acutely specialized—and the rest of the self must be abandoned to gravity, or removed elsewhere in imagination, though still just able to reply politely to remarks made in a soothing tone to someone addressed, oddly, by one's first name. Caught inside this merely material body, one realizes what is going on there as if standing in the corner waiting to get back, like a ghost. Then I get up and leave, light-headed: after all, one has to get one's teeth fixed. There is another metal patch now inside a tooth, a prosthesis rather than a tool, and so really a loss and not a gain. I am no longer quite what I was, but to just this extent one more object in an alien universe; a corpse, as it were, in advance. What causes stress is the obligation not simply to suffer such an invasion of my person but to consent to what denies me. This compulsion is either an insult or a sacrifice, and for the time being I cannot tell which.

The Body in Question would rank as a coffee-table book, with its colored illustrations from the corresponding television program, though in fact it harbors a significant philosophical argument. A more academic study which continues to influence recent thinking about the body is Mary Douglas's *Purity and Danger*. This is organized around an anthropological explication of the priestly regulations in Leviticus. The focus is accordingly not on the natural but on the communal possibility. "We cannot possibly interpret rituals concerning excreta, breast milk, saliva, and the rest unless we are prepared to see in the body a symbol of society, and to see the powers and dangers credited to social structure reproduced in small scale on the human body."[15] In other words, society in general is the meaning of which the boundaries or parts of a natural body cannot help but become so many

---

to others and so might more easily count as a first draft of what we have been calling the person.

[15]Mary Douglas, *Purity and Danger: An Analysis of Concepts of Pollution and Taboo* (London: Routledge, 1966) 115. Douglas's more recent *Natural Symbols: Explorations in Cosmology* (New York: Pantheon, 1970; rev. ed, 1982) repeats the same argument with additional instances from other cultures.

discrete signs. Whether ancients or moderns, we make use of our bodies in order to communicate cultural judgments that as such constitute the reality for which the several physical manifestations are at most clues. As with Miller, the concrete has thus become an allegory for the corresponding abstraction, the difference being that in this case the referent is a norm rather than an idea, and so initially at least social rather than intellectual.

But an implicit Platonism still seems to govern in anthropology as in medicine. For any social as well as for one or another of the "natural" sciences, progress is a successful reduction of hitherto mysterious or recalcitrant phenomena to evidence for some comprehensible system that would have to be realized by an impersonal and timeless (and therefore essentially modern) intelligence. Douglas's enterprise seeks out the "total structure of thought" which could be understood to govern such otherwise very disparate, not to say chaotic, affairs as accumulate in an unscientific encyclopedia like Leviticus. She discovers among these a universal requirement that individuals should "conform" to the "category" in which they belong. Ancient holiness, in such a reading, is simply modern order; animals are fit to eat if they behave in the way normal for creatures belonging to the environments in which they are found. So "swarming," for instance, renders species exhibiting this sort of motion unclean because it is inherently indeterminant, and so unassignable to the available categories of water, air, or earth.

Purity and Danger has become a hermeneutical classic, and the results of its method have impressed even biblical scholars, who are apt to be methodological latecomers.[16] It is, all the same, still possible to protest that this explanatory style converts the cultic practices of an ancient Near Eastern people into the epistemic structures of the modern West with almost suspicious ease. The intertranslatability of the normative and cognitive is a formula of our own intellectual universe, like the reduction of other modes of being to signifiers of this comprehensive reality. "Theory" in all its latter-day variants has come to mean one more analysis of this state of affairs that will at the same time legitimate its hegemony on the level of interpretation—as if to reflect the methodological and bureaucratic structures within which its practitioners must pursue their careers.[17] One's doubts need not reach to

---

[16]An appreciative use of Douglas's arguments is made, for instance, by G. J. Wenham in the New International Commentary on Leviticus, normally a conservative series.

[17]That the reduction of the body to an allegory of society has on the whole continued to prevail might be illustrated from a number of recent feminist studies. Nancy Chodorow's earlier *Reproduction of Mothering* (Berkeley: University of California Press, 1978), for instance, makes sure its reader understands that the disposition to mother should itself be understood as "perpetuated" through "sociostructurally induced psychological mechanisms" (211) rather than any "bioevolutionary" means, though her later *Feminism and Psychoanalytic Theory* (New Haven: Yale University Press, 1989) is prepared to be more "multiplex." A collection of essays offering "semiotic perspectives" and entitled *The Female Body in Western Culture* (Cambridge: Harvard University Press, 1986) is introduced by Susan Rubin

the specific conclusions drawn, which within the perspective adopted may seem quite plausible. But one could still "call into question," as the phrase goes, the concomitant deconstruction of the bodily as such, which might, after all, seem especially uncanny in such contexts as pollution and sacrifice. In a temple, as opposed to a university, the body, whether human or animal, cannot help but be all too embarrassingly present. One might go on to guess that this very bodiliness would still have to be at stake, however indirectly, in any scheme of interpretation as well as on the altar. Once again we seem to need a somatics as well as a "semiotics" to appreciate the full truth of the matter.

I suspect though that a rereading of Douglas's argument with a degree more regard for the actual corporealities involved might resituate without injuring the insights achieved. One might then propose that the purity regulations would in fact have at the core of their intention the integrity of what we have been calling the individual body. So both animals (chap. 22) and priests (chap. 21) should, according to Leviticus, be physically entire to be fit for sacrifice or to sacrifice. So too one should eat only animals that move in the way proper to their kind not only for categorical reasons but because motion is immediately expressive of the vitality of the body in question (chap. 11). Breaches of the boundaries of the whole body render the victim unclean, as with discharges from the penis (chap. 15), or menstruation and childbirth (chap. 12). "Leprosy" obviously interrupts the body surface (chap. 14). And for the same reason mixtures are not permitted: each kind of body must be allowed its proper identity (chap. 19).

The version of the body presumed throughout these regulations remains that of the individual, whether some citizen of Israel, the priest, or an animal. An imperfect beast is unfit for sacrifice; a deficient priest is incompetent to celebrate; an unclean person may be excluded from the camp. The issue throughout is what entitles one to admission to the nation assembled before its king. Bodily integrity is the prerequisite for social inclusion. Society as such, though, is *not* corporeal but legal. And the presumed criterion for judgment still remains implicit in the individual body of the citizen, priest, or animal offered up as a representation of either. The body is the truth of the system, that is, not the system of the body.[18] All bodies, it is presumed,

---

Suleiman with a firm reminder that the body, female or otherwise, must always be considered a "symbolic construct." And Jane Gallop's *Thinking through the Body* (New York: Columbia University Press, 1988), ostensibly a defense against just this disembodying approach, is in fact still too ensnared in the approved language to allow any imaginable body to emerge.

[18] The eventual dangers that might follow from the belief that the truth of the body is the system of ideas it can be made to support are effectively brooded upon in Elaine Scarry's impressive *Body in Pain: The Making and Unmaking of the World* (New York: Oxford University Press, 1985). Torture, she points out, is the infliction of deliberate injury upon some actual body in order to "substantiate" a social concept that is otherwise in danger of seeming fraudulent: allegory, in other words, not just discovered but enforced. The intersections of the body and ideology might also be illustrated from the essays accumulated

are inherently analogous. And every individual body dies. Its perfection, one might even claim, is revealed in just that conclusion. To sacrifice a singular body of whatever species is therefore to enact the destiny of them all in advance, as it were, of the common fact, so that everyone may realize the *telos* of this mode of being. It is accordingly what there is to do before God. So the cult "spells out" the condition of all existence. We need not condescend to Leviticus, then, as if we had somehow got ahead of it. Christians especially should recall that the gospel still presupposes the same truth, though it may advance another as well. But both cult and gospel either precede or transcend the scope of the cognitive paradigm presumed in any modern explanation of either. And the bodiliness they share shows how.

Mary Douglas understands ordinary housework as the maintenance of a system of ideas quite as much as the practice of an ancient cult. Dirt, she has famously observed, is "matter out of place": like its opposite, cleanliness, it has no meaning, as it were, in its own right.[19] So I vacuum the stuff up, Saturday morning after Saturday morning, and dust off the tops of the bureaus, where for some reason it accumulates. At breakfast and supper I wash the dishes, restoring each to its pristine condition. The bed as well must be "made," over and over. To "do" the wash or mend clothes is equally understandable as so much practical allegorizing, by means of which one labors to bring these materials back into coincidence with the relevant idea. The very repetitiousness of such tasks would seem evidence of their thoroughly comprehensible character.

But I suspect that in this context too an interpretation of such a kind, though accurate enough as far as it goes, would still confuse an order of explanation with the fullness of experience, as if the latter need count for no more than an instance of the former. In practice though I do not believe we find ourselves no better than slaves to some preconception, even our own. Housework is also often a pleasure, perhaps a sport, occasionally an art. To become absorbed in this activity is to follow a succession of invitations to give ourselves up to what in fact we are doing. We offer our proper bodiliness so as to re-create that of the things which surround us, and so reconfirm our own life. Each of these is almost a body too, or we would not care; it needs only a little nurturing from us to become itself again, and so alive for us. Housework is handwork, like nursing or the priesthood: I scrub or cut up or smooth out, over and over, not just as a repetition of an idea but in the rhythm of a routine. My gestures are somnolent as I move from one task to another, but in fact I am thoroughly awake and even enjoying myself. To be sure, this is my house, and I am the one who consents to what is being done. I am not the servant of some alien power. But it seems to me still that the invitations I respond to come not from an external imperative or even my own conscience but from the things themselves.

---

in the three issues of *Zone* printed together as *Fragments for a History of the Human Body* (Cambridge MA: MIT Press, 1989).

[19] Douglas, *Purity and Danger*, 35.

This floor *asks* to be mopped; that table top *needs* scrubbing. To accomplish as much I must indeed sacrifice myself, for this house is something of a temple too, but that is comparatively easy: I have only, as we say, to take the time. But this is enough. I am nearer the truth of things than I was, and pleased accordingly.

A more distinct and separable and so perhaps more "masculine" version of what in the end is still a common experience would be provided by repair or construction as opposed to maintenance. Slowly, summer by summer, I have also been redoing this old house, fixing up one room after another: one year the kitchen and bathroom, the next the cellar, the one after that the living and dining rooms. So I scrape old paint off the chestnut woodwork around a window and the door to the porch, or the baseboard and the molding between the walls and the ceiling. Then I stain the exposed wood to bring it back into coincidence with what it used to be. Finally I start on the walls and ceiling, painting each in turn, brushing on a second coat, and rescraping where paint has spilled on wood.

The habitual character of this work, hour by half hour, day after day, brings home what seems to be going on. When one paints, one is covering a surface while observing boundaries. These lines must be carefully traced and any mistakes corrected either immediately by thumb or tissue or later with a knife. So far the pressure of the relevant idea does appear to govern, though still in the service of an eventual integrity. For these lines distinguish where one thing ends and another begins: wall and doorpost, molding or ceiling, baseboard and wall. Bodies are not indefinite or unlimited, after all.

But a system of lines is still only a materialized idea. What gives substance to these is the body therein contained and renewed. And this is evoked not by the boundaries I trace so carefully but by the second coat. *The second coat*—why must we put it on? So as not to see through, one can realize, to the hazy ghost of the previous color, which looms behind as if to call into question the adequacy of the new covering. With a second layer I need no longer realize that older surface; a fresh and indubitable finish will provide that literally invisible third dimension we are really seeking all the while. For the surface is a boundary too, like the outlines, though in two dimensions rather than one. And within, that is, beyond or beneath it, is the rest of whatever is there. Substantiality is once again a sign that a body is almost present. All this surface needs now is some degree of motion, which my admiring glance will already begin to supply. A still life, or *nature morte,* is after all not really dead but alive.

In a painting, in the imaginative sense of that word, paint is laid on in two dimensions in such a way that its "subject" becomes visible in three. This is as true of abstractions as representational art, for even the most rigorously flattened picture plane will still be divided into segments of color, and to that extent evokes a sculptural presence. In painting, in the practical sense of that word, paint is laid on in two dimensions in order to evoke a third which as such is not visible, though we feel its influence. The practical would then be the only truly abstract art. Or one could say that the imaginary state of affairs revealed in a deliberate painting is a displaced equivalent for what is brought into actual being by simply painting a house, in which case the useful would be the only truly representational art as well. But it seems to me rather that neither the ostensible subject of a painting nor the real wall or ceiling upon which house paint is laid entirely corresponds as depth to the surface being covered. They stand in for this, without quite becoming altogether the thing itself. If one asks, what *is* this, one would presumably be returned once again to the body indeed. No merely individual body, imagined or real, can be entirely convincing to us, one might conclude, unless it also discloses some aspect of a most perfect whole. It is the absence of just this presence that I feel as I work. I want it still, like a lover deprived, for all I will end up with, I also know, is a somewhat cleaner place to live, which is not nothing, but not everything I would like. The result has to be less than I am left hoping for, though rather more than I began with. And that must do for the time being.

There can seem ways, then, to experience at least the memory or promise of an otherwise still unknowable and therefore either antecedent or ultimate body by way of the relation between the one we already inhabit and those others we can now touch. Touch is, we say often, the "language" of the body, or one more expression if not of knowledge then certainly of faith. Painting too is a kind of touching by way of the brush, wet on dry, stroke after stroke. There is accordingly a touch of the eyes: potential lovers, or perhaps enemies, look at each other across a room. Friends do not touch, except to shake hands, though members of a family may, as if to remember they were one body once. So one touches or is touched, physically or metaphorically, by those to whom one is related for the moment at least as if we were members of the same family after all. Touch reunites what has become separate, or initiates a union between those who began as autonomous. We see in order that we may touch sooner or later, or rather so that we may not have to touch all the time, like plants, but only when we want. It is the once and future child in us that longs for touch, hoping to be persuaded at last that we are not alone after all but members of some whole.[20]

In memory and desire, though, we are apt to forget that what seems missing ahead or behind is never quite absent up and down. We are always touching the ground still, or the floor, or the seat of this chair. Gravity keeps us in touch with the planet at least, like magnetism or the strong and weak forces, a mode of faith at the inanimate level that constantly unites us with the universe. This coherence seems

---

[20]The connections between touch, union, and vision are confirmed by a suggestion I found in W. W. Bartley's editorial introduction, "Philosophy of Biology versus Philosophy of Physics," to the collection of essays entitled *Evolutionary Epistemology,* already referred to. The biological reason, he proposes, why vision and photosynthesis make use of the same narrow portion of the electromagnetic spectrum (itself an intriguing fact) is that vision would have developed in the first place as a way to move closer to what would at the time have been "edible" light (29-30).

consoling: bodies hold together after all. At a certain depth all boundaries disappear. Cutting up cucumbers for a salad, for instance, I put the skins into the trash bag as I go, and the slices into the salad bowl. Something distracts my attention, and I recover to find I have thrown a handful of the dark corrugated strips into the bowl along with the pale and flexible flesh. On another morning, still in the kitchen, I cannot locate the old sherbert container I use to hold my store of mixed cereal on the bottom shelf of the refrigerator. Where could it have got to? Could my son have moved it the previous evening, or even taken it away with him? That seems too paranoid a suspicion. Then an obscure intimation leads me to the pantry cupboard. There it sits on the shelf where I keep its ingredients, the brown bag of granola from the health food store and the jar of toasted wheat germ. I have treated the combination as if it were still the things out of which it was made. I had forgotten the difference. The unconscious, we know, does not discriminate. It takes in as still or already united what "the mind" distinguishes as objects of different kinds or actions that ought to be kept separate in time or place. Such "accidents" testify not just to some concomitant absence of just this mind, though that can feel threatening enough, but more positively to a primordial unity of being, and if original, then perhaps eschatological as well.

Reciprocal

The integrity of an individual body, we have noticed, is defined by its boundary, which it maintains against other bodies like and unlike itself. On the campus path a dog pads from side to side ahead of me. The patches of red and gray hair on the backs of his legs balance, I am pleased to see: polarity integrates, as usual. He pauses at the corner of a building, sniffing, and then lifts a leg, to register his presence on this scene. The deposit overlaps, I can presume, those of other dogs, his predecessors and peers. So his world becomes a projection or emanation from his natural body, a repetition of its boundary at a further distance. My "territory" is wherever I am determined to roam freely, the limits of which I will defend or mark, perhaps, as in this case, with the remains of myself. Thus I make use of my death. That dab of urine is a signature: here have I been, and here I still am, as far as you are concerned. Language is my skin beaten thin.

I must have room, to live at all. In a display cabinet in this basement lie pieces of pottery from a recent dig on Cyprus. Two are set so close they touch, and I wish I could open the locked glass panels and separate them. *They* do not take pleasure in coming together, I am sure. An unwanted contact, however delicate, seems more threatening than a frank invasion, which at least is unambiguous: I can empathize, after a fashion, with the microscopic creature that swims in my blood, and so in imagination at least liberate it from me, and me from myself. But we all feel horror at lampreys or leeches that breach the boundaries of one body without properly becoming part of another or forming a third. Configurations that cannot be counted as either one thing or two are monstrous, like Siamese twins or multiple personalities. It is only discarded and so indistinguishable items that seem tolerable in a heap or stack, which thereby acquires by inheritance, as it were, a degree of the bodiliness abandoned by its elements. These have died that it might live.

Boundaries can be uncertain and may be challenged. An article from an old *Catholic Worker* by Robert Ellsberg reminds me that in a county jail of the sort activists used to end up at it was the practice to call out "Body only!" which meant the inmate in question should come out of his cell without toothbrush, bedding, or jigsaw puzzle, for he would soon be returning.[21] Ellsberg interprets the phrase to imply that a prison can hold only the body and not the soul, which does not seem quite the point. In fact, as some others of us also know, a jail is not in the least Platonic, but a tediously physical place where the soul is all too incarnate. "Body" would seem rather to mean your movable self, without portable extras but still including not just your immediate flesh but also clothes and glasses and whatever happened to be in your pockets. In fact Ellsberg does not hold to his own idealistic interpretation, for in another paragraph he tells of resisting a rectal search, which would situate the boundary between himself and others at just that most sensitive point. And for the rest of his time in jail he fasted, he says, another way of drawing the line in bodily terms. There is pride of course in such protests, and not just political or intellectual. What in fact prison does is cut me off from my previous environment, which I am *not* allowed to move about in. By reestablishing my limits that much nearer my proper center, I revenge myself on those who would break them down and so regain, as the saying goes, control over my life. The contest then is over who will draw the line. From a detached perspective this dispute is still an argument within the category: in any case there is a boundary, and both sides agree it defines the body in question.

In some contexts, as at the cellular level, this limit seems easy to trace; with complex plants, impossible except in imagination; with such animals as dogs and ourselves, ambiguous: how could a definite line be drawn from the corner of one building to another? Only by dots, perhaps, as we trace the edge of the universe. By way of such inscriptions, obvious or putative, this note of bodiliness at least may be assimilated to language, which does nothing else but define what is inside or out. And is not every line already a text? Or rather, cannot any text be reduced once again to a line, more or less twisted and chopped? But only symbolic bodies, which have already passed into or through language, need be conceived of as equipped with boundaries literal enough to stand as instances of "scripture." It would then be chiefly an imagined body that would find itself bounded by a real frontier, and a natural body only to the degree that this was already treated as if it were imagined, as when we gaze out on an actual "landscape" or see somebody's face against a contrasting background. The aura that surrounds a living body, at once revealing its

---

[21]Robert Ellsberg, "Long Days, Dark Nights in a County Jail," *Catholic Worker* 44 (July/August 1978): 1, 4-5, 8.

presence and betraying its environment, can seem rather a field of force than a barrier.

Even if we usually settle for thinking of the skin as the boundary of our own bodies, for instance, and so as a visible surface, or line swept round, we are obliged by such anecdotes as the one just repeated to recall that the most typical feature of this organ is not its power to contain or exclude but the several pores or orifices which so ambivalently breach that apparent rule. These are specialized for the incorporation or expulsion of other entities from within or without. The apparent wall is really a set of gates, including sight and hearing as well as mouth and anus, vagina and urethra—or navel before any of these. And there are simpler creatures, of course, that manage as much by way of gaps in the ranks of cells that border their parts, or even through the membranes that surround the constituent cells. A body is neither fortified nor imprisoned then but variously participative in a rhythmic intercourse with as much of the world as matters to it. This is perhaps clearest at the level of such events as the immunological reaction, in the news in connection with AIDS or the problems of transplant surgery. The practical boundary in any given context would then amount to this incessant reciprocity, inside or out of any "host." So I breathe, my bowels pulse, my bladder fills and empties; I sleep and wake; I walk about, one step after another, over and through this charged scene, which belongs to me more or less only because it also belongs to the other, in the nature of the bodiliness we share. Desire and repugnance, deficiency or superfluity, would then represent polar alternatives in a constant exchange. And upon these pulsations in turn would presumably depend the corresponding articulations of music or verse, complication and denouement, anticipation and nostalgia. Culture is a reproduction of the body too, which reproduces itself by way of just such rhythmic interactions.

And what is any "environment" if not the antecedent or incipient presence of other bodies of the same or different kinds, from which any individual must flee or toward which it may approach? My boundary is the constant possibility of what I may consume, or might consume me—or if of the same species, then what I must fight or love, and in either case acknowledge as equal and opposite. I do not merely sweep the horizon or experience a sensation of being in general but fix upon this or that which precipitates as already existing in its own right. And we are inclined to realize these as wholes composed of parts arranged about some "axis of symmetry" well before we know what they are.[22] If we add that we can notice anything only if it is moving, which is to say, alive, it becomes once more evident that bodiliness, our own together with that of the other, must precede culture and so cognition or textuality as well—which should seem reassuring to some of us at least. It could even make unnecessary what we would formally recognize as language at all.

---

[22]This is David Marr's phrase: see his *Vision,* 303-309ff., for a use of the idea to explain recognition.

One more dog story may illustrate: as I walk back along the corridor to my office, carrying a glass and a cup, both of which I have just filled at the water fountain, a German Shepherd gets up from where it has been lying at the door of the computer room. Dogs are forbidden in this building, but people do bring them in. This one approaches me, apparently aware of what I am carrying. I have often thought, seeing them asleep at doorways, how thirsty these creatures must become. And this one is; as we meet, he sniffs at my hands. I lower the cup onto the floor and he laps vigorously at the water inside. When its level has fallen too far down for his tongue to reach, I pour in more from the glass. Presently he is satisfied, and walks back to his place, nails clicking. We need not only consume or be consumed, then, as long as there is something else to offer in the place of one or the other. But this was an afterthought; what impressed me at the time was simply the ease of our communication. He had asked me a question, and I had answered, quite without words. Our bodies in motion toward each other had sufficed. That was already a language we held in common.

If the boundary of any body is linear shorthand for its intercourse with other bodies, and identity is once again confirmed as founded upon relation, the fact is still more or less obvious depending on context. Respiration, for instance, seems easy to explain without bringing in bodies at all. In plants and animals alike, the molecular form of oxygen, O_2, is consumed and CO_2, or carbon dioxide, is extruded, molecule by molecule. The process as understood in chemical terms would appear to include all that is relevant. Nutrition, though, is more interesting. Digestion would as such be thoroughly biochemical. But what is digested comes from a body as it serves to build up a body. Wholes incorporate wholes, though those of us who are not birds or fish usually find it convenient to chop these into bite-sized chunks, and may even mix one kind with another, or expose the results to some excess of heat. If we are plants, we wait until the bodies of the relevant others have been reduced to so many free-floating molecules—until, that is, they are not only dead but well done. If animals, we use our mouths and paws, if not butcher and table knives. These reductions may disguise what we are up to, like other forms of comprehension. The continuing truth is better illustrated by the habits of snakes and whales, or perhaps fraternity men with a bowl of goldfish. But in every case one creature is changed into another. Consumption is metamorphosis.

I pass a fence, behind which a flock of sheep are picking up hay scattered for them on the dirty snow. They raise their heads to stare incuriously, their mouths working as if to express a prim disapproval. Eating is what there is for them to do, besides grow the thick coats of wool. That too will be changed in due course, though not by swallowing. What whole body then are they so constantly and automatically consuming, I ask myself? This dun detritus seems as near nothing in particular as it well could be. But the answer is obvious—the plant. That is what is being reproduced as sheep while I watch—with a little adjustment on both sides to the exigencies of evolution and the season, themselves adaptations to this planet and its passage through time. These circumstances need not conceal that perpetual intercourse by means of which each body maintains itself as long as it can. The individual is evidently no better than a moment in this endless interchange. The flesh in which we now go about has been obtained from our neighbors in this world, to which it will sooner or later be restored—to be consumed, we may hope, in its turn. My integrity is founded upon an integration of these, though not of the same kind as mine or I should not hunger for them. But our differences only disguise the dependence we share.

This necessity is perhaps easier to observe in other creatures than among ourselves, though it applies across the board, and not only with respect to what one would formally admit could be consumed. Behind me in the checkout line at the supermarket was a grocery cart carrying a young child, naked in the hot weather except for a diaper and plastic pants. She stood upright on the mesh floor of the basket, reaching out for whatever was nearby. To see something apparently within reach was to try and get hold of it, regardless. Her mother stood behind watchfully, intervening from time to time to remove items that had been seized and return them to their places. At a checkout counter there are a fair number of these, in expectation of the grown-up version of just this response: candy, gum, razor blades, magazines, paperbacks. The little girl was very intent upon what she was doing. For her it was quite serious. The mother dropped what looked like a makeup case into the cart, hoping to distract her daughter, but this did not work for long; what was already on hand was by definition uninteresting. What indeed would the world consist of at this age? Things worth reaching for, which might, that is, be good to eat or at least to play with. The gaze in such cases involves the whole body, for the hand immediately follows the eye, and brings whatever exists back to the mouth.

But one might also return from obvious or displaced instances of consumption to such other metabolic processes as photosynthesis or respiration and discover at this level too some reverberation of the same creaturely necessity. What do plants eat, if not the sun? Or so much of that celestial body as they can make use of, which in practice may be no more than an electron or two. The radiant energy plants convert into chemical energy has of course been filtered through the atmosphere of the earth, from which they also receive carbon dioxide from the air and hydrogen from water as well as minerals from the soil. The whole body these creatures consume would then be represented not only by the sun or the decayed remains of other individuals but by the planet. But almost every form of life—which is to say virtually the whole of the "biosphere"—depends in the end upon radiation from the sun, deriving its nutrients directly or indirectly from that source. Solar energy moves into plants and from them to other creatures that consume plants, which in turn are consumed by others up what thus becomes a food chain. In the long run each of us is always swallowing a star. That is bread from heaven indeed.

A whole would still be consumed by a whole, then, though any metamorphosis might have to be reduced to a succession of sequences in order to be understood. A Venus's-flytrap is in that case not a gross exception but one more instance of the general rule, though this may apply in some gentler as well as an obscurer sense.

I too need air, not to mention heat and light, as well as this grass or these trees. And I too consume everything I can. So I am a microcosm of any macrocosm that may be imagined as much as any sprout of rice. For consciousness sweeps out a horizon of concern that would correspond to the life-world of animals and the all-embracing air and soil of plants. But if consciousness is still the center, the circumference would in principle and very nearly in practice be the boundary of the universe, wherever that might be drawn. The heavens would then be our branchy crest, and the charges of the atomic nucleus the tip of our rootlets. The whole of things is what I would in the end be endeavoring to devour. For the time being, to be sure, I or the specialists on my behalf must make do with this or that particle or quasar. That is what one can focus on, literally or metaphorically. But I know what these represent. I need not be deceived by images. The apple is the world, as in Emerson's dream of the angel. I would consume it at one bite and die happy.

Remembering as much, I am struck by an extrapolation of just such a kind in Emile Mersch's *Theology of the Mystical Body,* not exactly a textbook of biology. "A single plant of corn poppy or wild mignonette," this neglected theologian observes, could absorb and transform into itself the entire terrestrial globe in some ten years—supposing, of course, that the whole were assimilable and the plant's seeds suitably distributed. "After this, the whole solar system would be an affair of several years, and all sidereal matter of a few more: twenty at the most."[23] I could not know where he found his figures, but it was intriguing to follow an imagination that could casually set aside the usual contingencies in favor of so unqualified a possibility. Some actual population explosions have been in the news since he wrote, whether of red algae or crown-of-thorns starfish or deer or for that matter human beings, which might illustrate the same point on another scale. Mersch himself went on to pursue what for him seemed the psychic implication of such events, imaginary or actual, horrific or benign. Among the higher animals, he observed, sensation "already annexes the universe, not grain by grain or mouthful by mouthful, but at a single stroke, and by a movement so easy that it can be repeated over and over without being noticed. We may describe sensation as an exploit that consists in appropriating entire regions, oceans, and heavens by merely opening the eyes." In such a way it "brings back the whole universe as booty." In a perfected comprehension, then, the cosmos too would be taken in. We might *think* the "unity of the world," it would follow, even if we could not quite know it; indeed we must already, if only to appreciate the ideal privilege of the corn-poppy.

To eat anything, then, is in the end to consume everything, which must accordingly reproduce itself within my consciousness, if not quite as such, at least in thought. And an idea of the whole, however that might be formulated, would then amount to a re-creation of the universe in the mode of an ideal object. If so, even

---

[23]Emile Mersch, *The Theology of the Mystical Body* (St. Louis: Herder, 1951) 97-98. I shall be referring again to this remarkable book in connection with its formal topic.

objectivity (and any object is an idea) could in the end prove the surface or outline of the body indeed, and not just a convenient way of dealing with the remains or elements of natural bodies: the ultimate body in two or perhaps just one instead of three dimensions, to be sure, which is to say, as a circumference without content. But that would not be quite nothing either. The apple is still the world, which I would take in at a bite, after whatever fashion I might; for evil, we can easily read, but perhaps for good too.

Mortal

In any ordinary here and now, the individual body will seem to prevail, whether as myself or the other, and the usual notes of this mode of being will accordingly typify the possibility. But as soon as time is counted in, I must realize this confidence is not altogether trustworthy. Reproduction in the original as opposed to the derived senses takes time. And its slower rhythms notoriously enforce periods of somatic ambiguity in which the propriety of the singular body is put into question. Copulation itself already enacts what amounts to a dual body, though not for long—and this is not monstrous, though it must appear comic in most species. Pregnancy still more obviously generates a body at once singular and double, like mitosis before it. And the coexistence of mother and child extends well beyond birth, as we are sometimes embarrassed to realize, attentuating only with maturity—which begins the cycle all over again for another generation. "The family" can therefore seem almost another kind of body in its own obscure right, persisting beneath the lines drawn by an overexplicit individualism. Singular existence will then appear no more than a moment within an ongoing pulsation.

There are echoes of this somatic ambiguity within the arts too, as one might expect. At an exhibition of new pots at the museum, which for some reason has decided to take the crafts seriously, I think to myself, this is synecdoche: the pots are containers for the thing contained, which is *not* exhibited. But the relation between the actual presence and this complementary absence is as close as can be, like that of a mother and her unborn child (it was clearly not incidental that the potter was a woman). Thus bodiliness may repeat itself within itself almost as one with itself, and then, as at a birth, what begins as virtually coincident with the shaping hand becomes an independent being of still another kind.

The metamorphosis from a singular body through the ambiguity of two bodies in one, or one carrying another within itself, to the virtually eschatological emergence of two separate beings each with its own proper body is also reproduced within the tropics of language. Empathy, it is easy to see, is one with identification: I am whatever I take in or go off with by consumption or projection. In language this becomes tautology, or repetition without change. The next stage would be metonomy, which the manufacture of pots might illustrate. Here contiguity and association govern apprehension. Things linked in space or time stand in for one another. So hair and clothing and shoes reveal the self, or the knickknacks on a desk, or the tone of a voice. This would be the trope that governs friendship, in which I favor those close to me in tastes, attributes, or predicament. The third stage is full metaphor, in which confessedly different things nonetheless stand toward each other as reciprocally meaningful. Hereabouts might be located the possibility of marriage, for male and female are not in fact the same, any more than parent and child. So the several species of the symbolic body too might reflect, not to say depend on, the changes of the natural body through time.

But to entertain such analogies would anticipate a later phase of this argument. The civic repercussions of the slow wheel from singularity through ambiguity to individuality again are often less amiably positive. The abortion controversy would be a major instance here. One side affirms that the individual must preserve her right to control her own body. It is accordingly presumed that the contents of her uterus should count as a part of this through, say, the first trimester. The other side insists that the entity in question should count as a whole body, and therefore as already another person, from the moment of conception. The line dividing one individual from another might evidently be drawn at various other points along the continuum: when the fetus might survive on its own outside the womb, for instance. "Viability" could indeed serve as an elementary sign of independent bodiliness. But advances in technology have made this moment obscure, shifting the possibility further back toward the beginning of the period of uncertainty. Throughout, though, the general problem remains the same. On one side of the line there is one body; on the other, two. And both sides agree as well that any individual body should count for as much as any other of the same kind. No one doubts that bodies as such are morally as well as ontologically equal. Morality is equality between bodies, we might incidently conclude: justice is difference interpreted as equivalence. For in this context too identity precipitates as relation.

Both sides, it might also be noticed, are inclined to avoid the temporal aspect of the matter, though this is what generates the problem in the first place. Ethical controversy, like cognition, occurs in a timeless space where every instance of the body confronts all the others simultaneously, like members of a crowd each of whom must make use of the same sidewalk in spite of the competition. But if time is allowed back in, the issue need not seem only a struggle over who should occupy the same space at the same moment. A "fetus," that uncertain entity, is eventually revealed as a member of the next generation, which presumes not just a displacement but the disappearance of the previous individual. Temporality entails death as well as life. This is already hinted at in either of the bodily crises that punctuate the sequence: whether at ejaculation or at birth, I must "die" so that my child may live.

The time of the natural body is measured in generations. So our private sense of time is apt to be determined by our parents before us and our children after us. But reproduction is obviously not limited, at least in principle, to a brief sequence of moments in some repeatable genealogy. The theory of evolution has already provided us with a variety of narratives not just for some single family or even species but of every living kind through all the time that could ever have been required. So "controversial" stories appear from year to year of genetic studies that might identify, say, a possible mitochondrial ancestress for all current human beings, or perhaps the eocyte, or sulfur-consuming bacterium, which could account for all the other forms of life as well.[24] Such modern enterprises would share at least a motive with the corresponding ancient myths, which also sought to reimagine the contemporary many as the product of an aboriginal one, and so understand all actual bodies as reproductions of some singular prototype. Success in either genre would make us siblings after the flesh too in proportion.

We gaze back through indefinite sequences toward an ideal original; we look forward no more than one generation at best. The past is mysteriously long, the future dangerously short. So "this generation" not unreasonably understood their situation in New Testament times, only to find themselves mistaken, at least according to the flesh, which has gone on about its self-repeating business, as if without noticing. But it might be argued they were right still according to the Spirit, in which case a completion of time and the coalescence of all bodies in the body indeed would always be just that far off still.

Meanwhile our own mortality is a constant hint to the same apocalyptic effect. No wonder the sight of my own body in the mirror reminds me of how my father looked in what turned out to be his final years. There are photographs still of him working in the garden, dressed in baggy shorts and a straw hat, cigarette holder clenched between his teeth. In both images the same spare stringiness and slump of shoulders appears, though modified in shape and proportion, for I am my mother's son too. At the moment of such impressions, one's parents are apt to have been dead a while, so that we may see in the likeness an identity of fate. Meanwhile the same configurations are repeated in our children, with an equivalent set of differences: a certain weight of mouth, a lifted nose, the slope of a shoulder, perhaps a quick temper. This generational rhythm would amount to immortality on the scale of the genes, indefinite if not infinite. What I persist in imagining as the first person singular only represents this reproducibility for the time being. I am a verse in a poem I have not written the whole of, composed in a meter I did not

---

[24]The discovery of a possible genetic original for our variety of hominid, first advanced in an article entitled "Mitochondrial DNA and Human Evolution" by Rebecca Cann, Mark Stoneking, and Allan Wilson in *Nature* 325 (1 January 1987): 31-36, was announced to a wider audience in "The Search for Adam and Eve," *Newsweek* 111 (11 January 1988): 46-52. It has since been both reaffirmed [*Science* 253 (27 September 1991): 1503-1507] and undermined [*Science* 255 (7 February 1992): 686-87]. The bacterial possibility was announced in the *New York Times* of 14 January 1988, A:24, the source for which was a letter in *Nature* of the same date by James Lake (331:185-86), commented on in the same issue by David Penny (111-12). It too has been challenged (*New York Times* of 18 August 1988, A:10; *Nature* 334:609-11 and 564. Hypotheses must also struggle for existence. The controversies are reviewed in a popular style by Michael Brown in *The Search for Eve* (New York: Harper, 1990).

choose. But the pulse can still be felt, even if the blood does not belong to me.

The truth of the merely individual body would then be death, as time eventually reveals. Sooner or later that conclusion resolves all ambiguities, whether deliberately or in the natural course of things. The difficulty is to make this plainest fact of life accessible to the first person singular in something better than imagination. On the wall of the sheriff's office was a bulletin with mug shots of a young woman found dead by the side of the road almost a year before. The poster asked, reasonably enough, "Who is this girl?" Some particulars were added: 5'5", 120 pounds, lightly frosted brown hair, between fifteen and nineteen years old. She was wearing corduroy pants, a shirt, a windbreaker (information was sought respecting the brand of this). She had two rotten molars, had never received dental care, and never smoked tobacco or marijuana. The two photographs, a front and side view, showed a luminously beautiful Appalachian face, eyes serenely closed, neck propped on a rolled towel. The date assigned implied that no one had yet found an answer to the opening question. So there was no story to account for this body, though the imagination was teased to produce one. But that kind of reproduction had not yet begun, though the material for it lay concealed, perhaps, in the memory of some guilty soul. Meanwhile these facts remained, a reminder, here and there across the state, of what could so far be known for sure.

When the imagination has indeed become active over a case of this kind, the result is apt to seem merely melodramatic, however obscurely satisfying. It was a good cop movie, if nothing more, and could serve to remind me, if I did not already know, that (in popular tradition at least) "the body" means what is left behind after someone has been murdered. The rest of the story explained how this result could have come about, as if it were exceptional. In the fictional version the physicality of the entity in question has to be emphatically insisted upon, though our response is mixed with an awareness that the details must have been faked to seem so real: the blood on the bed and in the bathtub, the dusty disconnected halves in the vacant lot, the roughly sewn-together mannequin on the autopsy table. And as usual it is a woman's naked body. What else would seem worth the trouble? Murder and sex together recognize this mode of the natural body for what it is really worth, the myth affirms. So the cop, the priest, the whore, and the doctor become by a familiar tradition the guardians of our mystery, at once disenchanted and protective, at home with what there is at last to find out.

Suppose instead one went in the other direction, away from the popular arts and all the way through any merely repeatable facts or images to the thing itself? A while ago our local paper carried a story about a high school teacher in California who had arranged to bring a real body into his anatomy and physiology class. "He puts a group of juniors and seniors through about six weeks of lectures, reading, and lab work before he introduces the cadaver," the story explained. And he made sure to cover the face first, exposing it only later. One of his students is reported as saying that when he could see there was no life in the eyes, he ceased to be afraid, which sounds right: this body thereby became like a frog or cat—though holding the brain, it was admitted, did bring on a certain giddiness. The teacher had some difficulty obtaining a specimen for a high school class but eventually succeeded after persuading the curator of the local medical school that he too was a "professional." His principal was all for the idea: "achievement levels," he observed, were higher than ever.[25]

Obviously there had to be a good deal of framing here to control a reaction that might otherwise—what? Destroy the experiment? Release the true power of death from its hidden confines into the hearts and minds of these kids? The protective wrapping would include not just six weeks of lecture and a cloth over the face but the procedure employed to dissect the corpse, so that "dealing with" this would become indeed virtually the same as cutting up a laboratory specimen. Thus it might be reduced in the familiar style to one more accumulation of material facts that could find their meaning within a system of ideas. The body as such would disappear. Pseudoscience then corresponds to melodrama, with the additional self-protective wrinkle that the fiction involved includes a denial of its own presence.

Caught up in such imaginings, declared or concealed, we evade the truth of the matter—until some accident, as we call it, exposes at least the possibility once again. As I turn the corner I see on the far side of the road a body lying under a blanket with people clustered about and traffic backed up behind. A police car has just arrived, and the officer is walking up to the scene, arms akimbo. That is his fiction. An emergency van is parked across the road. It may have provided the blanket, which has an institutional look. A child's bicycle lies crumpled at the side of the road. As I glance at the hidden figure, I think I see a foot move, in which case the victim is still alive. I wonder if the car responsible is one of those parked nearby. It is a shock to come upon these occasions, even if a quick estimate makes it clear that all is being done that could be, so one passes on, part of the apparently heartless flow of traffic. Whoever sees, though, feels. Accidents reveal death: that is their function. The common fictions unsuspend themselves abruptly to expose what had been concealed all this while. And what is revealed is not an exception but the rule, which what we thought was the rule has kept us from taking in.

But here, as in the other instances I find myself assembling, the death in question still belongs to another and so remains imaginary yet as far as I am concerned. "The real thing is carefully hidden," observes Michael Lesy, introducing *The Forbidden Zone*, a report on his experiences as he followed some "death professionals" on their rounds. These policemen and pathologists, though, like their reporter (not to mention the reader), are necessarily at a vicarious distance still from the fact they must somehow deal with. Nor have I yet had occasion to touch the dead body of anyone I love, as the thanatologists now recommend for survivors.[26]

---

[25]*Ithaca Journal*, 4 February 1983.
[26]Michael Lesy, *The Forbidden Zone* (New York: Farrar, Straus, and Giroux, 1987). The thanatologist I have in mind is Lisa Carlson, whose *Caring for Your Own Dead* (Hinesburg

But the fulfillment of even this most intimate of parables would have to be my own proper fate, which I must suffer in the first and not the third or second person. Death is my boundary in time. So it would be the temporal equivalent of objectivity—the line drawn, but not yet. How then should I "know" it? Science is so much consciousness as corresponds to the object in space. What would be the corresponding subject for time? We have learned to call the action of that agent *appropriation,* following various authorities. Adulthood might accordingly be defined as an appropriation of the body not only in its need to maintain or its power to reproduce itself but in its susceptibility to death. The self is most fully itself, we claim, when it has "come to terms with" the implications of its own centricity. Of these sacrifice is presumably ultimate: one appropriates one's own death for the sake of some future body, individual or communal. But all possibilities of the kind remain mysterious, and so more easily revealed by example than formulated as a proposition. And an example is still a fiction as far as I am concerned, even when it is my own to myself. The other morning, for instance, I remember at last to carry away with me a fragment of tooth that had broken off some time before and had for an uncertain number of days been waiting on top of the radio, where I set things that need to be taken up to school. On my way I drop it from the bridge into the rapid waters of the wintry creek. That seems how I should dispose of at least this much of my own body. I have imagined that my heirs should do the like for the ashes remaining from the consumption of the rest of me when the time comes, depositing these, perhaps, in the little lake into which this creek flows. But for this piece I can do the job myself.

That same morning, by another coincidence, I also threw out, though not into the rigorous chaos of any descending water, an old bundle of typescript left over from a book published some years ago. This had remained in the back of a file drawer, using up space I needed for other records—which my heirs, to be sure, will want to throw out too. The book itself, I decided, would have to stand as best it could as the monument of another time. I could no longer make use of whatever had then been left behind.

On the path by the canoe shed a dead woodchuck showed up one day. No one had seen fit to shift the remains into the nearby lake, which annoyed me; you would suppose the Outdoor Club people could have done at least that much. But this was between summer school and the fall term, and nobody was around. When I came back the other way, the body had been moved to the side of the path. A stink was perceptible, and flies clustered. In another two days though I was surprised. We had some rain in the interval, which might account for what I now saw: a slump of fur spread out, the head almost unrecognizable, and over all a seethe of white maggots, the slender rods quivering like huge bacteria. Among them a few beetles crawled. I was pleased: this was how a body should return to the cosmos, as food for other

---

VT: Upper Access, 1987) emphasizes the desirability of the practice mentioned.

creatures. I sniffed, experimentally; the odor was no longer strong. Two days later still the black substance had disappeared, and the bones, an unexpectedly slender skull and a tan spine with a rib and a leg bone or two, showed through. The rest was no more than a vague ellipse of fur, which had already begun to blend into the surrounding leaves and twigs. It need not take long, I thought. That was reassuring.

Any sequence of examples should precipitate as at least a modest generalization. Death is the whole experienced, one might then propose, *in the negative.* If so, what would be the corresponding positive? To begin with, presumably, another life—of a different species, if the reproductive action takes place in the form we call nutrition, as with those maggots and their beetle friends, or of the same kind, if there is time. Among human beings an analogous metamorphosis will also have begun to generate stories, fanciful, perhaps, if only anticipatory, but more deeply imaginative in proportion as they are able to reembody the whole of what must in that case have had time enough to die. So I compose my report upon the woodchuck, to that extent in coincidence with what was so easily accomplished by the busy creatures on which I could look down. And so others have done more thoroughly in their time, and will again.

A sufficiently visceral instance of narrative conversion in one of the historical books of the Bible has struck many readers. A Levite from the hill country of Ephraim, Judges 19 begins, once took a woman of Bethlehem for a concubine. But she ran away from him back to her father's house. The phrase used puts the blame on her: she "played the harlot upon him." No infidelity is mentioned, but perhaps running away counts as harlotry enough. In any case, her master goes after her, "to speak to her heart, to make her come back," and apparently succeeds. Still she says nothing; instead we are told of her father's excessive hospitality, who presses the Levite to stay longer than he had intended. Eventually the pair leave and take refuge for the night in a Benjaminite town, avoiding still-pagan Jerusalem. At first the travelers must camp out in the village square, but an old man coming home from the fields takes pity on the couple and invites them to his house. That night a gang of "sons of Belial" assault the house, demanding that the stranger should be turned out to them, that "we may know him." The old man refuses, and offers his own daughter and his guest's concubine instead. The hoodlums still protest, but the Levite thrusts his woman out, and they are content to savage her for the rest of the night.

In the morning she comes back and falls at the entrance of the house. Her master opens the door to go on his way and finds her there with "her hands upon the threshold." Up, he says; let us be going. She does not reply. So he loads the dead body on his ass, carries it to his home in the hill country, and there cuts it up "according to her bones" into twelve pieces and sends one to each of the twelve tribes of Israel that they may learn what has happened and take action to punish the sin that has been incurred.

Through all this the woman has remained noticeably silent. Perhaps, if she has indeed played the harlot, she has sinned too, by the standards assumed. In any case she is most severely sinned against: by her father, by the old man of Gibeon, by the gang of rapists, and, most painfully, by her master. All this becomes entirely accessible to the reader, though apparently ignored by the narrative voice. The tale is told from the perspective of the "Deuteronomistic" compiler, for whom such a tradition seems merely to have illustrated a breach of hospitality of a sort that needed to be punished by the assembled militia. In this way the episode could be subsumed within a moral version of the covenant in the usual style of this historiography. The insensitivity of the narrator to the imaginative burden of the tale told thus becomes an accompanying atrocity of another kind.

The Levite's gesture at the close of the episode, though, recapitulates what has apparently been repressed through earlier stages of the narrative. The cutting up and dispatch of the woman's body does indeed serve to express everything she has not said for herself. The deed communicates more than is called for within the situation presumed, more than the narrative point of view would consciously tolerate. Such an action is archaic, cultic, and horrific in a virtually pagan style very remote from the ordinary dispositions of the Deuteronomic school, whose allegiances are firmly scribal, and so whether legal or literary rather "modern" than primitive. So it evokes, as any summoning of the body is bound to do, the alternative or priestly tradition within Israel—but here in an uncontrolled, aboriginal, utterly unclerical style.

The body of the woman, then, who should not have died at all but so miserably did, is not decently buried but cut to pieces, as if in a sacrifice or for some horrific consumption, and sent out (how? by whom?) as a multiplied word composed of just this much unclean flesh. Her corpse in its very disintegration thereby demonstrates the incoherence of the nation to which she is addressed, that combination of tribes which as a putative whole has been dishonored by the vicious deeds done upon her as a helpless individual—including, it may well be felt, the sins this nation would not consciously have recognized. The covenantal militia, a molecular assemblage of males, cannot restore her, or for that matter, themselves to life. (In this narrative it will take the establishment of David's kingdom to accomplish as much, which must wait upon the will of God.) But the sons of Israel can at least expunge the sin from among them by punishing so many of the guilty as they can lay hold of. Violence annuls violence to just that extent. For this purpose they gather "as one man" (Judges 20:1, 8, 11). The singularity of the original body is thus briefly reproduced in the transient unity of the host assembled. Many thousands die in the battles that follow. Benjamin is indeed punished by the other tribes. But then a new problem arises: the remnant of Benjamin will die out unless they can obtain wives, which the other tribes have sworn not to give them. So they are encouraged to steal women from an Israelite city that had not come to the muster, and from Shiloh. These secondary stories are in effect appendixes that repeat the initial state of affairs: a woman taken, more or less illegitimately, only this time on a tribal scale. On this dark note the narrative as a whole ends, and with it the book of Judges.[27]

---

[27]The story of the concubine has been examined in close verbal detail by Phyllis Trible

The best coda to the tale though does not appear until the eleventh chapter of the first book of Samuel, or two books farther on in the Deuteronomistic sequence. In that chapter Saul cuts up a pair of oxen and sends a piece to each of the tribes to call out the levies once more, this time against a non-Israelite king who threatens to cut out the right eyes of those who surrender to him. This time too the action may be subsumed within the covenantal ethic. The slaughter of the animals is in part sacrificial, as a prayer to evoke the response of the men at arms that follows, and in part proleptically punitive: it shall be for you as with these oxen if you do not come out. The liturgy is thus a repetition of the ceremony traditionally employed at the "cutting" of a covenant, when an animal is sliced in half lengthwise as a warning to the subordinate partner not to betray his new oath.[28] The dispersal of the oxen is to that extent a memorial of the original creature that had once served to establish the relation appealed to. The appeal works, as before: the militia are mobilized as one man, and Saul is successful in battle. He "saves" Israel by eliminating the enemy, as a prince is supposed to do.

By way of this link to the protocol of a covenant sacrifice one might return to the more impressive story in Judges with that much clearer a notion of what is going on. The Levite has in effect converted the victim of a crime into a reproduction of the founding sacrifice. The flesh of this creature, no longer merely animal and representative but immediate and human, becomes at once a warning and a call. And the result does indeed re-create the ruined body, however briefly, on the scale of the community. The nation evoked, though, functions not as an eschatological positive but only as a temporary negative or counterforce. Even the "prince," when in the second instance a version of him does appear, is defined in negative terms: to "save" Israel is not to bring about this communal body once and for all but to destroy such enemies as threaten the people at the moment. A movement from an individual through the symbolic all the way to the communal can be traced, then, but each phase of this ideal trajectory is still marked by a continuing absence: an oppressed victim; a dead, mutilated, and decaying corpse; a threat, and presently the accomplishment, of a violent project; the unavoidable deaths of many others; even, at the end of the story, a repetition of the initial crime. So we cannot yet read of an ultimate version of the possible action. But the narratives do throw light on what would be entailed in a complete version of such a project. And they help to link the fate of the individual body, which is always death in any case, with the chances for first a symbolic and then a communal reproduction of this. The stories offer us

---

in *Texts of Terror* (Philadelphia: Fortress, 1984) 65-91. For Trible it remains principally an instance of misogyny, ancient or modern; the symbolic and communal resonances of the event are not followed out. These are more nearly approached by Mieke Bal in *Death and Dissymmetry: The Politics of Coherence in Judges* (Chicago: University of Chicago Press, 1988).

[28]The connection is specified in the Anchor Bible commentary by P. K. McCarter, *1 Samuel*, AB 8 (Garden City NY: Doubleday, 1980) 203n.

somewhere to go beyond the reproductions of the flesh, nutritive or sexual. We are already moving in the direction of the End, even if we have not yet escaped the stress of the beginnings.

A second story of more recent date would return us to the abortion motif. Two columnists for the *National Catholic Reporter* were reporting on a conference held between representatives of the pro-choice and pro-life movements, presumably in an attempt to mollify the antagonism between these parties.[29] The issue that divided them was of course already a matter of concern to readers of this "progressive" journal, who, though Catholic themselves, might be expected to feel some degree of ambivalence with respect to the matter. So far the alternative responses involved could seem evenly matched.

But on this occasion the verbal and social predictabilities evoked by the safely middle-class term *conference* were unexpectedly interrupted by a group from elsewhere who forced their way onto the stage to condemn the meeting as a whole and unwrap, as a type of everything that was not being admitted, the body of an aborted fetus—a black female, evidently chosen, as one of the reporters disgustedly observed, for the political significance of its color and sex. The stern-faced figure holding this anomaly in a towel in the accompanying photograph was also female, though white and adult. The child, if that is what it should be called, was, the reader is informed, some four days dead at the time. The same writer, Jo McCowan, went on to protest the "deceit" and "violence" implicit in such behavior. How *had* this body been obtained? Was it not an insult to the dignity of death to exploit human remains in so crude and fanatical a way? The other columnist, Mary Bader Papa, was milder but equally convinced that the gesture was illegitimate. Her title was "The New Brownshirts."

The dead fetus evidently played a role in this context corresponding to the cutup body of the concubine in the story from Judges. And here too editorial framing was at once breached and confirmed. The columnists were as shocked as (presumably) most of the participants in the conference because an ostensive presentation of what they were preparing to argue about broke an accepted rule of such gatherings that all conflict should remain purely verbal—and so by definition impractical. The presumed hegemony of discourse was itself subverted by so gross a demonstration. The corpse displayed was *too* real, and at the same time all too superfluously symbolic too, as female, as black, as a product of the very process in question. *This,* the gesture implied, is what your sort of talk cannot either prevent or interpret. The exhibition of the body accordingly "closed" discussion, as we can well believe. The two columns deploring the result would then represent a recovery of language in exactly the sense that had been challenged. Yes, it was awful; but

---

[29]The conference was reported in the *National Catholic Reporter* 15 (23 February 1979) and commented on in the issue of March 23. McGowan mentions one fetus; the news story, if I have located the correct reference, refers to two.

here we are writing about it in the same style originally intended by the meeting—serious, concerned, responsible, and so forth. What we are objecting to did not conquer after all. It only interrupted for a short while. And my own irony at the expense of this recuperation should itself be qualified by an equivalent admission that I too am still writing about their writing, and so in the end a member of the literate consensus after all. The scribes always seek the last if not quite the final word.

In this context, as in the Book of Judges, the eucharistic overtones of the episode would not be hard to recover, even for a liberal. The gesture reprobated would in fact correspond to a display of the sacrament in a monstrance—itself, to be sure, a "traditionalist" practice these columnists and their expected readers might be inclined to deplore. So covenant is once again evoked in a new version. As with the Old Testament instance, what took place is still firmly in the negative throughout: a dead body, a practice deplored, a program interrupted. But the positive, in this context at least, is not far to seek. The body not of a dead but of a living child, whether in the womb still or outside it in our world, would become religiously significant as an equivalent for what is made ritually accessible in the eucharistic elements. A freshly conceived infant could only seem absolutely inviolable, after all, as an eschatological manifestation. "Natural law" will not quite reach that far. Therefore the corpse exhibited would *not* constitute a sacrament. It would instead be, to continue the parallel, what might be left over after a deliberate desecration of the consecrated elements. And in this respect too it might rhyme with the dismembered body of the Levite's concubine, which so forcibly alludes to a social union that does *not* obtain. To expose either corpse would then symbolize a state of affairs inexpressible within the prevailing discourse, argumentative or narrative. And the publication of a photograph along with the corresponding commentary would be a modern equivalent for the archaic dismemberment and dispersal. No wonder so many of those involved were shocked in the modern instance, and presumably in the ancient as well, though that reaction is only implicit in the fact that the story was passed on in the first place. Rationality of whatever kind can realize the body only from a certain distance, as we have seen. And distance is to that extent denial. But denial of any truth cannot remain perfect forever. The repressed will return, in one mode or another. For the body continues to reproduce itself, regardless. So we are sure to find ourselves once again in its presence, after one mode or another, sooner or later, dead or alive—and perhaps for good and all.

Chapter 3

Erotic

It all goes back, of course, to Adam and Eve—a story which shows, among other things, that if you make a woman out of a man, you are bound to get into trouble.
—Carol Gilligan, *In a Different Voice*

Central

Before going on to address the several modes of symbolic reproduction for their own sakes, it might seem appropriate to take a little more notice of the natural body's propensity to reproduce itself in the simpler sense of that word, especially among human beings, if only in parentheses. Sexuality would come before art, one might suppose, in any decent order of the possible metamorphoses. Besides, the different modes of our erotic experience already show versions of those varieties of likeness and contrast, nearness and remoteness, presence and absence that we have begun to associate with what at the level of language can safely be called metaphor. In the context of sexual reproduction though these polarities remain implicit in the mute encounters of the flesh instead of being recovered after the fact as a composition in words. So such elements of the erotic life can seem by comparison curiously innocent as well as primitive: silent, for all the accompanying talk, and however baroque, never quite just conventional.

There are advantages to the topic then that would justify lingering upon it, even apart from the inevitable attraction of an engagement so fatal for us all. What one wants in the first and perhaps the last place is not to argue a case but simply to notice the forms that already cohere to represent bodiliness in one way or another. We had better be modest in intention, if not quite in example. For what can in fact be realized cannot help but come out closer to ancient wisdom than any modern science. Is not "classical" Freudianism, indeed, almost a historical romance, offering as it does to explain how the erotic might be understood to evolve from the individual body? The result can seem closer to myth than knowledge. But the language for interpreting these interpretations is obviously still in dispute.

As I walk down the hall, I notice a student sitting on the sill of the big open window at the further end. She has turned to look out, and the curves of breast and buttock are prominent against the sunlight beyond. I feel a nostalgic pang, combining what by now is almost the memory of desire with a more lasting sense of awe. There she indeed is—and quite unconscious too, or so at least I suppose, of the gaze she may well be provoking in others besides myself. In these incomplete but interconnected curves I seem to catch intimations of a perfect whole somewhere beyond this scene, as if outside that window where I cannot see, though present still in just these elements of it. A traditional moment indeed, for which my interrupted glance could stand as a model for the relevant apprehension. Others may do better, but this is enough for me. I see these outlines, and fit them together not just as an image for but as a recollection of experience. And if I go on to think as well, it must be of the body. For what else is there either to desire or think about?

The female is the type of such initial images of the erotic body, we are all disposed to agree, men and women alike, including those who have protested the condition exemplified. For would not, the objection goes, such moments sufficiently illustrate the "specular" distance between a male subject and the corresponding female object, and so a domination of the unconscious by consciousness? In which case desire would, like the thought it introduces, have to be ranked among the species of oppression, and so implicitly as a denial of what is ostensibly admired. Yet in fact, one might respond, these occasions do not feel either so angelically cognitive or hegemonically masculinist as such a protest would declare. They seem rather introductory to a dialectical exchange, the commencement of an intercourse that would find its purpose in the developing disclosure of what can be no more than promised in such beginnings. And what is promised is never just "physical" but implicitly personal, however vaguely. We respond to surfaces of which the corresponding depths may yet become profound. But this is usually not obvious to start with.[1]

We all know in any case, whether as consenting or objecting, that the erotic body glimpsed at these casual moments is still comparatively *un*real—imaginary, however attractive. That need not mean it could not also ring true. A good deal may still be inherent even in such beginnings. It does not seem accidental either that it should be a curve that imports, whether of shape or movement. And this would hold, one also gathers, as much for the female as for the male, and not only reflexively, as when she learns to appreciate what thus becomes a reproduction of herself with an inspecting gaze borrowed from or anticipating the look of desire, but also more directly when, in our culture privately, she admires in the male the carnal analogue of what he finds in her. The notorious phallus, after all, and therefore that insinuating style that amounts to the aura or promise of this, is as constantly if less visibly interpretable as curvilinear too. Both modes of apprehension might still seem too "phallic" and so exclusive of a more intimate if ambiguous experience for a woman. But this too, however undifferentiated, "near," "fluid," a matter of touch

---

[1] That even the opening phases of the erotic life should count as personal is a special thesis of Roger Scruton's *Sexual Desire: A Moral Philosophy of the Erotic* (New York: Free Press, 1986). Such a conception of what might be called the teleology of desire would be confirmed from an unexpectedly chatty psychoanalytic perspective by Robert Stoller's *Observing the Erotic Imagination* (New Haven: Yale University Press, 1985).

rather than sight, would still be of the erotic body indeed, and in a version a member of the other sex can still recognize, as it were, from one more repetition of the inevitable distance.[2]

Would not in fact a chief contrast between the sexes with respect to the problem of desire and the desirable lie precisely in the degree of difference each experiences? It would appear that the female's experience of herself as also a version of the erotic body overlaps more completely and so more ambiguously with herself as an individual, so that the one can seem merely a duplication of the other. In males the individual body is comparatively asexual: the erotic body occurs as a specialized representation of this, a distinct signifier indeed, and so more readily separated in thought, time, and context. But such differences with respect to difference would still be distinctions within a developing exchange. Any more purely female experience of the erotic concealed behind an overexplicit "femininity" would therefore be inside of rather than outside this ongoing reciprocity. It need not be merely unconscious or repressed, but one more aspect of an unfolding whole along with the all too self-evident. If so, the ostentatious as well need not be understood only as an affront even at its most comic or vulgar. Our responsiveness to intimations of an ideal sphere is also engaged, after all, by the traditional shape of what is called by convention a heart, which reduces this from three to two dimensions and then from a radial to a bilateral shape. So it could serve to evoke either a pair of buttocks reversed or a swollen glans, and both more obviously than any pump. This is my valentine, we say: a gift of love, back and forth.

Reciprocity has always to be counted in, then, as well as metaphoricity, if only to complete the curve, which would otherwise remain broken, however undeniable. The erotic body promised by the female or initiated by the male has therefore to be formed if not finally at least fully by the couple, who in some flesh or other, physical or psychic or social, proceed to compose what may be enacted in this kind. That the resulting configuration may already be understood as a sufficient instance of the body indeed is the surprising claim of the New Testament texts on the subject. "And the two of them shall be as one flesh," says Jesus in Mark 10:8, quoting Genesis 2:24; "for they are no longer two," a repetition typical of that author continues, "but one flesh." The application follows: "What God has yoked together, man may not divide." "Flesh" *means* "body" here, clearly: whatever may

---

[2]The allusions are to language used in Luce Irigaray's *That Sex Which Is Not One* (Ithaca: Cornell University Press, 1985), which remains to my mind the most stimulating manifestation of contemporary French feminist thinking. Her arguments have predictably received criticism from within the movement as "essentialist," that is, too traditional. This polemic is reviewed and renewed in A. R. Jones, "Writing the Body: Towards an Understanding of L'ecriture feminine," *Feminist Studies* 7 (Summer 1981): 247-63; and more recently in S. R. Suleiman, "(Re)writing the Body," *Poetics Today* 6 (1985): 43-64; Toril Moi, *Sexual/Textual Politics: Feminist Literary Theory* (London: Methuen, 1985); and Diana Fuss, *Essentially Speaking: Feminism, Nature and Difference* (New York: Routledge, 1989).

be shared between and so revealed in the conjunction of man and woman in an unqualified marriage. This version of the ideal sphere though only God can bring about, it is said, by the same power with which he created the world in the first place. The composition formed by two complementary creatures in an absolute marriage would then rank as an equivalent to the same body on the scale of the cosmos as a whole—and so in due course, as the Markan narrative proceeds, to still another version at the Last Supper.

The gracious possibility that surfaces in Mark's pericope on the topic of marriage within the new covenant is also evoked by the argument of 1 Corinthians 7:10, where what seems in fact to have been passed on as a "word of the Lord" on the indissolubility of marriage is also repeated. This determination of the erotic body as at least in principle an eschatological possibility is alluded to again at 7:39, and in a negative form directs Paul's protest against the idea of uniting the members of a Christian with a prostitute in 6:15-16. It provides the core of his teaching on other contingencies of the sexual life in chapters 5 through 7 of the same letter, and is reflected at a greater distance in the otherwise embarrassing instructions on gender obligations in 11:1-16 and 14:34-40. This already-complex elaboration of Jesus' original word is itself repeated in Ephesians 5:22-33. The early tradition found various ways of spelling out the implications of a simple but sufficiently startling proposition: that the conjunction of a man and a woman should count not simply as a carnal accident or even as a social contract but as what a later mode of the new tradition would come to call a sacrament; which is to say, one more embodiment of the body indeed.[3]

In this, as in the eucharistic context, the New Testament texts employ the terms *flesh* and *body* somewhat carelessly, using *sarx* where *soma* might seem more appropriate and vice versa. But we can distinguish meanings more exactly here too, reserving *body* for the whole and *flesh* for whatever it may be composed of. In that case the flesh of the eschatological body in the sexual context would include not just the obvious complementarity of the generative parts, though these together enact the core of the rite that would correspond in this context to the celebration of the Eucharist on the scale of the community, or even the individual bodies of the partners as the rest of these might also take part, but whatever else the couple would find itself sharing in common, from the bed on which they lay to the family they generate to a history in time—not forgetting matters of the heart as well.

It is impressive how the issue here is not, as it must be elsewhere, the relation of the individual to Jesus or of Jesus to the community. It is determined entirely by the relation of each partner to the other—and so implicitly to God. Their mutual fidelity, assumed or asserted, would then become a specification of faith for just this

---

[3] We might accordingly read Andrea Dworkin's notorious protest against *Intercourse* (New York: Free Press, 1987) as the obverse of this eschatological opportunity. The violence of unbelief, as usual, mirrors what there is to believe in.

context. And that virtue would therefore have to be realized not only typically or crudely as an avoidance of adultery but in a mutual trust or consent to the moral and emotional possibilities of the common life. The corresponding negatives, an application of this version of the gospel might suggest, would also expose the same possibility—especially, perhaps, within the immediacies of the erotic as such. That which is *not* sharable in common but only desired, say, by one partner and (perhaps silently) refused by the other would remain unreal for both, whether as wish or threat, for what is yearned for and feared is still only imaginary for the individual. Couples notoriously find themselves divided as much by what they have not shared as united by what they have. In such cases each is inclined to blame the other, as the individual is apt to do, meanwhile entertaining one more version of the perennial If Only.

To form a new body, even for a moment, even in the flesh alone, it is necessary to breach the boundaries of those bodies that already exist, physical or psychic. We have noticed how the surface that most obviously bounds the individual is concentrated at those very openings which contradict it, through which an intercourse between itself and the rest of the world—which is to say, other bodies—becomes possible. No wonder these *stomata* are so acutely implicated in every version of the erotic life. We share our mucous membranes: that is, our half-skins, by so many doublings of inclosure and extrusion. This is a risk, and not only of health or pregnancy: that which defines us must dissolve, so that we might briefly and so at least representatively unite. And other differences too notoriously elide: pleasure and pain, sensation and emotion, intensification of life and anticipation of death. Union is therefore simultaneous with disintegration. It is perhaps not quite irrelevant that our urge to come together at such a cost should match in reverse the corresponding mode of reproduction among forms of life at the other end of the scale. Their mitoses would mirror our conjunctions. At that level one is two; at ours, two is one—in either instance, we might say, world without end.

Peripheral

If the dual body intimated in this or that moment of attraction may in fact be brought into something like full existence through the faithful intercourse, physical and psychic, of two equal and opposite partners, this potentially eschatological, if by now almost too traditional, possibility would also provide a norm in terms of which to situate what would then seem the various incomplete modes of the erotic life. One's examples here are sure to be accidental. My first is at once minor and vulgar. It has been a quaint custom for some years, I had occasion to learn, that pornographic magazines should focus on the exposed parts of the women photographed. The models are placed so as to make the most of this unusual view, as if it amounted to a revelation of everything that had ever been forbidden and must therefore be most desirable. The display could seem odd to an observer unfamiliar with the convention, for what is so appealing, on the face of it, about such a sight?[4] It might only make some kind of erotic sense, one could suppose, as a third in some imagined sequence from the clothed to the naked to the exposed figure. But in that case the real missing element would be the phallus, which should ideally fill this opening; or better still, perhaps, an image of the couple in action. But these are both as yet forbidden for publication. So a documentation of what Kingsley Amis once derisively called the inside of a giraffe's ear is provided instead. Nothing must stand in the place of something: the ugly and repellent for the promise if not the fullness of gratification. The very subgenre of romance that is most explicitly at the service of desire would thus subvert the very impulse it seeks to honor. The promise of the whole is travestied by exhibiting an abyss in the midst of it all, as if to invalidate in advance what is at the same time supposed to be as tempting as possible.

Other more familiar features of this literary kind suggest the same tendency to self-contradiction. Parts of the body, for instance, are often treated as if they were the whole, which as we have seen is inevitable to begin with, but with an exaggerated emphasis, as if to assert that they are in fact the whole already, with nothing more to be hoped for or feared—which even the most obsessed devotee must know is not really true. In a similar way the excessive deployment of language or decor so typical of pornography would seem to exhibit an underlying terror of whatever has to be either pre- or postverbal about the erotic life generally. An extreme cultivation of male dominance might testify as well to a dread of the natural power of the female in this realm. And the cult of perversion, like the hegemony of pain over pleasure, or difficulty over ease, or transgression over consent, would similarly overweight a sign with the value of the meaning it thereby contradicts and replaces. Pornography, which overspecifies everything, ends by omitting its own proper subject matter.

An emphatic absence would represent one reversal of value, of which a mocking concealment would be the satiric complement. On the inner wall of the pantry area of a campus coffee house the female staff used to put up centerfolds from *Playgirl* on the wall. These showed naked young men with brown California skins. In the photographs the genitalia are exposed: that is conventional for a centerfold in the female as well as the male version. But the workers in this place seriocomically added fig leafs of kitchen foil which simultaneously concealed and announced what lay beneath. One could think immediately that the several penises and testicles beclouded with ordinary hair would not in any case be what anyone of the gender addressed might wish or fear to see. The relaxed condition had to stand in for the still-forbidden erection. And one could go on to suppose that even if at some future time it might become legal to display what has so far to be only

---

[4] I learn from Linda Williams's *Hard Core* (Berkeley: University of California Press, 1989) that this "shot" should be called a "split beaver"—an accumulation of metaphors with their own burden of meaning.

hinted at, this too might not quite seem all that was wanted, for even the best image of the body as this might ever be desired could not become an experience of the event, which no photograph could show. And what would this be? The perfect orgasm? There at least this artificially lengthened chain of signifiers would appear to conclude for the time being. But even then one would not have reached a true signified, if only because orgasm is notoriously not a moment of possession but abandonment.

The little scraps of foil mocked the predicament they confirmed. Within the erotic life we are too often caught at successive points on the circumference of a center that continues to evade us, fascinated by figures that both promise and refuse their own fulfillment. "I want to suck big fat ones," reads an inscription in a toilet stall. A heterosexual censor has overwritten these letters, themselves big and fat, to read "fuck" instead of "suck." But the ontology affirmed as matter for a semipublic declaration of faith is the same in either case. Desire is indeed for substantiality or fullness of being, which either a part of the male or the whole of the female can stand in for. So the moment of completion is still anticipated—or its absence remembered. But apocalyptic fantasy is more prominent in this context than the wisdom of disappointment, for the latter turns back into the former almost as soon as it has been realized. Illusion, we know, is notoriously preferred to even partial knowledge in these matters.

Such comic or pathetic overvaluations of the stage just one step on from wherever desire first finds us would seem to invite a name ordinarily reserved for a subspecies of the general predicament. To treat the sign as if it already were what it means is fetishism; yet what else could one be caught up in, when some metaphoric sequence fails to conclude in fulfillment? To fasten upon any moment along the way as more than enough as it is would then become as absurd and reasonable a response to the intimations of an indefinite promise as any. So the repeated cultivations of desire in the absence of the desirable, as in masculine lust, or of desirableness in the absence of desire, as in feminine narcissism, could seem modest acknowledgments of the inevitable compared to the laborious pursuit of the perverse or the illicit (the usual male and female dispositions respectively) in the expectation that somewhere on the far side of transgression the perfect experience would reappear, complete at last.

To "interpret" a fetish would then mean to untie the immediate symbolic knot, releasing its original power of reference—which would not solve the erotic problem, but might at least gratify the intellect. To that extent insight could seize a secondary triumph out of the defeats of desire. The other year I heard a lecture by a fashionable critic taking off from Freud's well-known article on the topic of fetishism. As one might expect, the talk was frivolous and decadent enough to stand as a literary repetition of the condition in question. The distinguished visitor felt it at once his duty and his privilege to decorate and reambiguate the master's thesis—the core of which he passed around in a copy of a translation—in the approved style of the newer criticism. It was revealing that in the midst of these arabesques he did not challenge Freud's primary point, that a fetish must represent not just the phallus but that very mythological entity, the phallus as mounted by the mother. Real thought, it could seem to at least one member of his audience, might require objecting that though Freud was no doubt right as far as he went, he would also, on his own terms, have to be found incomplete as well. For in the process of explaining a fetish as a substitute, he was himself forced to "fetishize" its supposed original. This might in turn have to be re-understood in terms of the very argument he had set going as standing in for something a degree more obscure, which either could or could not exist somewhere as a *telos* for desire. The coincidence in Freud's account of a maternal body with the paternal member in a mythical union of female with male might suggest that the mystery of the whole composed by these two combined would be at least an intellectual terminus for the search, even when it could also seem a practical defeat; for who ever gets all they really want in this world?[5]

And the defeat, after all, need not be final on the scale of reproduction at least, however incomplete it may still seem to the individuals involved. We were each of us brought into existence by virtue of just this animal deed and are all capable, more or less, of the equivalent for the next generation; somewhat, it may be, to our own surprise. To that extent moments of duality do occur, and even repeat themselves. This fact alone might in the end explain the absolute value placed on them in evangelical principle. The erotic apocalypse is bound to happen in the flesh at least, pretty obviously more than once, or I would not be here, and neither would my children. What is still required of the critic is some way of formulating this much of the constant possibility without displacing it into myth. Thereafter one could proceed to identify the intermediate stages as best one could—without, if possible, overvaluing any one of these, as theory has too often seemed to do, fetishizing some explanation of fetishism.

But if the intermediate condition is in fact virtually universal, and obtains as often on the level of explanation as on that of desire, a degree of tolerance would also seem called for, as much for fashionable lecturers, say, as overdressed women or conceited men. If we are bound to find ourselves caught up in some excessive attachment to the sign, and so not yet in full possession of the thing signified either practically or diagnostically, that predicament may itself be understood as inescapable as well as problematic. Would not fetishism, translated into another language, become identifiable at once as sin, or that by virtue of which we are regularly disposed to take some part or aspect for the whole? Religiously speaking,

---

[5]The lecturer was Leo Bersani, whose views have since been expressed more elaborately in *The Freudian Body: Psychoanalysis and Art* (New York: Columbia University Press, 1986). Freud's original article may be found as "Fetishism," in *Works* (London: Hogarth, 1953–1974) 21:149-57. The metaphoric potential of this originally anthropological (or theological) term had already been recognized by Marx, as the republication of Georg Lukacs's *History and Class Consciousness* (Cambridge: MIT Press, 1971) has reminded more recent readers.

this overinvestment is idolatry, which is at least more obvious in the erotic life than in other contexts, as Paul's Corinthians could also be reminded. And there were presumably some unconverted but skeptical citizens of that city too. We need not, after all, quite believe in what we may not be able to avoid. To that extent tolerance could even become a species of detachment. And what we would then be detached from might accordingly be revealed as in its own misdirected way an act of homage still to the once and future body. The fullness of this might seem to remain some distance ahead if not altogether beyond us, but our several enthrallments cannot help all the same but display its indirect attraction. The more bemused or obsessed we may be by the several idols that parody its appeal, the more evidently, at least to others, we may witness to its true authority.

The temporal mode of fetishism would have to be repetition, as we have already begun to notice. And repetition evidently dominates all too much of everyone's sexual experience, perverse or "normal." It is aggressively present in the content as well as the form of homosexuality, for instance, which must provide one of the principal reasons for counting that erotic variation as ontologically deficient. To affirm our own partial identity over and over as if repeating a half would make it a whole by sheer force of will is all too evidently, one would suppose, a subjective as well as a generic untruth. And this would hold for the psychic or social versions as well as for the physical. Single-sex groups that assemble to affirm the identity they repeat may serve as agencies for "empowerment" but in the nature of the case presumed cannot claim to represent the whole either on the erotic or the communal scale.[6] Heterophilia (as opposed to homo- either philia or phobia) would at least admit the existence of another body not entirely identical with my own, and with that relation, which seems indispensable to sanity, not to mention spirituality, in any context.

But repetition clearly governs anybody's erotic experience, whatever his or her tastes, to that extent hindering the power of the sign to fulfill its own significance. In the life of the individual the manifestations of this rule are comforting as well as constitutive. We are not sorry our hearts go on beating or our lungs breathe in and out. We are not even bored with the reductive simplification of our stride. The cycles of day and night, with their accompanying routines, are on the whole reassuring. Sameness is security. But as soon as the possibility of something better is raised by the experience of desire, repetition is felt as frustration. Why should I

---

[6]This limitation would be contested by participants in the movement for a "women's spirituality," which has recently been so prominent in more than one ecclesial context. Rosemary Ruether's sufficiently representative *Women-Church: Theology and Practice of Feminist Liturgical Communities* (San Francisco: Harper, 1985) supplies explanations and examples from a comparatively moderate perspective. Other prominent names include Fiorenza, Schneiders, and McFague. But the peer group, sexual or racial, is not eschatological, as the rituals of the still-more-recent "men's movement" could easily demonstrate.

have to repeat the all too easily accessible sign at such a distance from its proper meaning?

The resulting impatience can appear in our recollection of the past as well as our hopes for the future. What we recall of our sexual experience is never the sensations that may have accompanied appropriation, to the extent that this has in fact happened. These disappear as they occur, leaving no trace behind. What we remember is the revelation of the desirable that prompted the attempt in the first place—and can still, as any victim of such memories well knows. Recollection is accordingly one with fantasy; which is to say, with desire in the absence of all but entirely imaginary instances of the desirable. Repetition in mind alone is indeed a fetishism: the painful redundancy of a ghostly signifier in the continuing absence of the signified.

Too often, we must still repeat, we do not get what we want, either in imagination or in "real life." The body we reach out for or suppose ourselves at last in touch with turns out to be only so much ordinary flesh of the same value as what we started out in, which by definition cannot be good enough. So we seek it another time, or in some other posture or version, hoping by increments of fictionality to compel the duality we still feel ourselves denied. But this strategy is only magic, which defeats itself; the very extravagance of the effort betrays the incredibility of the result. For a problem squared is not solved, only intensified. Indeed repetition is literally so discouraging that we must in practice pretend it is not taking place in order to survive it. We convert it to habit and call that comforting. But this retreat reduces the possibility from the dual to the individual once more, which of course is to lose precisely what is desired.

Meanwhile desire as such goes on being implicitly eschatological, as the biblical texts suggest and any personal evidence will confirm, even if, as Heidegger would put it, chiefly in the deficient mode. We want more than we get, but what we want is, in the nature of the case, more than we seem able to obtain. In this respect sex resembles food: the meal we hunger for is always more satisfying than what we end up having to swallow. Only the first sip of wine or the first lick of ice cream actually tastes the way the rest should. The fictions we settle for might accordingly be read most tolerantly as a species of premature poetry. If this could only free itself to be itself, we might even find ourselves with the exceptionality of art instead of the repetitions of sex. There are writers, after all, who have succeeded in converting their adventures and sufferings in this kind into explicit fictions of which these antecedents were no more than a first draft. For any satisfactory solution to repetition would always need to represent completion, if not in one mode, then in some other.

Meanwhile a revival of difference can occasionally rescue us from at least the banality of repetition. Some fresh promise of reciprocity will serve to lead us out of fetishistic dead ends, or rather through these into the freedom of what they really meant all the time. The frustrations associated with any intermediate phase of the erotic life cannot even be helped until the hope associated with complementarity revives—as it might, any time. For a true union of opposites is always ahead, however respectable the mere symbiosis in which we happen to be caught. So it can be reassuring for some of us, at least, to find the "traditional" differences between the sexes reappearing in some novel context, however suspect these may have become ideologically at the current level of middle-class consciousness. Invitation and initiative, offering and acceptance, ambivalence and focus, may then recommence their ancient dance—as always in the mode of surprise. To be sure, it takes tact to recognize the moment in its promise. Our manners must become membranes too, neither over- nor understepping the chances for mutuality that can become at once a shared boundary and an abolition of limits. This requires openness to that certain rare coincidence which seems yet once more to offer us everything at last—including a reversal of conventions it might seem ruinous to challenge explicitly. The social forms reflective or creative of the differences between the genders can sometimes function as an art of fate, an imaginative intercourse that can render playful what would otherwise have to be suffered or still hoped for.

Watching a campus production of *The Marriage of Figaro,* for instance, I am impressed by the young woman who plays Susanna. As good an actress as she is a singer, and exceptionally attractive besides, she mimes quite perfectly the attitudes that go with this comic, graceful, melancholy role. And the rest of the academic audience feels the same, laughing freely and clapping often. It occurred to me only later that it might be easier these days for young women to behave in such a traditionally, not to say exaggeratedly, feminine style if they had the excuse of a role to play. The theater would be a public version of what in private could occur only before a mirror; and feminists as well as "sexists" have already taken sufficient notice of that mode of representation. But if women, as Helene Michie has put it, must inevitably "become both metaphors for the unknowable, and metaphors for metaphor, their bodies figures of figuration," then any occasion that might render such a necessity deliberate could become liberating in proportion.[7] The nowconventional assumption that female identity is either physical or social, and in either case merely literal, might then appear one more philistine mistake. For if the truth of the matter is still at once metaphoric and reciprocal, the acting out of complementary roles in the theater of everyday life could become how we might articulate what would sooner or later have to fall into place regardless on the level of generation. A professedly fictive enterprise might be a way to come to terms with carnal necessity and erotic hope alike.

But if this much of the worldly difference between the sexes is better understood as imaginative than as either physical or social, then those aspects of gender could be redefined as limited objectifications of what would in fact flourish best in another key. The "physical" would become only whatever could be known

---

[7]Helena Michie, *The Flesh Made Word: Female Figures and Women's Bodies* (New York: Oxford University Press, 1987) 7. The mirror problem is discussed on pp. 1-10.

of the individual body from outside it, as the "social" would reduce to whatever might be known of the communal body from outside it. To appreciate as much would also underline the degree to which the genuinely imaginative in this context at least could never be merely singular in its mode of working. All living differences must be played out in the dual. It is not I but We who collaborate to demonstrate the merism in question. Sexual difference is a folk art.

And this would hold even if, outside of opera, we do not practice it very gracefully. Watching the couples of a Cambridge summer weekend as they sun themselves beside the river or stroll along the streets, it comes over me that men and women really do not get on very well together these days. They cannot, on this showing, seem to realize who the other is. The women want to please, that is obvious—but this is a weakness. The men want to show off, that is even more obvious—and this is a deformity. A man has a loose and physical notion of whom he is with. A woman has a loose and social notion of whom she is with. Neither seems to have a clear idea of what is over against them. It is all, as far as one can see, done by stereotypes. Yet the *telos* of the relation has nonetheless drawn them both, before and after or outside of marriage, in age as well as youth. Each still hopes for more than they have or may get. What they are oriented upon does not yet appear, but it governs their conduct all the same. So they continue to reveal the dual body by the very awkwardness of their failure to manifest it. And would not precisely this be the testimony of a hundred comic novels?

The possibility of injustice in the relation between the sexes, to which so much attention has recently been paid, would seem to arise only when difference shifts from a vital or imaginative to a metaphysical and therefore political idiom. This change of venue flattens what begins as polarity to hierarchy, which is certainly prominent, for instance, in the notorious passage of Paul's letter to the Corinthians where he argues (if this *is* Paul) so strenuously in favor of female subordination both in marriage as an institution (11:2-16) and in the church as a society (14:33b-40). His reasoning in both contexts presupposes that the differences between the sexes are exact repetitions, and always the same way round, of the larger difference between the flesh and the Spirit. As Spirit is to flesh, so must the male be to the female, the better to reinforce, he believes, the sacramental possibility in the dual and the communal context alike. It is true that a sacramental body may be understood as hierarchically structured, like other bodies, as we have seen in connection with the Eucharist, where indeed the wine would be to the bread as the Spirit is to the flesh, whether on the scale of the elected individual or on that of the endowed community. And hierarchy as such would not necessarily be unjust, even in strictly carnal contexts. It might be understood in fact as a boundary adjustment: the moment of tangency between two individual bodies is thereby articulated as an interlocking of super- and subordinate elements. Such effects are presumably experienced as acceptable to both sides because the combination repeats the top/bottom, center/circumference, or active/passive differences within any individual body. Hierarchical relationships would in that case amount to an explicitly defined reciprocity—or rather, a reciprocity explicitly defined. Society consists of the sum of these, so we should obviously not be surprised.

But one would, all the same, need to argue back against Paul that the ratio corresponding to Spirit over flesh in the context of a sacramental marriage would not be male over female but, as in the communal version, the Spirit as determining a whole formed by the combination of both. When and if this ever was in fact reproduced within the relation of husband to wife, Paul's ratio would hold—but not otherwise. And even such an internal rhyme would on his own terms have to be left open to the free motion of the Spirit indeed, or to what human beings would call coincidence. It could not be legislated ahead of time. Perhaps the wife might in fact represent the Spirit within a given relationship, or first him, then her—or neither in any assignable sense. To declare that the husband must invariably be to the wife, or the (male) leader always to the community, as the Spirit to the flesh would implicitly restore the hegemony of the Law—which Paul cannot afford to propose in this or any other context. By insisting upon such a rule he would reduce what had better remain pneumatic to the psychic once again, which is precisely what, earlier in the same letter, he has accused his Corinthians of doing. It has become almost conventional among recent exegetes to assign these uncomfortable passages to a more "orthodox" redactor. But we need not presume that Paul must always be beyond implicit self-contradiction on this or any other topic.[8]

We might incidentally conclude that any such translation back from the complementary to the categorical would regularly result in one more species of allegory, which in this as in other contexts might be defined as a premature interpretation of a promising metaphor in terms of what is already known, intellectually or socially. A truer resolution of the polarities by means of which the ghostly whole formed by the dual body is indirectly presented would seem to me to lie in the future so constantly prophesied by just this conjunction: that is, the always possible child. A baby would then be the happiest "meaning" of the composite sign offered, which need not in that case be fetishistically overinterpreted ahead of time so as to confirm the hegemony of such authorities as might already obtain. If marriage is indeed a sacrament, that is, a sign the kingdom is near, then the corresponding parousia might seem to come nearer yet at the moment of birth, which would at least prove that creation is still crescive after all, and incidently justify the dominical reference to Genesis.

I am abruptly impressed, as if in simultaneous contradiction to and confirmation

---

[8] A regression from the pneumatic to the psychic might seem precisely what has continued to prevail through too much "Christian" history after Paul. The issue has attracted a number of recent inquiries, notably Peter Brown, *The Body and Society: Men, Women, and Sexual Renunciation in Early Christianity* (New York: Columbia University Press, 1988) and Margaret Miles's *Carnal Knowing* (Boston: Beacon, 1989). Some cultural repercussions of gender hierarchy or polarity are recovered in Thomas Laqueur's *Making Sex* (Cambridge: Harvard University Press, 1990).

of Paul's doctrine, by the achievement of a French former surgeon named Michel Odent at an otherwise provincial clinic in Pithiviers, France. *Birth Reborn,* the book celebrating this project, might still be better known, I suspect, among feminist critics as well as medical professionals.[9] The problem generally acknowledged but rarely, except in such exceptional instances, ever solved would be how to re-create birth too not just as a "natural" but most specifically as a "sexual" accomplishment. At Pithiviers this has meant involving the whole bodies of the women concerned, who are shown naked and half squatting in midair (the photographs are startling), supported from behind by helping hands in their armpits, as they expel other smaller but still formidable bodies from between their thighs. In this practice the midwife (a role deliberately recovered) is free to catch and return the released infant to its now kneeling mother, who is then able to embrace and even begin suckling her baby without waiting for the placenta to drop or the child to be inspected, washed, or dressed. Thus birth is removed from an overwatchful medical system and restored as an experience to its experiencer. I am struck by how obvious the action then becomes: a body reproduces itself indeed, one whole visibly engendering another. One could be reminded too that this most thoroughly somatic event at the end of the procreative trajectory entirely matches, though with all the elements reversed, that of ejaculation at its commencement, where the male body comes to an equivalent climax. We might learn by such complementary differences a degree more respect for each other, gender by gender, individual by individual: this is what we can in the end do together, turn and turn about.

A child is, after all, the natural goal from which all the other reproductive differences radiate as more or less significant in proportion to their distance from this genuinely futural eventuation. Men and women are absolutely each other's other only in this respect: that the male cannot bear, nor the female beget, a baby. And even this apparently most radical difference would hold only for the long moment of the generative process itself. For the begetting and the bearing too are finally relative to the child, who in principle is always singular once more, and so must demonstrate a fresh reconciliation of opposites from the genetic level upward. And if we could recognize the child as the eventual unity from which every previous difference is spun off, from the most indispensable to the remotest tinge of style or attitude, we might then confirm the suspicion that any resting point along the way

---

[9]Michel Odent, *Birth Reborn* (New York: Pantheon, 1984). I found a reference to this experiment in Emily Martin's more recent *Woman in the Body: A Cultural Analysis of Reproduction* (Boston: Beacon, 1987), which makes a similar case from an anthropological perspective. The conflicts over childbirth are exhaustively reviewed by Paula Treichler, "Feminism, Medicine, and the Meaning of Childbirth," in *Body/Politics* (New York: Routledge, 1990) 113-38, a collection focused on the intersection of the (female) body with, if not quite science, at least feminist discourse. The complementary temptation to sentimentalize the premodern may be resisted with the help of Edward Shorter's depiction of "traditional" childbirth practices in *A History of Women's Bodies* (New York: Basic, 1982).

would indeed be metaphoric still in one mode or another. Even the dual body adumbrated in the rituals of intercourse, animal or cultural, would then be revealed as still a fiction introductory to the final truth of what, when it appears, no longer has an erotic coloration at all. For a baby, however appealing to both sexes, does not evoke sexual feeling. It is in fact the completion and putting to rest of all that—until next time, which in this context must wait until the following generation.

So the value of difference is in the end not just its power to mobilize the interactions of desire and the desirable but to enfigure the possibility first of complementarity, then of union, and finally of an entire future identity. Difference stands, that is, for its own opposite. The eventual signified is at last the ectoversion, or inside-outing, of the signifier. The reappearance of difference, we have said, can amount to a fresh promise that repetition need not be final. Repetition is sameness, by definition, from which the reappearance of the other is at least a rescue. But the other too, like the singularity against which it is properly matched, is in the end only a stage in a progress. Caught up in the figures of this dance, we should remember to expect a conclusion neither one of us will ever embody in our own persons. The fullness of the body is still ahead, then, in what happens not now but hereafter when we, as it were, are over at last—and a child is born.[10]

Eventual

If a child is both an origin for and the conclusion of our sexual life, the polarities which govern that would emerge out of a prior singularity and converge upon it once again. In that case we would need to allow for three moments of bodiliness within this reproductive trajectory: that revealed at the moment of attraction, which amounts to a reciprocal re-presentation of the individuals concerned as desirable and desiring; that which is enacted in the ritual of intercourse, and so anticipated or confirmed in any of the exchanges that may introduce this; and finally what is manifested in the living body of the next generation. In the first, an ideal sphere is visible but broken; in the second, it is complete but invisible; in the third, actual in principle if reduced in practice to bilateral fact. The movement through all three moments would then take up the whole of the relevant time, which we would need to allow for in estimating the significance of any mere present, however extravagant or intense. As in other versions of art, memory and promise include more reality than immediate experience can exhaust.

---

[10]The last essay in Irigaray's *That Sex Which Is Not One,* "When Our Lips Speak Together," elaborates on her principal figure: what might be "said" if the two lips of the vulva were to speak for themselves on behalf of their own pleasure. The result, however interesting metaphorically, is rather a mumble. But would an outsider be only rude if he suggested that in natural fact what the *labia* ex-press is simply the child—not the "name of the Father," then, but the body of the (son)?

As consummation allows us to situate the potential of such erotic phenomena as can be seen to precede it, so the moment of the child would enable us to estimate such dispositions as fall between the midpoint in the trajectory and this conclusion. Any focus upon a "sexuality" that would exclude the slower rhythms of procreation in advance, for instance, could then seem to exhibit not just a fiction of but an abstraction from the promise in question. Underneath the familiar arguments over birth control and abortion should lie an ontological concern: what is missed when and if we not only separate the erotic from the generative but forget that we have done so? The same doubt might inform the discomfort even a programmatic liberalism might feel at the hegemony of a "singles" life-style, with its medically and emotionally cautious exchange of favors between two individuals who dare not cease to regard themselves as no more than just that, or the related affirmations of homosexual privilege as a political cause. In such organized moods a contrary intuition becomes forbidden even before it has been formed.

Unfortunately the counter terms that the corresponding objections might employ, like "nature" or "normal," are themselves usually understood as deriving from the same universe of abstraction and so miss the imaginative, much less the spiritual, authority that might accompany them. The institutional church, stuck with the language of "moral theology," has notoriously had difficulty persuading even its loyal members, much less the rest of the world, of its views on homosexual behavior, birth control, or abortion. But any of these three judgments in particular might be interpretable with sufficient sympathy if still from a certain distance as founded upon an underlying unwillingness to countenance a rejection of the body at major moments in the erotic life, which as we have seen would include first a realization of the other, then intercourse, and finally the child. These systematic refusals of refusals, then, or double negatives, could be minimally justifiable as reflecting a care for the whole as this looms or may be enacted or in fact emerges. "Sexual morality" would need reinterpretation in terms of the body before it could seem a mode of common sense. But the same might hold for the ethical in general, which should, one could also guess, need to be similarly determined. The good *is* the body, we might then say, whatever the kind or context.[11]

One philosophical objection to self-protective sex that I have not seen raised might form part of such a broader recapitulation. The parts or potential thereby blocked off mechanically or chemically become parodic of themselves. A phallus without (effectual) semen or a vagina without (access to) a womb are condemned to mimic their proper functions within a whole which has already been denied. To

---

[11]Theologians have had to concern themselves of late with a number of bodily issues, medical or sexual, though so far to little general effect. J. B. Nelson's *Embodiment: An Approach to Sexuality and Christian Theology* (Minneapolis: Augsburg, 1978), for instance, is unfortunately too "pastoral" and therefore conventionally liberal in its sympathies to provide the help its title promises.

that extent they lose precisely the identity they insist upon, acquiring in its place a merely illustrative value for the relevant social imperative. Egotistic sex is necessarily ideological. One partner may own this or that, and the other borrow the use of it, but neither is free either to give or to receive for good and all, for that could occur only within and between members of a possible whole.

So we steal scraps from a sphere the possibility of which has already been prevented in advance without anyone concerned needing to realize as much. And in the process we necessarily devalue the very differences upon which we insist. If women abstract their "femininity," which thereby becomes merely narcissistic and exhibitory, men abstract their virility, which in proportion becomes masturbatory or violent. Both sexes interpret these abstractions as what they fancy to be their identities, which isolates each from the other. Then we are masters or slaves, performers and audience, borrowers or lenders—and at all times consumers. The erotic life is held up in external behavior and internal fantasy, and either way reciprocally alienated from what we might once have been able to become together.[12]

Our episodes of freedom from such a hegemony of the banal can seem virtually mythological in proportion, though no less impressive on that account. A climax in *Holy Days,* a book by Lis Harris on the life of the Hassidim, arrives when the author, Jewish but otherwise secular, decides at last to go to a *mikvah* or ritual bath. She arrives alone, after the birth of her second child. The features of the place and the procedures required are described for readers—who can be presumed to know nothing of such institutions—together with her own nervousness. This is assuaged by the motherly bath attendant, who treats her, we are told, like a bride. She steps into the breast-deep water and dips under the surface three times, instinctively adopting the fetal position. As she sinks down, she recalls all those others who have done the same, remembering especially her grandmother in extreme old age, curled up like a fetus on her bed, and her children as they had once been inside her own body. "I look up and see Brachan's [the attendant's] smiling face through the water. I feel good."[13] One more naked woman shares in a rite required of members of her sex in the way of life she is reporting on after childbirth, which she has in fact just gone through, meanwhile herself enacting the role of the fetus, remembering other

---

[12]Abstraction interferes at the level of explanation as well as practice. We have noticed how recent efforts by feminist scholars to recover the body can often seem compromised by the disembodying effect of the language employed. Lacanian "orthodoxy," like Derridian or Marxist, can be at least as dangerous to bodiliness as any medical or ecclesiastical equivalent. The collection of pieces assembled by Jaqueline Rose in her already-standard *Sexuality in the Field of Vision* (London: Verso, 1986) or by A. M. Jagger and S. R. Bordo in *Gender/ Body Knowledge* (New Brunswick: Rutgers University Press, 1989) might illustrate at large.

[13]I found this story in *The New Yorker* 61 (23 September 1985): 100, though it has since appeared in book form as *Holy Days* (New York: Summit, 1985) 144-49. It is probably relevant to the character of the experience reported that Michel Odent's project should also involve a pool to float in—though in that case before or even during rather than after birth.

figures from the previous as well as the next generation, and floating in water that for the time being at least renews her identity as a member of the relevant community. It is a striking combination of themes, though I think such an interpenetration of elements is in fact typical of such unqualified experiences of the body. At these moments the truth of the matter seems close at hand: we have only to express what is going on in words which will not fall short of what is realized. It is good that too was done in this case.

To come across an adequate rendering of such an experience is to be reminded by contrast of the absence of just those elements that make it up within that other religious action with which we first began. Jesus is a man; he never marries. Not only is his paternity in doubt, but even more to the point, he has no son. Though his prohibition of divorce (as well attested and uncomfortable an item as the tradition contains) would, as we have seen, testify to a willingness to confirm that marriage is indeed in principle as meaningful at the End as at the beginning of the world, he remains in his own person the singular individual as tenaciously as the Baptist before him or Paul after him. And within the eucharistic action, which we have taken as the central demonstration of his purpose, the erotic body is prominent by its absence, though the other major possibilities are all represented: the individual as himself, the metaphoric body as the polarized elements, and the communal version as the intended result. Jesus' "seed" would therefore have to be located in an agricultural rather than genital context, and even there at the furthest possible remove from the corresponding action of sowing grain, for it is baked bread he distributes, ready to eat: the result, not the beginning, of the peasant's labor. And as befits an apocalyptic intention, those who consume the symbol, and so acknowledge the possibility that they may become its meaning, are not members of the next generation (for in the Spirit there will be none) but siblings of the one who has initiated this communication—though after a fashion that transcends the repetitions of the flesh. As tribal heads of a penultimate Israel, they are all males. The action seems accordingly to take effect within a thoroughly masculine context. The clear and total differentiation between its several moments would further strengthen this impression.

At the same time it has always been easy to see the movement as a whole from the leader to his assembly as an act of intercourse between male and female—the wedding night, as it were, of the Christ and his bride, as the Song of Songs could be reread as proposing. We may recall as relevant to this image the fact that a marriage normally occurs between members of the same generation—which might as well then be the last. And the subsequent repetitions of the act that have reproduced the communal body as so many other bodies in space and time have not altered this condition. The Church is still contemporary with her bridegroom; her "children" are really only herself indefinitely renewed. For in this context the relevant single child has already been conceived and born, and no other is required. What can be celebrated anew is therefore the act of marriage itself. Beyond this moment we cannot yet go—the entire eventuation is hidden in the depths of an absolute future. It is accordingly the communal version of the body alone that would be able to recover what would seem to have been excluded from previous phases of the action.

If so, we could at least identify some misapplications of the feminine imagery this has regularly attracted. The other year a story appeared in the *Times* about the scandal generated by a crucifix exhibited at the Cathedral of St. John the Divine in New York that showed the *corpus* as a woman: a "Christa," in short. This aesthetico-feminist project had attracted the predictable support of one party among the cathedral staff and the equally predictable objections of another. So the figure could be interpreted either as an allusion to the need for all to share in the humiliation of the chosen one or as a trendy travesty of doctrine and history alike. In fact it would seem rather a displacement of the relevant truth. It is not the suffering but the risen Christ who could reasonably be enfigured as a woman. And this the tradition has already freely done, most obviously in the person of Mary, who continues to image the Church, though in the maternal rather than the marital mode. In any case, it would seem an abuse as well as an underestimation of her eschatological potential to oblige any female to rehearse the preliminaries to the communal possibility in her own person, even in imagination. That job has already been done—by a male, we could say, because the task in question was precisely to replace the masculine ideal of victory by violence. It is appropriate that it should have required a man to turn the inevitable presumption of all public action in this world inside out, for in every culture so far, that expectation has indeed been defined in male terms.[14]

There has always been a place, then, for a recuperation of the apparently excluded female as a figure for the community intended by the founding action. And this would in turn permit the climax of the erotic life to be understood as a metaphor at least for the corresponding moment in any liturgy that repeats the act. The eventual child too reappears in those images of Mary holding the baby as a retrospective parable for the body indeed in all contexts, including the cosmic. To that extent both intercourse and birth could seem confirmed as vehicles at least for the central event.

In a more skeptical mood one might recollect that even the last and apparently most final of these moments would reveal the body proper only with some qualifications. The possible child, we have claimed, would always be indispensable as an end in terms of which to estimate the value of whatever preceded or interfered with it. Yet once that conclusion had in fact been reached, the philosopher inside even the grandparent might feel if not quite cheated at least detached. For this completion of the sexual curve is in fact no more than just such another individual body as we each began in; from which, it has to be supposed, we have all the while been

---

[14]Hereabouts would also be the objection to Shaker theology. If Jesus has already enacted the apocalyptic role on the scale of the individual, we don't need Ann Lee—at least not for this purpose.

attempting in some sense to escape. Nine months have come to an end, and with them what amounts in principle to the entire preceding generation: and here again is one more infant, who must grow up to repeat the same cycle in his or her own turn. For the child, who unites the partners genetically as well as heuristically, has still got to be of one sex rather than the other, and to that extent therefore not quite an unqualified embodiment of the whole. The several moments of our erotic experience may indeed pass through versions of death and resurrection, but what emerges is still one more life of the same kind as we have already found ourselves burdened with. Even a birth might in that case prompt some distant equivalent to the melancholy that follows intercourse, which also returns us to our individual bodies after a moment of enacting something better. In either context one takes up where one left off, to recommence the trajectory all over again on this scale or that. The flesh alone cannot transcend itself; it can only repeat itself endlessly, always including the desire not to repeat. So *eros* would remain neither an origin nor a rival of *agapē,* but at best one of its figures.

As long as this limit has not yet been realized, one may detect a certain desperation, whether in our culture or some other. An article in the appropriate journal reports that a cave in the Himalayas has recently become an object of contemporary pilgrimage.[15] In the cave is a column of ice. This is interpreted as representing Siva, apparently by virtue of its capacity to embody the *lingam*; in that case the cave itself would presumably represent the complementary *yoni*. When the pilgrims finally arrive and touch the pillar, strewing it with petals brought from afar, they feel, the article observes, in the presence of the divine. But as they go out, there are sadhus standing at the mouth of the cave to mock them ritualistically. "You think you have achieved union?" they call out. So the pilgrims feel let down too. One understands why: all that distance, and at the end of it still no more than a pair of symbols, good as these may be— and of natural generation, at that, which all concerned already know too much about: the facts of life, as we call them, grimly. So the sadhus are right to mock. Yet the people are presumably right to come too, if there is nowhere else for them to go. At any rate, one would not wish the pilgrimage abandoned. A figure is not nothing, or even the figure of a figure.

It is perhaps the remoter parables that can prove most satisfactory, and among these the truly accidental may acquire the least qualified authority. The summer I was most concerned with the matters touched on in this chapter I was also painting the walls of my basement, a cave of another kind. By the feast of the Assumption in mid-August I had got to the central block of bricks that supports the chimney. It took a fair amount of time and much paint to cover this rough and thirsty mass, in the course of which it was possible to think again, as I had already done in connection with easier versions of the same task, that it was, after all, only the

---

[15]B. N. Azis, "Sacred Encounter at Amarnath Cave," *Natural History* 92 (July 1983): 45-50.

surface I could touch with my brush, however thickly loaded, however frequently applied. Yet in renewing this as any other wall, irregular or smooth, upstairs or down, I was in fact, I knew, paying homage to a depth I could not reach. I was, even if indirectly, acknowledging the substance of things. It was a mode of this I was making love to. And the boundaries of the body in question were just these interrupted surfaces of porous brick and crusted cement. Was the chimney in question then phallic, as in the magazine piece, or Melville's famous story? Not, it seemed to me as I worked, at this level. Here it was rather the house as a whole repeated as a solid block, a concentration of what I cared about most and was still caring for. At another season of my life it might have been the flanks of a woman that I was free to caress during just such an afternoon hour as I was now devoting to this homely task. The difference could seem pathetic, but I did not pity myself, for the thought of what each had in common with the other sufficed to do away with that temptation. I could not, as things were, make actual love; but I could at least fix up a house that had been left for me to look after. This was not nothing, any more than the other had been. And both could seem reasonable liturgies with which to celebrate the feast.

Chapter 4

Metaphoric

The pine lumber is unfinished inside the study; the pines outside are finished trees.   —Annie Dillard, *The Writing Life*

Practical

  We have often had to speak of the erotic life as if it were already a work of the imagination, though "in terms of" the body natural still, like sports, or dancing, or war. This is easier for the moments of attraction and intercourse than for birth, where the whole that emerges is so obviously one more body of the same kind as those that brought it about. And the sacrifice presupposed is also incomplete. The male survives his orgasm, though he does project his "seed," and the female is presumed to survive birth, though her child is a fully formed member of the next generation. Eros would then seem a comparatively unfinished art, which should therefore be situated somewhere between the individual and the symbolic body proper, where substance as well as form are changed. A fair number of other halfway instances might make a similar impression on the prepared mind.
  In Columbus, Ohio, for instance, the zoo is located outside the city, next to an amusement park. Some of us attending a family reunion were deposited there, to amuse ourselves for a while. I had not been to a zoo in years, so there was a degree of novelty in walking along winding paths from the elephants to the rhinoceros to the camels, and then to wider areas, surrounded by walls and moats, where various other species dozed or grazed: South American rodents, antelopes, vultures, ostriches. As one observed these beings, large and dusty, with awkward legs, the question arose, What were we gazing at? "Animals," one could say, which it was therefore not simply unjust to transport all the way to this middle-American city and imprison or train or inspect the feet of, as required. To begin with, it could be seen that they regularly exceeded in one direction or another whatever norm we might draw from our own bodies. They were bigger or faster or water-borne; their skins were rough; their tails sinuous. By a variety of exaggerations they summed up an alienated physicality, a dream or nightmare of unqualified flesh. And they were already remote in space. Africa and Asia were not where *we* lived, but mythical elsewheres for such beasts to lurk in as tempting or dangerous, beautiful or monstrous, rare and mysterious. Less obviously they ambled or dozed at a still greater distance from us in time. These creatures were older than ourselves, and

their archaic physiognomies evoked aeons of undisturbed existence before our race had come to kill or capture. Now they were here marooned; dependent, it might soon be, on such a protective imprisonment as we could contrive for them.

In all these ways they seemed alienated versions of ourselves as living bodies in some "natural" world. Their presence behind the concrete barriers testified accordingly to a mixture of fear and nostalgia in the species that now trickled along these paths, preoccupied with its own young, intermittently calling out the names it had given these other children of a greater family. Here were the rest of us, which we had given up access to in order to become precisely these crowds now exercising their curiosity at the expense of their cousins in life.

It was instructive as well to pass from the zoo across a parking lot to the amusement park with its own variety, this time of rides, games of chance, and food stands. And the two institutions seemed complementary in something besides a recreational or economic sense, for within the park the bodies in question belonged to the crowd itself. The rides offered artificial environments of one kind or another in which one's own body might be carried up and down and around on plastic horses or in cars on tracks, or (the most interesting instances) slide down chutes trickling with water to a pool at the bottom either by itself or clutching a yellow plastic skid. One *entered in*—that was the point—and then became subject to some extremity of movement sufficient to elicit pangs of fear and exhilaration, participation and helplessness. The purpose, I guessed, was to intensify these sensations of motion to the verge of nausea or ecstasy. Those ritualized shrieks seemed an equivalent to what in the erotic context would be the gasp of orgasm: a moment of *jouissance* that for any animal species would have to be exceptional. Here was bodiliness again, as at the zoo—and rather more our own, at least in principle, even if in so brief and artificial a context, as unreal in its fashion as the cages and compounds across the way. In both places we could be seen to have contrived imaginary versions of a body we were not quite able to take part in: the body, as Paul would certainly call it, of flesh still, for there could be nothing of the Spirit either in the idle animals on one side or the thrills and spills on the other. "That was fun!" the kids called out to each other as they came away from the more desirable attractions. "Fun" is the experience of *this* body, as best we can arrange for that. No wonder the word is often used for sex too.

Alienation or intensification would both be incipient fictions, then, halfway to a full reproduction; attempts, as it were, to break out from the limitations of the natural body in the direction of art. The rides in the park were not yet games, but on the way there; and games too, though not quite art either, came closer to showing how one or another species of that might emerge. On the Arts Quad two young men were playing frisbee. Both were exceptionally strenuous and agile, and a couple of catches—which I would have thought impossible—occurred successively as I passed. There went a running body again, the hand just reaching out, a quick clutch, and the familiar stumbling run to recover. What is a "good catch," then? I do not yet know. Each player served as a mirror image for the other, that much was clear;

they were really the same person pretending to be different, so the game might proceed. This was not so much of a risk as heterosexuality. But the frisbee was quite other than either of the players, a thoroughly if temporarily independent thing to be thrown back and forth, each participant in turn launching and receiving the disk; which is to say, a flattened sphere; which is again to say, a third body. By way of this entity they communicated, if only with themselves, if only as offering and accepting the same message, over and over. The toy would turn into a proper symbol, I could think, if it were given a chance; but that is not allowed by the rules: whatever whirls away with all the animal energy that can be packed into it must come back again the same as ever, for each partner will make up for the expenditure of the other with an exactly equivalent investment. Games of such a kind enact a naive immortality. Life need not end, if only one is quick enough, forever. No wonder this too is "fun."

A frisbee is very literally projected from the body, acquiring significance together with the energy that fuels its trajectory. Elaine Scarry, whose book on the body has already been referred to, mentions the extent to which the "artefacts" that surround us without apparent motion may also be understood as "projections," if not of the body as a whole at least of its parts. So the eye becomes a camera; the skin, a bandage or clothing; the hand or finger, a tool. Or it may be a function rather than some part that is displaced, as memory, say, in a library or computer. Most generally, she observes, it is the life of the body that is projected, as in the case of the frisbee: the inanimate is thereby animated, which in turn may "reciprocate" upon its original so as to "disembody" that, as when a chair allows whoever is sitting in it to become weightless.[1] Scarry's thought does not reach as far as reproduction strictly so nameable, where the whole body is recast into another whole of the same or some entirely different kind. But it could help prompt the corollary that a progression should be understood to obtain from (a predictably Freudian) "projection" through (an obviously Marxist) "production" to (something like a symbolic) *re*production as the terminus of this sequence of possibilities. The last might as usual provide a limit to situate less complete versions that precede and anticipate it. "Artefact" would then be an appropriate name for whatever replaced a part as opposed to a whole; which if it too appeared would seem in proportion what we could begin to call a work of art—or at least a game.

Artefacture includes manufacture, which would most literally apply to the crafts. A visit to our annual craft fair suggested a more inclusive way to formulate the difference between what we would still want to put under this head and what might count as art. A work of the former kind, it seemed, is still "useful," which is to say, centered upon the needs of the natural body in its relation to the environment, or other bodies like and unlike itself. The things fabricated are baskets, pots, clothes,

---

[1] Elaine Scarry, *The Body in Pain: The Making and Unmaking of the World* (New York: Oxford University Press, 1985) 281-85.

and such like, and so no matter how decorative or elaborate, still in the end expected to fit into somebody's usual way of life. They are metonymic, not metaphoric, and so not really meant to stand on pedestals and be admired—except at craft fairs, especially in the "court of honor," where they are treated as if they were indeed works of art for the time being. But even these most-admired objects would eventually, it could be presumed, be taken home and put to use or away. Such entities have not yet become independent bodies in their own symbolic right. They are still on the way.

In spite of this incompletion, there is always on such occasions an emphasis upon the several changes any substance must pass through as it is brought from a state of nature into the condition of an artefact at least. The makers contribute the labor of their own bodies, which had therefore to be boasted of and could be exhibited, for these things were definitely "handmade." It was interesting to observe how the sexual difference, which some of these amateur artisans might resist in other contexts, was allowed to be of some importance here. The "featured craftsperson" on this occasion was a young man displaying the stages required to manufacture baskets. He was pounding a log of black ash with a mallet. The loosened strips from successive rings of wood had to be pealed off, soaked, and in due course woven into baskets. That steady pounding took a strong arm. This was evidently a man's work, and therefore attracted an audience that seemed composed chiefly of other males. At other stations women and girls similarly clustered about weaving frames and spinning wheels or admired displays of lace. These were female skills. One moves up toward art, then, in such a context, and back again toward gender and labor—which could seem comforting, either way.

But games and crafts, like animals, wild or tame, are essentially mute as well as in practice all too repetitive. To move into art proper, one would need to include some language, verbal or otherwise. The attractive instances might still be as occasional as they become impressive. "At around age six, perhaps," writes Eudora Welty in the first of that sequence of lectures which have since been published as an autobiography of her life as a writer,

> I was standing by myself in our front yard waiting for supper, just at that hour in a late summer day when the sun is already below the horizon and the risen full moon in the visible sky stops being chalky and begins to take on light. There comes the moment, and I saw it then, when the moon goes from flat to round. For the first time it met my eyes as a globe. The word "moon" came into my mouth as though fed to me out of a silver spoon. Held in my mouth the moon became a word. It had the roundness of a Concord grape Grandpa took off his vine and gave me to suck out of its skin and swallow whole, in Ohio.[2]

---

[2] Eudora Welty, *One Writer's Beginnings* (Cambridge: Harvard Univ. Press, 1983) 10.

"From flat to round": an object of perception thus becomes a sphere, which is to say, a body in its own right, no longer merely part of something else but independent, as much in the world as the observer of the fact, and correspondingly awful to the remembered child. But this recollected moment of apprehension is simultaneous with a renewal of a word the form of which in the mouth reproduces this newly realized autonomy as a shape as well as a sound. That sound is then itself repeated in a second word, *spoon,* the likeness bringing together the analogous differences between a remote heavenly sphere, so heavy and yet so lofty, and the small hollow curve of a domestic implement familiar from infancy to us all. Distant and near, alien and familiar, cosmos and household, past and present, are reconciled through a sequence of translations from moon to mouth to word to thing. To be born with a silver spoon in one's mouth is to be privileged from the beginning, as Eudora Welty certainly believes she was from this moment. Nor does the metaphoric chain end yet: the whole substance of the moon, held in the mouth as a word as in a spoon held by a child's hand, is formally identified with the slippery bulk of a grape sucked out of its thick skin, a memory for the young girl and the old lady alike that also renews the difference between the globular moon and the hollow spoon as a contrast between the sweet flesh of the fruit and its tart membrane. And these ratios continue through the sounds of other words: *spoon* and *round,* for instance, or the consonantal links beneath *mouth* and *moon, grape* and *Grandpa, suck* and *skin, whole* and *Ohio.*

In all these ways the passage becomes a primary moment for the reader too of this splendid little book, who thereby shares an experience in its own way equivalent to the one described and rehearsed. We can be reminded accordingly that a sign seeks always to signify the whole: any sign, any time. It signifies another sign, or some part or aspect of the whole, only by default, through some violence of time and text we cannot help but suffer, though we need not altogether submit to or identify with it. Ideally, or rather eschatologically, the sign would still import the whole—including therefore itself. For we do wish to sum things up so as to comprehend everything at once, like the child a grape. It is the function of poetry, whether in verse or prose, accidental or deliberate, to reenact at least this desire. Meanwhile the instance at hand makes for *One Writer's Beginnings* indeed, which thereby becomes one more model for anyone else working in the same kind, and so for art as such.

Welty is re-creating a moment of poetry in childhood, toward which the adult voice that tells the tale stands as half a critic, distributing the mimetic elements for us to take conscious notice of. But more obvious poems too may be found to depend on the same coincidence of world and word. Seamus Heaney's "Toome Road" has for its occasion and subject matter an encounter between the author and a column of British soldiers on a country road somewhere in Ulster:

One morning early I met armoured cars
In convoy, warbling along on powerful tyres,

> All camouflaged with broken alder branches,
> and headphoned soldiers standing up in turrets.[3]

These opening lines supply the image that the poem goes on to develop as question, expostulation, meditation, and address. And this centers, it may readily be observed, upon a single word, "warbling," which may accordingly be identified as the probable seed of the whole biographically as it remains the core poetically. That such "tyres," huge and deeply treaded, should all together and at a certain speed on a narrow road produce just such a sound as would most properly be reproduced by the apparently very different associations of a term for a kind of bird song makes a metaphor that serves to concentrate all the issues of the poem: by what right is this force here, in Ireland? How unnatural its threat, already experienced by those alder trees, and how beautiful too the clean, repellent power! Here as with Welty the single word could not prevail so strongly without the support provided by the repetition of its enunciatory elements, which echo like those treads on the surface of a rural road. "Morning," "early," "armoured," and "cars" anticipate what "powerful" and "tyres" confirm and "broken alder branches," like "soldiers" and "turrets," repeat at a distance. These ripples of paronomasia extend the authority of the chosen word throughout the sentence it dominates, establishing the image generated as sufficient to govern the rest of the poem and so justify its remaining discourse.

What has variously been remembered as mimesis and objected to as representation might more justly be understood, then, as a species of incorporation. The alien body must take form anew as a body at home. When this happens inside some "language," the result is art. If that language *is* language, we have a poem—which may be, as these examples show, no more to begin or end with than one word long. Poetry is procreation in words. We may know this birth has taken place by what can be identified after the fact as some sort of metaphor. And the likenesses and differences that define the trope form complementary halves of a whole that amounts to a body once again—at least in figure.

This happens by way of an individual, who is apt to bear a name, Southern or Irish; but the medium of poetry is not just some idiosyncratic sensibility, however acute, but language. It is the actual bodiliness of the words we already share that surfaces in such formations, like a whale lifting its back above the water. Language gets its own way, pleasurably. It gets its way by getting in its way. It is tongue tied: so as to say what it might come to mean at last.

A full-sized poem would only need to show as much on a grander scale, where whole contexts might become metaphors one for another, so as to incorporate galaxies of history and culture as well as the immediacy of some private experience. In Richard Wilbur's contemporary classic "On the Marginal Way," for instance, the

---

[3]Seamus Heaney, "The Toome Road," in *Field Work* (New York: Farrar, Strauss, and Giroux, 1979) 15.

determining analogies are marshaled, stanza through formal stanza, as gracefully as deliberately, in this poet's characteristic combination of elegance and ease. The occasion is an afternoon walk along a well-known path that follows the rocky edges of the shore at Ogunquit, Maine. This is not a poem that disregards its source in the common world: courtesy to a potentially knowledgeable reader is at the same time a species of imaginative humility, which keeps past and present, shared fact and private association, and therefore world and word in touch, one with another. So the poet sees, as others might and have, an unusual configuration of rock along this path, in his words "sleek, fluent, and taffy-pale," which contrasts with the jagged fragments elsewhere and brings to mind how George Borrow once saw, beside a shore in Spain, "A hundred women basking in the raw": how overpowering that plenitude of female flesh with its "strew/Of rondure, crease, and orifice" must once have seemed, he thinks, as far beyond ordinary expectation as this somewhat too fleshly stone, an overflow of ancient lava. Here would be an initial metaphoric situation that (perhaps too easily?) brings together a familiar New England observation and an uncommon book, unusual nature and the confusions of eros, America and Europe, the eccentricities of a Victorian traveler with the reflective interiority of a modern academic on vacation. All this is very recognizably Wilbur as himself; we already feel we know this voice as it offers just these images, which could seem as much as anyone might ask from so well-known a poet.[4]

But because this poem is not just another lyric but almost an ode, quite in the best Romantic style, the two stanzas following bring in another image to correspond, the speaker tells us, with a change of light upon the rocks, which now "flush rose and have the melting shape/Of bodies fallen anyhow," this time not as a living panorama which once met a traveler's eye but as a heroic painting, a "Géricault of blood and rape," exhibiting the melodramatic aftereffects of an assault upon some desert town or caravan. From the rewording of an episode referred in a real book, we are shifted like the sunlight to an imaginary but all too imaginable painting of the same era and so at a similar distance from the observer in time and culture—yet he is the one, after all, who has read the book and seen such paintings, and so is his equally privileged though necessarily silent interlocutor, the imagined companion and actual reader, who has read books too and passed through museums and even, perhaps, walked upon the Marginal Way.

But then as the wind rises and "all is greyed/By a swift cloud that drags a carrion shade," the vision shifts once more, and the observer is reminded, if of bodies still, this time not of a scene recollected in a book or composed upon canvas but of facts photographed in stills and films alike, the "poor slaty flesh" of "Auschwitz" as that was "bulldozed at last into a common grave." And here too the presumed reader is easily with him, having shared in the experience of a generation

---

[4]Richard Wilbur, "On the Marginal Way," in *Walking to Sleep* (New York: Harcourt, 1969) 5-8; and now in *New and Collected Poems* (New York: Harcourt, 1982) 120-22.

that cannot help but sooner or later follow such repeated movements of the mind from the monuments of high (or is it merely precious?) culture to the facts of the history that has so regularly contradicted these. We too, it is assumed, can remember having seen, in grainy black and white indeed, just that tumble of stiff limbs before the bulldozer blade. The changes in the light of a single afternoon (with night, after all, coming on) combine with the impact of old and new events upon a mind remembering an identifiable if indefinite moment in the history of the American upper middle class. This combination is Wilbur's typical subject matter: metaphor as history, history as metaphor. Poetry is not timeless, after all.

To "take cover" from his last association, the poet recollects, as if in an effort to replace all his memories, amiable or horrific, that these rocks upon which he gazes were all the while a product of a sequence of moments in the course of which many-layered sediments were lifted and split by a volcanic infiltration that once sent bursts of "magma" out to cool into what future aeons of glacier and surf could turn into just these weathered forms. The geologic processes (in the handbook from which the speaker learned them already a set of explanatory hypotheses) are obliged under the pressure of his need for the full truth of the matter to become as charged with imaginative energy as the telluric events once were with inanimate force. The earth is still a body too, living or dead.

This meditation introduces the penultimate movement of the poem, which responds to a renewal of the peaceful sunlight, now falling not just upon rock but actual human flesh:

> And now three girls lie golden in the lee
> Of a great arm or thigh, and are as young
> As the bright boulders that they lie among.

With this rediscovery not just of the planetary past but of a present that is suddenly as attractive as it is actual, the poet is enabled to see again a "perfect day" and observe how "the waters clap

> Their hands and kindle, and the gull in flight
> Loses himself at moments, white in white

as if in reply to the implications of a newspaper that can also be seen spread out before somebody's face on an overlooking porch, with its news, as he writes this poem, of yet another war. "Joy for a moment floods into the mind," and the poem can proceed to its conclusion in a prayer that this momentary coincidence of air and flesh may indeed be trustworthy as a sign that all things, including human beings and their history as well as rocks and sea, might eventually be brought into unity by an equivalent if still vaster change. Geology, he has just shown, is poetry, rightly felt; may the same "motive" that has "found the manhood of this stone" in one deliberate metaphor after another go on, he prays, to "wash our own."

Thus Wilbur ends, very much in the style proper to poetry of the grandly humanistic kind so typical of him as an individual and so representative too of the period he re-creates and his poem now recalls. Its closure in a gesture toward the fulfillment of the metaphoric process in a religious reconciliation beyond the boundaries of poetry as such can seem gratefully acceptable in the work of someone who knows all too well what has so often been tried on that scale and what has failed. For precisely because what can be accomplished in imagination has in fact here and now been brought about, this remoter hope may still be accurately as well as generously placed as the ideal future of such a present as we have just shared—which has already so freely and fairly incorporated the corresponding past, natural and historical. A work of art is a successful revolution, which the other kind have on the whole not yet managed to be. On this basis poetry can become not only fun (as Wilbur also makes it easy to remember) but justified. The poet is whoever can actually tell the truth we are already free to comprehend while prefiguring something better still; and this is how.

But a Wilbur poem could also seem old-fashioned now, however "good of its kind": an instance of a cultural style already some distance back in what has since become almost as much our past as any of the contexts so skillfully evoked within it. The easy splendors of "On the Marginal Way" might then seem too much in debt to an academic mood of memory and allusion rather than immediate experience, and its metaphoric practice, convincing in its very elaboration as this becomes as soon as one has consented to the poem, might feel excessively self-conscious to stand for the full possibility of this or any art. Would not metaphor be too psychic an action in any case to represent the whole of what imaginative reproduction in words might amount to?

Such limitations have a historical dimension. Between the pleasures of this poem and any current reader must have intervened that other revolution in American verse of a generation ago, which forced upon all concerned a rather different idea of what this art might consist of. The principal names associated with the change would include not just the more flamboyant figures such as Ginsberg or Ferlinguetti but also Creeley, Ammons, Bly, and Snyder. In the immediate background of these figures and the many who have followed them since would be Williams and Pound, who in their different ways once seemed to have maintained an experimental attitude toward the form of poetry that had otherwise fallen into the background under the influence of Eliot and his poetical and critical descendants. The intention of this very unacademic cohort was to recover a more direct connection between experience and language than their teachers supposed was possible.

This common intention could accordingly be understood as therapeutic: to recover an active rather than a merely aesthetic integrity for a version of the symbolic body that could otherwise seem in some danger of losing what might be identified, and not just metaphorically, as its proprioception. A memorable moment in Oliver Sacks's well-known story of his recovery from a fall and an operation that had left him unable to recognize his own left leg as part of himself could supply an easy parallel "in terms of" the natural body. This very literary neurologist found that as he recalled a passage from a piece of Mendelssohn's and stepped out in the rhythm of this music, he was enabled to reappropriate the alienated limb. The music, the "kinetic melody" of walking, and the repossession of himself were thus simultaneous. The body rediscovers its proper identity, he observes, not in thought but action; and action for any body is inevitably periodic. Without such a rhythmic integration of parts into a whole there is, Sacks concludes, no "I," no opportunity for the emergence of an actual subject of experience.[5] The moral for poetry (or any other art) would not be hard to draw—and seems particularly easy to accept by way of just such an illustration on behalf of the generation of poets in question.

In the earliest years of the Modernist rebellion the hope of recovering the integrity of the symbolic body had seemed best exercised semantically: that is, by way of the "image," from which derived an initial name for one party in the movement. In that mode the experiencer must indeed reproduce the nature of things metaphorically—which is to say, within the scope of consciousness, and therefore, by a succession of inherited adjustments, to just such a model of apprehension as a poet like Wilbur would supply a happy instance of. For on that principle, the more "original" and therefore reproductive the image, the better the poem. But once the possibility of metaphor had itself become normalized as "imagery" or "symbolism" (not to mention its classroom decomposition into "tenor" and "vehicle"), any fresh reminder of the sheer bodily presence of the world would need to be arrived at in some thoroughly nonintellectual way.

The direction explored by the poets of the postacademic reaction had therefore to be subcognitive and presemantic. The available means, characteristically borrowed from jazz music, accordingly became rhythm; and the task of the several practitioners became to discover what sorts of rhythmic events in language could reproduce not just the look of things but the way they moved within and without. For meter by definition is fixed and traditional; rhythm, though, enforces an original relation to the universe as soon as it is felt at all. So it would need to be spontaneous and unpredictable, kinetic as well as aural, and therefore close to the emphases, balances, and rapidities of common speech. It would seek to reveal actual language as capable of embodying the motions of the world as well as its existence, and so the life and not just the substance of whatever body was in question.

The incipience of what could already seem poetry in this kind would emerge from the babble of toddlers, whose first words are at once metaphoric and rhythmic: *mommy* and *daddy*—or *abba* and *imma*. The routines of older parties might also illustrate, as when I leave the house in the morning or my office in the evening. To make sure I have in fact turned off the stove (for I do not trust myself to take such matters for granted these days), I look sternly at the switches to the burners, saying aloud as I take deliberate note of their positions, "Four up for Monday morning"—or whatever the day and time may be. Over the years this has become not just a statement of fact but a slogan, almost an advertisement:

---

[5] Oliver Sacks, *A Leg to Stand On* (New York: Harper, 1984) 146, 149.

Four Up
for Monday Morning

Each half evidently contains two strong as well as an indefinite number of weak stresses. So it has become a moment of free verse. When I leave the office in the evening, I check in the same way to see that the hot pot and its cord are both safely on their respective shelves and not by some inadvertence still plugged in, meanwhile chanting quietly to myself,

On the shelf, on the shelf, space . . .
for Thursday evening.

The order here seems to be a pair of units, each with two stresses, to make up what thus becomes a first line, but with the second stress of the second unit omitted, so that a pause is required to maintain the rhythm before what then becomes a second line, made up of two stresses as before, can fairly be rehearsed.

On each of these occasions I am persuading myself that a certain state of affairs does in fact obtain, so I will not have to wonder later whether the appliance in question has been turned off. For that purpose I fix a text within my mind, for such alone can reassure me: certainty *is* inscription, which can always be recalled even if the state of affairs to which it refers remains hazy. But this is no more than the science and therefore the prose of my enterprise. The poetry is in the rhythm, as a dance is in the finger I may raise to accompany my words. In both the world is reproduced for me not just as a sign branded upon my brain or an image before the eye of the mind or even as a voice addressing the corresponding ear but as a recurrent movement, which as such is not just imagined but performed. The several things in my environment, themselves already singled out by such acts of attention, are in this way converted into pulsations of my body— or rather, into the echo of these within the movements of speech.

It is noticeable that habits of this kind are formed upon rhythms already proper to the language spoken, and not just the character of the individual concerned, however obsessive. If one merely counts, for instance, one is bound to end up grouping the numbers one repeats in pairs, which themselves pair again as fours:

one, two, / three, four,
five, six, / seven, eight,
nine, ten, / eleven, twelve. . . .

This pattern is evidently intrinsic to such a series in English at least. And the faster one goes, the more obvious it becomes. If this four-stress combination in fact provides an intrinsic norm proper to the language, the next step up in rhythmic sophistication would be illustrated by one or another of those familiar sayings in which an expected fourth stress is omitted, so as to establish the remaining three as what can then be called a "line" indeed, as we have just seen. Another instance my generation will recall from Army days: "shit, shave, and shower." In fact the sequence of actions in question would be a shit, a shower, and then a shave. But the poetical form has the advantage of observing a sequence of vowels from closed to open. For a similar reason the question at the checkout counter these days is "Paper or plastic?" not "Plastic or paper?" Sound follows after and reinforces rhythm, as in metaphoric contexts it supplies immediacy to imagery. By such means bare repetition is converted into a reproduction of bodily motion—as in rap music, for another current instance, which also uses (a syncopated version of) the four-beat line. Rhythm "imitates" the *life* of whatever is going on: periodicity communicates momentum—and thereby hints at mortality and survival alike.[6]

By way of such familiar instances, one may become more alert to those unconscious collocations that produce the poetry of everyday life. The subtler cases, to be sure, require a cautious ear:

"I'll give you a ride
if you don't like the weather."
"No; as a matter of fact I'm
driving tonight."

Listening to this exchange from the hall outside my office, it seemed to me that the shorter or two-stress variant of the basic rhythm emerged of itself, along with the unexpected prominence of that break between "I'm" and "driving," which confirmed that this was indeed an enjambment and, as a feature of what preceded it, the huddle of syllables in front of "fact," which so unexpectedly took the second stress in what thus became a single line. Keeping one's ears open is indispensable in such cases; it is not possible to tell in advance how the stresses will sort themselves out in detail.

Attentiveness is especially required when one already knows ahead of time what

---

[6]Prosody is a crowded and contentious speciality, as any consultant of the opinionated abstracts in T. V. F. Brogan's exhaustive *English Versification, 1570–1980* (Baltimore: Johns Hopkins Univ. Press, 1981) can verify. Traditionalists like Fussell and Hollander are disinclined to admit any native rhythm in what they isolate as "free verse," though Derek Attridge's equally conservative *Rhythms of English Poetry* (London: Longman, 1982) is ready to concede the possibility of an aboriginal four-beat pattern (80-96). Even those explicitly recommending open forms are apt to redefine the bodily element in objective terms. For Charles Hartman, for instance, whose *Free Verse* (Princeton: Princeton Univ. Press, 1980) has become standard, lineation determines rhythm rather than the other way around. Donald Wesling labors to convert prosody into grammar in his *The New Poetries* (Lewisburg PA: Bucknell Univ. Press, 1985). And the pieces included in *The Line in Postmodern Poetry* (Urbana: University of Illinois Press, 1988), a collection edited by Robert Frank and Henry Sayre, are far too theoretical to allow themselves any descent to the level of rhythmic fact, even when the topic is black poetry. My own simplifications were originally prompted by an article in what I remembered as *PMLA*, though I have not been able to find it again.

the meter at least is going to be. Robert Bly's earlier poems, for instance, continue to presume a pentameter line, though in the accentual rather than an iambic form. But this means a reader must rediscover the necessary redistribution of stresses in each case for the first time:

> The darkness drifts down like snow on the picked cornfields
> In Wisconsin: and on these black trees
> Scattered, one by one,
> Through the winter fields—
> We see stiff weeds and brownish stubble,
> And white snow left now only in the wheeltracks of the combine.[7]

If a line of three beats presumes a fourth unheard stress at the end to divide it from the one following, a five-stress line would for the same reason anticipate a sixth inaudible beat to provide a pause between it and the line following. But a reader must still pick out where the five explicit stresses should be heard as opposed to how they might be felt if the same words and phrases appeared in some other context. We are invited accordingly to hear "the *dark*ness drifts *down*" without an emphasis on "drifts," though the phrase in isolation might attract one. We need also to hear a single combined stress on "cornfields," which might otherwise count as two. On the same principle, though with apparently opposite results, we had better hear all three words in the sequence "see stiff weeds" as held in a suspension of three equal beats, as if to bring out the rigidity of the frozen stubble, and so contrast this bristly concentration with the laxity of the line following, where one has to decide almost at random which of the four monosyllables "white snow left now" should receive the two stresses left once "only" has absorbed a third of the five to be applied. To follow each line of such verse is thus to find oneself recovering the casual and delicate modalities, as of a man walking carefully over rough ground, in which an American voice may be heard saying what there is, here and now, to say. Bly is not just using the pentameter then; he is reinventing it, each time.

A meter can be known ahead of time; rhythm, which embodies it, cannot. This imposes, or should impose, a special burden on the poet in such a kind. It is moving to see Gary Snyder, to pick another well-known and perhaps more original instance, listening to and taking down laconic remarks made over the radio between firewatching stations in the "Lookout's Journal" he kept during the indeterminate time of his early life before he became a poet indeed. "You're practically there," says "Sourdough radioing to the smoke-chaser crew,"

> "you gotta go up the cliff

---

[7]This is the middle stanza of the first poem, "Three Kinds of Pleasures," in Robert Bly's first and best book, *Silence in the Snowy Fields* (Middletown CT: Wesleyan University Press, 1962) 11.

    you gotta cross the rock slide
    look for a big blaze on a big tree."[8]

By writing down such accidental moments of colloquial discourse Snyder found himself unexpectedly provided with just what he needed in the way of a possible line for the poetry he was still hoping to arrive at. He could not learn as much from Milton or Chaucer, whom he was also reading at the time, though by firelight on a mountain side. What he heard as he listened to his fellow workers could then combine with the metaphoric import of the physical work he also found himself doing during those days, which in due course would supply the title for his first book as well as the subject matter of the last poem in that volume:

    Lay down these words
    Before your mind like rocks
        placed solid, by hands
    In choice of place, set
    Before the body of the mind
        in space and time:
    Solidity of bark, leaf, or wall
        riprap of things. . . .[9]

This labor proved a modern version of the same ascesis Thoreau had once practiced for *Walden,* which Snyder was also reading, requiring of both a consent to passage through the structures of convention, which in the elder writer's case had impinged as the discourse of commerce and in the younger's as the idiom of the academy, all the way down to those elementary modes of interaction with the concreteness of the world that are sure to engage hands and back and so the whole of one's own body with the wholeness of things. Only in such a way, the moral might be, does one discover something actual enough to make a metaphor of, as Thoreau did with his beanfield, or, in Snyder's case, find a reliable model for the placing of just such stresses as could produce a live rhythm in poetry. Upon the success of this renewal, then, would in turn depend the authenticity of his subsequent work in words, which remains notable for the contribution it brings to a project that in hindsight at least can seem the common intention of his generation of American poets. For to recover the world in one imaginative way or another is also to take part in the creation of what we can later call our national as well as a literary history. We are properly remembered for what we are able to pass on of the truth of bodies, which is tradition. And the active line was how this could be done for the time being in verse—and was done, by him and a few others. The result is something to be proud of quite as much as a good metaphor.

---

    [8]Gary Snyder, *Earth House Hold* (New York: New Directions, 1969) 9.
    [9]Gary Snyder, *Riprap & Cold Mountain Poems* (San Francisco: Grey Fox, 1980) 30. I have taken the liberty of omitting a period after "rocks," which looks like a misprint.

A few critical conclusions too might also follow from an appreciation of this practical achievement. If the special work of the poetical generation in question was to discover the extent to which rhythm too might communicate contact, and so provide kinetic as well as semantic instances of verbal reproduction, and if the search for a line that would generate such a rhythm was in fact sometimes successful, then in this context too we would have a norm in terms of which to discriminate good from bad work. We would be able to disentangle a central story from the surrounding context of shamanism, careerism, rhetoric, mimicry, and self-parody. We would have as well a redefinition of the genre. For the good work has shown all over again that poetry is always at least linearity, whatever else may be going on. A poem can do without a story or an identifiable speaker or even an image—much less a pattern of images. But it cannot do without a line. Even a one-word poem presumes a line to determine how that word will be heard. What a poem does at a minimum is enact this necessity. The news is how.

Practitioners as well as critics, though, have had difficulty finding an appropriate explanatory language for this dimension of poetry. "Modernism" began in a self-conscious rejection of the iamb and the rest of the metrical inheritance that seemed to go with it. But from that reaction to the present, the movement has never quite settled on an alternative set of terms for the rhythmic experiences it has sought and sometimes found. The various justifications successively proposed have often seemed inaccurate almost as soon as they were issued. Manifestos rarely count as thought, in any context. William Carlos Williams, for instance, had considerable difficulty explaining his own "variable foot" to himself or others. His epistemology could not explain his practice. For Elder Olson, another veteran with a strong effect on his many "sons," the line was a unit of breath. But a physiological explanation is really an unconfessed metaphor—which as such needs to be translated to make critical sense. Nobody has quite known what they were doing, except imitating each other, even when in fact they were doing it; as now and then (it is luckily possible to say) has indeed happened.[10]

Rhythm is more than meter as soon as it becomes actual. But all we can *know* of this or that rhythm is still a meter of some kind, as my argument like any other must presume. And if we do not quite know what there is to be known, practice will

---

[10] Paul Ramsey's article "William Carlos Williams as Metrist: Theory and Practice," *Journal of Modern Literature* 1/4 (May 1971): 578-92, simultaneously confirms the poet's inadequacies as an explainer of his own practice and exhibits the difficulty inquiries have faced in discussing these matters without falling into crankishness. I should guess that the strong influence of Charles Olson's midcentury manifesto *Projective Verse* (New York: Totem, 1959) was due less to his theory of meter than the character of his prose. Poetry, he affirms, must "get on with it, keep moving, keep in, speed, the nerves, their speed, the perceptions, theirs, the acts, the split second acts, the whole business, keep it moving as fast as you can, citizen" (4). Such exhortations already fall easily into lines defined by groups of stresses.

in proportion be divorced from criticism, or try to make do with bits and pieces of pseudocriticism, as has in fact occurred. In the absence of intelligence though practice has a way of becoming first a habit and then, as this becomes socialized, one more convention. By now the spontaneities of the original movement can seem to have turned into a new version of the "genteel" tradition, as widespread and debilitating as the state of affairs against which the first Modernists began by rebelling. The unspecifiable superfluity of the all too writable but quite unreadable poetry produced by our "creative writing" industry overwhelms all but the instincts of a few survivors. Mindlessness, at first a polemical clearing of the ground, has itself become institutionalized, and literary history as well as incipient ambition is baffled in proportion. But the evidence for a juster view of the situation does exist and may yet be responded to, though we do not know by whom.

One would not need to claim that the recovery of rhythm was or could remain a solution to every poetic problem. But on the basis of the successful moments, we could be reminded at least that a poem might indeed become the free motion of an imagined body—in words. The characteristic fault of "traditional" poetry might then be defined retroactively as an absence of motion. A body of sorts might still be present—the several forms of stanza and genre were means to demonstrate just that—but too often, an antagonist could object, the body therein composed did not move. But now that another generation has passed, it is also possible to detect a corresponding omission in the countermovement. In "contemporary" poetry, motion is free indeed—but too often no body is present. A hostile observer could say even in response to the best of what has so far been accomplished in this kind that it still represents too much of an abstraction from an ideal whole, the substance of which has in the meantime evaporated. One may recall a slogan Ezra Pound could find in Fenellosa long ago: "things in motion, motion in things."[11] The blood and the flesh of even the body of Adam should, after all, go together, in or out of any symbolic order.

Theoretical

Metaphor has long seemed the trope of tropes, or key to all the other figures, and so an obvious focus for critical attention, admiring or suspicious. And the key to metaphor is evidently bodiliness, which is what "tenor" and "vehicle" would have in common. Metaphor, we could then say, is the coincidence of bodies in combat or desire now revealed as a mystery of language as well. No one of the bodies thereby brought together could be the body indeed on its own but in their conjunction, being-in-general might still be indirectly apprehended. We must realize

---

[11]The formula occurs in a sentence of Ernest Fenellosa's legendary "Essay on the Chinese Written Character," published in *Instigations of Ezra Pound* (New York: Boni and Liveright, 1920; repr. Freeport NY: Books for Libraries, 1967) 364.

the body, it regularly seems, in a reproduction of bodies. And this, the recovery of rhythm could also show, is not a matter of meaning only. Rhythm would in fact be a species of metaphor: metaphor, as it were, in motion, where likeness recurs as a renewal of moments in time. In that case metaphor in the more limited or semantic sense would be a rhythm arrested at the singular instance; which is to say, a rhythm in which our own bodies are not yet engaged. To appreciate such likenesses between the modes of likeness would then amount to an experience of metaphor to the second degree.

Hereabouts would lurk the radical pleasures of art, as when elements abruptly combine that no one had thought to bring together but which turn out to rhyme after all, thereby testifying to a secret whole adumbrated in the form they share. At a concert to exhibit the resources of a newly reconstructed harpsichord, some Bach and Scarlatti were played, as might be expected. This was pleasant enough, but no surprise. Then, for an encore to the scheduled program, the performer played two pieces by Scott Joplin, including the tune everybody knows. The audience, that polite assembly (and what is more decorous than a musical gathering at a university?) laughed aloud in recognition and relief. Here was the Real Thing at last, and who could have hoped for it? For this careful "reproduction" of a baroque instrument and the ragtime music went perfectly together. Centuries, continents, and cultures were reconciled at last. We felt joy, and our own bodies bobbed, taking part in the sudden festival. For our flesh too was now a part in this unexpected whole, whatever else it consisted of. The body is contagious, and rhythm is that contagion. For a moment it was heaven on earth. So much even the arts can occasionally provide.

But the message conveyed would go deeper than what we usually call art, or art itself could not ring true. Nor would the most vivid instances necessarily be decorous, public, or pleasurable. When the dentist levered that upper back tooth out of its place in my jaw, I heard through my bones a snapping, crackling sound, like a limb being torn from its trunk. As animals, I could think, we are still like vegetables, and vice versa. The impression, or the similitude into which I translated it, seemed to testify to a corresponding unity in the nature of things. And would not all metaphors do the like, in proportion? In that case phenomena would already be pneumena, as it were, in incognito, which the sudden intercourse of any two contexts might abruptly reveal. The differences between this and that, or any two sets of either, would then count as variations in the flesh only. Difference is mortal; unity, we are thus prepared to think, eternal. Likeness shows one as the other. Metaphor, in other words, is metaphoric.

A physicist of my university named Michael Feigenbaum has been in the news recently for having discovered how to make mathematical sense of the rate at which closed systems break down into unpredictable chaos.[12] The dispersal of clouds and

---

[12] A current general book on the topic is James Gleik's popular *Chaos: Making a New*

the splatter of water falling on rocks have been offered as familiar instances of the problem. Would not metaphor too feel most typical and therefore most effectual when it worked to rescue or reconstitute some event on the verge of disintegration, so as to restore what was just then being lost as still bodily after all—though in another kind? Gazing at the strew of leaves fallen upon the path by the lake, I could recall, not for the first time, the term Hopkins once used for this product of the dying year: *leafmeal.* And that in turn reminded me of another word which had once occurred to me for the surface of a lake on such gray days in late autumn, when the water is lightly ruffled by the wind. *Pewter,* I had thought: such a literally incomprehensible surface is like soft hammered metal. So one reorders what is already a chaos to the eye into a newly apprehensible coherence of another kind. In such ways we create new wholes as the old decay, and then, by what may still be called a process of "association," move from one to the next, indefinitely. To live is to keep moving: to "imitate" life is to reproduce this motion. Behind that moment at which ragtime recurred upon a harpsichord were all the dis-integrations of time, which had long since dissipated whole worlds of musical practice, courtly or popular, as well as the accompanying contrivances of wood and metal, or fingers and feet, or mind and feeling. Chaos is decomposition—to which the only answer, except for the sheer love of death, is recomposition— which within the symbolic order means in some new set of terms. Each metaphoric act amounts to a miniature leap of faith. For which of us, still caught inside our own body, could ever expect another, except in faith?

The imagination practices, we might then say, a repeated resurrection—though still according to the flesh. We recreate as art what must already have confessed its mortality, or we should not need to "bring it back to life." Or be able to. Art does not replace religion, then, though that assumption has sometimes been made, but anticipates or recollects the work of the Spirit before or after the moment of revelation. So the individual work of art might be defined more carefully as two-thirds of a sacrament in form, as it is still one-half of a sacrament in content. For it has arrived at a symbolic rendering of whatever has already preceded its own possibility, while not yet incorporating its proper meaning, which would have to be one with the community that should discover what this was. It reproduces the past in the present, then, but cannot yet enter the future. With respect to content too, a work of imagination is still psychic, not pneumatic. But these deficits may also be understood as alternate modes of the same absence: for God is, precisely, the whole of the future.

All the same, art can show what resurrection is *like,* which, given the metaphoric mode both share, should be enough for the time being. Works of imagination can thus become the "testament" of a modernity otherwise inclined to settle for a merely

---

Science (New York: Viking, 1987). Gleik's own instances include the movements of cigarette smoke, the snapping of a flag, a dripping faucet, or the flow of oil in a pipe (5).

secular textuality, quite in the old style of typology or before that of *haggada*. Poetry is not the body of Christ but of Adam, we have repeated—and in words, not flesh (though words as flesh). But even so it can still typify what might in the end be meant by an entirely disalienated discourse, in which matter and form, past and present, tenor and vehicle were reconciled at last. All good poems, we know, are more or less elegaic. For the truth of the flesh is sad. But a good poem is none the worse for this fatality. The loss it reports, sometimes in advance, is after all restored for exactly the moment of our rehearsal of it. To be sure, that advantage is true only of good poems. But the other kind do not contribute to the definition.

Metaphor though has acquired rather a bad name of late among literary critics. The disposition to undo this trope into its allegorical or ideological constituents may be understood to have begun in what would now be called a "critique" of a doctrine that had once seemed indispensable to a previous generation. This was the belief that at least one metaphor was central to the very possibility of art, in or out of language—that by which any "work" would ideally at least need to be realized as a whole composed of coherent if conflicting parts so as to form an "organic" entity in its own independent right: a body, that is, though the obvious presupposition was sometimes forgotten. This article of faith, regulated for the classroom and the journal article alike as the New Criticism, had its immediate origins in the practice and propaganda of the first Modernist generation as these became conventionalized among successor authorities.[13] Behind such immediate beginnings, historians of the topic could in due course show, would be not just the French Symbolists or even the retrospectively reinterpretable Jacobeans and Metaphysicals but the explicit recommendations of Coleridge. His theory that the imagination accomplishes a "reconciliation" of "opposites" in a new and "vital" unity would once again display the merism as a crucial formula for that faculty indeed.[14] And behind him in turn,

---

[13]I. A. Richards, *The Philosophy of Rhetoric* (New York: Oxford University Press, 1936); M. C. Beardsley, *Aesthetics* (New York: Harcourt, 1958); W. K. Wimsatt, *The Verbal Icon* (Lexington KY: University Press of Kentucky, 1954); and perhaps P. Wheelwright, *Metaphor and Reality* (Bloomington: Indiana University Press, 1962), were memorably influential texts. Other names associated with the "classic" period include Auerbach, Barfield, Brooke-Rose, Burnshaw, Ransom, Sewell, and Wilder. Meanwhile Cleanth Brooks's *Understanding Poetry* (New York: Holt, 1938) and "Wellek and Warren," or those authors' *Theory of Literature* (New York: Harcourt, 1949), had communicated the doctrine among undergraduates and graduate students respectively. The era might be thought of metaphorically and therefore ironically as coming to an end with Barbara Herrnstein Smith's admirable *Poetic Closure* (Chicago: University of Chicago Press, 1968), which examined how poems conclude, that is, are released as bodies, thereby confirming their "integrity."

[14]The often-repeated definition of the typical poem as a "balance . . . of . . . discordant qualities" and of the imagination as that which "dissolves, diffuses, dissipates, in order to re-create" may be found at 2:16-17 and 1:304 respectively of the new standard edition of the *Biographia Literaria* (Princeton: Princeton University Press, 1983). The history of "polarity-

it has since become easier to realize, would also be Kant's isolation of the "aesthetic" as a category of experience to be held apart from knowledge or judgment, and so safe from either scientific or political reductions.

The attribution of the "organic metaphor" to works of literature, then, and so the disposition to accept these as imaginative bodies, would in the first place have been responsive to a cultural need for a symbolic bodiliness otherwise dismissed from modern modes of knowing and judging, which seemed to exclude it on principle. The "sphere" of the aesthetic could apparently provide a way to make at least a few representative bodies accessible to the imagination if not any longer to the mind or conscience. Such spectral entities would in this way take the place of the spiritual body as that might once have seemed accessible either in the Eucharist or in the Church—and therefore more obviously of the traditional but already discredited successor of both, the king and his "body politic." The arts might still be allowed, that is, to supply for the West what Christianity and the ancien régime alike had apparently failed to provide.

If so, a convenient way to summarize the difference between what has more recently become the old "new" criticism and the various theoretical mutations that have succeeded to its authority within "the humanities" would be to detect in all these latter-day modes of explanation a more or less systematic rejection of just this metaphor. "Deconstruction" might accordingly be understood historically as a completion of the long modern revolution. Once society ceases to be realized as a body, one finds oneself in the modern world. And once a work of art ceases to be experienced as a body, it loses its (metaphoric) integrity as an independent species of being. What is left in the absence of any such imaginable whole are so many disassociated and mutually disassociating figures in a verbal chaos without boundaries or predictable structure. The several epithets expressive of the condition subject to disassembly within the work of this school, essence, centricity, voice, propriety, presence, and the rest would then join "form" and "aura" as no more than "traces" of a lost body, natural or personal. But without bodiliness the individual "work" inevitably disintegrates into its constituent elements, each of which may be realized as it were chemically or mechanically but no longer imaginatively.

Nor would the particular metaphor which had for so long defined the apparent nature of a work of art be the only object of suspicion, though in practice it has

---

thinking" from Heraclitus through the German philosophers who influenced Coleridge is traced in Thomas McFarland's influential "A Complex Dialogue . . . " collected in *Reading Coleridge* (Ithaca: Cornell University Press, 1979) 56-115. The interplay between Romantic and Modern organicism and more recent anatomies of both is traced in this volume and in Christiana Gallant's collection *Coleridge's Theory of Imagination Today* (New York: AMS Press, 1989). The inheritance from Kant might also be followed through Goethe to Cassirer and—in still-rememberable times—Suzanne Langer, whose morphology of the imagination helped to reinforce the influence deriving more directly from Coleridge among Anglo-American critics.

functioned as the type of the rest. "Theory" has found itself obliged to adopt a critical attitude toward metaphor in general wherever it appears. Jacques Derrida's "White Mythology," for instance, a canonical text within this explicitly anticanonical sequence, attacks the view that metaphor should be understood as central to language, and so a source for metaphysics, on the ground that this presupposes that language is essentially a semantic process, in which names are reproductions of things. He proposes syntax instead as the key feature: sheer sequence should be understood as dominant, not representation. A looser and more recent example would be the disposition mobilized in another authoritative text of the movement, Paul De Man's *Allegories of Reading*, which variously seeks to reduce whatever metaphors may be encountered in the texts examined to their metonymic equivalents. Metamorphosis can thus be replaced by juxtaposition, which as such need not imply anything but more of the same in an indefinite and centerless proliferation.[15] No wonder the earlier phases of this intellectual reaction have themselves been followed by a succession of subsequent methods that under one heading or another have sought to move beyond the limits of any "literal" text into the social structures of production, comprehension, and expectation that implicitly determine these. If there is no body, there need be no boundary to the molecular interactions that can be followed. The multiverse of textuality would extend in all directions without horizon.

While literary criticism has been turning deliberately or automatically against metaphor and what had come to seem the aesthetic and political presuppositions associated with this trope, philosophy has during approximately the same period acquired a new and unpredictable interest in its potential value. For in this academic context the traditional prejudice has run the other way since Locke if not Descartes. The literal has regularly been privileged as a goal or standard for all relevant discourse, and figurative behavior remained under suspicion as ornamental if not deceptive.[16] But the immediate legacy of logical positivism left some practitioners skeptical of this bias, which prompted a reexamination of the epistemic function of metaphor, verbal or conceptual. The hope grew that it might be possible to legiti-

---

[15] Jacques Derrida's "White Mythology" appears most conveniently in *Margins of Philosophy* (Chicago: University of Chicago Press, 1982) 209-71. *Allegories of Reading* (New Haven: Yale University Press, 1979) is Paul De Man's second and least-obscure collection. Other names might be listed, but these will suffice to represent what has survived through death and scandal of the "orthodox" tradition. The contrast between metaphor and metonymy had long since been put into play by Roman Jakobson in his seminal essay "Two Aspects of Language," republished in *Fundamentals of Language* (The Hague: Mouton, 1956; rev. ed., 1971), and has been repeated in a number of modish contexts. The concomitant revaluation of allegory may conveniently be dated from Angus Fletcher's *Allegory: The Theory of a Symbolic Mode* (Ithaca NY: Cornell University Press, 1964).

[16] The distinction between the literal and the metaphoric as such seems to have been established by Aristotle. See G. E. R. Lloyd, *The Revolutions of Wisdom* (Berkeley: University of California Press, 1987) 172-214.

mate what had come to seem an inevitable strategy from within a continuing allegiance to the hegemony of cognition in general, which the success of science showed need not as such be doubted.

Here an appropriate sequence of names would begin with Max Black, whose initial article on the subject has regularly been taken to have initiated the current discussion. This piece distributes the possible perspectives on the matter under three headings. The *substitution* theory understands metaphor as taking the place of some literal proposition that could with an effort be made to replace it. The *comparison* view similarly presumes that a metaphor might be translated into an equivalent analogy or comparison. The *interaction* theory, which Black favors, proposes that metaphor "organizes" our knowledge by bringing to bear what we already know of the means through which we perceive whatever it is. One may observe that this explanation, like the two rejected, would still presume that a metaphor should be understood in terms of its contribution to understanding. It leaves the object to be realized as primary whether this has yet become known or not, and so leaves it essentially unchanged by the language mobilized to make at least introductory sense of it. We are still some distance from what could properly be called a reproductive view—if "view" would itself be the right metaphor for such a possibility.[17]

The discussion since would include such names as Goodman, Davidson, Ortony, Ricoeur, and more recently (and as it were intraprofessionally) Kittay or Soskice. Nelson Goodman's vigorous and engaging *The Languages of Art* has expanded the scope of the relevant instances to include such symbolic "systems" as dance notation and pressure gauges. Metaphor within and without these contexts becomes an inventive if still denotative transfer from "schema" to schema.[18] Donald Davidson has as regularly represented a counter-attack from an unreconstructed literalism: metaphor means only what it says.[19] Paul Ricoeur's *Rule of Metaphor* recapitulates a variety of thoughts upon the topic from Aristotle to Derrida from a perspective descending through the Continental as opposed to the analytic tradition. He too finds it difficult to formulate how metaphor might be understood to refer, though anxious like most participants to defend that possibility: what metaphor "creates, it discovers; and what it finds, it invents."[20] Thus it sketches, he proposes, so much of active being as has not yet become conceptual. If this formulation may appear too vague to be much help, the corresponding efforts among more technically

---

[17]Black's truly seminal essay appears as "Metaphor" in *Models and Metaphors* (Ithaca NY: Cornell University Press, 1962) 25-47. A subsequent article, "More about Metaphor," *Dialectica* 31/3-4 (1977): 431-51, has also more than once been reprinted. Black's terms "model" and "metaphor" reappear frequently in subsequent discussion.

[18]Nelson Goodman, *The Languages of Art* (Indianapolis: Hackett, 1976).

[19]Donald Davidson, "What Metaphors Mean," *Critical Inquiry* 5/1 (1978): 31-47. This essay, also often reprinted, has served as a useful antagonist for subsequent competitors. The remainder of this special issue is also devoted to the topic.

[20]Paul Ricoeur, *The Rule of Metaphor* (Toronto: University of Toronto Press, 1977) 239.

oriented members of the profession do not seem to me to supply better alternatives. Kittay's "perspectival" view or Soskice's emphasis on the "reality depicting" power of metaphor are for a reader outside the limits of the perhaps unavoidably self-complicating professional discourse scarcely more exact or promising.[21]

Most recent philosophical rehearsals of the problem, one finds oneself repeating, have not surprisingly maintained the allegiance to cognitivism that might be expected of this discipline. If, though, metaphor must be justified by its mediatorial potential within an epistemic structure already determined by a disembodied mind over against a correspondingly inert object, it can scarcely provide anything grander than "epistemic access," in my colleague Richard Boyd's convenient phrase, however indispensable this resource may prove in practice.[22] The professional bias of philosophers, like the shift upward into semiotics among literary critics, has continued to keep the language of explanation at some distance from the body. And without at least a gesture in that direction, metaphor seems bound to remain inexplicable indefinitely.[23]

Mark Johnson though does offer a startling alternative. His *Body in Mind* argues against the prevailing "objectivism" that our comprehension of the world is in fact governed by precognitive "image schemata" that sublimate what begins in physical responses as abstract concepts. A category, he observes, would need to be understood as fundamentally a *container*. What appears as logical consequence is in fact a species of *compulsion*. Numerical or moral equality is similarly based on the experience of *balance*. Other "schemata" include *in/out, from/to, front/back,* and the relation of a center to its periphery. The imagination, that is, should be understood as translating the ways in which a natural body encounters its environment into the grammar by means of which a mind comes to know its objects. This approach turns upside down the usual relation between the cognitive and the "physical," and therefore knowledge and metaphor: the higher faculty would be exposed as no longer the master of the lower but merely a sublimination of it in

---

[21] E. F. Kittay, *Metaphor: Its Cognitive Force and Linguistic Structure* (Oxford: Clarendon, 1987); and J. M. Soskice, *Metaphor and Religious Language* (Oxford: Clarendon, 1985). Both these studies, though reported here as disappointing, can be read as useful surveys of the discussion to date. Other names prominent in the recent renewal of interest in this topic would include Berggren, Casey, Cooper, Fogelin, Gumpel, Levin, and MacCormac.

[22] Richard Boyd, "Metaphor and Theory Change: What Is 'Metaphor' a Metaphor For?" in *Metaphor and Thought,* ed. Andrew Orotony (Cambridge: Cambridge University Press, 1979) 356-408.

[23] W. J. T. Mitchell's *Iconology: Image, Text, Ideology* (Chicago: University of Chicago Press, 1986), for instance, another recent survey of both the philosophical and the critical territories, reviews current ideas of and judgments between images, idols, icons, fetishes, commodities, figures, auras, and hieroglyphs—all without referring to bodies at all. A painfully contemporary need to privilege convention over nature makes any allusion of the kind inadmissible in advance.

what amounts to a minor key. Such a resomatized epistemology would make metaphor not just constitutive rather than introductory or rhetorical but absolutely original: the trope would in every case already be grounded in the body, however remote the derivatives and repetitions. It seems not just incidentally appropriate that Johnson should in the course of his presentation appeal to Kant, thereby linking the case he would make with a major source for the corresponding literary tradition. One weakness does already show itself nearer the surface of his case: it is still the body of the singular subject that is presumed as fundamental. The complementary body of the other does not yet appear; though allowing for just this possibility would help, I think, to avoid an imputation of solipsism to which this otherwise exceptionally attractive argument seems exposed.[24]

For duality does seem intrinsic to any unconstrained experience of bodiliness, whether within any singular instance or between some "self" and its other. Left/right, up/down, front/back, center/circumference, and toward/away would then be inward specifications of this familiar somatic principle, as male/female, or protagonist/antagonist, and prey/predator would illustrate outwardly. In imaginary space we may enfigure this fatality as a species of intercourse, whether in love or war. In imaginary time the same duality would become a succession of replacements: the beginning, that is, of rhythm. In nature the bodies in question may be of the same or different kinds. I may copulate or contest with members of my own species, but must eat or be eaten by those of others. Metaphor would be another such mixed relation, in which a natural and a symbolic body would associate in either a conjunctive or successive mode. If these must balance from the beginning, one need not privilege either the "tenor" pole of the relation, as the old New Criticism once demanded, or the "vehicle," as a philosophical somaticism might require. In metaphor the two bodies concerned are equally "interactive," as in the erotic and combative contexts. So in Eudora Welty's paragraph the word *spoon* unites moons and mouths, and *warbling* in Seamus Heaney's poem refers back to birds as well as forward to armies. Creativity, as Arthur Koestler once put it, may regularly be understood as a "bisociation" of two otherwise incongruous "matrices" of experience. Metaphor would in that case be intrinsic to all modes of problem

---

[24]Mark Johnson, *The Body in the Mind: The Bodily Basis of Meaning, Imagination, and Reason* (Chicago: University of Chicago Press, 1987). Johnson has also assembled a collection of articles, *Philosophical Perspectives on Metaphor* (Minneapolis: University of Minnesota Press, 1981), and collaborated with George Lakoff on *Metaphors We Live By* (Chicago: University of Chicago Press, 1980), a popular survey of the metaphoricity of everyday life. Lakoff's own *Women, Fire, and Dangerous Things: What Categories Reveal about the Mind* (Chicago: Chicago University Press, 1987) could seem overwhelmed by the language of cognitive science, though it too intends to carry on the campaign against "objectivism." His *More Than Cool Reason* (Chicago: University of Chicago Press, 1989), with Mark Turner, or Eve Sweetser's *From Etymology to Pragmatics* (Cambridge: Cambridge University Press, 1990), would indicate that the filiation continues.

solving, animal as well as human, imaginative and scientific alike.[25] For the contexts combined need not be officially cultural nor their conjunction strenuous. Intercourse is already metaphoric at the level of such "cross-modal equivalences" as allow us to realize, for instance, that what we see is the same thing as what we touch. And analogous reassurances arise from equivalently elementary relations between one body and another. Mothers, it has been observed, need not be taught how to converse with their infants by "attuning" their responses to whatever the child is doing, echoing the form and intensity of this activity in balancing gestures or words, as when a baby bangs its hand on a toy rhythmically and its mother repeats "kaaaaa*bam*" over and over to correspond.[26] We come together to realize who as well as where we are, and therefore what we are doing.

If there is still a latent difference between one pole of a explicit metaphor and the other, it would seem to consist not just of a contrast of kinds but between degrees of being. In front of the gas station at the Corners stands what I have more than once seen as a foolish spaniel, sitting with ears cocked in the driveway. As I drive closer, I realize each time that this is not a dog but a stump, black and white because from a birch tree. What is the difference between the possible identification and the actual? For one thing all the features of the scene cohere, none remaining inconsistent with the sudden conviction that this *is* a stump and not a dog, though it had indeed "looked like" a dog before, and might again. In that case "stump" could seem literal, and "dog" metaphoric. To be sure, one could on second thought reply that "stump" too is a metaphor, only now so appropriate we no longer recognize it as such. But on third thought the mistaken attribution still seems worth attending to. Something in me evidently wished or feared or merely expected that the entity in question would prove a dog. There was an element of disappointment as well as reassurance in the discovery that it was only a stump after all. That is a less interesting form or quantity of being. I suspect this disposition is general: we project upon the unknown as high a degree of existence as the circumstances will bear. Metaphor would then be heuristic in a double sense: not only as an effort provisional or successful to realize the nature of something alien but, as a concomitant of just this endeavor, an anticipation of as much as one could ever hope or fear. Metaphor is eschatological, we have already suggested, in tendency if not quite in effect. We prefigure more than we come out with, or begin as.

If we are moving toward more rather than less, the intercourse of bodies one with another would still be in the direction of the body indeed, whether or not we

---

[25]Arthur Koestler, *The Act of Creation* (New York: Macmillan, 1964). The general thesis at least of this cranky and encyclopedic "double" book remains alive.

[26]The example, like the terms *attunement* and *cross-modal equivalent,* I once again owe to Daniel Stern's *The Interpersonal World of the Infant* (New York: Basic Books, 1985). Stern's discussion of the metaphoric intercourse between mother and child appears on pp. 138-61.

ever got there. But this tendency need not mean that every transposition of the kind would always make most sense in the first instance, where the metamorphosis may be from a thing to a word, or the natural to the artificial, and therefore to some apparently "higher" use. The contrary shift may in fact surprise us with what turns out to be a latent potential for imaginative truth. As I walked to work a truck that must have just made a delivery passed by. On the truck's side was the usual logo as well as a supplementary message: "Here's the Beef." Some time had already passed since the question of which this would be the indicative form was in the news as a way of criticizing the lack of substance in a certain politician's claim to new ideas. In a short while, I thought, no one will remember that use, and the company will have to remove the phrase from their advertisements. But in the meanwhile it was still just viable. Beginning as a commercial complaint about the size of a patty in the hamburgers of a rival chain, the question became a metaphor, and, as it was picked up and repeated, almost an allegory. But here for one more moment at least it had returned to the original context. Beef is indeed meat, which trucks like this do in fact carry about from one place to another. This was a "second" literality, then, and so even more thoroughly metaphoric than any of the uses from which it immediately descended. Here's the beef: for us to consume as well as understand, the flesh of the flesh indeed if not yet quite the Spirit. The claim was reassuring: poetry was better off than one might have supposed.

In a postmodern age, what is left once metaphor has officially been done away with is allegory. Then the faculty that Coleridge named the "fancy" is instructed to take the place of the imagination. I once attended the opening of an exhibition at a friend's sculpture garden, thinking I might find some contemporary instances of the body as "original object." Wasn't that what sculpture was supposed to provide? But I was disappointed, though I should not have been surprised. The various entities arranged here and there on the slope overlooking the lake had the air of school projects, academic exercises intended to represent the current state of this art. And the art in question was evidently concerned not to reproduce a body, but with its own materials: steel and wood as well as stone but also unexpected "media" such as canvas or sheet metal or torn cloth. Indefinite quantities of such categories of matter were brought together to constitute some shape or combination of shapes. These seemed studiedly contrived to avoid suggesting anything in particular while alluding to a variety of other objects already familiar to the viewer: aircraft, fishing nets, slaughtered deer, or heavy machinery. The method seemed most "effective" when the materials in question ostentatiously clashed, as with a large cylinder of cheesecloth drenched in heavy vinyl. That really did seem to say something caustic about the relation between the domestic and the industrial, or the small and the immense. A comment was made, in the manner of a cartoon, upon the character of modern life.

But on the whole the show was merely depressing. "Materials," it seemed obvious, were substances that had already undergone a prior annihilation. A medium in the sense assumed was no more than so much abstract matter, the body of which had long since decomposed. This was chaos indeed, and therefore passively subject to the dominance of whatever category might be imposed. But all categories are inevitably conventional. The combination of materiality and convention is precisely what we mean by allegory, or the "art" of fancy: dead metaphor indeed. No wonder the chief value cultivated on this occasion had to be novelty, or some specious opposite of the conformity presupposed. If this sort of thing illustrated the prevalent rule, I concluded, I need not expect any surprise to emerge. For I already knew how the same game was played in other contexts.

One of these has been contemporary fiction. On my way to the library to look up a commentary on Thomas Pynchon, one of whose novels I had engaged to teach in the survey course, I passed some activities on the Arts Quad in commemoration of what was billed as "Earthrise." One of these was a huge earth-colored ball some six feet in diameter. Two young children were playing with this; a girl perhaps three years old and a smaller boy just able to stumble about. The older child was delighted to be able to push so vast a sphere and make it roll, which indeed she was doing unexpectedly well. Her little brother trotted after her or reached up to stop the ball as it rolled toward him. He would have liked to play too, but he wasn't quite big enough. Meanwhile their young parents looked on. The mother had a camera and took photographs as her daughter trundled the ball to and fro. That was her way of pushing it, as her husband's was to smile at all three, and mine to see this happening.

The episode seemed an answer in advance to the thoroughly postmodern author I was on my way to catch up with. We do not inhabit a void after all, I thought, but a world where bodies move, which it is a delight to see go. In this way at least we reproduce ourselves, who are already a reproduction, which is why the rehearsal gives us pleasure. Nor is this play an illusion, however unserious the occasion, but the solid earth in one or another of its endless modes. Balls are round for a reason, which will always suffice.

It would not follow that all works of fancy need prove insignificant, as at least one of the works in the sculpture garden had already hinted. The late Jason Seeley has acquired a certain reputation outside the boundaries of his profession and my university for his "bumper sculptures"—works of monumental art made out of old automobile bumpers welded together. The fact that such pieces of obsolete junk can be fused to compose a heroic horseman or a chair or even the "body" of a drivable car might seem only a slightly old-fashioned avant-garde joke, the repeated materialization of a single idea, almost a gimmick. But the joke does remain illustrative of something better than a fashionable cliché. These pieces take the leftover parts of one kind of thing and, without changing their physical appearance or recognizable shape, turn them into another kind of thing that may now be placed in a gallery as a work of art. The change is revealed as strictly contextual, which tells us something about the relation between utility and aesthetics in our social universe. It is sheer stuff, then, that connects the disparate regions of our culture. The bumpers are *un*changed: that is the comic point about them. A certain wry wisdom is transmitted:

Seeley's are new bodies of a sort, sufficient to occupy space in the corresponding environment. But they make use of the same old flesh. This is put in quotation marks, as it were, without losing its initial character. The previous use remains part of its current identity. A truer work, we could indirectly learn, would require the previous loss of everything—so that everything might once more be restored. Nothing less would be quite good enough for a full re-creation. These inventive constructions are not that, nor were they meant either as rebukes to or replacements for something of the kind, should it ever appear. They function, I would guess, as critiques: exposures, as it were, of the current state of affairs, technological as well as artistic, social and intellectual alike. The art of fancy would then be justifiable as a species of criticism in the mode of practice. In that case it might belong not just to fantasy or pretension or convention but to the subversion of these, like the other comic genres. It would be a prophecy, as it were, of a better understanding than has in fact celebrated it. If so, we might understand its implications a degree more securely than we usually do.

But how might one survive an excess of either fancy or criticism? An argument developed at the seminar for instructors teaching in the summer program. The topic for discussion was an article by a sufficiently modish critic who claimed that the purpose of criticism was to detect "cultural codes" in the literature it examined: sexism, for instance, in the work of Hemingway. A young Marxist in our circle made a point of showing how he could in his turn detect a code in the essay as well: "relativism" in this case. It came over me that exposing somebody else's "ideology" necessarily meant imposing one's own, which a third party could always top. Criticism would then become successive one-upmanship, terminating in an ideal totalization from which nobody would be able to escape. No wonder, I thought, that graduate students are so anxious these days. But how might this tedious process be evaded, if not by some return to the concreteness of the language from which one began, so as to feel whatever degree of bodiliness this showed: the "pleasure of the text," as one participant put the possibility in a currently acceptable terminology, or "the sensuous surface of the signifier." In that case one might even be able to realize art as a liberation from ideology, whether of the writer or the reader. If we use works of imagination only as battlegrounds for critical combat, we miss the chance to experience their power to rescue us from the very fate we would impose upon them. But there was something pious as well as old fashioned in such notions, which prevented them from seeming altogether convincing even to their entertainer.

As I walked home from this argument, I passed a portion of the road that had recently been resurfaced. Embedded in the fresh asphalt was a small stone. It is one of my habits to kick loose pebbles that give the impression of being stuck, and as I walked, I tried; but failed. The stone would not move. Nor could I pry it free with my fingers. I was annoyed but not yet willing to seem even to myself a mere victim of obsession, so I went on—thinking, though, that if I had a long spike of some sort I could knock that stone out. And half seriously I scanned the ground ahead of me in search of such an instrument. By coincidence, exactly what I had been fantasizing appeared before my eyes: a four inch nail, rusty and a little bent, but perfectly suited to the purpose. This seemed a hint it would not be merely compulsive if I were to retrace my steps. So I did, meanwhile looking out for another stone of suitable size to use as a hammer. This too was easily found, and I proceeded to where I had come across the embedded stone. There was a moment of panic when I feared I would not be able to find it again. But presently there it was. Glancing about to make sure I was unobserved, I set down my newspaper and lunch bag and addressed myself to the task. Sticking the nail in at an angle, I struck it sharply, and the stone came loose. Throwing away my hammer, I picked it up. A clot of fresh asphalt clung to its underside. As I pried this off, dark odorous stains were left on my fingers. I walked back once more on the way I had been going, debating what to do with the stone now it had been freed. Disposal of the nail presented no problem; I could drop this where I found it, perhaps for someone else to make use of. I thought of throwing my prize into the lake, but that would have meant going out of my way. The best place to deposit it, I thought, would be the creek, over which I would have to pass in any case. So when I came to the bridge, I stopped and cast it out over the rapid waters as they descended from ledge to ledge on their way to the lake. There it would be free forever. And I felt the episode had come to a satisfactory close.

Besides, there was a story to tell that I could rehearse in the first place to the psychiatrist I was then consulting for a problem I had been having with impulses of what he politely called anger. And in due course I could also repeat it in writing, first in a notebook and later in a form that somebody else might read. What was the story "about"? There seemed at least three contexts within which it might be read. The therapeutic was the easiest: I too wished to become unstuck somehow, and my concern for the stone made an appropriate allegory of this wish. But would not a "symptom" be an as yet insufficiently liberated symbol? If so, the episode could also be read as a rehearsal of the issue that had arisen at the meeting. A work of imagination, I had been arguing, must be freed from its natural or social circumstances before it can function as a symbol; but once that has begun to happen, to seek out its remaining constraints would only reattach it and so prevent its emergence into what might otherwise become its proper mode of being. A symbol should become a free body, I could think, like my stone: more than a pebble, though less than a rock, three-dimensional, solid, of a certain tangible shape and weight. And to liberate a symbol is to share in the freedom one may thereby enable it to achieve. The imagination *is* that freedom.

So a third context within which the episode might be understood could be a universalization of the first two. We can get as far as the symbolic body at least—in imagination only, but that is good enough for the time being. We are able to liberate the sign, which is the gesture of art. And any sign is meaningful, that is, full of meaning. We cannot by any effort of our own enact the whole of this import in advance. That is beyond us in the corresponding community, which therapists or readers can only approximate, and "interpretation" can do no more than outline. We are caught at the signifier, then, as the familiar saying goes. But this is not nothing, provided it too is a body of some kind. For the body in every context is a promise, which might after all be kept, if not now, then perhaps in the End.

Eschatological

The Book of Proverbs can seem the dullest in the Bible. It is hard even for scholars to maintain interest from one saying to another or from one collection of these to the next. And the relentlessly regular meter only emphasizes the banality of the content. But the character and function of these traditional maxims can help mediate between the possibility of literature as we ordinarily understand it and the art of Jesus as the Eucharist and his other words and deeds exhibit this. The Hebrew name for the book is *mishlei,* the construct plural of *mashal,* which means both "rule" and "likeness." The term accordingly covers more than the English word *proverb,* taking in within a single loose kind not only folk sayings but the verbal or acted parables of the prophets and the riddles of the sages: whatever is most concentrated, gnomic, or enigmatic within the wisdom tradition. To the degree that such teachings are cryptic, they are sure to be metaphoric as well: the saying or story proposed affirms a likeness between some phenomenon of nature or human life and the covenantal differences between understanding and folly, justice and wickedness, judgment and salvation. And by way of this tenor one might see a connection to the other root meaning of the word. The poet, one could say, is he who rules by making likenesses. Wisdom would then be to realize the truth concealed within such indirect communications, so as to take part in the nation at once addressed and created.[27]

In Proverbs a *mashal* is typically transmitted from "father" to "son": which is to say, from sage to disciple. The process is thus a literary analogue of the patrilinear transmission of identity that determines the physical survival of the people from one generation to another. Wisdom is an inheritance, like the name of the father, which at circumcision becomes the name of the son. To pass on a *mashal* from one generation to the next is accordingly to repeat it until it has been memorized or to "write it on a tablet." These alternatives make no practical difference, since the traditional oral process is really another species of "writing" too.[28] Sheer repetition has got to be textual in the nature of the case. When the scribes came to understand the Torah as a whole, or the verbal inheritance in its entirety, including the Law and

---

[27]A convenient article summarizing research on the genre as such may be found in Timothy Polk, "Paradigms, Parables, and Meshalism: On Reading the Mashal in Scripture," *CBQ* 45/4 (October 1983): 564-83.

[28]The implicit textualization of deliberate memory has been persuasively demonstrated by Birger Gerhardsson (though the argument has since provoked some objection) in his influential *Memory and Manuscript* (Uppsala: Gleerup, 1961).

Metaphoric 141

the Prophets as well as the Writings, after the model provided by the practice of wisdom in which they were trained, it became natural to think of revelation too as passed on in the same fashion from father to son. In this way the privileges and duties entailed by the covenant could be sustained on the human side of the relation through the vicissitudes of history, external or internal.

In all these respects one could appreciate the differences as well as the likenesses between the wisdom tradition in general or such a collection as Proverbs in particular and what Jesus can be seen to be doing, in or out of the Eucharist. In that action, we have claimed, he transmits his identity in the body rather than some message as a word. His art is therefore altogether instead of only allusively somatic: the fullness, as it were, of what metaphor promises in the mode of resemblance. And he stands toward his disciples not as a father to his son but as the elder to as many younger siblings, male or female, within what is in apocalyptic principle a single—and therefore the last— generation. His transfer of privilege and obligation alike need not then entail repetition as an essential feature of what is being done, however often the act itself may in fact be rehearsed, for it is always from the individual that the community receives its gift: the same individual, the same community. The remotest recipient in our indefinitely extending space and time is still as nearly related to him, and in the same way, as any of the first participants. The Church is "apostolic" not by descent but by equivalence. And what we find ourselves doing, still more obviously, is not conning a lesson but enjoying a feast.

Nevertheless, the Eucharist remains generically a *mashal,* quite as much as any maxim attributed to Solomon, that other "son of David." A definition is offered, a metaphor proposed, and a communication effected—which thereby generates the corresponding community. So Jesus' action at the Last Supper replicates the wisdom tradition in a successive as well as a contrastive sense. His is the wisdom of God, as Paul would put it, and not of man. But as Paul could also imply, the wisdom of God *is* the body of Christ.

And the same principle may be traced through the other "genres" within which the Jesus of the narrative gospels is portrayed as acting. Here may be found cures and exorcisms, parables and sayings, feedings and symbolic actions as well as a final meal. In each of these ministerial contexts a bodily event, physical or psychic or imaginative, is brought about in such a way as to bear a spiritual import. In all of them too we see a Jesus who gives himself away, virtually at random, to whoever appears upon the scene, always concretely, always meaningfully, invariably with a view to a completed community that would no longer be merely human but altogether of God. So persistent a disposition is difficult to attribute only to the several versions of the imagined character. It seems more consistent with the pervasiveness of these motifs to attribute them to the original as well as the evangelical Jesus. If so, we might reasonably judge that all his words and deeds should still be counted as *meshalim* of one sort or another. It looks as if, that is, he never did or said anything merely literal—though some of his disciples, then or since, may have wished he had, and gone on to recast his words or deeds to make them so. He rules, it might be fair to conclude, in metaphor and not otherwise. So one might say, picking up both meanings of the word, *moshel,* by parabolizing, *mashal,* he has reigned. His poetry *is* his power. But if *his* "lordship," in contrast to all the others, is indeed metaphoric in every context, then we would also be in a position to realize that the imagination need not be thought of as terminating somewhere short of the End, like the other faculties which have sometimes boasted their superiority to it. On the contrary, it would require only the appropriate *metanoia* (whatever that should consist of) to become capable of revealing the presence of God in the very midst of what was otherwise not yet changed. The imagination is the one carnal power Jesus not only allows for but makes personal use of. Eros he brackets, which has puzzled some; violence he renounces, which has annoyed others; but what *we* call art he not only does but is—in *his* sense, to be sure. We could not simply claim, like Herder or Blake in a later age, that the imagination already *is* Christ. But what long after the fact becomes a typically Romantic counterassertion could not unfairly be reversed: the messianic possibility, as Jesus enacts it, is inherently imaginative—and may be fulfilled accordingly, after one metaphoric mode or another.[29]

All of which might be realized most economically with respect to the Seed parable, which I referred to briefly in the first chapter. Mark, the most creative among the synoptics, appropriately chose this as the key to all the parables. "Lo," it begins in his version, "a sower went forth to sow. . . . " The critics have labored to distinguish what Mark or the homiletic inheritance immediately behind him might have added to the language in which this most memorable of Jesus' explicit *meshalim* was originally formed. I find myself impressed with a sequence of pieces by J. D. Crossan, which began by detecting within the clauses supplied by the evangelist's text a pattern of triads that could be identified as oral in character and so perhaps as original.[30] These would begin, Crossan proposes, in a Semitic as well as a Greek or English triple play on the verb for sowing in the introductory sentence: "A sower went forth to sow, and it happened in the *sowing*. . . . " Then would come, in his reconstruction, three results of this imagined action, each with its own verbal triplet. "Some fell by the road, and birds came, and ate it up" would be the first and least

---

[29]I owe an appropriate sense of these Romantic alternatives to James Engell's by-now-standard *Creative Imagination* (Cambridge: Harvard University Press, 1981), which follows up earlier histories of the faculty in question by Abrams and Bate. Herder and Blake are summarized on pp. 218-25 and 244-56 respectively.

[30]"The Seed Parables of Jesus," *Journal of Biblical Literature* 92/2 (June 1973): 244-66, was the first of these, which Crossan reedited for *In Parables* (New York: Harper, 1973). A more thorough review appears as the central chapter in *Cliffs of Fall* (New York: Seabury, 1980) 25-64. Other recent names in what has remained a lively specialty include Carlston, Donahue, Drury, Linnemann, McFague, Perkins, Scott, Tolbert, Weeden, Wenham, and Wilder, as well as such older authorities as Dodd, Jeremias, and Perrin. Craig Blomberg's "Interpreting the Parables of Jesus: Where Are We and Where Do We Go from Here?" *CBQ* 53/1 (January 1991): 50-78, is a convenient review of research to date.

Metaphoric 143

encumbered of these. The two sentences following have apparently attracted supplementary additions obscuring what may originally have exhibited the same structure. There has been disagreement over which clauses should be thought of as added and by whom. Initially Crossan disentangled "and some other fell on stony ground . . . and when the sun rose, it was scorched," which would throw the emphasis on the verbs. In a later review of his own reasoning, he preferred to isolate "some other fell on stony ground . . . and immediately it sprang up from not having depth of soil . . . and through not having a root, withered." This would produce a triad of nouns—in Greek as clumsy as the English. Other readers before and since have proposed additional alternatives, none to my ear absolutely convincing.[31]

A third larger unit of the same kind has been easier to extract: "and some other fell into thorns, and the thorns grew and choked it." The Marcan text supplies a fourth unit to this penultimate series, summarizing the result of all three: "and they did not give fruit." This addition seems unnecessary; of course they didn't. The real fourth unit would instead contrast with rather than summarize the previous three: "but some fell on good ground, and gave fruit . . . and bore . . . ," requiring us to bracket only the obviously supplementary "growing and strengthening" attached to the second element of what otherwise would become still another triad. And then, to complete the whole, the final verb in this fourth sequence of three would break out into a justifiably exuberant triplet to reveal the results of the action imagined: "and bore one thirty, and one sixty, and one a hundred." Once again critics have disagreed as to the meaning, agricultural or otherwise, of this divided yield, with which the other synoptics (as well as Thomas) already had trouble. But the rhythmic effect is obvious: the parable concludes in a characteristic flourish of the same style in which it began. For the art of such a *mashal* is as thoroughly kinetic as it is obviously metaphoric.

Crossan's analysis—initial, corrected, or contested—would thus allow us to see through the text of the Evangelist to a possible oral version of the parable which we could appreciate as better composed, more a whole made up of coherent parts, than what could then seem the comparatively prolix and even distracting narrative we are otherwise obliged merely to read. To the extent that we are persuaded, we would in that case be at least imaginatively in touch with a more "organic" body, the dancelike motions of which would rehearse the rhythm of folk art as well as the purpose of prophecy. Such traits would certainly be consistent with what the scholarly consensus has already been able to advance as typical of a rhetorical style we might fairly attribute to the "historical Jesus."[32] And these elements of formal

---

[31]Other possibilities for eliciting an original triad are advanced or referred to in Joel Marcus's *The Mystery of the Kingdom of God* (Atlanta: Scholars Press, 1986), which surveys research on the Seed parable in particular (19-71). His focus, though, is on Mark rather than on Jesus.

[32]A useful summary of what might amount to a portrait of Jesus as "primitive" poet may

bodiliness would also consist very well with the immediate import of the tale told, which recuperates a mode of reproduction familiar to villagers of any age: the death of one body, a seed, in order that another, the resulting plant, might, through however many successive if advancing stages of failure, grow all the way to maturity—where it could bear many new seeds in its turn.[33] Jesus' metaphors, like his origin, are very Galilean.

But we may notice too, as we shift our attention from the possible form to the hypothetical import of the parable, that if this, like the other mysterious deeds and sayings, is recognizably a work of the imagination, it must be an instance of eschatological and not this-worldly art. The Seed parable already plays upon a double valency of the image provided, overtly engaging only the agricultural import while not entirely obliterating its procreative sense. That seed, or *zerah,* is "physically" passed on from father to son and so begets the human race as a whole as descended from Adam, restored in Noah, and repeated first in a sequence of sons and then as an amphictyony with Abraham. But Jesus scatters his "seed" not in the womb of some chosen mother of a privileged descendant but at large and at random, as the sheer announcement that the promised Kingdom already obtains here and now. Such a gesture is indeed more obviously comparable to a peasant in his field than a father at work upon the task that defines him. The Seed parable thus reveals the method all the parables presume. Its content is their form. And because *this* "sowing" happens all at once, in what amounts to a single penultimate generation, no inheritance, sexual or documentary, is required. The word is now immediately oral or bodily—though still indirect. And whoever has ears to hear is always its intended recipient, male or female, Jew or Gentile, who therefore need no longer have just the right father in the flesh.

Jesus' metaphors are of the Kingdom of God. The metaphors of ordinary *meshalim,* biblical or modern, are of what we may call in New Testament language the "kingdom of men." The difference needs to be kept in mind, perhaps especially by literary critics.[34] It is most readily marked, we have already seen, in terms of time: human art reembodies the past, while the art of the eschatological agent

---

be found in the opening pages of Joachim Jeremias's *New Testament Theology* (London: SCM Press, 1971) 1:1-75. The special features identified, besides an obvious devotion to metaphor, include a preference for the "divine passive" (typical of apocalyptic as a genre); a tendency to employ antithetical parallelism; the use of two-beat, four-beat, three-beat, or three- and two-beat (*qinah*) rhythms, and frequent paranomasia for sound. In other words, Jesus is *not* prosaic.

[33] My attention was called to this implicit forward movement by John Donahue's *Gospel in Parable* (Philadelphia: Fortress, 1988) 34.

[34] Stephen Moore's *Literary Criticism and the Gospels* (New Haven: Yale University Press, 1989) offers a knowingly skeptical review of the influence recent criticism has had on New Testament studies. He recapitulates the changes in Crossan's address to the Seed parable in particular (137-46).

preembodies the future. The contest is therefore for possession of the present as a sign, for that is when all signs signify. The question is, In what direction? What Jesus is showing, then, is that a sowing of the *spiritual*—which is to say the futural—seed can in fact be done even now in the midst of things as they still are by someone who gives himself over to just that task.[35] And we have already seen him sowing one or another variety of this grain in Mark's own narrative, chiefly up to this point in the form of cures and exorcisms. God's Kingdom, we have learned at the beginning of this version of the story, is "near." So whatever is done in such a way as to amount to a demonstration in other terms of what is accomplished parabolically in the scattering of the seed will show as much. The fullness of that kingdom has not yet "come," either in Jesus' day, or when Mark's work was composed, or when that in turn can be taken apart again by a contemporary critic. For the completion of God's reign would have to be equivalent to the harvest promised in the conclusion to the parable. But however discouraging the task on which he was embarked, we could imagine Jesus as "saying" to himself and us, he remained confident that his work would indeed bear fruit in the End—though still another kind of seed might have to be sown first.

If so, we would also have a way to reunderstand the explanation of the Seed parable, which is offered in Mark immediately following its presentation. When he was alone, the story continues, Jesus' disciples asked him what this (and the other) parables meant. The secret of the Kingdom, Jesus replies, is given to you, but not to those outside, who can only hear a *mashal* as *in*comprehensible. And he explains to these insiders that "what the sower is sowing is the word," so the various categories of soil correspond to different kinds of unresponsive listeners: the inattentive, the over-enthusiastic, and the worldly. Those who "bear fruit" would then be those who hear the word and put it into practice. Their "harvest" would consist of their good deeds. This explicitly allegorical explanation is evidently cast in terms of the Christian preacher and his congregation rather than Jesus and either the crowd or the disciples. It has therefore been understood as a matter of course among the critics that it must derive from the tradition rather than the source, though Mark has installed it in a place of honor, thus illustrating his own typical concern with explanation in general as that may follow from in order to reinterpret the enigmas of the initial deliverance. His own text as a "gospel," it is fair to say, amounts to an explanation at length of Jesus' parabolic presence.

But it would not be enough merely to identify the generic limits of the interpretation as contrasted with the original "poem," useful as this may be. What any mode of interpretation, ecclesial or Marcan or critical, would eventually need to take into account is the premise on which the original is based. And if this is

---

[35]The eschatological possibility is precisely what Crossan's recent *Dark Interval* (Sonoma CA: Polebridge Press, 1988) denies: the parables, according to this version of his ongoing argument, subvert this world without embodying the other.

indeed eschatological, then *any* translation of its metaphoric burden into this-worldly terms, didactic or theological, would be at best anticipatory and at worst obstructive. For in the End the parable would have to be "interpreted" not by any human being of whichever generation but only by God. The image of the harvest would be exchanged for the truth it prophesies at *that* moment—and not one instant sooner. A truly eschatological parable, whether verbal or practical, could not by definition be properly construed except by the arrival of the completion it enfigures. Jesus' art is therefore in principle *in*comprehensible. It cannot ever be got the better of either morally or intellectually. It can only be entered into, so that we too might become a part of the parable as well as explainers of it. And that has presumably been the point of rehearsing it ever since.

Such a hermeneutic condition would hold even more acutely for the Eucharist, the true *mashal* of all *meshalim,* and so the type not just of the explicit parables (which the Seed parable might otherwise remain) but every other demonstrative word and deed as well, and so of the very possibility that there could ever be such a thing as an eschatological as well as a worldly deployment of what we would still want to call the imagination. The most obvious differences between this central action and any carnal work of art, however otherwise successful or even canonical, will serve to point the contrast. In our world a work of imagination begins in a certain indistinct coalescence of experience and desire. This antecedent matter, however indispensable, is scarcely coincident with the whole being of the imaginer in question. Nor is that self ordinarily "inspired" in its own view or that of anybody else. Whatever it may consist of, the matrix in question is duly reconstructed as so many words, forms, or substances that as such are alien to it. The result, as we have seen, may indeed become an embodiment of sorts—but by no means of its originator as a whole, who usually survives to live and very likely compose again some other day. And the third moment amounts to still another concatenation of circumstances. The book, let us suppose, either is or is not read: in any case it is one of many like itself. For a brief while, perhaps, it is commented on; in a few cases, it becomes a "classic," which is to say, it is rehearsed for those not yet interested in the classroom. The community toward which it looks forward and which, if that came into being, would become its meaning has to be represented by the occasional individual for whom it may prove formative. And what is this person likely to do? Write another book.

In all these ways the ordinary work of the imagination exhibits by contrast the exceptionality of Jesus' accomplishment. The whole of him, we have proposed, including his endowment by God, is reproduced without remainder in a new whole composed by the polarity established. The eucharistic act is Jesus' autobiography—though in a most thoroughly altered sense of *autos, bios,* and *graphe* alike. So *his* final "poem" can afford to be utterly identical with himself, as is, ideally, the community that receives it. If there is still a gap, it is obviously at this end of the trajectory. Israel is not yet fully herself. But that is not his fault. In the flesh, difference rules over all three moments of the creative process. My poem is not myself, nor are you who read it one in being with it, as you are surely relieved to realize. But in his case authorship, work, and audience remain the same: to begin with in practice, and even to end with in principle. Form confirms content. There is only one body, throughout.

And in order to convey as much, he must clear away the intervening space. This makes sense: the first necessity for any artist in such a kind would have to be to disalienate and so disestablish all merely human symbols on this side of the relation with God. One would need to reappropriate whatever had become displaced onto other creatures, and so into the temple, where these were sacrificed, or for that matter upon the text, which continued to repeat all the other obligations. The entire structure of reality would need to be consumed in the consent of a single individual. The effect within the order of signs, and so for the imagination in general, is to leave the power of representation altogether on the other side of the relation. Metaphoricity as such, that is, has been moved from here to there, out of this world and into the world to come, once and for all.

If we may understand Jesus as appropriating his world by abandoning himself so that the eschatological sign might come, as it were, altogether into its own, we might also as an incidental consequence appreciate why the "historical Jesus" is so apparently uninteresting to the historical Jesus. For he gives himself over to the symbol and therefore to the community that might turn into its meaning so entirely there is nothing left over for any other obvious record or monument—even, the story goes, a dead body. To seek out some idea of what Jesus was like before he did precisely this would contradict the implicit intention. The result must inevitably remain a retrospective hypothesis, the content of which has got to be more or less imaginary—in our terms, that is, rather than his.

What we can have instead is evidently the constant suggestion made by the example provided. And if the art of God must always be some anamnesis or recapitulation of just this action, then any full reproduction of it, ritual or ethical, would need to include what is already presupposed to begin with: the oblation of the individual—not just *this* individual, but any and each instance of that species, wherever and whenever he or she might appear upon the scene. The presence of the sign or the community, or more exactly the community as a sign, would then regularly entail just such a personal appropriation as a condition for the legitimacy and efficacy of what might thereby become reproducible yet once more. The flesh reveals the Spirit on just these terms. The art of God is indeed a reproduction of the whole, and the whole always includes ourselves, but upon this condition—which it may take some time to feel the force of in one's own case.

This necessity would be the grim news within the communication effected, or rather just previous to its emergence as a communication. The symbol is liberated to mean what it "says" at the cost of life, we could conclude, his or that of anyone else who comes along: but then it is indeed free to accomplish its transhistorical task, a part of which is to convey not just the content but the form of the message.

What Jesus hands over, that is, includes his own parabolicity.[36] Just as he begins as a parable of the Kingdom, or its presence on the scale of an individual, so he keeps that possibility alive by transmitting this power of eschatological representation. The absolutely typical parable includes the authority to create other parables of the same kind: even to become parabolic, like him. The Eucharist would then amount, we could say, to his "Directive," or "Supreme Fiction," or "Four Quartets"; a last will and testament of himself as poet. What John's gospel must imagine retrospectively as a long final speech, Jesus has in fact already provided in a simpler, indeed virtually a wordless form. For the propositions enunciated, however indispensable, are essentially rubrics. They are not the message but its anticipatory explanation. They frame what is conveyed, which must occur for us in the midst of an implicit silence. That, after all, is how a *mystērion* should be communicated.

But the sheer fact that such a parable, or such parables, or such parabolicity, is somehow abroad even in the midst of what we must still call this world might also suggest that metaphor as such, given its susceptibility to such an extraordinary use, may already be incipiently eschatological wherever it appears, in or out of apparently "secular" poetry, found or formal. In that case any natural thing or event, the parable of the Seed in particular might imply, could just as it exists, or rather just as it is realized to exist, supply a more or less adequate symbol for the Kingdom indeed. In which case too it would not be merely interesting that Jesus happened to use metaphor, as if he might have chosen some other trope, if such existed, or none at all. Nor would the point be simply that his special calling required such a manner of communication, though we know this is true too—as if the rest of us might get by with other rhetorical means for our profane purposes. It is rather that by acting as we seem to see him doing, he "baptizes" metaphor in general. We could learn accordingly not only that the Kingdom of God is perpetually present to some extent in this or the like specific (if apparently exceptional) fashion, but that all things are similarly suspended at what amounts to the like distance from their eventual completion. If the Kingdom may even now be accessible at least in metaphor, then wherever metaphor may be found, the Kingdom should indeed be present—in proportion. And where is there *not* some degree of metaphor, even in the language of those who have gone furthest out of their way to do away with the possibility? Like the Kingdom, and for the same reason, it is both omnipresent and irresistible, however small the seed.

---

[36]Other inquiries, I find, have also been sensitive to this aspect of the "inheritance," among them Sallie McFague, whose *Speaking in Parables* (Philadelphia: Fortress, 1975) argued for a theology more responsive to the example provided. Her later *Metaphorical Theology* and *Models of God* (Philadelphia: Fortress, 1982 and 1987), though, seem to forget that to advance metaphors, however well suited to "our age," from this side of the relation is only "remythologizing" in the pejorative sense. The difficulty of distinguishing "religion" from revelation persists in Stephen Prickett's *Words and the Word* (Cambridge: Cambridge Univ. Press, 1986) or Garrett Green's *Imagining God* (San Francisco: Harper, 1989).

Chapter 5

Communal

Nothing is to be preferred to the Work of God.
—*The Rule of St. Benedict* 43.3

Historical

Works of imagination tend of themselves, we have been saying, to produce communities that act out what thereby becomes their meaning. "Meaning" means, in fact, just so much community as may result. Individual works of art are created, one might then say, in the hope that the corresponding mutualities of affect and attitude might sooner or later come into being, the better to exemplify the possibility at least of community as such. For that is what we yearn for—if only in imagination. So the character of any culture would depend upon such imaginative acts as it has agreed to publish and rehearse. The sheer variety of these would suggest that we are constantly being offered almost as many "gospels," though some would surely overlap. The "canon" in any genre would then include any assemblage or sequence that had already become more or less accepted as potentially meaningful, and therefore exemplary, though it might not yet be clear of what. Wedding ceremonies, hockey games, Frost poems: we rock in the eddies of them all, some disappearing on their first occasion, others recurring at ritual intervals to mark the moments of a lifetime or a civilization. The feelings and impressions that any work of art leaves behind would then amount to as much community as has actually precipitated in the individual or group concerned. The scandal arising from Salman Rushdie's *Satanic Verses* could show that this effect may occur in the negative as well as the positive. In either case, a feeling would make sense only as one more element in or a violent subtraction from a possible community the rest of which had not yet come into existence.[1]

So much we could see to be true simply in the flesh. Within the regime of the Spirit the same rule would hold. But here the result is by contrast immediate and

---

[1] It is interesting that even such strict "intertextualists" as Hillis Miller and Robert Scholes have recently begun to entertain the notion that reading might involve an ethical or political dimension. David Cooper's suggestion in *Metaphor* (Oxford: Blackwell, 1988) that the figure in question generates "intimacy" (152-74) comes nearer the case advanced here.

unqualified—at least in principle. The eucharistic action, original or reproduced, has in the very nature of the case supposed the power to generate just what it means, then and there, here and now, in full. To consume the elements, we have already argued, would of itself bring the *ecclesia* of God into existence, even if this version of the body had never existed before—as perhaps, in some sense, it has not yet. The body of Christ as symbol is completed in the body of Christ as community. What has to remain suggestion in the flesh thus becomes presence in the Spirit. *This* work of art already creates what it means: to comprehend it is most "literally" to become just that much.

One could then fairly ask, What has happened since to the very idea of a final symbol that would of itself turn into its proper meaning? Paul's letters to Corinth, we have already seen, may be read as showing how well he understood the intention of the founder—if this is in fact what we have identified. Colossians may or may not also be his work in whole or in part; in any case, it repeats a thoroughly somatic definition of the communal possibility with further variations. Ephesians, more obviously by a disciple of the next generation, renews this interpretation still more elaborately, with other differences to suit changes in the cultural context. And in due course the Fathers, Greek or Latin, continue to speak of the Church as the body of Christ in the mode of community and even of a connection between this and the Eucharist, though for the most part indirectly, as we have also seen. The scholarly labors of those modern theologians of the time between the wars in our own century who sought to confirm that the current Church too should be thought of primarily under the same title helped to recover traces of the idea in the writings of the late imperial period. De Lubac, Congar, and Mersch between them brought forward the references to be found in Irenaeus, Origen, Athanasius, Hilary, Chrysostom, Cyril, Leo, and especially Augustine.[2]

It has been shown accordingly that the idea at least of the Israel of God as a completed communion in the import of its principal symbol was by no means lost through the several centuries between the closing of the canon and what we think of as the beginning of the medieval synthesis. But it would not seem unfair either to conclude that the focus for those chiefly concerned was no longer on this eschatological privilege. It is therefore plausible for such standard historians of the period as Chadwick or Kelly virtually to ignore the spiritual possibility without intellectual or narrative embarrassment.[3] From the perspective they adopt it is not the bodily but the hierarchical and dogmatic aspects of the Christian universe that

---

[2]The major instances as they appear in translation include Henri de Lubac, *Catholicism* (New York: Sheed and Ward, 1958); Yves Congar, *The Mystery of the Church* (Baltimore: Helicon, 1960), and less well known though more thorough than either, Emile Mersch, *The Whole Christ* (Milwaukee: Bruce, 1938).

[3]Henry Chadwick, *The Early Church* (London: Penguin, 1967), and J. N. D. Kelly, *Early Christian Creeds*, 2nd ed. (London: Longmans, 1960) are still on every ecclesiological bookshelf. I am indebted especially to the latter for the facts here summarized.

take public shape through these carnal generations. Controversies over and therefore the sequence of changes in ecclesiastical government and ideology necessarily occur in the midst of this world as a matter of past fact and present discourse alike. *Schismata* are of the flesh in the nature of the case, as Paul already had occasion to observe. The relation between church and state cannot help but be disturbed or determined by arguments and decisions that in practice reduce both to secularity. The line between orthodoxy and heresy must be drawn in the same dust. It is accordingly the history of the church as institution that can be repeated. The Church proper, we might then recollect, would have in truth no history, all of which she would at once transcend. But that identity cannot provide much material for historians, whether of deeds or ideas.

Not that what thus becomes so prominent need be considered altogether irrelevant to the apocalypse of the body in the mode of community. It is clear, for instance, that the central theological issue through these early centuries is Christological. The dogmatic declarations all focus upon the identity of the Son in relation to the Father. And the key term in the corresponding controversies, as everyone also remembers, is *homoousios,* "of one being." The expression is not poetic but critical, and so philosophical rather than biblical—which apparently upset some participants at the time. It is therefore a specimen of language about language, of the kind likely to be used by a collective seeking agreement within itself on what should constitute certainty with respect to the question at issue: theology, that is, not revelation. But what the term affirms does in fact very carefully define the connection between the poles of what a modern could identify as a metaphoric relation. It asserts that these are, when functioning within the metaphor (which is to say, as an "object" of faith rather than reason) identical one with the other. The Son, as one would say in language closer to the original, is indeed consubstantial with the Father. One might put the relevant objection to the alternative formulation in an equivalent terminology. If the Son is no more than *homoiousios,* or like the Father without being identical with him, then metaphor has been reduced to simile—and the figures compared are still bodies in this world. Arianism is normal for the flesh, where likeness and difference presume juxtaposition. But an infinite art would have to be absolutely metaphoric and therefore determined throughout by identity. And that much, the controversy and its result could show, can indeed be known: we may define the form at least if not the content of revelation from a rational perspective which as such must still fall short of what can nonetheless be affirmed.

And if the Son as an individual is indeed a perfect metaphor for the Father, it would follow too, though this was not on the agenda at the councils and therefore does not appear in the official declarations, that all modes of this metaphor must be in the same relation to its ultimate meaning. Identity would be implicitly affirmed of the several species of the "vehicle" as well as of the relation between any one of these and their eventual "tenor." The Christ whose nature is affirmed in the definitions is throughout understood as the singular person who was begotten, died, buried, and rose again. That which is to be trusted in for the future is still, that is, formulated in terms of the past. But this retrospection is itself structurally metaphoric: the individual (and so apparently exceptional and distant) Christ becomes as it were a typological prefigurement of the total Christ, who may always be shared, and so participated in without alienation. All manifestations of an eschatological metaphor would need to be admitted together as long as any one of them is. What the Fathers would have thought of as the historical and we would now call the dogmatic Christ thus carries along with him, as it were, the eucharistic and the communal modes of his identity. The apparent paucity or marginality of explicit references to these other versions of the central parable may thus be compensated for by a sufficiently generous understanding of what in fact they were obliged to focus upon.

We might understand the creeds, then, as representing a collective effort to define the structure at least of that which as such must transcend reason in rational terms: to trace the axis of the other world, as it were, by way of a schematic history of this. In that case even the organizational and ideological conflicts of the time would exhibit the same principle of homage to the Spirit, however carnal the practical or literal results. In the age that follows, though, what can seem like a counter-movement may from the same distance be detected. The identity found explicitly assignable to Christ (and therefore implicitly to his Church) can be seen to migrate back in among the powers of this world, there to recast these in sacral language.

The standard modern study of this phenomenon has been Ernst Kantorowicz's *The King's Two Bodies,* which might virtually on its own allow us to fill in the next gap in the sequence. In his account this would extend from the earliest Middle Ages to the verge of Modern times.[4] He finds an origin for what becomes the Medieval and in due course Renaissance and later "classical" notions of royal and national bodiliness in the very patristic definitions of Christ and the Church we have just glanced at. The two "natures" of Christ, human and divine, reappear in early Medieval times, he argues, in the corresponding notion of the king or emperor's identity as combining the profane and the sacred. Somewhat later a complementary transfer seems to have occurred with respect to the collective as well as its head. What had been true of the Church alone could then be affirmed of the "body politic" formed by the nation headed by its monarch. In similar ways the idea of martyrdom, already shifted to the church militant as a way of justifying service on a crusade, became in due course a sufficient explanation for death in war on behalf of the *patria*. The eternity of Christ with God could in a similar fashion become the perpetuity of royal or legal establishments.

An intermediate stage in this migration of a completed bodiliness from the realm of the Spirit back into the flesh was provided by the progressive sacralization

---

[4]Ernst Kantorowicz, *The King's Two Bodies* (Princeton: Princeton University Press, 1957). This classic study carries implications well beyond its announced topic, the development of medieval political theology.

of the institutional church and especially the papacy, which occurred at the same time. An important moment in this transition would be marked by the bull *Unam Sanctam* issued by Boniface VIII in 1302, which not quite incidentally established the term *mystical body* as normative for the church in this as well as the other world.[5] It thus became possible to think of the Pope as the "head" of this displaced body as well as if not quite instead of Christ. The church-as-state thus helped mediate a transfer of the body image from the Church indeed to the state-as-church. It is painfully amusing to read Kantorowicz on the ways in which the two powers swapped symbols back and forth. "The pope adorned his tiara with a golden crown, donned the imperial purple, and was preceded by the imperial banners when riding in solemn procession through the streets of Rome. The emperor wore under his crown a mitre, donned the pontifical shows and other clerical rainments, and received, like a bishop, the ring at his coronation."[6]

As a result the kings of the emerging nations and the composite bodies they now formed together with their peoples acquired the sacredness of being that had in the first place been associated only with the divine community and its founder. If the original amounted to the body indeed in the mode of community, these derivatives became at least bodies of a special kind—and in certain respects the more apparently substantial of the two, for a nation had the force of arms at its disposal as well as the simultaneously actual and ceremonial presence of the monarch and his servants. The question, legal or political as well as theological, then became what sort of body could legitimately be predicated of a king or his nation or both, and what claims these entities might properly make on other species of bodiliness, carnal or celestial.

From a critical distance this question does not seem hard to settle: a carnal body of whatever kind beyond the "body natural," and that too as soon as it has been formally taken into account, must be at least but no more than imaginative—which is to say, a work of human art. For it is a great and painful part of what is revealed in the revelation that any unqualified version of the communal body would have to remain eschatological only. Firmly carnal and from the beginning predicated on force as they were, these new copies of what had once been a spiritual body indeed would for that reason alone have to be ranked as parodic in proportion to the religious quality of their claim. In the light of the exchanges, not to say contaminations, explored by Kantorowicz, one would need to reunderstand both so much of the institutional church as succumbed to the appeal of the model

---

[5]In the earlier Middle Ages the term *corpus mysticum* had meant the consecrated host. The communal body was referred to, following Paul, as the *corpus Christi*. In the twelfth century these terms came to be reversed under the pressure of the transubstantiation controversy. Boniface's bull formalized this exchange, which incidentally though only implicitly continues to exhibit the close connection between these two modes of the body. The argument in Kantorowicz, *King's Two Bodies,* 194-99, is worth following carefully.

[6]Ibid., 193.

provided and those national and legal bodies that formed themselves wholly upon it as unconscious surrogates for the true *ecclesia,* carnal figures consuming rights and authority that could rightly belong only to the body of Christ proper. In the West, history has notoriously preempted eschatology, and this phase of the former could stand as one of the more formidable of several unfortunate instances.

I have sometimes wondered if Shakespeare's special prominence at the beginning of the Modern period might not be attributable in part at least to what might be called his therapeutic recuperation of royalty for the *un*ambitious imagination. His plays could be taken to demonstrate that what had been or might yet become brutally political was only theatrical after all. If England had in fact absorbed this curative message, the first of several modern revolutions might have proved unnecessary. But if so, Hobbes's *Leviathan* could in a similar way exhibit how absolutely the suggestion was not taken up. For this formidable theorist's "Common-wealth" is not only an "Artificiall Man" but a "Mortall God." The "Soveraigne," singular or plural, amounts to a "Person" whose unlimited authority all subjects must understand themselves as having consented to, whether by deliberate institution or submission to conquest, for it is most certainly exercised by divine right. The state *is* the church, and whoever directs its powers is entitled to appoint pastors and determine what doctrines shall be taught by the "Publique Reason." The monarch is even free to preside at the Eucharist. For in Hobbes's view the Kingdom of God does not as such obtain even in parable: it has been put off until the Second Coming. Christ has therefore no current authority—much less the Pope, whose rule is no better than a "Kingdome of Darkenesse." That title might seem better suited to his own vision, which would seem to provide a formula not only for the autocracies of his own century but the totalitarianism of ours.[7]

One could also trace, as another repetition of the same general shift from the spiritual to a carnal idea of the communal body, the history of what has also continued into our own day of the "corporation." This would have begun in what remains a sufficiently Pauline discovery that the *ecclesia* might be understood as occurring on more than one scale: as household, city (and therefore diocese), nation, or in due course *oikoumene.* As the empire in general became "Christian," the smaller versions not only reproduce but concentrate the whole, whether as monastic communities in the desert or papal conclaves in the capital. So far the inevitable representations of the initial possibility would still count as spiritual, at least in principle. But with the decline of civil authority, one or another of these modes of the body proper not unnaturally attracted secular responsibilities as well. Ecclesiasti-

---

[7]It seems typical of our inability to grasp the impressive (if peculiarly monstrous) case that Hobbes is making that the editor of the Penguin edition (Harmondsworth, 1968) should understand him as introducing no worse than a "bourgeois" ideology. The progress of the body image in English history and literature from Henry VIII to Hobbes is traced in detail by David George Hale in his *Body Politic* (The Hague: Mouton, 1971).

cal "bodies" were in due course founded that could count in canon and civil law alike as *personae*: diocesan chapters, abbeys or orders, and later universities and charitable endowments. The secular analogues these in turn inspired included boroughs, guilds, companies, and staples. Later monarchs not unexpectedly found such "fictive persons" useful for trade and government as the early Modern age began. In America too the original transition was repeated at still another remove: these entities were in the first instance churches, charities, and cities, and only later banks, canal companies, or railroads. As modernity took hold, corporations escaped from political subordination to become universally available devices for the accumulation of capital and its employment under regulations to ensure limited liability for individuals. A process of demystification necessarily set in: the bodily, not to say personal, metaphor was gradually exposed as no more than just that; though autonomy and some degree of immortality did survive. Wall Street too, we could fairly conclude, still derives from the Eucharist—though by now the successive stages of the transformation take a while to puzzle out.[8]

The history of the corporation from its ecclesial beginnings through the medieval or absolutist repetitions of these to the contemporary transparencies would put one in a position to appreciate the special task of the Modern age in all contexts, but especially the communal. For what the Enlightenment has set itself to accomplish is evidently the annihilation of what could thereby be understood as a parodic body wherever this might be found. The principal figures and movements have severally labored to reveal by thought and action alike that there is in fact no such thing—except perhaps as a harmless figure of speech. The recovery of a disenchanted reason has everywhere functioned as a critique of some false positive within this world. And the falsity of such positives has always seemed insufferable in proportion to the bodiliness they claimed. A nonbodily positive is simply a fact or an idea or a text; in social terms, a structure or system, and therefore at least in principle without sacred authority. Modernity would then amount to a deconstruction of the specious body wherever it might be found and its replacement by one or another mode of whatever is *not* bodily. With respect to the spiritual body, this tendency has been explicitly atheistic; with respect to the natural body, human or cosmic, dangerously technological. With respect to imaginative bodies, I have already suggested, this critique has too often been unnecessarily destructive. But with respect to the body politic insofar as this had become a spurious imitation of the first of these, the result has surely been salutary as well as critical. In this world collectives had better not become bodies—except in imagination—nor our leaders messiahs, even in metaphor.

---

[8]The history of the corporation is a topic with a variety of byways. I have found such earlier authorities as Davis, Machen, and Pollock and Maitland more convenient for my own digressive purposes than such moderns as Berle, Drucker, Friedman, Mason, Seavoy, or Tierney, though each of these is a specialist in one or another aspect of the subject.

156   *Some Bodies. The Eucharist and Its Implications.*

"Historians long ago began to write the history of the body," observes Michel Foucault, and no one since Kantorowicz has contributed more to this typically postmodern project. His comparatively early *Discipline and Punish* especially has helped set in motion many other inquiries of the kind besides his own.[9] Even those who have not read this genuinely seminal book will be sure to recall from it the two major instances in terms of which Foucault dramatizes the difference between the ancien régime and the revolution, or what he calls the "Classical" as opposed to the Modern period. The first of these is the notorious description of the death of Damien the regicide in 1757, which provides his introductory image: a man pinched by red-hot implements and torn apart, with some difficulty, by horses. The second is Jeremy Bentham's ideal Panopticon, designed to permit a central gaze to supervise a multitude of prisoners, patients, workers, or pupils isolated in banks of cells about an architectural and therefore social circumference. These stand as exempla for the social presuppositions of their respective eras. In the first, authority becomes concrete in the flesh of a victim exhibited as a spectacle of public torment. In the second, authority is systematized as an impersonal surveillance of a crowd reduced to objects in a structure of knowledge materialized as social "discipline." Between them these instances become types for the change from a world founded upon a speciously unifying bodiliness to the bleak but factual universe of cognitive and social categories.

The upshot of the Foucauvian contrast is therefore the familiar Modern point: that though the body once seemed everywhere modular, now organism has been replaced by organization, ancestry by norm, ritual by convention, membership by citizenship, and status by measurement. Foucault and his followers have concentrated on the grand shift from bodiliness to disembodiment as one passes from one episteme to the other. One might notice in reply to some of the more totalizing accounts of this change that it need not be understood as complete even in the political arena with which it has usually seemed natural to begin. The "corporate" state lingered on as an ideal for Catholics at least into living memory in Austria between the wars and in France and Italy as well as Spain since. More recent assassinations could also remind us of the degree to which even a republic founded upon a most explicit repudiation of royalty can still experience crises associated with the older form. And outside those larger social contexts within which the change has indeed been most evident, the manners proper to the old body politic may still be found to obtain here and there. The family would be one obvious context; another is the erotic life, where a bodily polarity generating a reciprocal

---

[9]Michel Foucault, *Discipline and Punish* (New York: Pantheon, 1977). The sentence quoted appears on p. 25. I have not found his later history of sexuality as useful for an earlier phase of our topic. The Foucauvian project has prompted a continuing critical fascination with the more or less disgusting bodiliness of this or that period in the past: research, one might think, as morbidity.

fascination still maintains its disquieting power. Hence perhaps the erotic coloration such social practices as Foucault is reconstructing can take on in hindsight at least. Such "history" is not only imaginary but fantastic.

The modern age, though, evidently remains under the domination of a alternative intention that may readily be recovered after one fashion or another by the historians of its emergence and what it emerged from. We have already called the effect a deconstruction of what may, within a perspective that includes the eschatological instance, be called the parodic body, or body out of place. This operation may be found to have occurred first in the context of pure thought. The Cartesian annihilation of the body image as irrelevant to knowledge of the cosmos and its replacement by an impersonal mind and a correspondingly material universe would typify the initial stage of the process. The decapitation of one monarch after another could then seem no more than an allegory of this founding accomplishment in the belated language of action. Both revolutions, intellectual or political, could still seem no more than partial stages toward an elimination of the body from all contexts where it ought not to be found. Something always remains, we have observed, of the older presupposition. But the critical successes of the Modern project have ensured at least that these instances must suffer under an imputation of illegitimacy, as with the erotic instances just mentioned, or unreality, as with the aesthetic examples, or mere privacy, as with the individual body we are still left to inhabit. And the spiritual body, though in principle untouched by the destructive attention devoted to its competitors within the flesh, has in practice been assumed to have shriveled into incredibility long ago.

The continuing enactment of this disembodying intention would at least prevent any of the very unbodily structures that have proliferated since from surreptitiously acquiring the privileges of the model they replaced. The subject, it could then be concluded, would be no more sacred than the object—in spite of Hegel on one side or Marx on the other. And the state would a fortiori be exposed as essentially if not yet practically no better than profane, and therefore unbelievable in principle however indispensable for the time being. An unqualified critique would do away with everything that remained of what had begun in the first place as an illicit displacement. But it might do more than that. Cognitive or social positives, thoroughly desubstantialized, would eventually become transparent, if not to the mind or conscience at least to that in us which is still capable of faith. The process of disembodiment would eventually leave, at least in principle, a perfect blank at what we might still call the "heart" of each. A foreseeable end of the Enlightenment, then, should ideally amount to a perfect negativity. Such an apocalypse of the Modern would in theory dissolve knowledge itself, together with the texts in which it must inhere, in the same way that an unqualified revolution would, as some have already hoped, do away with the state. And across the vacancy thus exposed the body indeed might then prove uninterruptedly visible once again to the eyes of faith at least, as if on the far side of some desert, or the other shore of an ocean. But such a renewal of the initial apocalypse is obviously still to come.

The suspicion felt for a body out of place, which historical retrospection can identify as central to any modernizing intention from the beginning to our present, has more obviously left in its wake a variety of reactive swirls. One result, often remarked, has been a withdrawal to and reaffirmation of the natural body as the only remaining ground of value.[10] This reaction would be easy to trace through the history of economic development or medicine or popular culture. The difficulty is obvious: the individual body is mortal. Its own death is always at the core of whatever it can be certain of. And without hope for some identification with a stronger mode of the body, real or illusory, mortality becomes not merely central but implicitly total. It seems characteristic accordingly that absolute death, whether in war or extermination or some nuclear or environmental catastrophe, should haunt the memories and fears of any consciousness so reduced. The natural body, individual or familial, could all the same be understood as the religion of Everybody in any situation in which the alternatives had lost their traditional credibility. Multiplied, this faith becomes the association or peer group, whether in a generational, sexual, racial, or national form. In any of these cases, though, it is still an aggregate rather than a community, whatever the rhetoric. The corresponding faith of the first person singular, or Somebody, is apt under the same circumstances to focus upon the possibilities of the symbol. Once the body politic disintegrated, what did in fact survive the representative revolution were new versions of the imaginative body. Bodiliness, evicted from the cognitive and the ethical, took refuge in the aesthetic, where Romantic hopes could justify an "organic" concreteness and coherence that had come to seem only superstitious or reactionary outside the arts. Poetry, painting, and music could not merely survive but even flourish amid the failures not merely of the traditional regimes but of their revolutionary successors. Modern historians of Romanticism and its successor movements have had no difficulty tracing the results for the imagination of its abrupt emergence as compensation for the loss of communal trustworthiness—and the only apparent means for any transcendence of mortal existence.[11]

The difficulties implicit in this reactive efflorescence have also been easy to detect. The aesthetic body, whether melodramatic or ironic, operatic or imagistic, has

---

[10]Many examples might be provided, in and out of "serious" thought. One is supplied by John O'Neill's *Five Bodies* (Ithaca: Cornell University Press, 1985), a protest against the overorganized society which has precipitated from science on behalf of a "radical anthropomorphism" that would restore bodiliness to family, polis, cosmos, and "discourse" alike. Once again I can recognize a project akin to my own across the inevitable differences.

[11]I am conscious here of the case developed in M. H. Abrams's *Natural Supernaturalism* (New York: Norton, 1971) and carried on since by other scholars. The Romantic hope for an aesthetic body, affirmed anew by Modernism and then apparently lost again, has since been reasserted in an appropriately polemical style by Murray Krieger, most recently in *A Reopening of Closure: Organicism against Itself* (New York: Columbia Univ. Press, 1989).

necessarily been weakened by its removal from the contexts it has had to abandon in order to preserve its own autonomy. Modern art as such was obliged to settle for fictionality, not truth, and can only very indirectly claim any ethical consequences, which may or may not always seem a happy irrelevance. On the whole it has boasted of this isolation, through occasionally new cognitive or moral claims based on the aesthetic have been advanced, as if to reconquer these lost territories for the imagination. But these efforts have invariably failed, sometimes at a considerable cost.

For Romanticism, or the imaginative reaction to the Enlightenment after the fact of its apparent triumph, is as soon as it attempts to take effect on the scale of the collective no better than the beginning of fascism, as too many instances have proved. The most ostentatious version of a newly communal body of Adam on this scale in our times has of course been the violently resomaticized nation. Robert Lifton's well-known study of the medical aspects of the Holocaust is more than incidentally relevant to any recapitulation of this history.[12] Medical personnel were necessarily involved in that consequence—for which a defensive ideology was accordingly required, since natural bodies were being destroyed rather than preserved. One story has often been repeated: a Jewish doctor victim asked an SS doctor how he reconciled this (she pointed to the smoking chimneys) with the Hippocratic oath? "When an appendix is gangrenous," he replied, "it must be cut out." The application of the metaphor enforces what could then appear a strictly "medical" choice: it is no longer the body of the individual which counts, but that of the *Volk*. And this version of the carnal body not only as reimagined but restored to power had already been defined by Party doctrine and its deeply Romantic sources as the body indeed; that which, in other words, should in fact replace the body of Christ in the allegiance of any merely nominal member of that obsolete entity—not to mention the simple bodies of so many disposable Jews.

In this most Modern of all the instances, then, the corporate community of the ancien régime was resurrected, as it were, with a vengeance, accompanied by a newly absolutized version of the same rationale that had once prompted its medieval antecedents. The flesh claimed not just to take the place of the Spirit—for in the apparent absence of that possibility, this decision alone might seem innocuous—but to seize what had once seemed its rival's privileges, messianic and communal alike, of which a manifest bodiliness would be primary. And once this challenge had been raised, extermination, whether of the mentally unfit or criminals or of any other elements "unworthy of life," could indeed become one more therapeutic task like the eradication of vermin or bacteria. For violence was in that case merely an

---

[12]Lifton's argument, for some time familiar in essay or lecture, has now been elaborated in his *Nazi Doctors: Medical Killing and the Psychology of Genocide* (New York: Basic, 1987). The story is continued in more general terms in Robert Proctor's *Racial Hygiene: Medicine under the Nazis* (Cambridge: Harvard University Press, 1988).

antibiotic in the service of a "higher" life.

Given so prominent an instance of the return not just of the repressed but of what had once seemed securely decomposed, the critical disposition inherent in modernity from its beginning might seem all the more necessary—if only as a genuine as opposed to a spurious therapy. And this critique would continue to entail a persistent suspicion of communal bodiliness in all its forms on the obvious ground that anything of the kind is almost sure to be more or less seriously out of place. Any such investigation, though, would in turn raise a general question: Could there be no innocence on this scale at all? To which one might respond by suspecting the universal application of the suspicion: the very constancy of the phenomenon suggests some degree of legitimacy within the complications offered by any instance, however horrific.

I would propose accordingly that the communal body is innocent in proportion to the presence of imagination within it. The aesthetic is always as such free from guilt. This was Nietzsche's thesis, which has since been bequeathed to an odd variety of heirs. Even the Nazis might pass this test sometimes—in their parades, say, as the famous movie once seemed to show. If innocence seems unusually prominent within the realm of the female, for another questionable instance, or simply in the safety of the past, this would presumably be because one's distance from either would necessarily re-create them both as imaginary as far as *I* was concerned—presuming, as usual, a masculine subject at loose ends in the chaos of the present. If so, apparently communal but not yet spiritual versions of the body might remain plausible just so far as these were still or also or only works of art, or so near that as to share more or less in the corresponding privilege. Hence the reassurance so regularly offered by ceremony, as at a graduation or weddings. We take courage from the suggestion that whatever else we may be up to in the name of the collective in question, it may still be felt as subsumed in the relevant holiday. On such occasions we can reimagine our several institutions as imaginary after all, and so innocuous, in spite of everything we cannot help but know about them.

At my university, for instance, the freshman class of the Architecture school has been accustomed to celebrate St. Patrick's Day by constructing a large green dragon out of painted cloth and wooden framing. Inside and around this fragile artifact they have perambulated the campus, accompanied it may be by a band, floats, little green figures to pull and lift, and a cheerful crowd carrying green balloons. The ritual thus amiably reverses the legend of the saint, who is best known for having abolished snakes from the island of his mission. Here is *the* snake back again, revived for one day at least on the grandest possible scale, with a head thirty feet or more in the air, and teeth, scales, and wings in proportion, as well as a long tail supported from within by invisible myrmidons. The event makes for an old-fashioned carnival, when what is forbidden in ordinary time, not to mention a season of penance, is briefly obligatory. Such demonstrations would exhibit the feral generally, which in these ways compensates for civilization and its discontents. It is curious too that a neopaganism of such a kind has to remain morally improper even, or perhaps especially, in an otherwise thoroughly post-Christian context. But the Green Dragon is of course not a "serious" instance either of primitivism or the transvaluation of values. It is too flimsy to be real, and celebrates a mock phallicism, the resurrection less of the unbaptizable flesh than of illusion. At the close of its brief life, already a little the worse for wear from a snowball and egg gauntlet in the engineering quad, it goes up in flames near the place from which it started. But now I learn that this apparently reliable tradition may be discontinued—too many bottles thrown, the authorities claim, I do not know with what justice. I should have thought that the danger intimated was already safely deflected by a mock celebration of what was in fact all too well under control. In the university, after all, a body of whatever kind is no real threat to the hegemony of mind. The dragon is likely to revive accordingly.

Meanwhile the triumph of modernity has produced a variety of effects, if not quite on the church's proper identity, then at least on the ways in which her members have been able to realize this. I have proposed that a migration of bodiliness from the Spirit to the flesh served in the first place to sacralize the institution and thereby generate "Christendom" in all its misplaced concreteness. But the emergence of a critical reaction to this displacement, which has in due course come to seem the common element in the several manifestations of modernity from Descartes to Derrida, has had the effect of challenging not only the plausibility of such parodic communalities as might be inherited or invented but the credibility of their supposedly spiritual original as well. The ecclesial body, already too closely identified either with its own or some royal version of the body politic, could only suffer in principle and practice alike from the deconstruction of the latter. Church and state decomposed together, or else reasserted themselves in spasmodic reactions that outparodied the parody exposed. Such efforts could not help confusing the religious with the imaginary, not to say the superstitious or neopagan. A disposition to overvalue essentially profane aspects of the composite inheritance, a doubt (often unconscious) that the spiritual could be trusted to take care of itself, and a generalized refusal of the Modern critique from within as well as from without came to seem intrinsic to the legacy. Meanwhile the Eucharist, still at the core of daily practice, continued to convey, however implicitly, an invincibly pneumatic and therefore absolutely otherworldly intuition of the corresponding communal body. Such experiments in community as have punctuated the modern history of the Church in and out of the Roman allegiance may accordingly be understood as practical interpretations of the metaphor thereby communicated, whether these were explicitly monastic or loosely popular, radical or conservative. And a remoter effect of a similar kind may be detected in so much ecclesiological thinking as has sought to recover the body as a major name within the Catholic tradition.

It is easy to locate evidences of the last within comparatively recent history. We have mentioned De Lubac, Congar, and Mersch as typical authorities for the period between the wars, when this image seemed for a brief while newly triumphant. A revival of the conception for Modern times had in fact already commenced early in the previous century, in part therefore as what retrospectively can be associated with other manifestations of the Romantic reaction. By the third decade of this century though, the body image had come to seem ripe for full acceptance—if the necessary sources from the inheritance could be specified, which these theologians endeavored to supply.[13] The French thinking especially of these years was in due course officially validated in Pius XII's encyclical *Mystici corporis* in 1943, which accepted the Pauline formula as a master metaphor for the Church's self-understanding—though after a fashion, to be sure, that conformed it to the inherited status of the institution. For the Pope, the solution was simply to identify these: the body was the institution, and vice versa. For Congar, the sacraments mediated between the two. For De Lubac, obedience to one became a means of entering into the mystery of the other. The allusions to his own appropriation of this evangelical necessity are among the more moving moments in his text. The problem lingers for those who must somehow accept both, to be resolved in one way or another.[14]

Meanwhile the position that has dominated a more recent phase of ecclesiology internationally and in America would find an equivalent type in Avery Dulles's popular *Models of the Church*. These are, according to him, institution, community, sacrament, herald, and servant. Under the heading "community" he places both the newly traditional idea of the body of Christ and a more recent conception for which the formula "the people of God" has since become familiar. The Church as sacrament could be assimilated without difficulty to the older formula: if the body can indeed manifest itself in this world, it must be as a sacrament, whether explicitly symbolic or implicitly communal. "Herald," a Protestant conception, and "servant," an identification easier to associate with liberation theology in the Third World or social action in the first, is understandable only on the supposition that they compete with or supplement the first definition, or "institution." For all three would refer to aspects and activities within a human rather than the divine context.[15]

A skeptical critique of Dulles's survey might accordingly prefer to distinguish

---

[13]De Lubac's *Splendour of the Church* (New York: Sheed and Ward, 1956) reviews the history of the idea in the century previous to its acceptance by the magisterium (61-67). Other portions of the argument of this book approximate the case already made here. "The Church produces the Eucharist, but the Eucharist also produces the Church," he observes on p. 92, and in the course of supporting this generalization comes perilously close to the idea that the eucharistic action should accordingly be understood as communicating the messianic identity from the individual to the community. But as usual this does not quite happen.

[14]Louis Bouyer's *Church of God: Body of Christ and Temple of the Spirit* (Chicago: Franciscan Herald, 1982) should probably be ranked as a latecomer to the French prewar discussion. For him, the institution is justified as contributing to a unity founded in the Spirit.

[15]Avery Dulles, *Models of the Church* (New York: Doubleday, 1974). His contribution to the discussion is continued in a sequence of later books: *A Church to Believe In* (New York: Crossroad, 1982); *The Catholicity of the Church* (Oxford: Clarendon, 1985); and *The Reshaping of Catholicism* (San Francisco: Harper, 1988).

"body" and "sacrament" as intertranslatable epithets for the Church *kata pneuma*, which would make it easier to connect both with the Eucharist and through that to an intention of Jesus. But it is characteristic of Dulles's book, so representative of what has become virtually an establishment liberalism since Vatican II, that the question of Jesus' intention is never raised. The assumption throughout appears to be that members of the church are free, more or less, to choose which model they prefer. Nor, it may also be remarked, does the place of the Jews come up as an issue, though if the phrase "People of God" has a literal sense, it must refer to that nation. If so, it should behoove any Christian using the expression to explain the relation between the literal and any metaphoric meanings it might take on, and so between Judaism and Christianity. But this problem does not arise either.[16]

Another influential authority within recent ecclesiology has been Hans Küng, whose *Church* does at least raise the issue of Jesus' intention as relevant for any self-definition by members of the entity in question. But he quickly decides that Jesus did *not* establish anything of the kind. The church, in his view, is merely a fellowship of those who happen to believe in the resurrection. It is therefore entirely a human creation. The "body of Christ" formula is therefore *not* original, nor does Küng bring up the Last Supper in connection with it. It is incidentally interesting (and perhaps evidence of some inconsistency) that Küng is satisfied with a traditionally sacrificial understanding of the Eucharist, though a sentence or two is devoted to what we have called the strictly sacramental possibility. This alternative, though, is repudiated, apparently on the ground that such an interpretation would overprivilege the institution, toward which he is in a polemical relation throughout.[17]

---

[16]In taking this easygoing line, Dulles was supported by at least some New Testament scholarship of the period. R. S. Minear's *Images of the Church in the New Testament* (Philadelphia: Westminster, 1960), for instance, asserts that "no one figure can be selected as the dominating base line of all thought about the Church" (222). But if the eucharistic action may be understood as establishing the body as precisely such a figure, the image it transmits would have to take precedence. One would then be obliged to interpret the other images found in the canonical writings by way of this central motif. Of these the nation would presumably be first among equals, given Jesus' choice of the Twelve, followed perhaps by the temple. The city, vine, woman, harvest, and so forth would accumulate as secondary reproductions of these. There obviously is no lack of metaphor within the tradition.

[17]See Hans Küng, *The Church* (New York: Sheed and Ward, 1968) 223-34 and 227, followed by 236-37 and 239-41, for the two halves of this argument. Küng's language, like De Lubac's, is strongest at those moments when he is willing to entertain the riskier possibility, though in the end he refuses to be tempted: "Those who eat the body of the Lord themselves become a body. By receiving the body of the Lord, the community reveals itself as a body; their share in the body of the Lord makes the believers who eat it into the body of the Lord. In the Lord's Supper the community is constituted as a body" (223-24). One could hardly put the case more explicitly. It is ironic that two of the more influential competing ecclesiologies of recent times should so nearly approach an interpretation of the situation as a whole that might avoid the other disadvantages of both. More recent discussion on the German side

But his principal argument would allow at most for one or another of those titles that presume a profane understanding of what would in that case become not really a community at all but simply a collective or congregation, actual or potential, made up of adherents to what would then only in theory have to be the same faith.

Both these sufficiently typical theologians may be understood as deriving from a disposition that could understand itself as more or less sanctioned by *Lumen gentium,* the constitution on the church as determined by Vatican II, as earlier authorities may be understood as anticipating the corresponding encyclical of Pius XII. In this document, the idea of the church as "the people of God" occupies an independent chapter, which has served at once to sanction and dignify that appellation, whatever its connotations for progressives and conservatives then or since. In popular American practice, the term has become virtually a code word for the progressive party within the church generally and therefore an attractive alternative to the expression advanced by the older authorities, which by virtue precisely of its acceptance in the previous generation had come to seem compromised by too close an association with the institution. The difficulty for both liberals and conservatives has been that what this formula sums up and what the magisterium maintains cannot help but take shape as antagonists inside the same category: which is again to say, within the horizon of the flesh. Meanwhile the potential implicit in the body image is once more comparatively neglected—at least as an idea.

The fact that the institution has remained a stumbling block within the ecclesiological debate of the last two intellectual generations would offer an opportunity to raise a more general question: Why should there be an institutional church at all? Any satisfactory answer would have to revert, it seems to me, to the offstage presence, so often neglected, of the Jewish people. The continuing existence of this nation through the whole aeon dominated by what has preferred to think of itself as the Israel of God is at least an interesting scandal. We might then put the two problems together for a tentative solution to both by entertaining the possibility that the institution, as it has developed and persisted as a conundrum for theologians ancient or modern, has in practice stood in for this apparently absent though still embarrassingly present nation. The Jews have not as a collective passed through into the eschatological phase of their own possibility, a Christian would need to say, a possibility that the Church claims to actualize. But here they still are, the "people of God" indeed.

We might accordingly decide that the body of Christ, if this is indeed the proper title for the gracious moment in the apocalyptic sequence, would need to be thought of as still missing, if not quite its central core (the "remnant" may be understood to have provided that much from the beginning), then at least the immediately surrounding layer. There is still, we may accordingly imagine, a hollow ring within

---

at least is summed up in Robert Kress, *The Church: Communion, Sacrament, Communication* (New York: Paulist, 1985).

the total sphere. What should fill it remains on the hither side of the boundary between this world and the next, *l'olam ha ze* and *l'olam ha ba,* and remains there, a collective defined by the text of Scripture. But for just this reason the nation in question is unable to assume a position as the authorized premessianic complement of another Israel according to the Spirit, which from any perspective within it cannot yet exist at all. It seems accordingly not a phase of the Christian but "another" religion, both to itself and its putative rival. An absence is disclosed therefore not just within the world of the Other but in our world as well, though the first is real and the second, from a wider perspective, illusory. It is actual enough, though, to prompt the usual process by which a vacuum is filled. An institution has been constructed, we could then say, to substitute for the nation as this still is—and in due course, we can observe, the new entity has attracted some of the habits and privileges associated with the long-since-alienated collective. And this surrogate development in turn has made it harder to understand not just the history of Christianity or the proper relation of that to Judaism (or vice versa) but the more general relationship between a text, upon which any institution, Jewish or Christian, has to be founded, and the body—which by definition (as such, textual too) would transcend the text.

The philosophical issue though is a problem for a separate discussion. One need only conclude our historical sketch of the communal body by repeating a question once asked by Emile Mersch, still the best of the classic modern theologians of the Church, in his second and more speculative book, compiled (after his death on the roads of Flanders in 1940) as *The Theology of the Mystical Body*. "What, in Christian teaching," this Belgian Jesuit asks his readers, "is the point, the aspect, the mystery which is present in the whole and in which the whole is present? What is the thing which makes that doctrine one by enclosing it in itself? What, within the very heart of Christian teaching, is the first intelligible with respect to which the entire doctrine is one and intelligible?" His answer is "the whole Christ," or the "fullness of humanity but also the fullness of divinity in the fullness of his Unity"—which is to say, what we have been calling the body indeed. In such evocative formulations Mersch could be understood as doing for the communal possibility what the theorists of the patristic period had done for the individual: establishing, as it were, the eschatological entity in its situation as well as a definition in this world could do that. "All dogmas," he goes on to say, "discourse of the whole Christ," who is therefore simultaneously the content of Scripture and the one true object of theology. "There is nothing but the incarnation." It is difficult to avoid quoting phrases that seem to concentrate the central intuition so splendidly, though this insight of course is supported by a more conventional tissue of argument on this or that topic of theology to show how each may be understood to imply what he is still obliged to call the "mystical" body as both its ground and result.[18]

---

[18] The passages quoted in the preceding paragraph from Emile Mersch, *The Theology of the Mystical Body* (St. Louis: Herder, 1951) may be found on pp. 50-51, 111, and 24.

If Mersch's work had been better known sooner, so as to become as influential as that of his French peers or German successors, it might already have proved easier than has recently seemed possible not just to adjudicate satisfactorily among the titles for the Church and in particular to find some way to articulate an ideal relation between the body and the institution or its liberal and radical antagonists, but more important, to maintain a clear notion of the identity entailed by the principal image. If one keeps in mind that the community in question is eminently the body, whatever else it or she or we may also be called, then the perennial (as it has proved) temptation either to displace this image or to substitute implicitly secular definitions would be easier to resist. The real presence of the body indeed in the form of a self-acknowledging community would obviously reduce the inclination to overvalue such other intimations of communality as we might continue to lament or desire or even enjoy and so enable us to interpret these too as prefigurements with their own legitimate (because strictly imaginative) power. For history as well as doctrine would then confirm that there could in the end be no more than one such body on the scale of the community—and that this would indeed have to be eschatological, if present at all.

One might accordingly conclude that the special task for those professionally concerned would be to reeschatologize ecclesiology. We are by now used to thinking of Jesus himself as the agent of the End. Biblical scholarship has effectually normalized this understanding over the last century or so. We are even more or less ready to suspect that the eucharistic action might conceivably import as much. But at least in recent times (and from the beginning as well, if in other terms) the Church has not quite become accustomed to thinking of herself too as a equivalently parabolic manifestation of the Kingdom of God—except in ways that have embarrassed friends and further alienated enemies. To employ otherworldly language to describe a this-worldly state of affairs is obviously idolatry, not self-recognition. The church of this world has accordingly preferred, on its less triumphalist side, to think of what therefore can fairly be called "itself" in the mode suggested by the prevailing sacrificial understanding both of its founder and its founder's symbol, and therefore as a repetition of both in the midst of any current social praxis. Such modesty is ethically as well as theoretically safer. But it is not yet all that might be. For the Church could also allow "herself" to be a reproduction, we may allow ourselves to be reminded, of the resurrection as well as the passion: which is to say, of the nearness of the End as such. Such a thoroughly eschatological community, we could also realize, would never be more than one day old, nor would it (or rather in this case most certainly "she") have longer than just half a lifetime yet to live. But she would never cease to enjoy exactly this much of all the time there could ever be.

Such a communal body would indeed be the eventual Israel of what could then be identified as the original intention, to which all other variants, anticipatory or parodic, Christian or Jewish, could therefore be related after whatever conceptual fashion we might manage. And every other body too, natural or symbolic or even approximately communal, could then occupy at least a metaphoric relation to this all but entirely ultimate whole, which would in that case be able to stand even for unbelievers as at least the regulative idea in terms of which these other versions of bodiliness might severally be understood. For then the Church would more obviously appear as the community of communities, the promise fulfilled of all the others, from family to nation, university or party, army and agency. In that case even the institution might be easier to recuperate as a type for what it prophesies, like the Law a "shadow," in the language of Colossians (2:16-17), of things to come, which the gospel, however that may be "preached," can afford to claim has already, to just this extent, become true. It takes a body, after all, to cast a shadow—a body with the light behind it.

Textual

Modernity, we have been proposing, is most generally any critical process by which a body out of place is either re-placed where it belongs or done away with. The first context in which this can be seen to have occurred is natural philosophy, where a scholastic or Renaissance analogism was replaced in theory and practice by what could thereafter deserve the name of "science" indeed. The second context is still more obviously the political, where revolution has repeatedly disintegrated one version or another of what had come to seem a specious communal body together with whatever representative individuals came to hand. A third context, one is by now aware, is the realm of the aesthetic, which for so long seemed immune to or exempt from either cognitive or ethical attack but has since also become subject to a "critique" that refuses to allow even works of art to retain any traditional attributes of bodiliness. In all three contexts, what has succeeded is in the first place chaos; in the second, so much of this detritus as might still be categorized, organized, and distributed: the object, physical or mental; the institution; the text. And all these recombinations, the most recent of these movements would allow us to say, are in the end assimilable to the last.

If so, we might also observe that these successive triumphs have raised a second-level question: How might the text itself be "deconstructed"? But for this metaproblem modernity offers no solution in any of the terms it has sponsored. Philosophy has not yet proposed any convincing way for knowledge to culminate in its own annihilation. Epistemology has repeatedly examined the elements of the cognitive paradigm—but only from a perspective within it. The state, alas, has certainly not withered away, however often it has been reconstituted. And the demystification of art has so far produced only an embarrassing surplus of fanciful theory and theoretical fancy. Nor has anyone, apparently, whether in theology or in practice, found a way to undo the institutionality of the institutional church so as to reveal the bodiliness of the body indeed without interference or qualification. In every context the text, literal or social, remains apparently triumphant.

The last of the second-level problems mentioned, though, might at least suggest a direction in which to look for an older context within which this "problematic" of the text might appear not only to have been raised but, at least in principle, to have been solved as well. I have just suggested that the insecure relation between the institutional and the charismatic modes of the Church could be regarded as a repetition in medieval, modern, and postmodern times alike of a deeper and quite literally crucial difference between "Judaism" and "Christianity"—though these all-too-ideological names would as such misrepresent the polarity in question. If so, it should be possible to revert to this, the aboriginal version of the problem, where the text is simply the Torah, and the corresponding institution is therefore the nation of Israel. For in that context the act of deconstruction to the first degree may already be seen to have taken place as this nation established itself within the land of Canaan. An explicit structure based on a covenant with God was to the social and religious environment of the Late Bronze Age what the Enlightenment has been in modern times to "Christendom." In both cases, a revolutionary disembodiment was succeeded by the hegemony of a text. But in the ancient context this dominance would in due course be challenged by an apocalypse that proposed to replace the text by a new mode of the body. Nothing of the sort has yet occurred within the context of modernity—unless in fear or fantasy. We might well attend accordingly, even as unbelieving critics, to what could still be learned from the one sequence within which an ideal trajectory could in fact be followed from the beginning to something nearer an End than we have otherwise been able to arrive at.

That what became Judaism, and therefore a definable identity for the people in question, has from the start been founded upon not just *a* but *the* text, has always been sufficiently evident. The Torah is ostentatiously a *written* document from the beginning, whenever that moment may be dated in traditional story or scholarly hypothesis, and however many times the founding instance may have had to be supplemented or reconstructed, generation after scribal generation. The "documentary hypothesis," itself now a tradition under attack, has in modern times proposed a sequence of compositional moments from J and E through JE, balanced by P through R, with Deuteronomy, as the Greek name implies, as an intermediate recapitulation.[19] The books of prophecy accumulated in a similar fashion and were in due course added to the deposit, along with the other "writings." But the process may be seen to continue through the Mishnah to the Talmud; and by now there are many books on the Talmud. In precanonical times each act of interpretation resulted in an addition to or a rearrangement of the inherited text; in a postcanonical age, the same act produced one more commentary upon the text. But the principle is the same: text produces text, indefinitely.

Texts typically include within themselves an explanation for the authority they

---

[19] I am relying on what has remained, somewhat shakily, the conventional wisdom among modern biblical scholars through the argument that follows. The apparently old-fashioned "documentary hypothesis" has recently been energetically revived by R. E. Friedman's popular but acute *Who Wrote the Bible?* (New York: Summit, 1987).

claim. For the Torah this legitimation is, to begin with, ambiguous. According to the story rehearsed in Exodus, intercourse between God and human beings is oral on both sides until Moses writes the key words down at the ceremony establishing a covenant as the permanent form of the relation (24:4). In 24:12, though, it is the Lord himself who writes on the tablets of stone, and this is repeated at 32:16. Both of these are apparently J passages. The second set of tablets, which are reinscribed after the first have been broken, is also ambiguously attributed. In 34:1 the Lord promises to write on them. In 34:27, though, he instructs Moses to write; and in 34:28, which continues the scene, "he" could refer to either person.

By the time Deuteronomy is composed, this ambiguity at least has been resolved. In that book the Lord himself not only speaks out of the fire at Sinai but also writes down the commandments that specify the covenant on the tablets (Deut. 4:13; 5:19; 9:10; 10:2, 4). To make God write the key words is to absolutize the text, a position in due course taken over by Islam as well as other varieties of fundamentalism—which is, in every context, a religion of the *literal* generally. There are further repercussions of this resolution within Deuteronomy: a continual emphasis on *writing* is very noticeable, whether in connection with laws, stones, or simply a bill of divorcement. The explicit use of the covenant formulary, which can be found to structure the book as a whole, would reflect the same disposition, for the document of any covenant must, by ancient Near Eastern practice, be composed according to a conventional order of parts. And the notorious rigor of the D version of the relation presumes an equivalently explicit definition of the moral situation: a line is drawn to divide what should be done from what must not, and penalties are established to enforce the difference. The slash, which defines the Deuteronomic "not/but" in all contexts, is the very blade of the chisel or point of the pen, separating what is from what is not, being and nothingness, positive and negative. And the literary predicament presumed by such a project exhibits the same principle. To repeat the Law yet again in a still more compelling version is to accept textualization as properly determinative of whatever may have been obscured by the vagaries of oral tradition, cultic or popular or royal. This enterprise of a scribe, who must also have understood himself as a prophet (presumably the one predicted in 18:18, though as a writer rather than the speaker there imagined), is thus recognizably very "early modern" in character. Deuteronomy is, as it were, the Protestantism of the Old Testament. And as in the later case, retextualization can also be felt as overtextualization.

At the close of the central block of Deuteronomy, which is devoted to the detailed stipulations for the covenant occupying chapters 12 through 26, the narrative switches back to the story with which it began in order to commence a coda. At the beginning of this, in 27:18, we read that on the day when the tribes pass over the Jordan to occupy the land the Lord their God has given them, they are to set up and plaster stones, one for each of the twelve tribes, and write upon them "all the words of this law" (27:3, 8). In context this must mean the text of Deuteronomy itself—understood, that is, as an expanded version of the Decalogue on as many additional surfaces as that would take. And if the stones represent the tribes, to write upon them would become a way of impressing the instructions they record on the hearts of all the people. The blessings and curses that follow in chapters 27 and 28 repeat the model of a liturgy that may at one time have been employed at a ceremony of covenant renewal. On such occasions a shorter version of the central document could have been read aloud and sworn to. Such a ritual would itself be repeated in another form whenever the intended reader of Deuteronomy went over it—ideally, we are also to understand, as the obedient king, but in practice as any congregation of the just.

In other words, the text is repeated not just before entry into the promised land, as one might expect (for would not inhabitance have to be post-textual, and so bodily?) but within it as well, on the other side of the river. The text lays claim to the land in advance. And this directive is represented as carried out in the Book of Joshua, which was later assembled along with the rest of the "Deuteronomistic" history under the same auspices as Deuteronomy itself. We are told how the ark bearing the tablets was carried across the bed of the Jordan, miraculously laid bare for the purpose, and the twelve stones were erected on the farther side to memorialize the crossing. Any other sort of future than that which should still be dominated by the instructions received and inscribed must therefore be understood ahead of time as illegitimate forever. History can thus be rediscovered after if not before the fact as a serial exemplification of the ethical difference determined by the text in the form of successive episodes of corruption and recovery, wickedness and punishment, arranged to display as narrative what has already been spelled out as commandment. Even song can be recruited to this didactic intention, as chapter 32 of Deuteronomy shows, where Moses is represented as composing yet one more "witness" against any future apostasy. His last words function accordingly as still another stone to specify the obligations of generations to come, as the larger text for which the hymn supplies one of several concluding moments functions as an occasion for repetition to the Levites. Text overlaps with text as Moses places his new book "by the side of" the ark containing the tablets (31:26) .

One might conclude a review of these conclusions with a custom referred to, appropriately enough, in a note to this chapter in the Hertz edition of the Pentateuch, where, a latter-day scribe myself, I can read that the verse commanding Moses to write down the song (31:19) was understood by the rabbis as a recommendation that each Israelite should write out a copy of the whole Torah for himself. In later times this was accomplished representatively by allowing each man in the congregation to fill up one letter of several at the end of a scroll left in outline for the purpose.[20] To worship in such a mode is to read, but to read is to rewrite; and

---

[20] J. M. Hertz, ed., *The Pentateuch and Haftorahs* (London: Soncino, 1972) 889-90n. This remains a convenient edition of the Torah for the amateur Hebraist, though now in the process of being replaced by the new Jewish Publication Society commentary edited by Nahum

to rewrite is at each stage to renew the authority of whatever has already been or is just now being written, generation after generation, world as if without end.

The closest cultic analogue to the version of the relation we find written out in Deuteronomy as commandment would seem to be not the temple ritual but an older domestic rite which, unlike the public cult, has persisted to the present. The "order for the covenant of cutting" to be found in the modern *Prayer Book* is most explicit that circumcision should be understood as an imprinting of the relevant text upon the body of the infant.[21] The model is Isaac, who was sanctified when the "statute was set in his flesh," so that thereafter his offspring should be "sealed" as a "sign of the holy covenant." To *cut* the flesh of the male generative organ is to *inscribe* an initial and therefore representative commandment upon this equivalently representative part of the natural body, as if to take possession in the name of the Lord of what might otherwise become an idol. Other features of the traditional rite would support and amplify the implications of this central action. The *mohel,* or "cutter," who is traditionally appointed to do this work of the hands, and the godfather on whose knees the child is held, are evidently surrogates for the father, who at just this moment accepts this child as his son indeed, and therefore a successor in the sequence of generations as Isaac was for Abraham, into whose ancestral version of the relation the boy is thereby inducted.

In the rite of circumcision a father accepts his son; and simultaneously prepares this new body in advance for the same holy work that has just been completed in his own case. Circumcision is not then an abbreviated castration, as has too easily been supposed. It is rather a hallowing of that member by which the continuity from father to son may be carried on. The transmissive power of the male must be set aside for the Lord, for the tribes are his, and therefore the sequence of generations from the beginning into so much at least of the future as has with the birth of one more male become predictable.

On the level of language, this most typical action is repeated in the assignment of a name, which takes place on the same occasion. In the older tradition a son was named after his father, *as* his father's son, in so many words: X, son of Y, thus becomes the father of Z, son of X. Those lists of names in more than one book of the Bible, which endlessly define sons in terms of their fathers and these again as sons of the fathers before them, thus serve as repeated exemplifications of the principle by which sexual becomes cultural representation. The death of the individual in one generation is literally survived by passing his name on to a

---

Sarna and Chaim Potok.

[21]J. H. Hertz, ed., *The Authorized Daily Prayer Book,* rev. ed. (New York: Bloch, 1948) 1024-29. My argument presumes the historical (and therefore Judaic) form of the rite, which in a prehistoric (and so pre-Israelite) version may have been performed as a preparation for marriage by the bridegroom's father-in-law. In that context the sexual meaning would obviously have predominated over what has since become the textual.

descendant as the sign of continuing citizenship in the nation constituted by a permanent relation to God. Hebrew idiom generalizes this strategy: "son of ___" in any context means "belonging to the category typified by ___." Conceptual status too is thus enfigured by descent: what is in Greek (and therefore modern) thinking an *idea* is for Hebrew culture an *inheritance*.

The private rite rhymes with its ancestral analogue on the scale of the collective, which establishes just such a covenant as a child of any era is being inducted into. On those archaic occasions the body of a representative animal would be most literally "cut" in two lengthwise, as a demonstrative confession: so might it be done to the party concerned should he not keep the terms of the treaty thereby constituted. The edge of the knife that split the victim may accordingly be understood as already drawing the line that initiates writing, as a "covenant document" under the throne of the relevant god would amount to the same line broken up into as many letters. To "cut a covenant," whether aboriginally or repetitively, is then to decompose a natural body in whole or in part so as to constitute the relevant text. The father writes, the son reads; and the text is passed on as an inheritance that defines them both as who they have got to be within the relation.

The rite of circumcision has over time been normalized so as to emphasize the hegemony of the literal text among these ritual equivalences. Earlier stories make more of the phallic and memorial elements. In Genesis 28, for instance, Jacob journeys from Beersheba to Haran in search of a wife. On his way he sleeps and dreams; and in his dream the Lord renews with him the covenant that had already been constituted with his father and his grandfather, repeating anew the promise of the land and a future increase in his "seed." When Jacob wakes, he sets up the rock on which he has slept as a pillar to mark this new encounter and pours oil upon it, giving the place a new name, "the house of God." The phallic *matzebah* would then manifest a species of textuality *avant la lettre,* an *aleph-taw* out of which the other elements of the alphabet would in due course proliferate. In such a tale we seem to catch the moment of translation from member to stone to tablets to parchment.[22] An upright stone is regularly a constant witness to the prevalence of an agreement, as when Jacob and Laban make a treaty of peace and marriage in Genesis 31. For a stone is permanent, extending the scope of the relation it signifies from one generation to another. A circumcised penis would then be, as it were, a living stone. Objectivity, which a stone typifies, would from the beginning be coincident with textuality even before any writing was in fact inscribed upon it. By the time of Deuteronomy, though, such patriarchal physicalities have either been translated altogether into their literary equivalents or dismissed as pagan corruptions: in Deuteronomy 16:22, for instance, setting up a pillar is expressly forbidden. But

---

[22] It can seem more than incidentally interesting that these multiple meanings should continue imperative for the "phallus" (so prominent in and out of the Lacanian version of psychoanalysis), which has to count both as a physical organ and the representative "signifier."

circumcision survives to manifest the principal connections nevertheless.

A fully scriptural and adult analogue to circumcision might then be discoverable in the custom of "binding" the words of the Shema, which includes just this command, "as a sign on thy hand, and as frontlets between thine eyes" (Deut. 6:8). "Literally" to wear these words would then be to reenact an inscription or branding of the text upon the body on a daily basis but without immediate appeal to the more equivocal if original symbolics of the flesh. In this way a responsible citizen of the relevant collective could still testify without ambiguity to the unqualified character of his commitment to those *other* words he would then proceed to repeat. And this confirmation of purpose would in its turn be reinforced by the supplementary custom of writing the ayin at the end of the first word of the initial verse of the prayer, that is, "hear" in "Hear, Israel, the Lord our God, the Lord is One," together with the final letter of the last word, the daleth of *echod,* so as to form the word meaning "witness." This verse, then, together with the other verses that make up the Shema and the practice that accompanies their repetition, make up a composite act of testimony. Witness is the legal form of sacrifice, as procreation is the sexual. To concentrate the pretextual instances within the text or the usages that accompany its repetition would make what can be done in just such terms absolutely normative. In all such cases the body would be either subordinated or excluded—or hoped for as altogether futural, the sons of a son not yet even begotten, the anointed one indeed.

It has often been observed that textuality and repetition necessarily go together, as we have just found ourselves rediscovering, not for the first time.[23] Rhetoric would then repeat repetition, to render the principle self-evident, and so make a game of necessity. There are certainly sufficient instances of this, casual or prominent, in Scripture, whether as psalm verse or narrative recurrence. Repetition is, to begin with, a species of multiplication, which extends the text in time and space, as inscriptions become copies, commentaries proliferate, and readers repeat these and themselves, generation after generation. But by exposing the common element, which is in fact repeated from one set of circumstances to another, repetition can also serve the apparently opposite purpose of condensation or reduction. We are invited by the very recurrence of the accidental to seek out the essential: some formula that might concentrate the multitude of local sentences into

---

[23]The "iterability" of the text has been influentially reaffirmed for contemporary criticism in Jacques Derrida's essay "Signature, Event, Context," now most accessible in *Margins of Philosophy* (Chicago: University of Chicago Press, 1982). His rendering of the link between repetition and the signature has helped determine the order if not the conclusion of my own argument. A concern for the latter theme persists through other Derridian texts, including especially *Glas* (Lincoln: University of Nebraska Press, 1986), though to no repeatable effect that I have been able to discover. Peggy Kamuf's still more recent *Signature Pieces* (Ithaca: Cornell Univ. Press, 1988) is, I am also afraid, too "orthodox" to be helpful except for titles.

a master proposition which would govern them all. This disposition too is reflected within the tradition as the search for a single commandment that could sum up all the others—or within the history of the text, as the repeated effort to fasten upon a "canon within the canon," or utterly typical instance.

One candidate not often mentioned for this role would illustrate the aesthetic as well as the didactic uses of repetition. Psalm 119 may at one time have served as the concluding psalm for the collection of sacred songs as a whole. It could have been installed in that position when Psalm 1, with its promise of happiness for the one who obeys the law and murmurs it night and day, was placed at the beginning to introduce a psalter already divided into five parts—which would thus repeat the five books of what had by then become recognized as the Torah indeed. Psalm 119 might even have been composed by the editor responsible for this arrangement, who could thus have intended this poem as a last word for sure, a repetition and concentration of all the others, not just the hymns it thereby concluded but the rest of Scripture too. If so, we should date this psalm of psalms some time in the late exilic period, when so many of the previous texts too were being put into what was, upon the return, to become their final form.[24]

The principle on which Psalm 119 is organized is wonderfully demonstrative of the intention it seems to represent. Each of the twenty-two stanzas contains eight verses of two lines apiece. Every verse of each stanza begins with one of the letters of the Hebrew alphabet, in the corresponding order. And each employs a word from a set of synonyms for the instruction provided in Scripture generally. These may be variously translated: M. Dahood lists the principal words as *law, testimony, way, precepts, statutes, commandment, ordinance, word,* and *utterance.* There is no apparent order to the sequence of words within any one stanza. Dahood points out irregularities: instead of one of the usual words, *truth* is used once, in a stanza governed by the letter *lamed* (ל), and five verses, he thinks, are defective because missing a term. In fact a careful reading would reduce these to one instance in verse 122 of the *ayin* (ע) stanza, where no master term appears at all. Once in *nun* (נ) there is a double repetition: *word, ordinance, word, ordinance.* Once in *samech* (ס) there is a repetition of *statutes* in successive verses. In *beth, vav, resh, shin,* and *taw* (ב ו ר ש ת), verses with two major words appear. An author as skillful as this poet could presumably have avoided these irregularities if he had wished. They may accordingly have been deliberate, to avoid perfection. He had already imposed two additional "laws" upon himself, the better to manifest his devotion to the Law

---

[24]The suggestion concerning the intention of the putative author of Ps. 119 I owe to J. W. Rogerson and J. W. McKay, *Psalms* (Cambridge: Cambridge University Press, 1977) 5. The role of the "Torah psalms" has been reviewed by J. L. Mays, "The Place of the Torah-Psalms in the Psalter," *JBL* 106/1 (March 1987): 3-12, and Jon Levenson, "The Sources of Torah: Psalm 119 and the Modes of Revelation in Second Temple Judaism," in *Ancient Israelite Religion,* ed. Patrick D. Miller (Philadelphia: Fortress, 1987) 559-74.

indeed. But no one can be sure, these defects might imply, of one's righteousness by any standard, divine or human, metaphoric or imperative.[25]

Each verse is made up of a single sentence, and each sentence is centered upon one of these major words—which incidentally reflects what appears to be a universal rule, that a sentence is essentially a single word in context. Since each of the repeated major words means virtually the same thing, each verse too in effect repeats all the others. Twenty-two times eight is 196: the number of repetitions without *significant* semantic variation is overwhelming. Synonymy is identity, with a vengeance. As a song this meditation is therefore *all* antiphon—a bold stroke, indeed intolerably so to some minds. For there is, this poem would relentlessly demonstrate, only one thing really for any speaker to confess, no matter how many times it must be said. This subject speaks in the first person, and to God, not his peers. The psalm is therefore a prayer that rehearses the relation established by the covenant on the scale of the individual. Here, for instance, is the letter *hē* (ה)—chosen at random, as should be appropriate for such an purpose. (Psalm 119:33-40 in most English versions. Once again the Soncino translation is employed.)

> Teach me, O Lord, the way of Thy statutes;
>   And I will keep it at every step.
> Give me understanding, that I keep Thy law
>   And observe it with my whole heart.
> Make me to tread in the path of Thy commandments;
>   For therein do I delight.
> Incline my heart unto Thy testimonies,
>   And not to covetousness.
> Turn away mine eyes from beholding vanity,
>   And quicken me in Thy ways.
> Confirm Thy word unto Thy servant,
>   Which pertaineth unto the fear of Thee.
> Turn away my reproach which I dread;
>   For Thy ordinances are good.
> Behold, I have longed after Thy precepts;
>   Quicken me in Thy righteousness.

As with the same covenant on the scale of the collective, this cumulative affirmation of allegiance is also and without qualification a written document, no matter how many times one "says" it over. The alphabetic structure already determines as much. The several synonymous words repeated, the sentences that

---

[25] I owe the information repeated in this paragraph to Mitchell Dahood's Anchor Bible edition of the *Psalms,* AB 16, 17, 17a (Garden City NY: Doubleday, 1966–1970) 3:193, even when I disagree with aspects of his reading.

convert these into declarations, and the paired verses that reinforce or contrast with what each affirms are in effect spellings out, letter by letter, of what is for each stanza already entailed by the initial introducing each verse—a governing factor that cannot be represented in translation. It is not hard to conclude that all writing is thus in principle subsumed into this stunningly final inscription, which so unswervingly rehearses the covenantal presuppositions of every other possible text. "The alphabet is a ready metaphor for totality," as Will Soll observes in his recent monograph on Psalm 119—the totality, one would need to add, of the text.[26] For simply as such it testifies to whatever is elsewhere registered in terms of the signs it supplies, as a catalog sums up a library, a dictionary a language, or an encyclopedia a culture. Writing *defines* relation, says this poem, and here that thesis is proved true once again, over and over.

Meanwhile the single word all the master words might be translated into does not as such appear among them. That word, which should in principle concentrate all the synonyms and therefore any one of the additional words that support these to form sentence after sentence, seems as such unsayable. It would therefore be at the same time unwritable, for it would need to be made up of what all the letters of the alphabet together would spell at once; and that word does not exist—as an element in any language. On the side of the relation in which an individual can repeat this poem or a nation compose its constitution, this inaudible and illegible master word would therefore have to be heard or read as a plurality of other words. As in other contexts, the many reflect the one—and in a broken mirror at that. But a reflection as carefully oriented as this poem is no chaos. Psalm 119 could accordingly stand as a formidable instance of what one might mean by the text of all texts, or the text indeed. What that would amount to "literally" would remain implicit in the poem's formal conduct. But there it may be read, from a suitable distance, which is all the while precisely as close as prayer.

How though could one in fact move from several actual synonyms to a single ideal word, or more literally still from the many letters of the alphabet to some single letter that might concentrate the purport of them all? Another Old Testament instance could provide a clue. It occurs in Ezekiel 9:4, when in the prophet's vision a figure clothed in linen with the equipment of a scribe is instructed to mark the foreheads of those within the city who have sighed and cried out at all the abominations for which the rest of the inhabitants are to be punished by six angels, now waiting with their instruments of destruction in hand. The pen is to the sword, then, as one to six, which would also be, presumably, the proportion of the just to the wicked. The mark to be set on the foreheads of those who should be spared is a taw, the last letter of the alphabet—which in the archaic Hebrew orthography is

---

[26]Will Soll, *Psalm 119: Matter, Form, and Setting*, CBQ Monograph Series 23 (Washington: Catholic Biblical Association, 1991) 27. Soll's suggestion that this psalm should be attributed to the exiled king Jehoiachin seems only eccentric.

formed by a cross.

The vision recalls Exodus 12:21-23, where the mark in question is made in the blood of the Passover lamb upon the lintels and doorposts of each house in order to distinguish the Israelites from the Egyptians. On that occasion the means is cultic and the distinction national. The attitude presumed is accordingly from a later viewpoint almost pagan, like the still-earlier parallel, the mark placed on Cain in Genesis 4:15. For Ezekiel, though, writing in exilic times, the mark imposed is explicitly a letter, not a splotch of blood or a tattoo. And as the last of the alphabet, it may as a result be understood to sum up all the others and so in effect all the words that might ever be inscribed with those letters, as in an alphabetic psalm. It thereby becomes in miniature the entirety of the Law in a single sign.

The Apocalypse of John picks up this image and repeats it in the form of a contrast between those who bear the name or number of the beast on their hands or foreheads (Rev. 13:16-17) and those who have been "sealed" with the name of Jesus and his Father (Rev. 7:3-4; 14:1) written on their foreheads. These later versions of the idea seem less carefully scribal: the "brand" or "seal" is apparently imposed in letters of visionary fire, and the sign itself is left ambiguous: is it a word or a number, two names or one? But the mark in question is evidently to be understood as a species of signature, or sign manifesting the possessive rights of the person or persons concerned. And this association is genuinely useful.

We may follow it up by reverting not to an earlier prophet but to one of the Writings. Job's complaint, in the book of that name, concludes with a long speech in which, as the narrator puts it, "the words of Job are ended" (31:40). Just previous to this moment of closure Job cries out, "Behold my signature!" as if he were indeed in court, and in this way attested that he stood behind what he had been saying: "Let the Almighty answer!" (31:35). The Hebrew term for "signature" is in fact the letter *taw* (ת), employed as a word instead of the name for a letter. The cross that originally formed it could then represent the testimony of someone who did not know how to spell his own name, letter by separate letter, or could not afford a proper cylinder with a name or symbol in relief upon it to roll out against the clay. At this point in the *mashal* that the story of Job has become, the term acquires a special significance. In the version that determines this narrative, the unjustly afflicted individual complains at length. In another version, which may still be detected in what is now the introductory portion of the book, he may have remained silent. In either case, the signature attesting to the validity of the words employed or simply to the presence of the person concerned is still a cross. With that mark Job signs himself in before God. From that point on it is his divine opposite who must do him the justice of replying to what has thereby become his last word indeed.

Should one wonder, then, if this final initial also becomes, as if by accident, the constant sign of the individual Jesus? Thus does he "make his mark," as Robert Frost used to observe sardonically. The crucifixion is in fact his first and last document. Thereby he inscribes himself once and for all. The cross is indeed the end of the line. In that letter the text terminates for good. Paul very well understands this consequence, which informs his doctrine that the double stroke of timber and flesh should be understood as concentrating and thereby replacing the Law in its entirety. So he wonders at his foolish Galatians, before whom, he repeats, Jesus as the Christ had already been "written out" as "crucified" (Gal. 3:1), as if upon some one-word, or rather one-letter, poster. That reduction, we are to understand, is as much of the gospel as may be *understood,* that is, stand out as legible in this world. It is a mistake accordingly, Paul reports himself as having found out the hard way, to depend on any other sort of "sign" or "wisdom," Jewish or Greek, besides what is testified to by an event that has in effect consumed all other texts whatsoever. Colossians 2:13-15, if we may trust this much of that letter as Pauline, is equally emphatic: Jesus is described there as "nailing" the Law, and so the debt of sin this document incidently attests to, upon the same cross. In just this individual flesh, then, the text at once triumphs—for what more complete *titulus* could there be than that which converts the whole of the body natural into a single letter?—and is erased. A taw of such a kind would indeed enact and cancel any other signature. Whatever followed could not possibly be in writing, whether physical, literal, or social. In Job what in fact follows is a long speech of the Lord, displaying the mysterious wonder of creation. In the case of Jesus, what follows is what can be proclaimed as the resurrection. In both, the text as such has in principle already come to an end—though in both too we may also guess at this result by way of a narrative that must itself be read as a text. For all readers are still in this world, however much they look forward to the next.

A signature, we would ordinarily say, terminates the text to which it is appended. It is therefore in principle and often in practice the last *written* word; the period, as it were, beyond which the extratextual, whatever that might turn out to be within the situation in question, would have to be thought of as commencing. In a tale like Job, or any one of the narratives that have since been repeated of the life and death of Jesus, it would only be natural to place the end of the line as near as possible to the end of the story. But this position need not be inevitable, even for terminal signs set down from within our side of the covenantal relation, which is what we must necessarily be concerned with in the case of Psalm 119 or Ezekiel or Job or so much of Jesus as could be put to death. A signature might also "authorize" what follows at the beginning of a text—on the title page, say, as with a book we give to a friend. Or it may be found deep within the text, at its center, or even scattered about broadcast, as a hint so many times repeated that it cannot easily be taken in.

The last is most evidently the case for the "signature" of God himself—who as such would obviously be on the other side of the relation. The textual manifestation of this conclusion can be quite explicit within scripture as the Holy Name. It is well known that in Jewish practice the tetragrammaton, or "four-letter word," should not be read aloud as it appears in the text but instead should be replaced by "the Lord" (literally "my Lords," Adonai) as an oral surrogate. In the Hassidic tradition the same person is referred to still more indirectly as *Ha Shem,* "the Name." A related custom is less familiar to Gentiles. Once the Holy Name has been written down, it should not be erased—even from a classroom blackboard, as I once found to my embarrassment. This prohibition was deduced by the rabbis from Deuteronomy 12:5, which requires the people to seek the Lord only in the place where he has chosen to "place his Name there." The text thus becomes a sufficient successor to the temple, where the God of Israel was once understood to tabernacle precisely by way of a ritual repetition of his Name. The practice of preserving the Name in Hebrew characters even in Greek translations of the Scriptures would presumably reflect a similar understanding of its special status. So would the custom of burying worn-out texts in which the Name appeared, instead of destroying them by fire or otherwise.[27] For the essence of the text, as concentrated in the Name, would in principle be indestructible. That signature at least could be thought of as inscribed forever, *l'olam,* as if in stone that would never wear away. Erasure is thus understood as inconsistent with the very idea of writing: if a text can be blotted out or thrown away, it cannot have been altogether real in the first place. From an ancient point of view, a disposable text is a contradiction in terms.

The written Name thus attests not to the absence but to the distant presence of the One who has authorized the surrounding text—literally enough, according to Deuteronomy, as we have already seen. In that case it would be at last this signature that would most satisfactorily concentrate the surrounding context of Scripture as a first, last, and often-repeated word. No wonder that in the cabalistic tradition the Torah could be understood as spelling out precisely this Name of names—though cryptically, so that only adepts might in fact find it there. The Zohar repeats this thesis as the proposition that "the entire Torah is the single holy mystical name."[28] How, then, should the literal Name itself be understood? To say it aloud was already forbidden, for that might bring all too near the presence it conceals as well

---

[27]The first practice is cited in Moshe Greenberg, *Ezekiel 1-20,* Anchor Bible 22 (Garden City: Doubleday, 1983) 65; the second in Hertz, *Pentateuch,* 800n. The permanence of the text exactly as written was as such a familiar motif in the ancient Near East, as with the "laws of the Medes and Persians," which could not be altered once written (Dan. 6:9), or the Laws of Hammurabi, as cited in Louis F. Hartman and Alexander A. di Lella, *The Book of Daniel,* Anchor Bible 23 (Garden City NY: Doubleday, 1978) 199.

[28]I quote the translation offered by G. G. Scholem in his *On the Kabbalah and Its Symbolism* (New York: Schocken, 1965) 39n. The permutations of this way of reading the text are reviewed on pp. 37-44. Scholem's more recent *Origins of the Kabbalah* (Princeton: Princeton University Press, 1987) reverts to the earlier beginnings of the interpretive tradition that led up to the Zohar. The translation of this climactic text by H. Sperling and M. Simon offers another rendering of the difficult medieval Aramaic, which attributes the key proposition to a presumably fictional Rabbi Eleazar: "To study the Torah is like studying the Holy Name . . . the Torah is all one holy supernal name." See their edition of *The Zohar* (New York: Rebecca Bennet, 1962) 4:395.

as intimates. Once upon a time the high priest had been entitled to call out the Name as a blessing over the crowd assembled for the Day of Atonement. At such moments the owner of the Name could indeed inhabit his temple by proxy at least. But now there are no high priests and no temple. The Name must apparently remain silent. But it still may be read—if only with the eyes.

And if it is, letter by letter, it would also become possible, with the help of a later and rather different interpretive tradition, to realize that the word thus formed is not only a sacred noun but a common verb. It may in fact—though this continues to be contested—most probably be parsed as an archaic form of the third-person-singular imperfect of the verb *to be*. If so, the likeliest translation would become "he will be," which in turn would need to be read as an abbreviated version of the fundamental covenantal promise: the God of Israel may be known as the one who will indeed be with his chosen ones, individual and plural, through the rest of the future as he has been with them in the past.[29] To declare as much is then to "name" him from without, in the style of one human being speaking to another or formally announcing who he is to the people gathered together to acknowledge just this identity.

If this understanding of the literal meaning of the Name is accepted, then the form in which it appears in the text would already be a circumlocution. For the third-person version would be an objective incognito for the first-person form, which as such appears explicitly only in the narrative of Moses' first encounter in Exodus 3. There the Lord reveals in answer to Moses' question that his true Name is *ehyeh asher ehyeh,* or "I will be who I will be" (Exodus 3:14). In the same verse the Lord puts even this most intimate version of his Name back into quotation marks, as if to protect it. "Thus shalt thou say to the sons of Israel, "*I will be* has sent me." Some scholars have understood this crucial verse as a subsequent explanation inserted into a narrative that would originally have assumed that the Name revealed was in the third person throughout.[30] But if, as has long since become conventional

---

[29]The principal alternative interpretation of the Name within the American scholarly tradition has been William F. Albright's theory that it represents an archaic *hiphil,* or causative form. In that case the Name would mean "I cause to be," emphasizing the creative power of the one to whom it may be attributed. This grammatical decision has been passed down to Albright's "sons," David N. Freedman, Frank M. Cross, and R. S. Boling. Eichrodt and de Vaux, among the European authorities, prefer the imperfect of the *qal,* or indicative. Such recent reviews of the problem as Parke-Taylor, *Yahweh,* or C. R. Gianotti, "The Meaning of the Divine Name YHWH," *BSac* 142/565 (January–March 1985): 38-51, support this second preference, which seems to me necessitated by Exod. 3:12 and 4:12 in the immediate context of the formal revelation of the Name as well as by similar language at other covenantal moments (e.g., Gen. 17:4, 7; 21:22; 26:3, 24; 28:15, 20; 31:3-4; 35:3; 39:2-3, 21, 23; 46:2-4; 48:21).

[30]Parke-Taylor (*Yahweh,* 47, 51) as well as the ambiguous Brevard S. Childs (*The Book of Exodus* [Philadelphia: Westminster, 1974] 61-70) and the more decisive Martin Noth

to presume, the episode of the burning bush should be attributed to the E source, we could find reasons to see the declaration made in Exodus 3:14 as entirely consistent with what occurs in earlier stories regularly assigned to the same author. When Jacob wrestles with the mysterious figure in Genesis 32:25-33, he obtains a blessing and a new name for himself—but *not* the name of his antagonist, though he asks explicitly. And in the same patriarch's vision of the night in Genesis 46:2-4, though God identifies himself merely as the "God of thy father," the divine speaker repeatedly emphasizes the first-person pronoun: it is *anochi* who is this God; *I* will go down with you to Egypt, and *I* will surely bring you up again.

The first composer of these stories could accordingly be understood as deliberately holding back the true form of the Name—until it could be revealed to the man for whom that privilege was reserved. In that case Exodus 3:14 would be the carefully contrived climax to a sequence of cryptic hints, all of which would presume that the first-person version of the Name would indeed be its pre- as well as post-textual form in Spirit and in truth as well as in the necessarily imaginative rendering we are obliged merely to read. We could accordingly appreciate a prophetic as well as a narrative meaning in the promise of future support and accompaniment which is already expressed in Exod. 3:12 and is soon picked up again in the list of wonders that are to be performed, as well as in the assurance that *this* Lord "will be with" Moses' mouth as he speaks to Pharaoh (Exod. 4:12). The motif is persistent enough to confirm that a continuing presence in and out of the story should indeed be understood as the proper meaning of the Name in all contexts. For presence, in Hebrew *panim,* literally "faces" (which is to say, the two sides of what we would call one face) is precisely what effectuates the promise of relationship that the Name affirms.

An eschatological reading of the third-person version of the Name would in that case be the first-person version—whenever that might be spoken aloud or in silence, not of course by one person to another, or even the high priest to the nation assembled, but by the Lord himself—which would certainly have to occur beyond the text. When the one so repeatedly named becomes present to his people in the midst of the vicissitudes of their history, or to any individual among them for whom, as the phrase goes, he "comes near," then he would in effect be saying his own Name of himself, for that is what he would indeed be enacting. The textual version would be at last fulfilled, as nomination from without dissolved into a presence renewed. "The letter," as another interpretive tradition put the contrast long ago, is always in the third person; "the Spirit," in the first.

There are several contexts within which it is possible to see the third-person version of the Name approaching the first, though without, except for Exodus 3:14, quite arriving there. The most frequently repeated of these would be the intermediate

---

(*Exodus* [Philadelphia: Westminster, 1962] 43-44) share this view with varying degrees of emphasis.

form *ani* or *anochi yhwh,* which combines the third-person form of the Name proper with a first-person pronoun. "I am," this formula would in effect affirm, "indeed the one to whom you refer by way of the Name." We should probably count in as well such parallel formulas as *ani el shaddai* (Gen. 17:1) or *anochi elohei avraham* (Gen. 26:24), which convert other titles, specific or general, into additional synonyms for the Name. Whatever follows such self-introductions would therefore have to be understood as revealing the present will of the Lord, in or out of the narrative. A variant better known to Christian readers is the *ani hu,* or "I am he," so prominent in Second Isaiah, where the nominative element is replaced by the corresponding pronoun in order to introduce the one who is to reveal his presence once again as he leads his people back from exile. The modern German theologian Walther Zimmerli, reviewing all the scriptural variants of the self-introductory formula in what has become a classic essay (appropriately titled "I Am Yahweh"), concluded that the repetition of the mixed expression should be read as testifying to a conviction that the function of narrative, liturgy, and prophecy alike was to manifest the presence of the Lord as this would eventually be revealed in an apocalyptic enactment of the Name by the one to whom it belongs.[31] The end of Scripture, in other words, would be the transcendence of Scripture. The text must be sooner or later fulfilled in theophany; distance, in presence. The Name in the third person, we might accordingly conclude, is the constant *kethib,* or what is written; the Name in the first person an ultimate *qere,* or what is to be spoken—but not, it is clear, by us.

A most interesting paper by the contemporary critic Sandor Goodhart offers an opportunity to trace this always potential metamorphosis of the Name from the third to the first person in a very significant though ordinarily unexamined instance.[32] The *Tanakh,* or Hebrew Bible as a whole, may be understood as surrounding the Torah so as to supplement, repeat, and interpret it. Torah itself, if a center must be found for all five of its "five-fifths" in turn, would presumably need to be thought of as focusing on the "ten words," or the modular obligations of the covenant, as these are typically rehearsed in Exodus 20 and Deuteronomy 5. One of these passages is

---

[31]The article has been published with four supportive pieces under the same title as *I Am Yahweh* (Atlanta: John Knox, 1982). The second and third essays in this book emphasize that the "knowledge" of God called for or provided is accordingly a response to the divine self-disclosure, which is to say, an acknowledgment in faith. Zimmerli does not take deliberate notice of the difference between the third- and first-person versions of the Name, but his argument is most usefully confirmatory for any thesis that does.

[32]Sandor Goodhart, "Biblical Differences: Reading the Ten Commandments," an essay always on the verge of being published. The next four paragraphs follow his argument. Goodhart omits a third repetition of what may still be called the Decalogue in Lev. 19, which assembles, as one might expect, a sufficiently priestly set of specifications. But there as well the formula *ani Adonai* is repeated throughout, as if to punctuate and connect the separate instructions. And this version too, one may learn from a note in the Hertz edition of the *Pentateuch,* was identified by the rabbis as summarizing the essentials of the Torah (497n).

evidently a repetition of the other, though scholars continue to disagree which should be considered the original. These differences, though, need not interfere with a reading that focuses on the Name. If the Ten Commandments are indeed at the center of the Torah, we may go on to ask which among them should have priority. The answer is clear: the first.[33]

Then comes another difficulty: how far should the scope of this commandment be understood to extend? Jewish tradition identifies it with Exodus 20:2 and Deuteronomy 5:6, which are identical: "I am the Lord thy God, who brought thee out of the land of Egypt, out of the house of bondage." This declaration is understood accordingly as already commanding belief in the existence of God. The next verse, "Thou shalt have no other gods before me," also the same in both versions, is taken as the second commandment. It falls into the shape of a negative instruction after the pattern that is followed thereafter and might therefore in another count stand as the first commandment. The next three verses are traditionally understood as an amplification of this second instruction, though the first two of these begin with independent negative instructions, "Thou shalt not make unto thee any graven image" and "Thou shalt not bow down unto them." Exodus 20:7 and Deuteronomy 5:11, requiring that the name of the Lord not be taken in vain, is then received as the third commandment. The fourth, a positive instruction to observe the Sabbath, marks a clear break. But everything that precedes it seems to cohere as what might reasonably be interpreted as a single double imperative. This would fall into place logically as the two contrasting halves of a typical not/but: the Lord must be your God and not the idols of the Canaanites.

In the course of this ideal double commandment, three references to the Name appear. The first comes at the very beginning of what is now counted as the initial element in the series, where the Lord declares himself in the familiar style: "I am the Lord your God," or *anochi adonai elohecha,* where *adonai* stands for the tetragrammaton, as usual. If the Exodus version of the Ten Words comes from the "E" source, as the scholarly consensus has held, we need not be surprised to find an almost hidden repetition of what we have identified as the literal import of the Name in a negative formulation of the corresponding repudiation: "There shall not be [*lo yehiye*] to thee strange gods before my face," where the verb is in the usual form of the third-person singular imperfect as contrasted with, but also in parallel to, the archaic form fixed in the Name. Two verses further on, the reason given for not bowing down to images of natural creatures is that "I the Lord thy God am a jealous God," which also repeats the language of self-declaration with which the sequences began. And a concluding instruction requires that "Thou shalt not lift up

---

[33]The German theologian Werner Schmidt has anticipated this much of Goodhart's thesis from a tradition-history perspective in his *Faith of the Old Testament* (Philadelphia: Westminster, 1983): "The history of Israel could be written as a history of the first commandment" (76).

the Name of the Lord thy God as a nothing." Taken as a whole, then, what can be read as the first commandment does indeed center upon the Name—as all the other commandments, however discriminated, would center upon the first. And all the other instructions of the Law may be made to gather themselves about these Ten Words.

At this point Goodhart offers a most suggestive reading of the fundamental not/ but provided by this first commandment. What is repudiated is idolatry, or the worship of that which is not the true God. What is positively required therefore is recognition of and obedience to this actual Lord. But who is he? Exactly what his Name implies. To understand this, though, requires interpretation. To interpret is to overthrow whatever idol stands as an obstacle before the face. To take the Name "in vain" is to misuse it for human purposes—to employ it, that is, as an idol. To the extent that there *are* idols, there cannot *be* the presence obscured by such inventions. To read Scripture successfully is accordingly to see through whatever is merely textual and therefore objective in what one confronts, so as to encounter the true Other as an absolute subject: that one whom it is in fact always possible to meet, face to face.

Interpretation would then end in a conversion of the third person into the first, which in the case of the Name means realizing this not just as written down or even as read aloud by one man to another but as completed in its true meaning by the very one to whom it indeed belongs. The opportunity for just this final metamorphosis is at its height here in the first instance of the Name's appearance, which the others reinforce: that is, the opening words, *anochi adonai*. For these scarcely disguise a corresponding statement in the first person. "I am what you call 'he will be'; that is, I will be who I will be." Thus God in effect interprets his own Name by saying it over again as he once did to Moses. But this, the true Name, or rather the truth of the Name, cannot in the nature of the case be written down.[34] It is indeed altogether beyond the text, though it must always be anticipated as the meaning of the text. The signature of God, that is, of itself implies the presence of God. To reread that signature the right way round is to come into his presence at last and so to experience the fulfillment of what promises precisely this event. Even the Holy Name itself may be an idol—until it is rightly understood. But that *can* take place. And if it might occur for this word, which concentrates all the other words, it should in principle be possible for them all. At the end of the line, then, at least one absolutely typical text would successfuly deconstruct itself. To interpret

---

[34] G. G. Sholem (*On the Kabbalah,* 30-31) mentions a cabalistic doctrine that what was revealed on Sinai was no more than the first *aleph* of the first use of the word *anochi* in this first commandment—all the rest of the Torah was supplied by Moses, as interpretation. This engaging idea we may in turn understand as an analogous attempt to isolate the first person—by way though of a letter still, which however reduced either to the first, as in this case, or the last, as in our own earlier proposal, would as such remain in the third person.

Communal 185

the text *is* in the last analysis to deconstruct it, or rather, to deconstruct the *text* (as opposed to one or another of the carnal bodies, immediate or spurious, that may precede it) is in fact to interpret it, once and for all. To arrive at just this point would therefore be, in the Pauline phrase, to "lift the veil of" (2 Cor. 3:15) the Torah; that is, to read it eschatologically. Reading is ideally an apocalypse. And the End of the textual universe, Paul's image also implies, would be to find oneself face to face with the One whom we are seeking—or fleeing from. Here would be at last the Spirit of the letter indeed, for weal or woe.

We may perceive as well that such a conversion of the third person into the first would have to occur by way of an intermediate change from the third to the second. *He* (or *she*, or *it*) can become *I* only when addressed as *Thou*. Interpretation turns into encounter as reading becomes acknowledgment. And this hermeneutic apocalypse would be simultaneous too with an appropriation of the relevant subject on the near side of the relation. For what corresponds to the divine person addressed and revealed within a relation that may be confirmed by precisely such an endlessly possible fulfillment is the complementary human person, singular or plural. But in the nature of the situation disclosed, this subject would have to realize itself as no longer positive in its own previous right (for that would now be idolatrous too) but negative: in a self-abandonment before the presence encountered, which is to say, a sacrifice. Of this sacrifice, prayer would once again be the obvious verbal mode, especially on the scale of the individual, who is *not* always in the temple. A phrase from Ps. 109:4 puts the result succinctly: *ani tephilah*, "I am prayer." This verse could accordingly provide a formula for the human identity that corresponds to the post-textual meaning of the Name. This is who can say *hineni*, "Here I am!" "Before the face" we are each and all of us present as the disestablishment of our previous identities, whatever these might consist of. In that case "I am prayer" might indeed define the precise degree of being it would be proper to assume within the relation. I am present, we might say, *as* my own absence—which is once again to observe, as a sacrifice.

If interpretation should in the end be understood, then, as the first stage of prayer, and if prayer is a species of sacrifice that may still be carried out on the scale of the individual, the general category within which all three might fit would appear to be what has most appropriately come to be known as the *kiddush ha shem*, or sanctification of the Name. For to honor the Name would sooner or later mean to stand face to face with the One who reveals himself by way of it, whether in so many words or otherwise. The references to this general possibility in the Torah and Prophets are for the most part indirect and tend to focus on what ought not to be done, the *hillul ha shem*, or profanation of the Name.[35] But what should

---

[35] In Lev. 22:2-3 and 31-32 the profanations to be avoided are technical and priestly. Moses is represented in Num. 20:12 and Deut. 32:51 as being refused entrance into the promised land because of his failure to sanctify the Name. Jer. 34:16 and Amos 2:7 similarly

be done positively is already implicit in the phrase once inscribed upon a gold plate fixed to the headdress of the high priest as he went about his service: *kodesh l'adonai*, "Holy unto the Lord" (Exodus 28:36). Zechariah 14:20 anticipates an eschatological future in which the same formula would appear even on the bells of the horses. In postbiblical times the rabbis developed the idea as a recommendation for individual conduct, positive and negative, at moments of crisis, and therefore as a rationale for martyrdom. It was so applied from the time of the Maccabees to the revolts against Rome, and thence through Christian assaults on Jewish communities during the Crusades or the later medieval persecutions. It has accordingly recurred in modern times as a formula of interpretation during the Holocaust, as when a group of villagers brought to the edge of their common grave by the *Einsatzkommando* heard their rabbi invite them to understand what they were about to suffer as a *kiddush ha shem*—though no one knew then that anyone would survive to tell the story.[36] Christians too are offered an opportunity to appreciate the meaning of the phrase in the second clause of the Lord's prayer, which (presumably in allusion to the Kaddish) asks that "Thy Name" be "hallowed."

All these usages might exemplify what would amount under this heading to a single possibility, in which the subject could appropriate its own abandonment as a concomitance of encounter with the one who names himself as the one he is. Such a confession would always be a sacrifice in principle even if not without qualification in practice, ceremonial or historical, verbal or carnal. The act in general would in that case be what there was to do in the long run and therefore what has in fact been done now and then, in solitude or company, by whoever lived to do it. It should be of some interest to discover that the act of reading a text too might count as a mode of this action, if only from a certain distance. Even criticism, then, need not be altogether out of touch with what there is in the end to bring about.

Nominal

The Scripture of Scriptures, the previous section enables us to conclude, has to be the Holy Name. The Name is at the head of the Ten Words, as these introduce the other commandments, which in turn secure whatever else may have since been added to successive layers of the text as supplement or commentary. The Name is therefore central, wherever it may be found: all the other words, anticipatory or consequential, spell this one out, more or less explicitly. The tetragrammaton functions accordingly as the type of what might ever be inscribed, whether on stone or in flesh. But a written version of the Name remains in the third person, as befits

---

rebuke profanations among the Israelites at large.

[36]This happened at Kelme in 1941, according to Martin Gilbert, *The Holocaust* (New York: Holt, 1985) 194-95. Similar episodes are reported for other places too: see pp. 482 and 659-60. There may well have been some that will never take their place in any narrative.

a narrative made up of sentences composed from outside the relation depicted, or a set of laws transmitted from one generation to another. Within a text there can be no true "I" or "thou," but always at best some fictional "he" or "she" or ideal or factual "it." So the Name too is inevitably displaced from person to patriarchy, relation to history, revelation to instruction. To just this extent the God of the tale told and the commandments conveyed cannot help but function as an idol—until the inscription is properly read. The Name is a promise that comes true as soon as it is kept. The end of scripture is a restoration of presence. Interpretation concludes in encounter. The deconstruction of the text is an eschatological event: an "apocalypse" in the strict sense of that term, which might on principle take place at any time.

If so, we would now be in a position to admire anew how Jesus reproduces the Name, and not just in the third person (for the taw of the cross may be understood to repeat that literally enough), but in the first. For to become the "face" of the Father in the midst of any concrete here and now must in the nature of just that possibility be to enact the true meaning of the Name—in the first place as an individual and then, we began by arguing, as a community: as an "I," that is, which in due course becomes a "we." The body, it is thereby disclosed, is *how* the full meaning of the text cannot merely be intuited or even voiced but realized. The body of Christ in all its modes is then the substance of the *I am,* the actuality of presence—the incarnation, we can now properly say, of the Name indeed.

The first generation of believers and others since have searched the Scriptures for clues to the legitimacy of just this extraordinary strategy. The most impressive of those that have to do explicitly with the Name, as I have already mentioned, is probably the repeated use of the formula *ani hu* in what we now call Second Isaiah. "I am he who" will accomplish the return from exile, that author repeats. Like the *anochi adonai* of the initial commandment, the phrase is a close approximation to the Name in its first-person form, which suggests that this prophet knew very well what he was doing and why. The Johannine *egō eimi* would then correspond exactly to this usage, which the Fourth Evangelist appears to have studied with special care. For in his narrative, Jesus is literally the one who is free to say the Name of himself in the first person, thus manifesting the presence thereby announced for as many contexts as he finds himself in. *I am,* this Jesus declares, the Christ, the bread of life, the living water, the light of the world, the Son of Man, the gate of the sheepfold, the good shepherd, and the resurrection. Implicitly he also makes himself the wine at Cana and the temple in Jerusalem. All these predicates become parables of him, any one of which may be converted from its previous status as a sign into the presence it means by way of whatever occasion offers the opportunity for encounter. But in our admiration for John's insight, we should also recall that the actual as well as the reimagined Jesus would also have read and indeed, we must gather, did read Isaiah quite as carefully as his latter-day disciple. What matters in the End, we are always forgetting, is not how some Evangelist may have read Scripture, much less, or even, a medieval Kabbalist or modern scholar, but how

Jesus himself read it. And from the obvious results we can gather enough of what must have happened to realize that he need not have *said* "I am" in any language to have found himself enacting what the formula expresses, in a way sufficient at once to fulfill Isaiah and anticipate John.[37]

A question already raised—Why did Jesus not himself write, as Moses apparently had?—would also be easier to answer in the light of such an appreciation of his vocation. Whatever could be written down had been. There would therefore have been no further need to supplement, much less comment on, the inherited scriptures. If his role was in fact to act out their eventual meaning, there was nothing else for him to do within the space they already occupied—except signal their completion. And this conclusion the cross may almost ironically be understood to accomplish, bringing the text to a close in what amounts to a final letter indeed. Nor need he be understood as authorizing the composition, after his death, of anything that might subsequently come to function as a "new" testament. This too had in effect already been supplied: at the very center of the "old." All that was still necessary, as ever, was to read the inherited text the right way round.

What he does instead, we have also noticed, is speak and act—freely. Whatever is said and done is then left entirely to the memories of the participants, who may or may not recall either. And the principal actions performed are, according to the narratives, cures and exorcisms, which most vividly enact a transmission of creative power into the bodies of other people. The Name, after all, promises accompaniment, assistance, support. That this anticipation should be proved true most convincingly and intimately in the flesh of those who could benefit from his presence would in itself offer good evidence of his self-understanding. Jesus gives "himself" over. He does not keep himself to himself. For the identity he appears to lay claim to is intrinsically communicative.

The eucharistic action would then be not just a final but an utterly typical action within a ministry where all the other deeds and words seem more or less to participate in the same intention. For this demonstration of the Name too is thoroughly transitive. Absolutely nothing is held back. According to Isaiah 42:6 and 49:8, the servant of the Lord is himself to be the covenant for his people. The constitutive "text" for any eschatological version of the relation could not in that case be separate from the person of the one establishing it. His identity—which is to say, his body—would itself have to become the latter-day equivalent of those documents that had specified the demands required in the previous age. The Eucharist is an eschatological "signature," inscribed not in stone or on parchment but as the body: to begin with, his own, then that composed by the elements to be

---

[37]My first chapter has referred to Ethelbert Stauffer's attempt to historicize the Johannine "I am" in his *Jesus and His Story*. One could add here Thomas Altizer's *Self-Embodiment of God* (New York: Harper, 1977) as a painfully sophisticated endeavor to recuperate the formula in another idiom. The effort at least should be recognized.

consumed, and finally that of the new Israel which receives the blessing thereby conveyed. John quite properly calls it the bread on which the Father has "set his seal" (John 6:27).

We seem close to the mind of Jesus in Isaiah 25:6-10, a passage that stands out as virtually independent of its context. On "this" mountain, which is to say Zion, the Lord will prepare for all peoples a feast of "fat things" (*sh'manim*), and wines left to settle on their lees (*sh'marim*). At that time he will do away with the veil of mourning that covers the people: he will "swallow up death for ever." Then it shall be said, "This is the Lord for whom we waited that he might save us (*yoshieinu*); we will rejoice in his salvation (*yeshuato*)." The word played upon is of course Jesus' "own" name. In these verses we seem very near to an expression of the intention enacted, for the eucharistic action is set in motion on the mountain of Jerusalem and includes both "flesh" and wine. The Last Supper would accordingly be a feast of the End times anticipated, whose elements combine to imply their meaning, like the very sounds of Isaiah's words.

Another fragment of Scripture also seems relevant. "And he blessed the people," says 2 Samuel 6:18 and its repetition in 1 Chronicles 16:2, speaking of David after the ark has been removed into the midst of the tent at Jerusalem and sacrifices have been offered "in the Name of the Lord." For this David's latter-day "son" does too. He blesses the people in the persons of their twelve leaders and in the Name of the Lord indeed, not just by calling out the third-person form of this over them, as a high priest had to do after the exile had replaced kings by clerics, but by reincorporating the corresponding first person within them. We could, after all, very easily realize the declarations ever since transmitted in an impersonal indicative in the first person too, as in fact John does for the first of them (6:35): *I am* the bread, *I am* the wine—and so therefore must *you be* who consume this food and drink. Such an dissemination would amount to a most complete blessing indeed. In the next verse of the older story, as if to confirm what had just happened, David also distributes food to the people: sweet bread and (the translation is difficult) perhaps wine as well.

If the eucharistic species thus become in combination the key "document" that attests to the prevalence of this new version of the relation, then the rite within which these become accessible over and over is also the covenantal renewal ceremony proper to the eschatological condition thereby established. To celebrate it is accordingly to reproduce the moment of revelation, and so recreate the corresponding community. No other sign or mode of transmission would in that case be either authorized or indispensable to anything like the same degree. The other texts of what we have come to call the New Testament would in the light of this action need to remain secondary, however useful in that place. With the exception of the rare moments of prophecy they also seem to include, they belong to teaching, not revelation; in Mark's convenient distinction, they are *parrhēsia*, or that which may be passed along openly, not that which is inherently mysterious, or *parabolē*. And if the Eucharist is the true "document" of the new covenant, it would follow too that the command to repeat the action might very well be original rather than ecclesial. Jesus could have known as well as any scholar since that a covenant needs to be regularly renewed by some ritual means or other. If this action amounts to the moment at which the community is as constantly brought into existence, it might follow as well that the rite would have to be repeated not just once in each generation or even once a year but every day. The eschatological body reproduces itself endlessly, we can realize, until the End, and this is how.

The ark of the original covenant, the story goes, was eventually placed in the holy of holies of Solomon's temple, and inside it the stones on which were inscribed the "Ten Words." Such a mode of deposit for the relevant document was conventional for ancient agreements of the kind. When the Babylonians destroyed the first temple, they seem to have done away with these stones. No one has known since what became of them. Perhaps they were deliberately smashed into dust. When the holy of holies of the second temple was erected after the return from exile, there was therefore nothing to put in it, and very wisely the space was left empty. It would then be possible to understand the action accomplished at the Last Supper as filling this space at last. So a text would be succeeded in the first place by an absence, to provide as it were a decent frame or margin and thus anticipate a future restoration. And this in turn would be brought about not by way of another text (as Jer. 31:31 might seem to expect) but by an impersonation and so incarnation of the Name. That whole body would then count as at once a fulfillment of the text and its replacement. The Eucharist, we could also say, is the fruit of the tree of life now eschatologically restored, in which case the tree of knowledge is the text of Scripture itself—that by which one learns, precisely, the difference between good and evil.[38] Less extravagantly, the Eucharist would serve as proof of the new version of the covenant that Jeremiah can also be reread as anticipating. But what had once been a redoubled centricity is in this version a freely generated circumference. The relation can be proved to obtain, not by the contents of a sacred chest in the innermost room of a special building in the royal city of a chosen nation, but by way of a symbolic action susceptible to ready reproduction anywhere at anytime and, one might also add, by anybody. Instead of other nations coming to worship at Jerusalem, as had once been foretold, the secret treasure of the city has in effect been scattered among the nations—and not by way of theft either, but as a gift. The seed was and still is being sown.

On one side of the relation, then, is the text; on the other, the body. The text determines *l'olam ha ze,* or the world as it has so far had to be. The body manifests the age to come, *l'olam ha ba.* On both sides a signature may be found. On one side, this is exposed by a reduction of the text to its key term—which must still be

---

[38]Some of my readers may have seen an engaging cartoon (originally German, apparently, though often copied) showing a very naked Adam and Eve accepting a heavy volume from the mouth of a serpent coiled around a tree: a figure for precisely this point.

read the right way round. When it is properly interpreted, its meaning will be found upon the other side; or, as we have also seen, the text may be reduced still more literally to the letters out of which it is composed, and these in turn to the final letter, or taw, the signature of someone without a worldly identity to call his own. As a singular individual, Jesus reduces the text to the cross, his one "written" word. In the resurrection he radiates as the community. The two signatures match each other on either side of the relation; literal and metaphoric, textual and bodily, historical and eschatological, patriarchal and personal, human and divine. Jesus signs himself in both ways: the first in order to reveal the second. His *kiddush ha shem* is at once unqualified and all-inclusive.

And this doubleness is rehearsed in the experience of any latter-day congregation, who pass from baptism, in which each individual reproduces the passion, to communion, in which all together participate in the resurrection. As a ritual means of entry into the body, baptism stands in a complex contrast to circumcision, by which citizenship under a national version of the relation is established. Circumcision, we have already observed, re-presents the triumph of the text. That flint knife is the letter of the Law indeed, turned on edge. So the covenant in question is not inappropriately "cut" into the body of the male individual who is thereby recruited for service under the Lord of hosts. To be circumcised is to be confirmed within a tradition that continues in one's own person. To be baptized, though, is to suffer a death by water, instant and unqualified, leaving behind no remains to be buried, as if in fact at sea. The natural body is not merely nicked or written upon (or even ritually washed, as seems to have been the point of John's baptism) but done away with altogether—at least in principle. Nothing is precisely what is left of it. Upon nothing whatsoever no writing is possible: the possible text is erased as it were in advance, for without *some* materiality, flesh or stone or parchment or computer screen, nothing can be inscribed. Through baptism the individual, male or female, is abandoned to nothingness—so that he or she may be reborn into the eschatological community. That community accordingly exists post-textually, as a new body of an absolutely other kind.

The same difference could be recast in terms of the implied role of temporality within the contrasting dispensations. In the Israel constituted by circumcision, each generation of sons learns to acknowledge itself as in the same situation as that which was born of Abraham's seed or came out of Egypt. Time is measured by the sequence of these generations, each of which transmits the relevant identity to the one following. Patrilinear repetition marks the moments of what is in principle a permanent covenant. The text is that which must be handed on so as to guarantee the persistence of the collective. It is the canon of the necessary culture.

Within an unbounded version of the relation, there is in principle no text at all, and therefore no significant phallus, no patriarchal "seed," no patrilinear nomination. So the sacrifice of baptism is open to members of either sex and any nation. Procreation and its differential functions are irrelevant, since within the sphere of the resurrected body no more than one generation is ever to be found. Within this body we are, as "coheirs" with our elder brother, at the same time brothers and sisters of each other. The Father alone is the parent not just of his firstborn Son but of all the latter's siblings as well. Thus we are always contemporary with Jesus, no matter how many generations may have passed. These are no more than so many moments in the flesh out of which the penultimate generation is constantly being reproduced. So we "inherit" not a text but the Spirit, or that which is constantly forming us into the body indeed. The Church grows but does not descend. Spiritually speaking, we have observed, there is in consequence no such thing as a "history of the church," any more than there need be, strictly speaking, any "new" testament as a merely written witness to the fact of the relation. In the body we are beyond all that, now and forever.

This privilege need not mean that what we have come to call the New Testament cannot also be read as testifying to precisely this eschatological shift from text to body that we have already observed can be read as anticipated within the Old. In 2 Corinthians 3, for instance, Paul begins by boasting that his community in that city is already a true "letter" of recommendation, so he needs no other, as his rivals within the apostleship may have hinted. The instance of the body of Christ he himself has helped to form is as good as (Paul means much better than) any written document attesting to the merely carnal identity of the bearer. For this bodily and so freely metaphoric "letter," he goes on to observe, is "written" not with ink, that black (*melas*) substance of death, but in the (white fire of the) Spirit, and therefore not on stone (he shifts back from papyrus to the ancestral material) but on the "tablets" of human hearts. The parallels continue as he formally contrasts the old and new versions of the covenant. Familiar Pauline polarities accumulate: a written code and a life-giving Spirit, a fading glory on the face of Moses and a steady glory emanating from the risen Christ, a veil and a naked face, slavery and freedom. Verses 3:14 and 15 focus the central contrast between Scripture as it must still be read by those who cannot penetrate its "literal" meaning and the text as it can now be understood by those who are able to follow their leader—and his apostle—all the way through it. For "only through Christ" is the "veil" removed. The metaphors severally rehearse what we already know to be Paul's constant thesis: the text is to the body as the Law to the Spirit, and so as figure to meaning, or prophecy to fulfillment.

The passage from 2 Corinthians could be linked with a daring image in Colossians 2:14-15. In these verses God is praised for having "cancelled" the "note" that represents our indebtedness (literally *wiped out* the *handwriting*) by nailing this to the cross. The language conjoins the carnal body of the man so treated with the *titulum* that explained the "crime" for which he suffered and both with the Torah scroll. The death of Jesus, an implicit argument would go, should therefore be interpreted as a consumption at once of the Law and the judgment it registered. An unqualified enforcement of the text would at the same time be its undoing. The Law is used up in the very act of being carried out, once and for all. And if we are reluctant to credit even so striking an image from a dubious letter, we may find a similar reference in Galatians 3:1. There Paul speaks of having "written out" (*prographein*) Jesus Christ as crucified to his addressees when he preached the gospel to them for the first time—and they accepted it. To propose Jesus as an expiatory sacrifice is then to define his individual suffering as an utterly physical reduction of the text or, as we have already put it, to see the cross as the last letter of the alphabet indeed.

To concentrate on the cross is to understand the still-more-explicit proposition offered in Romans 10:4, that "Christ is the end of the Law" (*telos gar nomou Christos*), in the first of the two senses of that ambiguous word: the death of Jesus terminates the text. But *telos* may also mean "goal," in which case the assertion would parallel as well as anticipate the instruction presently advanced in the same letter that "he who loves his neighbor has fulfilled the law." The commandments, Paul observes here as before in Galatians 5:14, are "summed up in this sentence" (more literally, *recapitulated* in this *word*), "you shall love your neighbor as yourself" (Rom. 13:9). As the verse following affirms, "Love is the fulfilling of the law" (Rom. 13:10). This version of an interpretation of the text as the body allows us to identify *agapē* as the good word indeed, which would in practice name the presence not just of a sacrificed but even more evidently of the glorified Messiah. For to love in the style this term recommends is precisely to reproduce the body on the scale of the community and thereby to prove the resurrection true. Paul's repetition of what had already become a familiar Christian formula will serve as well to link him with the other authors represented in the New Testament. For the doctrine held in common by all, that the commandment written down in Leviticus 19:18 should be understood as summing up and so as potentially transcending the rest of the Law, would already serve as a communal reflection of the principle that the Name is the best clue to the identity of Jesus and therefore of his followers. For the first-person plural as opposed to the singular mode of the Name would presume an actualization of what can only be referred to from a normative distance as *agapē*. "We are" precisely to the extent that the love of neighbor has in fact become incarnate once again.[39]

Paul supplies the most formidable instances to illustrate how the text of Scripture may be converted into the body of Christ in the style of argument, as one would expect. In the style of narrative, the best examples are, somewhat surprisingly perhaps, to be found in Luke's two books. The obvious examples from his histories

---

[39] The text from Leviticus also appears in Gal. 5:14; Matt. 5:43-48 and 22:39; Mark 12:28-34; Luke 10:25-28; and James 2:8-9. Wayne A. Meeks, from whose edition of *The Writings of St. Paul* (New York: Norton, 1972) I take (with numerical adjustments) this list, observes that the choice of Lev. 19:18 as a key verse was already familiar within pre-Christian tradition (89n). This point is somewhat irritably confirmed by Hertz's edition of the Pentateuch in a special note devoted to the topic (563-64). The thesis that the import of the text is always the community it prefigures has been argued with respect to Paul's interpretation of Scripture in general by Richard Hays in *Echoes of Scripture in the Letters of Paul* (New Haven: Yale University Press, 1989).

of the ministry and of the church include those episodes in the combined work that show somebody interpreting Scripture as fulfilled in the presence of the Messiah. Luke 4:16-22 is the first of these: Jesus in the synagogue at Nazareth reads from the scroll of Isaiah and then tells his audience, "Today this scripture is fulfilled in your hearing." The Emmaus story, at the other end of this author's initial narrative, presumes the same conception of what is going on: in Luke 24:13-15 the risen Jesus, still in incognito, explains to Cleopas and his companion "in all the Scriptures that which concerned himself" before revealing his proper identity "in the breaking of the bread." In the second narrative there are three cases of the kind. In Acts 8:26-40, Philip too is shown interpreting Isaiah for the Ethiopian eunuch in that official's chariot. In 17:2-3, Luke's Paul argues from the scriptures in the synagogue at Thessalonica to prove that Jesus is indeed the Christ. He does the same at Ephesus in 18:19 and again in 28:23-18 before the Jewish leaders in Rome. In all these instances, Luke is presumably reproducing the normal practice of Jewish Christian missionaries in the earlier period of the church. The principle assumed is as clear in the narrative examples then as in Paul's argument: the meaning of the text is the bodily presence of the Messiah, whether before or after death.[40]

Both versions of the case presume that to read the text successfully is to assume it must be meant apocalyptically. Even if this might not have seemed so once, Scripture must now be understood in that Spirit. Interpretation is either eschatological or incomplete. And if Luke, the most "historical" and least extravagant of the narrative Evangelists, can nonetheless be found to presume such a hermeneutical principle, it should be possible to extend the generalization we may derive from his instances as well as from Paul to reach our own apparently very different predicament as well. The texts available for an ultimate reading in the first ecclesial generation consisted of the Tanakh and perhaps a few pseudepigraphical supplements. In modern times we are clearly not so limited. This is the age, we may well complain or boast, of the text triumphant, not to say explosive. But the principle upon which even Luke as well as his immediate predecessors and successors found themselves free to interpret *ta grammata* would presumably still be accessible in our day too in proportion to our readiness to appropriate the opportunity. The Bible might then seem typical rather than exceptional—or irrelevant. For if Christians are, religiously speaking, still within the same generation according to the Spirit, then we should in principle be liberated hermeneutically as well as chronologically.

One difference between our respective predicaments is all too literal: there are that many more texts to read, and the chaos they accumulate as is a good deal

---

[40]The hermeneutical principle in question, as illustrated by the Emmaus story in particular, forms the climax of a thoroughly post-Derridian yet equally Christian argument in Jean Luc Marion's *Dieu sans l'être* (Paris: Communio/Fayard, 1982) 210-14. Unfortunately he must deny himself the use of "being" and "presence," not being free to admit their bodily sense, which weakens what otherwise seems a parallel interpretation of interpretation.

harder to organize into canonical chains, even here and there within what is still called "the humanities." More important, the texts that seem most characteristic of the modern situation have proliferated outside the very idea of relation—indeed, in defiance of or as substitutes for that—outside relation as such, that is, not just the covenant with God, old or new. This predicament can confuse even religious readers, who not unnaturally find themselves forced back on repetitions of one kind and another, marking time, as it were, for lack of something more conclusive to do. For the apocalypse has apparently been postponed, at least as far as interpretation is concerned. So we are left without orientation and ready to argue there can be none. But if, as the biblical instances still seem to imply, the essential interpretive move is still a conversion of the text into the presence or voice or, most convincing of all, the body it implies, then in principle all texts should be susceptible in their degree to an equivalent reading—as soon at least as relation is counted back in, whether to God or simply other persons. *Something* of the gospel might then prove readable in virtually any text at almost any time or place. In which case it might even be fair to claim that there is in fact nothing in the end to read except the gospel—which is to say, the advent of the Kingdom, the *mashal* of the Lord, the person of the Messiah, the body of Christ indeed.

And if the body is always the meaning of the text, this eventuation should prove as true for the social as for more literally literal versions, old or new. In that case, one might also be able to find in just the conversion called for a way of reconciling the institutional and the "charismatic" Church, a problem that we have already found has proved difficult to solve for at least two recent generations of ecclesiologists. The Church as the body of Christ reproduced on the scale of an eschatological community might then be understood as the *meaning* of the church as institution—whenever this interpretation could in fact be realized. The church as institution would not in that case need to make ultimate sense as such except as a repetition of itself in one set of terms or another. It would be, that is, always and everywhere a continuing supplement to itself, still the "shadow" (*skia*) of the *sōma* yet to come (Col. 2:16-17). But it could indeed make sense as "fulfilled" in quite the biblical understanding of that expression as soon as this body was in fact revealed by way of the corresponding completion. The institution would then function as a social version of "the Scriptures" for this latter day and would invite the same interpretive obversion. For in the modern as in the ancient instance, the third-person sign would have to dissolve into its first-person meaning in order to function as such. The sacraments, and the Eucharist especially among them, would then amount to the ritual moments of just this conversion. These at least have never been avoided! In other contexts the record is obviously less unambiguous.

In any of them, though, the necessary event, it is still clear from the exemplary instance, could occur only after a preliminary reduction, which is to say, a passion. If the institution cannot act this out in other than ritual ways, its citizens may find themselves obliged to make up the difference on its behalf, visibly or invisibly. Sometimes this reduction may be comparatively easy, as in the intellectual case.

Sometimes what is required must take place in moral terms. Then the individual concerned may find himself or herself a victim of injustice, which by virtue of exactly that fact is at the same time an opportunity to enact the import of the very institution that inflicts it by enduring just so much of the necessary interpretation in one's proper person. De Lubac, I have already mentioned, is especially moving at those moments in his argument when the application of this rule in his own case may be glimpsed. And there have been other examples before and since, private or public.

But in or out of the explicit church, we are ordinarily caught a stage or two further back from any such crisis, aware, it may be, of the crucial difference between the text and its meaning, and therefore between institution and body, but unable for one reason or another to share in the necessary conversion. Then we may find ourselves, to point the obvious moral, doing no better than formulating arguments against the finality of the text in what amounts to nothing better than one more version of the text. Repetition repeats itself endlessly in this world, which it thereby defines. In the midst of that milieu, even the most devout homage to the idea of the body will not of itself reach all the way through to the body indeed. In such a case the possibility is in effect handed over to the reader—who may in turn feel the same frustration on his or her account. But theology need not apologize too profusely for not being sacramental as well.

Chapter 6

Cosmic

Also in this he shewed a littil thing, the quantitye of a hesil nutt in the palme of my hand; and it was as round as a balle. I loked thereupon with eye of my understondyng and thowte: "What may this be?" And it was generally answered thus: "It is all that is made." I mervelled how it might lesten, for methowthe it might suddenly have fallen to nowte for littil. And I was answered in my understondyng: "It lesteth and ever shall, for God loveth it; and so alithing hath the being be the love of God."
—Julian of Norwich, *Revelations of Divine Love*

Physical

There can seem almost too much to say of the communal body, within which we are all eager to live after one fashion or another, and too little about the cosmic body, though if one might obtain in the form disclosed, the other should seem probable as well. The question would be, On what terms? Paul's principal contribution here is the well-remembered Romans 8:18-25, where the apostle unexpectedly anticipates that even the *ktisis,* or rest of the natural world, will eventually come to share the apocalypse of the sons of God. The cosmos, he claims there, was made subject to futility not through any sinfulness of its own but as a reflection of the punishment inflicted upon an erring humankind. So it too can still hope to be set free from death to enjoy the ultimate freedom of the justified. Until then he imagines that it "groans." But Paul's vision of an absolute future for the natural universe should, if it may indeed be entertained as a prophecy of the Parousia, also entail a penultimate condition for the same form of being. In fact his invocation earlier in the same letter (1:19-23) of the wrath of God against the Greeks who should have been able to realize the work of God in creation would appear to presume as much.

There might be room, one could therefore suppose, for what would accordingly rank as a "sacramental" version of the body of Christ on the cosmic as well as the communal scale. The verses quoted from Colossians to introduce my own project would offer a post-Pauline hymn to just such a possibility. If the Church can in fact be, even now, so should the equivalently gracious mode of what we could then most properly call creation. We would in that case be able to look about us to some purpose, not entirely without hope of seeing what was there to be seen—if only in some version of faith.

In the clear evening sky glowed not just a quarter moon but two golden planets, Venus and, I could presume, Jupiter. They looked stunning against the dark blue, off at whatever distances they really were from each other and this ball on which I stood, its own sunward side no doubt glowing as well with the same reflected light, though this I could only guess at by the pink tint over our western hills. I was on this sphere then, not one of those. Even the unilluminated portion of the moon shone too, it seemed as a further reflex of the same earthshine. So these four bodies hung neighborly together in silent space, mirroring the radiance of the star they shared—once upon a time, one also knew, their original. One could see where we were.

The sun radiates, one could also think, and gravity compacts. Both modalities form spheres, whether of expansive energy or inert mass. By virtue of the first I could see the results of the second, through eyes molded to take advantage of the former on top of a body contrived to resist the latter. I would be a sphere too but, as things are, cannot quite. The same forces that have composed these others have prevented that in my case. There is always a certain satisfaction, though, at the sight of this perfection of form, even if only in a universe of what one has learned to call so much inanimate matter. No wonder it has prevailed as a principal figure for the nature of Nature since Anaximander at least.[1] Among plants, it is possible to observe, growth would approximate the shape of a sphere as near as might be. The corresponding circle is established among animals, we have already suggested, by the principle of mobility, which traces an imaginary horizon for its inhabitant. For human beings the same line would presumably be drawn by consciousness, though I could not see that as I gazed into the heavens. Where is the boundary of the universe? In any case, it framed what I did see. But this, like most other circumferences, has to be ideal; in the actual world, the appearance of perfection had better be sought at a lower level of being. The celestial, we have known for some time, is not really heavenly but even more utterly carnal than ourselves. These bodies, though, would still illustrate the potential of them all. The several forces reduce so much apparent inertness to just such an image of perfection. What most minimally is, then, though on so grand a scale from where we stand, coincides, one could say, with what altogether might be. Omission simplifies, and we see what we would otherwise have to presuppose or imagine.

Astronomy is only physics on a macroscopic scale. Standing in the hall at home, looking through a window at the sunset again on another clear evening (they

---

[1] Walter Burkert's standard *Greek Religion* (Oxford: Blackwell, 1985) affirms as much (307), referring to Charles Kahn, *Anaximander and the Origins of Greek Cosmology* (New York: Columbia University Press, 1960), which would indeed support this case (75-81, 92-94, 115-18). A more recent authority, though, G. S. Kirk et al., *The Presocratic Philosophers* (Cambridge: Cambridge University Press, 1983) does not find the spherical image quite so prominent. As usual, specific attributions are hard to be sure of.

are not common where I live), I observe just above the western horizon a sickle moon and this time can actually see it descend at what seems an almost terrifying rate of speed. The illuminated fringe arced about its lower edge reflects light from a sun already well below the horizon. And now this too blurs and winks out in spurts of brightness, the last of which glows a brief while before going out. Our local balls do not just hang as in a picture, then, but roll round each other with another version of the same motion as that of the cars now moving up the hill just outside my window. These were going home from work, but the planets are always on their way, over and around, their motions a near repetition of their form. To be sure, I could also think, the traffic is really tracing another species of the same line, an endlessly repeated orbit outlining the circumference of this planet, each vehicle with its own two suns casting their light before it. That is what this nation is up to, as one can tell even better from the air approaching some city at night. The apparently animate may seem no better than inanimate too, if we stand back far enough. Even thought, we could also realize, is more nearly a mode of gravitation than radiance, for does it not attract like to like, compacting its minimal objects into units of comprehension? Scale, as the heroes of this theme have so often shown, makes no real difference with respect to being.

Bodies in motion—it is surely one of the simplest ideas possible. A review a while ago of Daniel Boorstin's *Discoverers* conveniently included a revealing quotation from Newton's *Opticks*:

> It seems probable to me, that God in the Beginning form'd Matter in solid, massy, hard impenetrable, movable Particles of Such Sizes and Figures, and with such other Properties and in such Proportion to Space, as most conduced the End for which he form'd them; and that these Primitive Particles being Solids are incomparably harder than any porous Bodies compounded of them; even so very hard, as never to wear out or break in pieces; no ordinary Power being able to divide what God himself made one in the first Creation.[2]

For Newton the atom could already be a thing-in-itself, as more or less it remained, this review could remind its readers, until the close of the last century, when that entity too began to show itself "porous" after all, and mass changed, at first in thought, then in practice, into the corresponding energy. It was for him, then, the essential unit even of creation, as the sky seemed to exhibit and analysis could confirm for earth as well. But this apparently most reduced and, to that extent, ultimate body had to be understood in terms of the most material, which is to say the deadest, flesh: the absolute, as it were, of dust. Hence the air of allegory that hangs over such a description, at least in hindsight. These atoms were what could at the time be posited as knowable in the end, and therefore what should be

---

[2]The review was by Jeremy Bernstein—who supplied the quotation from Newton—and appeared in the *New Yorker* 60 (12 March 1984) 158.

believed in too. To that extent such bodies might even have stood in for the body indeed, if any had been in a position to apprehend the possible parable, as one gathers did not in fact occur.

Such a metaphoric hint might seem easier to pick up in more recent times, now that it has become possible to look back over almost a century in the course of which the apparently irreducible atom has suffered a gradual disintegration into its component elements: first the electron, then the nucleus, then the components of the nucleus, and most recently the particles of these parts.[3] The "massy Solid" has in the process been revealed as a concentration, not to say an incognito, of extravagant forces—and so as virtually alive too in its own alien fashion. The atom is now an even better model, then, for the universe than in Newton's day, since to comprehend the elements of this least of bodies is simultaneously to understand the origin of the whole. One may observe too that the spherical character of the entity in question has apparently persisted from the older to the newer understanding.

Apparently this figure continues to obtain on all scales. An article in the *Times* announced a while back, for instance, that at the age of 10^{-35} seconds the universe was no larger than a baseball. In that case, one could suppose, the notorious "big bang" must really have been a very small bang indeed, scarcely a pop, however immense the expansion since. We could once quite literally have held the world in the palm of one hand, had any of us been around at the time. Another week, as if to confirm this confirmation, came two other stories, one of the discovery of a way to photograph the virus of infantile paralysis (a twenty-sided polygon of atoms, it turns out, and to that extent almost a sphere too) and the other of a project to place a telescope outside the atmosphere of the earth that might extend our perspective (it was then hoped) to the boundary of the universe. It is already possible, another photograph showed the other day, to take in the supernova Cassiopeia A, 10,000 times the size of the solar system, as a full, if somewhat lumpy and fulgurous, "fireball," like a coal in a grate. And larger units like galaxies approximate the same form as best they can, with arms spiraling about a core and a canopy of gas above and below the more obvious disk to fill out the shape. Meanwhile too one learns from the same popular distance that quasars should now be understood as the origins or products of their gravitational opposites the black holes, the probable nuclei of galaxies in general. Additional discoveries are sure to complicate whatever simpler narratives an outsider may be permitted to construct. What role should a "wall" or even "ripples" play in any imaginable version of everything?

But the "*uni*verse," however this may be defined, seems for the most part some kind of ball still, though now we are inside and cannot see to the skin of it yet or

---

[3] I owe my own sense of this most typical of modern intellectual histories to Abraham Pais's excellent if dauntingly technical *Inward Bound* (Oxford: Clarendon, 1986). The equivalent story for the reduction of the cell to the molecular and thence to the atomic level is retold in H. F. Judson's *Eighth Day of Creation* (New York: Simon & Schuster, 1979).

know for sure when and where such a surface could be. It is attractive to learn, from whatever distance, that cosmology should be so boldly endeavoring to comprehend the entirety at least of our physical circumstances and have already come near making contact, even if suppositional, with the center of everything and its circumference as well. This project is indeed, though after another fashion, to think "according to the whole." There is something otherworldly about the ambition of science in any era, and never more so than in these active times. Some might accordingly be prompted to press a metaphoric step further and understand the eschatological community of which we were just speaking as also a universe to the second power, and the moment therefore of its emergence as a focus for infinitude indeed, a singularity *kata pneuma* rather than *kata sarka*. But that might get too far ahead in the argument, forcing an allegory where at best one might find a suggestive likeness. But if a likeness, then perhaps a parable too.

The analogies do multiply in spite of one's scruples. If the universe may be thought of as originating in what amounts to an absolute point or moment concentrating all the forces, objects, and dimensions that have ever since determined its form and contents, these must then have been raised to an infinite and therefore inherently incomprehensible pitch. A "singularity" is by definition an event in which infinitude prevails—but infinity is by definition beyond the knowable and so in a most literal sense supernatural. It is intriguing that a variety of later and more local events within the universe which has in fact come about may apparently be understood as reversions to this original moment. A galaxy reproduces the cosmos as a whole from as near the beginning of that as it can get back to. A star reproduces its galaxy, from as near the beginning of that as it can get back to. And a planet reproduces a star, but on that scale gravity is not powerful enough to ignite the counterforce of radiation, so the bodies in question remain apparently inert, though still hotter at the core, as if to provide a hint of what would happen if it might.[4]

What in that case would reproduce the planet? In the first place, one could say, life in general, which in all its varieties through every era has done its best to alter what had begun as physical to suit the biological. "The biosphere is all of a piece, an immense, integrated living system, an organism," affirms the introduction to the appropriately named *Microcosmos,* a recent book rehearsing this thesis, which focuses on the effects detectable at the cellular level.[5] Such enthusiastic language

---

[4]There have been a number of books recently intended to inform outsiders of these mysteries. I have profited from Steven Weinberg, *The First Three Minutes* (New York: Bantam, 1984); Heinz Pagels, *Perfect Symmetry* (New York: Simon and Schuster, 1985); John Gribbin, *The Search for the Big Bang* (New York: Bantam, 1986); and Stephen Hawkings, *A Brief History of Time* (New York: Bantam, 1988).

[5]Lewis Thomas has supplied the words quoted in his introduction to Lynn Margulis and Dorian Sagan's *Microcosmos* (New York: Summit, 1986) 4. The initially shocking "hypothesis" in question was first proposed by James Lovelock, who has more recently reaffirmed it in *The Ages of Gaia* (New York: Norton, 1988). Thomas Berry's *Dream of the*

may, to be sure, betray a confusion of scales or at least a mixing of metaphors. One might feel safer shifting directly to particular living beings, which would at once more obviously and more securely appear to re-create not just the surface of the planet but the universe as a unit. Any individual, then, of whatever kind, might be understood as recapitulating the cosmos as best it could and as completely as conditions permitted. Death is then one more instance of gravitation, as development would be a species of radiation. First we expand, then we contract: from nothing all the way to nothing again, rehearsing the systole and diastole of the whole in terms of each living body that inhabits it. On the largest scale, though, the original explosion is continuing. The "big bang" is what we are still in the midst of. So we cannot yet experience the contracting phase of that body, if indeed this is to be expected, and may not survive as a race to see the "blue shift" that would announce its coming. In that case our individual bodies would already realize more of the total rhythm than the cosmic version. We are an answer to the question we would put, in this as in so many other ways.

Like a galaxy or star, the individual body, whether oak tree or human being, goes back as near as it can to the beginning of things in order, we have noticed, to reproduce its own kind. Procreation is regression, as germination would be the moment at which expansion recommences. But in that case too we might also allow ourselves to think that each celebration of the Eucharist is a recovery of the resurrection, that "big bang," we have just been tempted to suppose, of the corresponding pneumatic universe. We must go back to start over, whatever and whoever we may consist of. And all the species of this necessity rhyme, which again we should expect. If the physical universe can indeed be read as a parable of the spiritual, we would then be doing no more than following the lead provided—which, after all, the first parables would have been doing too.

Philosophical

But "physical" bodies, celestial or atomic, could be perfect only in proportion to their remoteness from our own, and to that extent at best figures for, rather than instances of, what we have been calling the body indeed, though their motions and their beauty may continually suggest what the objects in themselves will not as such provide. And astronomy and physics, we all know, could only recommence the ancient cosmological project at the beginnings of modern times by accepting a radical reduction of all lively or integral bodies as indispensable for the purpose of understanding nature as opposed to imagining it. We cannot examine or even think of the objects of these sciences, or any other that has adopted the same model, otherwise than as these entities have in fact been discovered to be, the random result

---

Earth (San Francisco: Sierra Club, 1988) could represent an echo of this impulse as communicated among some theologians.

of so many indifferent interactions that must be regarded from a correspondingly impersonal point of view. The cognitive paradigm of object and subject, or matter and mind, has inevitably prevailed over any of its merely fantastic or empathetic alternatives. We all know too that this hegemony has been repeatedly challenged without as yet, in the modern West at least, suffering any serious defeat on its chosen grounds, though one or another critic has always been ready to remind whoever would listen that a philosophical tradition which divides what thus becomes at best an inanimate body from what as a result remains an anonymous intelligence has sooner or later to be realized as a double abstraction from some indistinct unity that would either precede or transcend it. The difficulty has still been to appreciate, however indirectly, what this suggestion could possibly amount to—without falling back into myth or some language that continues to be governed by the very structure one is endeavoring to recover from.[6]

Historians, as contrasted with philosophical analysts of the structure in question, have had an easier time with it: they can at least point to a period previous to our own in which a cosmic whole could still be understood as bodily in some more coherent sense. Leonard Barkan's *Nature's Work of Art,* for instance, can take formal notice of the figural interplay between commonwealth and cosmos during the Renaissance, when at least in retrospect both could seem easier to comprehend in terms of some antecedent unity of being.[7] The coalescence of discordant elements into an integrity organized by some unifying principle can accordingly be found as a governing motif not only in such learned pursuits of that age as astrology but in poetry and architecture as well. The "premodern" might in such a way be associated most generally with the proliferation of analogy from one context to another on the basis of their common dependence upon this central trope. We have already observed how some of the more inclusive histories that have provided this critic with his method have indulged a grander version of the same vision in the political context, where it has been easier to follow the bodily model back to its ecclesiological and therefore liturgical origins as well as forward to its social deconstruction in the age of revolution. In matters of knowledge, though, and so for any theory of

---

[6]The more serious modern and postmodern critics of the cognitive paradigm include, in approximate chronological order, such names as Burtt, Husserl, Schrodinger, Neumann, Maritain, Ryle, Toulmin, Jaki, Nagel, and Rorty. The alternative difficulties mentioned might also be variously illustrated among them.

[7]The full title is *Nature's Work of Art: the Human Body as Image of the World* (New Haven: Yale University Press, 1985). Let me anticipate my next reference to Francis Barker, *The Tremulous Private Body: Essays on Subjection* (London: Methuen, 1984). These authors have more than almost a last name in common; between them, they may be taken as carrying on the critical project already typified by Foucault's *Discipline and Punish* to cosmic as well as communal concerns. Carolyn Merchant had already reviewed the same shift from a Renaissance to the Modern understanding of nature from an "ecofeminist" perspective in her *Death of Nature* (New York: Harper, 1980).

what might ever be realized of the universe at large, this motif was to be evicted comparatively early. Philosophy, mathematical or natural or both, modernized itself well before statecraft.

Francis Barker's equivalently recent essay on *The Tremulous Private Body* could represent another reading by a member of the same critico-historical school of the transition from a traditional to the "bourgeois" age. It is, conveniently, a degree more concerned with the intellectual side of the change in question. So he instances ways in which the "spectacular" body to be found in royal or punitive ceremony or in theatrical performance is replaced by the schematic body of, say, an anatomy text as this must be defined by a consensus of experts. Rembrandt's "Anatomy Lesson" accordingly becomes Barker's principal example of the cultural revolution, though he also rereads Marvell's "Coy Mistress" and moments in Pepys and Milton to the same effect. The arts of this transitional time are perhaps not the best contexts in which to demonstrate the philosophical point, though of course it is a part of such a historian's purpose to show that the imagination too finds itself subordinate to the new epistemology. To be sure Barker, like Foucault before him, does not go on to remind us that this premodern body, once omnipresent in so many contexts, would already have a previous history through Christendom to its origins in the Eucharist. But that sequence had been traced in another intellectual style, as we have already been able to see.

It might be possible to propose from a still-wider historical perspective that something like what we have agreed to call the shift to modernity has happened before in other cultures besides our own. The problem of knowledge, after all, begins as far as the West is concerned well before Socrates. It may even be that the Buddha, who was clearly not called "the enlightened one" for nothing, should in fact be thought of as having carried through an equivalent initial deconstruction within the context of ancient Indian culture. To be sure, the first of these revolutions, which certainly succeeded intellectually, never took hold politically or technically, though it did arrive at the beginnings of science. And the second took place entirely within the context of wisdom, and so as a critique of desire rather than as a structure for intelligence.

For an unqualified manifestation of what can thereafter be recovered from subsequent instances in social or imaginative contexts alike, we must probably remain satisfied with the canonical point of origin for the Western version of the perspective in question, that thoroughly modular moment of illumination in which Descartes discovered himself as minimally an instance of mind—and the world thus became so much matter. With him, as if all at once, the paradigm did in fact seem to establish itself in full—and can accordingly serve from then on to explain not just all subsequent cognitive practice in terms of the structure provided but any such previous activity as could be assimilated to it. No wonder that epistemology becomes the next strictly philosophical reduplication of the initial moment, the science of this newfound science, as Husserl would call it, or knowledge knowing itself. Sometimes the subject has been redefined in terms of the object, as in empiricism. Sometimes the object has been defined in terms of the subject, as with idealism. But in either case the polarity itself has remained essentially undisturbed, its continuing dominance as decisive for its enemies as for its celebrants. To redefine the object as in point of fact linguistic, as the latest school of criticism has made a point of doing, and the subject therefore as a product of this, or object of an object, is still to employ one of the innumerable strategic options already implicit in the paradigm as such. So too would be the apparent counter to this maneuver, an overattachment to the subject conceived as liberated in the mode of an imagination for which all species of objects are happily "fictive" and so *un*real. Our postmodern literature as well as our science, "hard" or human, is still governed by what all concerned have agreed to suspect without so far being able to give up.

One connection I have not seen any historian of ideas make should have already become comparatively easy. The modern establishment of the paradigm, we have said, presupposes that any previous body has been split in two, so that the soul, which once reproduced the whole, is now separated out and generalized as an impersonal point of view, while the abandoned flesh drops back into a correspondingly chaotic and indefinite extendedness. The "mind-body" problem would then be insoluble within precisely these circumstances where it cannot help but be repeatedly posed, for the body sought has not just been placed out of reach but must have already disintegrated in order to produce the very consciousness that entertains the issue.[8] All that the common mind can know, given the all-determining initial step, is so much intrinsically disorderly matter: objects, facts, ideas, particles, sense data, "raw feels." And these are obviously no longer the body proper, if that ever did or might still exist, but its decomposed remains. So the complementary intelligence is left floating like a ghost in the space that has succeeded to what might once have seemed "the encompassing" environment or "life-world."[9] Indeed it is, more acutely considered, precisely that space itself; consciousness, as Sartre once famously observed, is within the paradigm *no-thing*, the negative implied by any known positive. It cannot be accidental that the corresponding political

---

[8]C. A. Peursen, for one instance, surveying the "problem" in *Body, Soul, Spirit* (Oxford: Oxford University Press, 1966), has no trouble rehearsing the initial critical move. But then he finds himself, as others have before and since, in difficulty as he attempts to discover an adequate language for what the apparently unavoidable abstraction is *from*. "Mind" or "I," however redefined, have already, alas, been captured by the enemy.

[9]The phrases in quotation marks are respectively the expressions offered by Karl Jaspers in his *Philosophy of Existence* (Philadelphia: University of Pennsylvania Press, 1971) and Edmund Husserl in *The Crisis of European Sciences* (Evanston IL: Northwestern University Press, 1970) for whatever would *not* be assimilable within the paradigm. Phenomenology, as we have seen in connection with Merleau-Ponty, cannot help but suffer a familiar imputation of vagueness. The "ghost" image for the mind was made familiar for Anglo-American philosophy by Gilbert Ryle's *Concept of Mind* (1949); the (rest of the individual) body becomes a "machine" to match.

revolutions should have been publicly marked by the decapitation of a king. The royal person, we might repeat, embodied the commonwealth, as this in turn, we could now add, reproduced the accompanying cosmos. To divide such a figure's head from his trunk would then indeed have made a most appropriate "sacrifice" of what had once prevailed, however spuriously, in the name of what should now obtain, however limited. The king is dead, one could repeatedly cry out: long live pure Reason. With *that* body out of the way, no others need apply. Or so for a while it could seem.

For we have also noticed how, in proportion to the hegemony of the paradigm, all other bodies, innocent or guilty, individual or representative, erotic or religious, became in principle superfluous, not to say embarrassing, and therefore either subordinate to some abstraction or set aside in some deliberately marginal realm of the private, the aesthetic, the feminine, the primitive. To be sure, resistance has never quite ceased, whether from philosophers or psychologists, novelists or adulterers, fanatics or soldiers. But religion was safely isolated comparatively early in the process, and the other powers, including desire, which some might have supposed invincible, were obliged to retreat to regions where they could be allowed free play at the expense of losing any ontological privilege. The hegemony of the paradigm has continued secure, even in its apparent multiplication, dispersal, routinization, or even fragmentation. On the social scale the problem is posed by the antipresence of the text, as we have seen; on the cosmic, by the omnipresence of the object—and therefore the *cogito* that must intend this object. In both "contexts" we are still awaiting a deconstruction to the second power, which would amount to the corresponding apocalypse. Who shall reduce modernity for us, which has reduced everything else besides?

The summer I began to address these matters a good deal of construction was going on in my building. Its inhabitants could not help becoming reacquainted with some of what was involved in this process besides noise, dust, and the need to keep away from both. I was struck among other impressions by the extent to which what was being done seemed to enforce the hegemony of the structure with other aspects of which the philosophers on my hallway were presumably concerning themselves. Strangers from what I could feel was the old-fashioned American working class, which we do not often have to do with in the academy, were putting together so many measured surfaces: ceilings, floors, and especially walls. These last had to be carefully built up, layer by layer, upon a wood framing: at first a metallic mesh, then three successive layers of plaster, a coarse grey, a finer grey, and finally a white, called, as I learned by asking, *scratch, double-up,* and *finish*: names already, as so often in such cases, a kind of poetry. And once the last coat of plaster had been swept on, the painters followed with their rollers. The materials that rendered these successive surfaces solid and opaque were evidently chaotic: so much dust, literally or essentially, mixed with water and troweled or brushed on: matter at its most thoroughly reduced, shear extendedness for sure, ground down so as to be shaped into an abstract form, itself defined by a line crossing another line at right angles: the text, I could therefore think, indeed. Those lines then represented the domination of matter by mind, and so these artisans by the invisible architect. There was some horror mixed with my curiosity and occasional admiration, as at the manual skill of the plasterers, or my impatience to have the job completed by term time. A house (of sorts) was being built: that was the satisfactory import of the project. For a house is still a kind of body, and therefore satisfying to the imagination.

But these steps to that end seemed to disclose the comparative unreality of any such merely imaginable whole, which was, after all, not in fact what was literally being put together. That labor merely repeated and materialized the ideal object in an endless process which as such cannot satisfy the imagination, though it helps keep the economy going. We were being shown against our will, though ostensibly in our interests, how invasive the paradigm has in fact become. There was no use romanticizing it then, or its victims, among which a university, after all, might in some respects consider itself one more. The *cogitata* were still very much with us; the *cogito,* it could not help but follow, continued as lord of this world. How then might either or both be overthrown—or changed together into something else? History could expose the situation and perhaps identify origins, but the problem remained philosophical; if there might be a solution, it would apparently have to be worked through in those terms.

How then, in thought at least, if not yet in practice, physical or professional, might one hope to recover from the disembodiment enforced by the paradigm? And not just nostalgically but ideally, in terms therefore that could hold for any period or culture? For there should be some way to confirm the suggestion constantly offered by any actual body, however near or far away, that the cosmos does indeed exist, and might even be realized as such. Meanwhile the apparently obligatory abstraction is perpetually preventing what might otherwise become a convincing presence, as the corresponding impersonality already denies in advance whoever we are that have begun to feel it. To disestablish this structure it would clearly be necessary to exchange history, which by definition can report only results, for philosophy; but perhaps also to leap back, for a sufficiently promising instance of what still seems required, to a cosmology that could reasonably claim innocence of modernity and the premodern alike. For our local sense of the once and future body, communal or cosmic, must now suffer the imputation of imaginative displacement and to that extent incredibility. We cannot wish to repeal a justified revolution, intellectual or political, and had better not try. In the textual or social context the Bible, we have found, could provide an exemplary instance previous to both Christendom and the modern West within which a sufficient reduction could in fact offer a glimpse of transcendence. In the same way a stronger version of a possible origin might supply a more satisfactory figure for what the corresponding apocalypse should ideally consist of within the order of cognition. The subjective pole of the paradigm, it has become conventional to suppose, clarified with Descartes. The objective pole would have to be traced at least as far back as Plato, if not, therefore, to Socrates. In that case we could accept the implicit suggestion that what we must accordingly call the "pre-Socratics" might offer an account of the body at once innocent and cosmic, antecedent and anticipatory.

More than one of the obvious names could indeed be read as supplying just such an example. The idea of the One, for instance, which in the nature of the case proposed would seem to supply our best clue to what is desired, is already present in Pythagoreanism, where as we might also expect, it begins as it continues: ambiguous. The One is divine or arithmetical or musical or all of these. The mathematical unit repeats itself geometrically as a point, and then as an atom of existence, or, for the living universe as a whole, as its procreative seed or warming fire.[10]

But the stronger instance would surely be Parmenides. In the "Way of Truth," or primary section of this thinker's compressed but frankly heroic poem, the Odysseus-like seeker is driven in a chariot as far as the gates of day and night, where Justice is persuaded to let him pass on out to another scene where he learns from a second and more welcoming but never named goddess (is she Wisdom indeed?) that there can indeed be only one One, which is therefore identical with *to eon,* or Being, or "the subject," or that-which-is—the possible translations seem unavoidably various.[11] What is *not,* he quickly learns too, has therefore absolutely nothing to do with this, whatever it is. For something cannot be nothing, or even the opposite of nothing; if anything exists, something does. Yet this can indeed be known: reality is what can be spoken of or attended to, for thought must always be of something (as Husserl would repeat some generations later). It follows too that whatever is must be previous to all differences, including those so important for later philosophy as idea and matter, temporality and eternity, finitude and infinity, or surface and substance. Whatever is, we could therefore add, would have to precede or transcend language, which presumes and establishes difference as such. No element of any polarity could therefore refer to anything real. Dualities of every kind are simply illusory, *doxa.* (It is appealing to remember in this connection that the discovery that the morning and evening stars were in fact the same entity was traditionally attributed to Parmenides.) If the truth of being is pre- or postdifferential, it must always already but also forever be present, entire, and utterly unique: "whole, singular, and as unmoving as complete," as the fourth verse of the eighth

---

[10]My summary here is dependent on F. M. Cornford's introduction to his classic commentary *Plato and Parmenides* (New York: Liberal Arts, 1957). Walter Burkert has more recently argued in his *Lore and Science in Ancient Pythagoreanism* (Cambridge: Harvard University Press, 1972) that Pythagoras is really too prerational to count even as a source for any post-Socratic thinker. But the idea at least of the One seems a clue worth pursuing.

[11]A. S. Mourelatos points out in *The Route of Parmenides* (New Haven: Yale University Press, 1970), one of several recent studies of this author, that the language associated with the goddess of instruction connects her with ideas of constraint or compulsion (26-29). It would fit the tone of this extraordinary poem if we should understand Parmenides to be implying that fate was wisdom, or wisdom, fate.

fragment puts it.[12] These attributes are then the "notes" (*semata*) of what is, which may properly therefore be imagined as resembling a massy sphere, perfectly symmetrical from all directions.

The mysterious authority and suggestive power of this intuition, as formidable as it is archaic, could prompt the question, is the Parmenidean entity perhaps already the body on the scale of the cosmos, though in what has to be a pagan and so a quasi-mythical or prephilosophical form? His version of the possibility would have the immense advantage over subsequent definitions of "incorporating" at once the abstract and concrete aspects of whatever is, which would allow us in principle at least to take a major step if not quite forward at any rate decisively backward from the limits of the paradigm. Plato was presently to idealize this unity, as Aristotle was in due course to materialize and distribute it, thereby prefiguring between them the contrasting options for a succession of intellectual choices in time to come.[13] But here Being is as yet undivided, indeed indivisible. To be sure, some complementary disadvantages would need to be admitted. The fixity, externality, and therefore separation from the subject so strongly insisted upon would seem to make *to eon* rather a figure still for the body proper than a complete version of it. Jesus, after all, does *not* refuse but on the contrary accepts precisely those appearances and contrasts that Parmenides dismisses under the heading of the "Way of Seeming." Phenomenality, polarity, metamorphosis, even negativity are evidently included within the individual, symbolic, and communal modes of the body indeed, as we have seen—and should in reason be expected to obtain for any cosmic version as well. Nor does Parmenides, for that matter, employ the word *soma*. Within the poem outlining the doctrine, these refused or omitted elements would seem indirectly dramatized by the mythical situation imagined as a frame for the central deliverance. Who *is* the nameless goddess, then? Or rather, what is the actuality of which she is so ostentatiously an imaginary version? What is missing from the philosophy may still be latent in the poetry.

But if *to eon* is not yet quite the body indeed, it is at a minimum identifiable with what in modern terms might be called the unavoidable *it*, or rational but also simultaneously actual object, whatever that happened to be; the line, as it were,

---

[12]The form of this saying is variously identified and translated in the current standard edition, David Gallop, *Parmenides of Elea* (Toronto: University of Toronto Press, 1984) 64 or by Leonardo Taran, *Parmenides* (Princeton: Princeton University Press, 1965) 88-92.

[13]My review of the possibilities will skip over Aristotle, in part because what that post-Platonist meant by *ousia* seems to have remained uncertain for his students, whether ancient, medieval, or modern. The *Metaphysics* appears irresolvably ambiguous. Is Being plural or singular, concrete or abstract, transcendental or experimental? The surveys of the alternatives in Joseph Owen, *Doctrine of Being in the Aristotelian "Metaphysics"* (Toronto: Pontifical Institute, 1978) or Mary Louise Gill, *Aristotle on Substance* (Princeton: Princeton University Press, 1989) suggest that an outsider had better avoid the topic; though even from a distance it could be observed the ambiguity leaves room not only for Aquinas but also Heidegger.

reduced backward or forward to the corresponding point. Parmenides, we could say, is the first to think in terms of a singular universal, which would make him a protomodern as well as a pre-Socratic. His idea of being could then function as at once the earliest and (still after its fashion) the best formulation for what we could in that case think of as, if not the body, at least the universe: the cosmos, as it were *kata noun*. For the account he offers could not *not* seem minimally true of any such knowable entity, minute or grand, original or terminal. Parmenides would to that extent already anticipate the best results of his successors, if not quite the corresponding apocalypse. This position would make him at least a prophet of cognition—perhaps almost the last, as well as the first, of that most unusual kind.

After Parmenides would come Plato, whose own dialogue devoted to and named after his precursor offers a notoriously puzzling meditation on what might or might not be made of the earlier thinker's substantialization of the Pythagorean One. In the course of this inquiry that dense entity is first reduced to nothing and then expanded again to everything, as if to see what evacuation and elaboration alike might make of the master's intuition. The first "hypothesis" does away with the several *semata* of that-which-is, first subtracting its integrity, and then successively arguing that it must be aspectless, shapeless, placeless, timeless, neither in motion nor at rest, neither the same nor the other—not even, strictly speaking, there at all. In this way a reimagined Parmenides, who conducts the analysis himself, is made to argue away the truth of his own idea, reducing this thought not just to a rational core but to the nonexistence even of that. The One itself, or *auto to hen*, becomes as a result barely intelligible, for without some degree of being, how could such a focus of attention even be thought of? The second thesis allows the One that much once more, as if as a concession, and from this starting point develops a multiplicity first of numbers and then of things, and so through all the other attributes of physicality, motion and rest, and temporality, in such a way as to include even the features that the historical Parmenides had dismissed to illusion.[14] Such a double movement is a "reading" of the original poem with a vengeance, quite in the most modern style of that dangerous activity. But what could a reader of this reading conclude should be Plato's own decision on the point at issue? It has proved difficult to determine; which might be an aspect precisely of the point to be understood.

We would apparently be better off with the *Timaeus*, a late dialogue devoted explicitly not to Parmenides' argument but to his subject matter. Some familiar

---

[14] I am indebted again to Cornford's own reading, still in *Plato and Parmenides*, esp. 116-22, for my summary of the first phase of the argument and 203-204 for the whole. The contribution of the dramatic context to this dialectic provides a focus for Mitchell Miller's more recent *Plato's Parmenides* (Princeton: Princeton University Press, 1986). Plato also criticizes Parmenides' idea of being in *The Sophist*, pointing out the difficulty of subsuming it under an appropriate form. See Cornford once more in his *Plato's Theory of Knowledge* (New York: Liberal Arts, 1957) 220-28.

motifs do reappear, and within a similarly mythical framework. We should understand the first craftsman, the principal speaker explains, as having created the world as a single coherent spherical living entity that might reasonably be called a god in its own right, though it is still a creature containing all the other creatures. We seem closer here to a reproduction of the older philosopher's idea, and so once again to a glimpse at least of the body indeed. The later portion of the dialogue elaborates on how such a universe might be supposed to have been put together in what amounts to a scientific rather than a poetic style. But before this alternative commences we have already learned that the cosmos in question is not in fact all there is. As a merely created whole it is only an image for its real model, the "highest and most completely perfect of intelligible beings" (1.4) or "eternal Living Being" (1.7) or "Perfect intelligible Living Creature" (2.7).[15] In that case our world, though undoubtedly a living body, is not yet the body indeed: that possibility, if it could still be raised, would have to be reserved for the model or ideal and therefore *in*visible (because only intelligible) being of which the cosmos is a copy. This anomalous figure a latter-day Christian reader might, it could seem on first reading, be tempted to identify as a philosophical prefigurement of the preexistent Son. I have wondered accordingly if any Platonically minded figure within the Johannine branch of the tradition at least might have entertained some such notion. My informants, though, do not recall a case of the kind.

I suspect in any case that even if this temptation should ever have been or still might be felt, it had better be resisted. The *Timaeus* as a whole invites a reading that would remain skeptical of the very mythological language that governs its presentation. Myth, like dialogue, is preliminary or rhetorical for Plato, not final. It is indulged in only to be seen through. A suitably demythologized version of the argument presented would therefore have to translate the tantalizingly ethereal figure in question into yet one more image, this time for the complex of all possible Forms sufficient to supply a set of instructions to replicate the actual universe.[16] For the radical difference between the empirical and the rational, time and eternity, becoming and being, and so of the plausible and the certain would for Plato take precedence over, and therefore implicitly determine, the meaning of any merely imaginative mode of presentation. To be sure we are still left wondering, once such a preliminary reduction has taken place, how any complete system of ideas—if that *is* what the "perfect intelligible living being" stands as a figure for—should itself be thought of as organized. Would there not have to be, to follow up in Platonic style, a Form of all these Forms, or most general genus for every species and subspecies, moral or mathematical or intellectual? In the *Symposium* this is the

---

[15]I follow the translation by Desmond Lee in his convenient edition of the *Timaeus and Critias* (Harmondsworth: Penguin, 1971).

[16]This is Desmond Lee's solution, which he repeats in his introduction as if representing the scholarly consensus (*Timaeus*, 10).

Beautiful, as one would expect from the subject matter of that dialogue. In the *Republic* it is the Good, as befits an examination of justice. The aspect of the last idea that confronts even the wisest evidently varies according to context. The domains of desire and will, though, are notoriously resistant to reason. It seems safer to stick to the One as the least limited and therefore most neutral name for whatever can in the end be known for sure.[17] The *Parmenides* makes obvious that this terminus should be conceived as altogether an essence without existence. The *Timaeus* does not tell us clearly how its own contribution to the question should be read. But we need not doubt that Plato would prefer us to end with a rational rather than a religious conclusion, if only for the time being.

The Hellenic canon could supply some suggestive instances, then, of whatever-it-is that would need to be understood as preceding or underlying if not yet quite transcending the differences imposed by what we have been calling the cognitive paradigm. To be sure, we can also notice, even for the earliest of these, some movement in the direction of what presently clarifies as a species of objectivity, rational or factual or still ambiguous, and to that extent the emergence of what looks like one pole of the structure in question. The doctrine of Forms in particular could be read as securing once and for all a reasonably clarified version of this result, as the *cogito* of Descartes may be understood as determining once and for all a sufficiently reduced version of the corresponding subject.[18] To that extent we would find ourselves still with one more history of the emergence of "modernity" in the mode of cognition, and so with yet another repetition of the problem instead of some way of advancing toward a solution.

But we need not seek only among ancient authorities for approximations to some idea of the cosmic body. The problem of relating the One and Being after a fashion satisfactory to both reason and faith was repeatedly discussed among the scholastics too, who added "truth" and the "good" to the "transcendentals" to be accounted for. If though we are seeking not just an antecedent and so inevitably mythical or traditional image for this possibility but an explicitly eschatological disclosure of the case, we would though probably do better with a more recent and therefore challenging instance, if one could be found. And here, luckily, it is not hard to settle on a major specimen of just such a kind. Of the older but still distinctly "Modern" authorities, Kant would surely stand out as primary. His *Critique of*

---

[17]Plato may in fact have delivered an unpublished lecture "On the Good" near the end of his life that assimilated even that apparently final form to the One. Burkert, *Greek Religion,* 324, refers me to Harold Cherniss, whose *Riddle of the Early Academy* (Berkeley: University of California Press, 1945) reviews the possibilities from a more skeptical perspective.

[18]It could be argued that Plato also uncovered the subjective as well as the objective pole of the paradigm. His soul is deathless and therefore preexistent; it already remembers what the *agon* of dialectic must struggle for. The immortality of this interior power could then be read as a mythical version of what a modern would identify as the impersonality of the mind.

Pure Reason already represents as formidable an examination of the paradigm itself (though still from within a repetition of it) as there has ever been. But its interest in this connection derives from Kant's insistence, as a product of precisely such an analysis, on the simultaneous indispensability and unknowability of what he names the "thing-in-itself." For knowledge, as the process of cognition structures it, can only, on his account, be of appearances in space and time, which should themselves be understood therefore as modalities of the Understanding.[19] What from within the activity of this limited faculty we are prepared to call objects or things or even bodies would in that case amount to no more than representations produced by a coincidence of sensation and the relevant concept. What Kant reserves as the Reason, or the subject thinking most generally, would though still require that we posit as the source for these several appearances something else that might then be understood as a truly transcendental "object," an *ens realissimum* that could serve to unify and support our otherwise all too chaotic experience of the world.

To be sure, Kant sometimes speaks of things in themselves in the plural, as if there might be many such, in which case he would appear to have in mind something like what his predecessor Liebnitz called "monads." In that case it would be individual natural bodies he is referring to rather than any cosmic body. But as his argument continues, the expression occurs more frequently in the singular, and by the time he arrives at the section "The Ideal of Reason," which should be crucial, it has already come close to meaning a single transcendental entity. This in turn soon modulates into an idea of God rather than of some unique whatever, which would seem to overleap the problem, though in an interesting direction. But in any case one might seem to have in the preceding analysis of the Understanding sufficient permission to suppose that the thing-in-itself would have to be singular, on Kant's own terms. For a plurality of entities could only be established in space and time, which are how we differentiate one body from another. If these, though, are concomitants only of the Understanding, the "object" of Reason, which transcends all times and places, must necessarily, it would appear, be unique.[20]

In that case we could understand Kant as once again rehearsing the import of Parmenides, but now after the fact not only of Plato but also of Descartes, and so

---

[19] My language presupposes what remains a standard translation of the first critique by Norman Kemp Smith (New York: St. Martins, 1965).

[20] It is embarrassing to discover that Schopenhauer agrees with me, though in a Romantico-naturalistic style that identifies the thing-in-itself with "will," or materialized force. Of the standard authorities Cassirer and Paton do not see a problem. More recent critics (Strawson, Walsh, Guyer) so disapprove of the general idea that the issue does not arise. H. E. Allison and J. N. Findlay are ambivalent; the latter's *Kant and the Transcendental Object* (Oxford: Clarendon, 1981) does at least affirm that an original Leibnitzian plurality seems to come together at last in a "single supreme thing-in-itself" (348), a "monad of monads" (351), or "whirling wheel of Being" (354). It seems fair to conclude that Kant himself was not yet quite Kantian enough on this central point.

as much on the far side of the paradigm, at least in principle, as the oldest of these authorities would be previous to it. He would seem accordingly to come as near as any Western thinker has yet done to outlining, if not quite the absolute reduction of reason we are still seeking, at least the wilderness through which any quest for this would have to pass.

Kant would in addition suggest a way of avoiding the danger to which Plato could feel Parmenides had succumbed—that of attributing too positive a character to the being it was still necessary to presume. For the Modern theorist the thing-in-itself is liberated to remain always and everywhere what he is careful to call it, a regulative idea, not a constitutive one. There is no way to avoid presupposing it, that is, but no way either to argue from its ideal indispensability to its actual existence. We must attribute a certain unity of being to the cosmos in order to make sense of the bits and pieces we have to do with, but we cannot prove that it makes a whole. We must simply act and think *as if* it did. This scruple very neatly preserves, it seems to me, the remaining difference between whatever might be thought even at last and what, if it could still be posited at all, must therefore be believed in rather than known. If the body exists on the scale of the cosmos, this restraint would seem a very necessary condition for our comprehension of just that.

In late spring the students are nearly through with their academic obligations, and games are got up to express the corresponding mood. One afternoon, as I headed toward the library, I passed a group of boys who had pushed a great ball onto the grass. Its covering was a coarse green cloth, on which were painted images of the continents, somewhat dimmed by time and wear. This was a more advanced version, then, of the game I had seen the two young children play a term or two before. The ball was filled not quite full of air, so as it rolled it slouched, like a huge pillow. What one tried to do with this soft sphere was jump on top and if possible rise to one's feet and walk along with the ball as it rolled. But I saw no one succeed, though several tried, running over and over to leap up onto the yielding surface, arms spread out and knees clutching. Some clambered for a while desperately, but all soon found their own bodies out of sync with the ponderous motions their very efforts produced, and pitched or slid off with exclamations of mock despair. It was mostly a male game, I observed, though a couple of girls tried too and even more quickly gave up.

This enterprise could be read as demonstrating the truth of Kant's scruple, I thought, as well as the repeated efforts since to prove him too pessimistic, beginning perhaps with Hegel, that Paul of our modernity. But we cannot know (which is to say, dominate) the thing-in-itself, even in a university, where some might be expected to try. For whatever it is evades and slips out from under our best attempts, however strenuously we throw ourselves upon it. Meanwhile the entity in question remains more or less obviously the wholeness of the whole. The arts quad is at the center of our local academic galaxy, so it could seem appropriate that this game should be played there, as if in mockery of the institution to which in their workaday mood these young people would, like their teachers, be subordinate.

Exams, after all, were still ahead. But it was evidently possible to have fun anyway, before and perhaps after too.

In his first critique, Kant remains utterly noncommittal with respect to the qualities or character of that which he still finds himself presuming on what for him are the self-evident grounds that whatever absolutely is cannot be brought within the horizon of an impersonal mind's attention to its objects, material or conceptual. The cognitive paradigm, that is, must do without precisely what it cannot help but continue to found itself upon. And for Kant, as for the age his thought at once criticizes and advances, cognition continues to take firm precedence. His own subsequent analyses of the moral and aesthetic possibilities of human experience literally come second and third respectively. The *Critique of Judgment* in particular has often seemed a comparatively minor or even dubious portion of this master's work.

Yet this text too may be read as suggesting a significant addition to the otherwise unspecifiable idea of the thing-in-itself as the first critique had left this. As one might expect, Kant is clear that aesthetic judgments are noncognitive and therefore neither objective nor logically derivable. This determination would situate the imaginative in general within the cultural province it has in fact occupied throughout the modern period, as we have seen; licit, as it were, in its own right, yet without any metaphysical rights, all of which have been preempted by cognition. For our pleasure in any recognition of beauty, Kant goes on to say, accompanies the mere representation of whatever there may be to the subject—which is, he proposes, consciousness-in-general, or the Understanding and Imagination at free and disinterested play. The apparent object of such judgments is then only a purposiveness without purpose, and so distinct from both the pleasant and the good. This account seems on the whole somewhat condescending; though the report of the "sublime" that follows his analysis of the "beautiful" was in due course to sanction grander visions of the Imagination among some of this philosopher's poetical heirs.

But Kant also reviews his own case from the perspective of the Reason as well as the Understanding or (what for him is the sibling faculty of) Imagination. And from that perspective, something further is exposed. Aesthetic judgments invariably presume their own universality. If I decide that something is beautiful, I must by this very determination expect that anyone else is bound to concur—whether or not in fact they do. This implicit universality is subjective rather than objective. But it is still unavoidable in principle, however confused in practice. Kant then asks himself what could legitimate such an a priori expectation—and finds that this must once again be the "supersensible substrate" upon which the Reason was found to rely within the context of knowledge.[21] In the case of aesthetic experience, animal

---

[21]The phrase quoted is the one used in the translation of *The Critique of Judgement* by J. H. Bernard (New York: Hafner, 1951), still a familiar textbook version. My acceptance of the Kantian argument would seem naive to Paul Guyer, whose *Kant and the Claims of Taste* (Cambridge: Harvard University Press, 1979) is strongly critical of the philosopher's

or verbal, any such entity would still be inaccessible as such. It remains a normative idea, not a provable (or in this case, an enjoyable) actuality. But something about it is all the same disclosed by a careful return upon a presupposition of the experience addressed. The central act within what has otherwise continued to seem only a subset of our cultural life would to this extent coincide with the axis of the master faculty of cognition. Both would then presuppose the same transcendental "object," upon which human consciousness in general would ultimately be oriented. Indeed, aesthetic judgment might provide a better clue to the full truth of the matter than cognition, for beauty would in that case be a reliable clue to or symptom of being, the like of which would still be missing in any merely indispensable object of reason. But this hint has been difficult for subsequent thinkers to develop.

Nietzsche might, to be sure, be read as endeavoring to advance the claims of aesthesis from the compensatory position in which it had been left by his post-Kantian predecessors. But the aesthetic seems for him rather an elaboration of the natural and so a function of the imaginative than an introduction to the cosmic. A more serious instance would surely be supplied by Heidegger, whose protest against the authority of the paradigm would have to stand as the most trenchant in more recent times. His appeal to a premetaphysical *Sein* that could even now prove uncoverable beneath the abstractions of the "ontic" would indeed look forward not just to a recovery of the aesthetic but to the coherence of that with the manual in the work of the artisan as a type of what should ground the experience of human being in the midst of our world. The note of his meditations on this primordial level of existence has from their commencement in *Being and Time* been bodily in what can seem a startling as well as a satisfying degree. No wonder, one could feel, that he considered himself virtually a pre-Socratic—or that Parmenides should be an explicit precursor. Heidegger is a most serious Romantic, for good or ill, and so might represent the next step on from Kant, ontological or aesthetic or both, whether or not one remembers his immediate precursors within the "phenomenological" movement.

There would still, though, be some limits to the promise of even this apparently most radical of the modern challenges to the sufficiency of the paradigm. Heidegger's central thought could in fact appear, as it develops through a powerful sequence of texts, rather less than more suggestive compared to the Kantian thing-in-itself, whether that remains merely ideal or already beautiful. For him Being remains indefinite, omnipresent, hidden: "under erasure" indeed, as a late text calls it, and so rather a concept diffused, or thought dispersed almost to chaos once again, than any eventual coalescence. There is, even in imagination, no such *thing* as Being. What exists are still beings—which is to say, bodies. The background hum of being-in-general would then amount to the copresence with whatever else we

---

effort to prove the intersubjectivity of aesthetic judgment and positively scornful of his "misguided" regression to the possibility of a supersensible substratum.

were then and there engaged upon of all the other things there might yet be in the world. Heidegger has a profound feeling for the bodiliness of the human subject—his celebrated account of the ontological implications of the hand is often recalled—but that which has yet to be grasped is more often left vague. *Dasein*, or human being, is surrounded by the "ready-to-hand" without quite being able to lay hold of anything equal in density to itself, much less confronting another presence as good as or even superior to its own. It seems typical of what is still unresolved in the Heideggerian version of the human predicament that the ground or soil back toward which his language is repeatedly calling us would in metaphor at least continue as the surface of our planet. It is the whole of that body to which we are held regardless; and if so, this might practically serve to enfigure a corresponding solidity that seems missing on the scale of being-in-general. It is not unfair accordingly for Derrida to repeatedly reemphasize the inevitable inaccessibility of any Heideggerian hope. I have seen this latter-day critic draw the letters for the word *Sein* most deliberately on the blackboard at a lecture—and then cross these over with a large and equally demonstrative *X*. "The text," as his version of the necessary objection would put it, can only mark the absence of any presence.[22]

Heidegger would seem open to just such a reification of his own qualification to the extent that his proper thought is not yet Heideggerian enough—has remained, that is, still too absorbed in the potential existence of the natural or individual body to seek out what might eventually become a final body—though as a Jesuit seminarian he could once have known something of this too, as it were in advance. But had he continued along the dusky wood-path he chose to follow as a dangerously free thinker, it is still possible to guess that he might have come nearer where there is in the end to go. His Being, if no longer only the obscurity of evening, is perhaps already the dawn of which the body indeed would then be the rising sun.

Heidegger's slow movement through the woods must continue in general as an impressive if obscure intimation of what might yet be accomplished on the scale in question. For a somewhat more explicit adoption of the hint supplied by Kant's third critique, one could turn such a project as that of Urs von Balthasar, who *did* become a Jesuit for a while at least—and endeavored on the basis of precisely the suggestion made to construct an explicit "theological aesthetics." Beauty, he argues

---

[22]The Heideggerian source for the motif is his *Question of Being* (New Haven: Twayne, 1958) esp. 81-104, though Derridians are apt to attribute it to their own master rather than his precursor. Derrida's *Of Spirit* (Chicago: University of Chicago Press, 1989) 2, though, could remind them that the *kreuzweise Durchstreichung* was not originally inscribed in French. His own essay at a formal aesthetics characteristically omits both the idea of a subjective norm and the possibility of a posttextual presence which this might imply, though he reviews Kant's third critique at some length in *The Truth in Painting* (Chicago: University of Chicago Press, 1987) 37-147.

in the first volume of what eventually became a trilogy, is the key note of revelation, not its rival. The constituents of the beautiful, he finds accordingly, are "form" and "glory," which as demonstrated in what he can formally acknowledge as the typical event would identify Christ as the form of which God is the glory. Faith is therefore "seeing the form," a formula that supplies a title for his initial volume and might, one could also suppose, apply to other contexts as well.[23] The complexity of this post-Platonic idea expresses a unity that cannot be realized all at once, though it amounts to an entire image of divine power. The project seems promising and might rhyme easily with what we have either observed or desiderated in our other authorities. But Balthasar's own vision is perhaps too firmly "Christocentric" in a dogmatic and therefore limited sense. The historical Jesus is for him only an inference to be reprobated, and the Church too (though he was a conservative churchman, and honored accordingly) is in his eyes comparatively subordinate. Bodiliness is mentioned, but its relevance for the view proposed is not carried home: though such terms as *equilibrium, harmony, attunement,* and *simplicity* for the Christ-form would imply that it is in fact always one mode or another of the body that is being acknowledged. The key difficulty seems to be that the language of revelation is aestheticized rather than aesthesis in general Christologized. So the cosmic opportunity silently proffered by the very person with whom he can afford to be explicitly concerned is not quite taken up. The opening supplied by the initial Kantian insight is not yet passed through—on the way, we are still obliged to hope, toward a more thoroughly Parmenidean apocalypse than has so far occurred within any context, ancient or modern. But Balthasar can at least represent a serious theological variant of the ideal possibility that as such remains alive, in or out of one academic "field" or another. Thinking need not, after all, be contained within such categories of what may easily be identified as the social equivalents of the Understanding.

Or so one continues to hope as well as suppose. While in search of further philosophical instances for the inquiry here rehearsed, I spent what at the time seemed the better part of a summer reading F. H. Bradley's *Appearance and Reality*. I might have chosen R. G. Collingwood's somewhat briefer *Idea of Nature,* or perhaps something by Bergson or Whitehead. For there have been within what could still be identified as comparatively recent times more than one attempt to seek out alternatives, if not quite solutions, to the problem of the paradigm. Bradley could in fact seem one of the more serious of these. He clearly knew his Kant as

---

[23] A full title would include other names: Hans Urs von Balthasar, *The Glory of the Lord: A Theological Aesthetics* (San Francisco: Ignatius; New York: Crossroad, 1983). Only the first volume, *Seeing the Form,* seems immediately relevant for the issue addressed. Frank Burch Brown's *Religious Aesthetics* (Princeton: Princeton Univ. Press, 1989) reviews the overlap between the contexts named from a cautiously post-Balthasarian perspective and James Alfred Martin's *Beauty and Holiness* (Princeton: Princeton Univ. Press, 1990) summarizes the opinions of various other authorities. The question remains: Is beauty revelatory?

well as some of that master's more dubious successors. Perhaps I was then, it also occurred to me, the only person in Cambridge, or for that matter in America, to have embarked on a reading of just this text during those weeks of what at home was summer school. Even so I could not read every sentence or understand all I did read. But that was not fatal. I found myself edified regardless: Bradley's "Absolute" did indeed seem one more reflection of the thing-in-itself, this time in a late-Victorian, high Oxfordian, and therefore sufficiently aesthetic style. What else, I could almost decide, but the body indeed could any Reality be that was simultaneously *one* and *experience*? It was reassuring to discover that someone else had determined just this much and gone on not only to write his thought out but get it published too. He was even in paperback, I also knew, though my edition was older than that, and evocative in proportion. For I could recall as well, walking those brick sidewalks down leafy streets, that T. S. Eliot had once spent an equivalent period of time with the same book in an earlier edition still. There on one of the houses I passed was a plaque to prove as much. That part of the world does not change much physically, however different the inhabitants and whatever is on their minds.

One could see too how Eliot might have felt it necessary to move on from what is still unsatisfactory about the doctrine of this book toward Christianity proper—which Bradley had felt himself safely beyond. Does not "The Waste Land" in fact look ahead from within the chaos it so frankly dramatizes all the way to the Eucharist itself? The bread, after all, is how the journey to Emmaus concludes in Luke, if not in "What the Thunder Said," and the wine is what the grail would have contained, once upon or rather before even any legendary time, and so ever afterward as well. That double absence could accordingly function as the very type of the presence mirrored in reverse by the heterogeneity that precedes; upon which, as if to come to an end for the time being, the last speaker subsides at what for this poet and his reader alike is rather a stopping point on the way than anywhere to call home. Perhaps poetry, then, was still a better clue than philosophy or even theology, though I had yet to read a fair amount of both.

Terminal

Nostalgia, though, however appealing to its victims, is though one of the weaker forms of aesthesis, and should not be allowed to obscure the prospect of a rational resolution to the problem of reason, if that is still possible. For cognition continues the central action within which any promise of the body restored would need to be reformulated for modernity at large. It is not by evading, then, or even supplementing what is knowable but by completing what is already implicit in the structure of the most typical instances that one might approach the verge at least of what would in such a case become at last an other world indeed—the world, that is, of the Other. And the cosmos would have to be the context within which this fulfillment did or did not take place for the obvious reason that knowledge is always of the cosmos, micro or macro. The university, we must boast or admit, can only contemplate the universe. We will never know more or less than everything, in one set of terms or another. And this predicament is as inevitable for us as ever for the Greeks, who at least knew when they were composing cosmologies, heroic or skeptical, even if the opportunity must now be felt in so much more fragmented, complicated, and dispersed a degree.

But if the body is to prove recoverable on the scale of the cosmos for modernity as well, then the paradigm would need somehow to be teased into deconstructing itself, so that subject and object together would, as it were, conflate or collapse from within, leaving nothing of either behind—but something else altogether ahead. To dissolve the object into the subject, as idealism once promised, would be no more than half an apocalypse. To reduce the subject to the object, as empiricism or materialism and more recently "theory" have successively proposed, would still leave some form of the latter in what thereby becomes total possession. But suppose we were to revert not just to this or that pole of the structure in question but to both at once. Then we could appreciate the paradigm as the dividing up of a once-living body, cosmic or communal, as the historians have suggested. Or we could situate it as an abstraction from what, by *not* taking thought, we could still experience in our own natural bodies, as the phenomenological and existential tradition has proposed. Or we might finally also take it to be promising by the very violence of its structure an eventual recombination—as whatever would then become of it. In any of these ways we could preserve some degree of confidence in an eventual reduction of what has otherwise seemed so invincibly resistant to the very idea of the body, much less its real presence—all the way to the idea at least of just that. This hope might then amount to one more version of the Parmenidean expedition or the Kantian scruple, and seem no less promising accordingly.

There could of course be a variety of approaches to the problem. If an object of cognition is in any case an instance of what we have agreed must be a text, we should be prepared to find that other attributes of that genus might become relevant to the problem posed by this species. So we could presume some advantage in recalling even the most literal matter of fact associated with the general case: for instance, that a text is typically a sequence of letters written from left to right or right to left or from the top down. These form an ideal extendedness as soon as they have been untwisted and connected end to end, as happens already in handwriting, where each word is formed out of an uninterrupted line, and to that extent has already become a single "letter." We could recall too that the separate rows of type on an ordinary page are not, as in poetry, significant units in their own right but physical compromises: a prose text, however long, is really all one "line." What *is* this line, then?

It makes a difference, we regularly say: in fact at least three obvious differences. The paradigm, we have repeated, divides the body into mind and matter; in its political application, that line becomes an ax blade or guillotine, as we have seen. The natural model for the resulting polarity is then the relation of head to trunk. The moral difference, with which the biblical texts are chiefly concerned, is between what should not and should be done. It therefore directs without destroying the body, over which it assumes command in the name of a higher authority. The model for this ethical not/but is presumably the bilateral symmetry of the individual body, which may turn either to the left or the right. The final or religious difference would be between the flesh and the Spirit; which is to say, between any body and the body indeed. And the model for this contrast in turn would be the relation between one body and another, or myself and the person I meet. Or is it my own death? But to encounter another is in principle to die already. That is one reason I resist the possibility.

If we think of the line as dividing the body, definition is destruction—which is to say, textuality and therefore objectivity is violence. If we think of the line as tracing the outline of the body, definition is discovery—which is to say, inscription is love. In that case the line, and by extension the text, would do no worse than the body already seems to do of itself, which is to declare its own bounds, though now in two rather than three dimensions: an ideal if indefinite sphere can always be projected as an actual though limited circle. The text terminates the body, then, in one way or another.

Still following the figure, we could then remember that either line or circle would eventuate without difficulty as a point, that dimensionless dimension from which all dimensions must begin. We have already noticed by another route that the text would reduce to the taw, or final letter of the alphabet, which both the ancients and ourselves could inscribe as a cross. But would not a cross too reduce to its point of intersection? That dot, however arrived at, would then amount to the metaphysical minimum, or whatever either is or is not, and *is not* only as another mode of *is*. No wonder, one could feel, that sentences, true or false, end with periods, or that calculation began with *calculi*, mere pebbles to be counted one after another. Total objectivity, then—which is to say, the unavoidable text at once absolutized and reduced—would, it seems to me, be most perfectly exemplified by what would also appear as the arithmetical unit, which brings us back to where we left off. For in classical and modern science alike the "language" in terms of which what can be known becomes knowable is sooner or later mathematics. Explanation is reduction, as we have seen, and reduction is, to begin with, metaphoric: biology becomes chemistry, and chemistry physics. But physics is already mathematics, and as one approaches that *telos,* likeness becomes identity. The arithmetical unit is the universal metaphor. And what is knowable mathematically has already been predefined, Pythagoras once told us, as some complication of the One. To precisely this extent the universe of cognition could be preunderstood even before any specific investigation has begun. The ideal *telos* is at the same time an *arche.*

In that case we had better continue to read Plato too as "Platonically" as possible, acknowledging without reserve the strictly intelligible character of the cognitive atom. And as he offers us a chance to see the doctrine of Parmenides reduced from the obscurity of the mythological to the clarity of the rational, so we could also retroactively reduce his successor Plotinus from the mystical to the rational back again as well. *Reduce* is in that independently very interesting case not quite perhaps the right word: *prescind* might be better. For to Plotinus the rational unit he inherits from Plato is at the same time perfectly transparent to a divine One. No wonder, we could say; the incarnation is precisely what has *not* happened in his case, so there is no eschatological body to fill up the "space" between thought and God, and thereby rejustify the claims of the flesh that he very naturally assumed would have to be left behind. For him the rational immediately predicts its own transcendence. The ultimate sign, that is, coincides perfectly with its divine import. But if so, we might as well stick with the older authority, as long as our intentions are philosophical rather than gnostic.[24] The One, we might then say, is then at least a Hellenistic if not yet the Johannine logos—the Baptizer, as it were, rather than the Baptized. And of this identity the mathematical unit would continue as a constant core, which persists through all stages of the Greek tradition as it has for any modern reproduction of that from one epistemological complication to the next.

Within this most concentrated type of all that could ever be meant by the *univ*erse, then, everything would indeed prove utterly knowable—if never more or less than just that, no matter how high or low the count, for all subsequent sums and divisions, formal or factual, would necessarily engage this cognitive singularity as presumed and repeated. An explicit philosophy of mathematics is apt to concern itself with comparatively advanced problems like infinity, or the square root of two, or fractions. But the only strictly theoretical issue would, it seems to me, remain the first, which is once more to say, the bare unit. Zero too is after all only one less than one, as two is one and then another one.[25] The One already abolishes difference, since difference must invariably be accounted for by means of it. And all further arithmetic or logical operations presuppose the same elementary step.

To be sure, the several schools seem uncertain how much if any metaphysical status to attribute to this rational minimum. Jacob Klein's proudly modernist book on ancient mathematical theory argues, for instance, that the Greeks never did become quite rational enough about the nature of numbers, attributing to them still rather too much countable being; whereas the early moderns, improving upon their predecessors, succeeded in distilling an ever more perfectly conceptual and therefore sufficiently universal idea of what they were dealing with. Numbers thereafter were

---

[24]This gap does not mean it could not be worth following the One through the no-longer-standard-but-still-classic translation of *The Enneads* by Stephen McKenna (London: Faber, 1962). In the third edition as revised, the most relevant passages seem to include 247-50, 369-79, 406-08, and 614-25. Plotinus is a reading of Plato, as Plato of Parmenides; the next step, which we (if not any of these) could imagine taking, would therefore indeed be the gospel according to John.

[25]It is interesting how the argument of Gottlob Frege's century-old *Foundations of Arithmetic* (New York: Harper, 1960), a founding text for what was to prevail as the "logicist" party, continues to circle about 0 and 1 as test cases for his or any explanation of what is going on.

not of objects but objects in their own right.[26] Morris Kline's more recent and therefore perhaps more pessimistic recapitulation of this history traces a similar trajectory in another key; from an initial confidence that the truths of mathematics must coincide with the facts of nature to a system of subspecialities that has come to hold itself apart even from physics, not to mention the other sciences.[27] What Klein approves, that is, Kline regrets—a difference that would itself reproduce the issue. "There is no truth in mathematics" is one version of the latter's cri de coeur, and "any attempt to find an absolute basis for it" is, according to him, most probably doomed. Nonetheless this increasingly empty science of sciences is somehow still applicable to nature, and in that mysterious applicability lies the promise we have been pursuing. The articles collected in Benacerraf and Putnam's still more recent but already standard anthology take for granted the predicament Kline laments.[28] They develop a variety of names and justifications for precisely this alienated state of affairs, which can therefore continue to seem repellently aprioristic or "platonic" (with a small *p*) to those who would like to restore some explicit relation between mathematics and the rest of the world. As might be guessed, Russian Marxists have been prominent on this side, and with them a school of American "realists.[29] So the problem persists. But could not, an outsider might suggest, the One, capitalized or not, perpetually offer some hint of the kind either repudiated or wished for?[30]

For this constant focus of attention, and thereafter of calculation, combination, or division, would already have to be what anything at all has in common with everything else. It would amount therefore to the speed of light, as it were, of the rational universe, the *hilastērion* (Rom. 3:25) or *kapporeth* for any cognitive sacrifice—the "is" therefore of every proposition as soon as that had ever become a

---

[26]Jacob Klein's *Greek Mathematical Thought and the Origin of Algebra* (Cambridge: MIT Press, 1968) was first published in German in the mid-1930s.

[27]Morris Kline, *Mathematics: The Loss of Certainty* (New York: Oxford, 1980). The quotations that follow appear on 99 and 312.

[28]Paul Benacerraf and Hilary Putnam, eds., *Philosophy of Mathematics: Selected Readings* (Cambridge: Cambridge University Press, 1983).

[29]The Russian contribution may be found in A. D. Aleksandrov et al., eds., *Mathematics: Its Content, Methods, and Meaning* (Cambridge: MIT Press, 1963). A representative "realist" might be Philip Ketcher, *The Nature of Mathematical Knowledge* (New York: Oxford University Press, 1983). I have also found assistance in Tobias Dantzig's long-familiar *Number: The Language of Science* (London: Allen and Unwin, 1962). G. C. Granville's *Logos: Mathematics and Christian Theology* (Lewisburg PA: Bucknell University Press, 1976) has not, I fear, proved helpful, in spite of a promising title.

[30]An outsider cannot read Benoit Mandelbrot's already classic *Fractal Geometry of Nature* (San Francisco: Freeman, 1982) except metaphorically—but would not the One most literally reappear in his novel strategy, where a single figure is made to repeat itself indefinitely on successively different scales, the better to make mathematical sense of processes that would otherwise remain chaotic?

question. It is already the very possibility of metaphor, which is sure to hold regardless of individual likenesses and unlikenesses. Within the paradigm it manifests itself indifferently as the objectivity of the object, or the interpretability of the sign or the disinterestedness of the subject: the "eye" of the "I" indeed. No wonder that in English at least the arithmetic unit and the pronoun share what is virtually the same mark. The axis of the real is always some coincidence of these. But coincidence *is* singularity. Each instance of knowledge necessarily exhibits what must in the end typify them all. The One is the constant synthetic a priori, for it cannot help but prove repeatedly rediscoverable within each and every case there could ever be—or for that matter not be. The "always already" of cognition and the eventual presence of being would then seem to meet or not meet at just this point, to which the skeptical X which at once cancels and acknowledges transcendence could readily be reduced.

If *Sein* is at a minimum the aura or intergalactic cloud of what should sooner or later precipitate as the cosmic body indeed, we need not be surprised that what at once proclaims and denies precisely this possibility should once again take the shape of a cross. The Form of all Forms, we might even be able to profess, is precisely what would be enacted by that figure in thought as well as in cult or morals—not to mention history. Mathematics begins, we could realize, where the rest of this world ends, though it may never get any further than just so far. The One, or (to avoid, or rather bracket, the inevitable mystical allusion) oneness, *henōsis* as we might more neutrally name it, would then seem in principle at least an ideal solution to the mathematical and the metaphysical questions alike—not to mention the natural or the supernatural as soon as either of these was raised.

And once what would still need to be qualified as the bare thought of such a thought has at least been entertained, some supportive even if not quite confirmatory instances from a variety of other contexts do suggest themselves. The Greeks, and not just the Greeks, may not have been perfectly rational by modern standards, early or late. But like other ancient peoples, they certainly possessed the wheel. And would not the invention of this most typical convenience suffice to indicate that the idea of an indefinitely repeatable unit as the essence of the knowable case would already have been implicit long before there need have been any declared lovers of wisdom? I have wondered too whether the notoriously exceptional "monotheism" of Akhenaton, the only intellectual pharaoh we know of, might not also involve a similar intuition. The Aton, or "sun disc," would indeed appear an analogue in Egyptian terms to the Pythagorean, if not quite the Platonic, idea.[31] And within the

---

[31] The authorities I have consulted (Aldred, Redford) would not, alas, confirm this possibility, though they do not prevent it. The current disposition is evidently to downplay an earlier enthusiasm for Akenaton as a religious revolutionary. It is of some incidental interest that his symbol makes an appearance in the Hebrew Scriptures too. "There will come," says Malachi, "for you who fear my Name the sun of justice, with healing in its

otherwise very different context of the Hebrew revolution we could locate a similar (and therefore to the mind, at least, an identical) emphasis in the familiar affirmation of the Lord's exceptionality; who is, the Shema has regularly declared, one indeed: *echod*. It is this always potentially infinite singularity that is communicated by the Name, as we have already realized by another route.

A One generalized in such a fashion would in that case amount to a rational analogue for the Holy Name within the biblical text. Indeed the One *is* the Name, we could assert, but only in the context of cognition—which is to say, as translated into Greek, which is again to say, in modern terms. And this indispensable unit would remain, like its scriptural analogue, in the third person, for in the act of cognition there is obviously no second, and the first has already evaporated into the impersonal *cogito*. What then might be a truly eschatological version of this version of the third, the I not as subject but as Other, who might in that case fulfill the rational *it* as well as the biblical *he*? If the One is indeed the rational equivalent of the Name, we would still have to say: whatever might present the presence of God; which is to say, the body; which is therefore once again to say, the person of Christ. But how should this completion obtain on the cosmic scale, to which we are necessarily limited? There has been no messiah to complete Greek philosophy, nor any Church (though *The Republic* did what it could, like the university since). Nor has there been any equivalent apocalypse within the modern version of the cognitive situation, though here at least one or two messianic pretenders have in fact appeared, in and out of philosophy. But we should not, if the relevant context has indeed to remain cosmic, expect any simple repetition of what once occurred on another scale. What we could expect is simply what is promised. And a promise does seem inscribed in the One. Like the Name, the One is always ready to be converted into whatever it finally means. A cosmic eventuation need not be individual or communal if it is already noumenal. Parmenides and ourselves would then always enjoy the same opportunity, which any one of us might in principle exercise at any time or place. In this context, thought would already be a species of prayer, and science or philosophy a *kiddush ha shem* too after its own kind.

And to remember as much would allow for a recognition that by way of the One we are able to anticipate the accomplishment of what has already been advanced, if only in fancy, as an ultimate desideratum, the conflation of the paradigm in its entirety. We are regularly obliged to talk in terms of the object, for that is what is sure to confront us. But the ideal singularity of that focus is equally true of the corresponding subject—and therefore of any imaginable resolution of the difference between them. The One, we could by this time allow ourselves to say, is what both halves of the polarity have in common. In that case the mathematical unit would be not just an indispensable element in the knowledge anyone might have of anything but a secret name for the structure as a whole: the axis, as it were,

---

wings" (3:20).

that might, like any other line, reduce to a point at last. By whatever route we follow, then, we return where we began. The One is the end of the line, period.

I have sometimes thought rock music might provide an imaginative analogue to the means and end of the cognitive expectation. For the rhythm of this most popular art is virtually identical with the unit of rational inquiry. One, one, it says to the crowd in us all; and to feel the message is already to begin a dance, that is, to incorporate the rest of any individual body within the loop from one otherwise unvarying beat to the next. Melody would then supply an elaboration of this inclusion, and rhythm and melody together an equivalent for what the calculator takes in as at once the constant and the contingent. Bodies rhyme with bodies, luckily. Literature seems by contrast rather less well off. There has to be more than one letter in any actual alphabet to accommodate the irrationalities of a spoken language. Poetry, and still more obviously prose fiction or history, is by no means an a priori art, nor would it ordinarily lay claim to possession of the end, human or divine. It amounts to the omitted middle most of the time: loose and baggy, as it may admit or boast. So its orders remain diachronic and intermediate, making the most of differences that are not, for the time being at least, to be resolved. In that mode even to free some image of the whole might seem virtually impossible. How could one draw the line, where "the point" could *not* be arrived at—except in criticism, which surely does not count?

Once again it seems possible to revert to the biblical context for an instance that might typify the possibility of a literary analogue to the philosophical quest for a perfectly adequate cosmology. There the imagination (though not working under that name) did for once find itself free to compose a narrative that could stand as a sufficient equivalent to the work of reason, though in so apparently opposite a style. The priestly author who, it has been supposed, must have put together the first account of creation which stands at the "head" of the Torah, presumably as the best possible preface to what at the time would have seemed the standard edition of this final text, can appear in retrospect to have known very well what he was doing and therefore how this might be done. We do not know his name, obviously, or even for sure that he ever existed as an individual, though it is hard to credit any committee, however learned and devout, with the subtle artistry of the P work generally. And nowhere is this constructive care more evident or suggestive than in the first chapter of Genesis, as one of his most faithful disciples, Umberto Cassuto, has helped a recent generation of readers to appreciate.[32]

---

[32]Umberto Cassuto's *Commentary on the Book of Genesis* is itself divided into two volumes, *From Adam to Noah* and *From Noah to Abraham* (Jerusalem: Magnes, 1964). As these titles suggest, the project was broken off at chapter 13 of the text: Cassuto died. What remains is the single most indispensable work of Old Testament criticism in modern times, though I have profited from the work of other scholars, including Brueggemann, von Rad, Rendsburg, Rendtorff, Sarna, Vawter, and Westermann. My account of differentiation in the

What this narrative poet, as we may now reimagine him, had to do was comprehend the cosmos as a whole—and not as an idea only but actually: which is to say, as the free creation of the same God who had already been acknowledged, since the revelation at Sinai, as the lord of history. How might the full unity of that extraordinary whole, the cosmic body, become accessible at least imaginatively in a sequence of personal actions? It is clear that this writer abandoned from the start any thought of representing the entirety of things mimetically. (We could say with the benefit of hindsight that such an attempt would have reduced him instantly to a mathematical silence, as in other cultural contexts it has others.) Nor is creation, whatever else it might be, the same as what human beings may do by the labor of their hands. The full truth in this context has therefore to be distinguished from whatever falls short of that by its own special verb, *bara*. He who alone can create indeed is thereby situated on the far side of the horizon that limits what human beings can take hold of by themselves.

How, then, could one more individual text that necessarily elaborates itself within these bounds succeed in testifying to the whole of what is so absolutely beyond it without falling into what this author would identify as idolatry or we could understand as the philosophical equivalent? P's solution is another verb, the causative form of the word meaning "to divide," or *hivdil*. Differentiation, already the defining note of his ethical allegiance then and since, thus becomes a way to spell out the full apocalypse of being as a sequence of contrasts in a humanly imaginable time. So difference, instead of being reduced to identity, as reason would demand, is in fact emphasized, as if to seize upon the direct opposite of unity as the best possible representation of exactly that. In the same way, a thoroughly diachronic sequence, itself placed at the beginning of a chronology structured to continue as far as writer and reader alike, can be forced to stand in for an otherwise utterly inexpressible synchronicity. The primary distinction is accordingly of light from darkness. "Let there be light," says God to begin with, and light was. The Hebrew enforces an exact echo of word and being, *y'hi-ōr, v'y'hi-ōr*. The words that articulate the breath of God produce what corresponds to them instantly, in an ostentatious inversion of the order obtaining among human beings, who must wait to reproduce what has already come into existence in another and weaker vocabulary. It is a formidable instance of what a contemporary philosopher might recognize as truth by disquotation.[33] The new presence of light then stands over against the uninterrupted darkness, which had prevailed before and still persists—but

---

first chapter follows Cassuto.

[33] The definition in question is attributed to Alfred Tarski, whose "Concept of Truth in Formalized Languages," most recently republished in *Logic, Semantics, Metamathematics* (Indianapolis: Hatchett, 1983) 152-278, has proved seminal. More familiar examples take such a form as " 'Snow is white' is true if and only if snow is white." Tarski's formula would also hold for the eucharistic propositions.

now as an opposite of this novel fact, and so within a human order of difference. Then comes the "firmament," or vault, to divide the waters (which, like the darkness, also preexisted creation) into the corresponding elements, the waters above being separated from the waters below. The third step is to divide again one of the halves just divided, so that the water under the firmament may be distinguished from the dry land, or the earth from what can now be redefined as "seas." Each step is "good"; that is, it *is*.

And so the sequence of differentiations continues, each successive part being in turn divided again to supply a new contrast, as the earth is instructed to produce, on the one hand, seed-bearing plants, and on the other, fruit-bearing trees, and the light first created is reapportioned between the day and the night, and therefore the sun and the moon with its stars. In the same way the waters, which had already been separated from the dry land, are filled with living creatures, and birds are supplied to fly above the earth. These two kinds are then paired against those that belong to the dry land, whether tame or wild. The process concludes with the creation of humanity in the form of two sexes, male and female, "after our image," *b'tsalmenu,* and so in a relation of dominance over the other living beings, who must eat the foliage of the same seed-bearing plants and fruit-bearing trees of which human beings may eat the produce. This likeness in difference is repeated in the power to reproduce, a reflection within creation of what God alone can do from outside, and so, in the second creation story, which P inherited from his sources and placed after this introductory narrative, by the power to call things by their names. Authority, generativity, and nomination thus make up human equivalents for the power that God is shown as exercising, with each facet of this likeness displaying its dissimilarity as well as its closeness to the divine original.

The constant contrast between difference and unity thus becomes an imaginative equivalent of these delegated authorizations. Polarity repeated in successive acts of division is *how* a human mind can reproduce what as such is neither divided nor successive but always and forever a constant whole. The imagination does homage to unity not by enforcing a reduction, as would need to be the case for the reason, but by accepting differentiation, which is thereby legitimated as the expression as well as the opposite of what it means. Once again the merism appears, not though in this very Hebrew context as one more rhetorical device among others, but as the one figure that is in fact most perfectly suited to the situation in which the author finds himself, for it reenacts the very principle of the act of composition he is embarked on. The predicament that at once prevents and defines him thus becomes an enabling form for a genuinely imaginative "creation" of his own.[34] And with this

---

[34] A vision of cosmic unity by way of the conflict of opposites is also intrinsic to Heraclitus (who came, appropriately enough, before Parmenides). Charles Kahn, *The Art and Thought of Heraclitus* (Cambridge: Cambridge University Press, 1979) would supply an instance, though this is not quite his translation: "The god: night, day; winter, summer; war,

realization to orient his work, he can accept as well, with almost casual generosity, the pluralities of his own language and along with these whatever mythical remainders the enemy nations can supply as so much material to be reused. P is very far from being naive or "primitive," though his sophistication is that of an ancient priest rather than a modern artist or critic. But with the help of the ethical structure of what has already become by his day a repeated inheritance, he is able to allow just what prevents any direct experience of unity to testify in its own contradictory fashion to exactly that. In this way difference is at once allowed the fullest possible scope and done away with; it is honored and subordinated; resituated, as it were, to show what it might be good for after all.

Difference accepted thus becomes a means for the imagining faculty at least, or that which P would probably call wisdom, to "come near" the fullness of cosmic being, and so bring a reader too, as he would also put it, before the face of God. A rereading of Genesis that would take sufficient advantage of the reading already supplied by Ugo Cassuto would accordingly be in a position to appreciate precisely this much—and to generalize the case illustrated as far as an equivalent modern predicament. But a second movement commencing with the first chapter of Genesis might also be worth following, for it leads to another version of what we can still call the same end, though it could not be assigned with the same degree of confidence to any imagined author. If the first might be called a reading of difference, the second would become a reading of results—which is to say, an explicitly eschatological reading, for it concludes in the same revelation of the Name we have already found to be central in connection with the Decalogue.

This sequence too would start with the creation of light on the first day, taking notice this time of the content rather than the form of the moment. Both light and the darkness that is redefined by contrast with it are permanent but, we can also observe, utterly unformed and therefore inanimate modes of being. They are in fact the very simplest sort of thing: not the nearest in kind to their creator, as the chronology might seem to imply and much allusion since has presumed, but in fact the remotest. The corresponding command is therefore a straightforward "let __ be"; and God himself is obliged to name the utterly passive result. We seem to be offered almost a biblical equivalent for the universe produced by the "big bang," a mere seethe of particles other than which there could only be whatever is not.

The firmament created on the second day is scarcely better organized except by contrast with the equally chaotic waters that it separates. On the third day, though God distinguishes and names the earth and the seas in a similar style, he also commands the former to "put forth" grass, herbs, and trees. Vegetable life appears, if so far only as a set of very generalized species, and therefore *un*named. On the fourth day we revert, as if to recapitulate, to the elements first made, but this time

---

peace; full measure, famine." Genesis 1 could then be read as the whole poem that corresponds to these fragments.

see them given bodily form as sun and moon, and with that dominion over an otherwise indefinite day and night. On the fifth day we repeat the creation of living organisms, now in the air and the seas, which are accordingly commanded to "swarm," "fly," and also "be fruitful" and "multiply": the sea monsters may even be understood to take dominion over the waters, as perhaps the more noble birds, though these are *not* mentioned, would in the air. Indefinite being, *haya*, has thus become bodily life, *chaya*—a play on words that asks to be taken advantage of by author and reader alike. By the sixth day the same intensification has been brought about on the earth as well. Cattle, creeping things, and finally human beings are created and commanded as before to be fruitful, multiply, and, in the case of the last at least, who is created after "our image," not only to fill the earth but subdue it. The principal difference between unformed or passive being and formed or self-reproductive life is thus paralleled by further differences between "resource" and "utilization," or subordination and dominance.[35] There is more and more *to* existence, then, as we pass from the beginning of the week of creation to its close.

And to become aware of this ontological doubling and redoubling from the first to the third and again from the fourth to the sixth day is to become alert as well to what seems a continuation of this process beyond the limits of the first chapter into the rest of Genesis as well, and indeed all the way to the revelation at Sinai in the third chapter of Exodus. In the second creation story, which follows immediately after the Sabbath rest on the seventh day that concludes the first, the power of nomination too is given to humans. "The man" names both the other creatures with which he shares the earth and "the woman" who has been created to share dominion with him.[36] After the command that establishes relation has been issued (and almost immediately disobeyed), both partners acquire *personal* names as well: Adam, no longer just "the man," now calls his wife "Eve," which no longer means merely "life." Relation, even if refused, brings with it individual existence, to which a corresponding style of nomination testifies. The naming of persons continues significant throughout Genesis. Either Eve (4:25) or Adam (5:3) names Seth; thereafter women often name their children. Names, as the excerpts from the "book of generations" that punctuate the separate episodes of this book make evident, serve to establish the identities of the persons mentioned as members of successive generations and therefore as potential and sometimes actual agents in the associated stories. Nomination both implies and enables inheritance and agency alike, which

---

[35] The words quoted are used by Nahum Sarna to differentiate the two halves of the creation account in his recent commentary *Genesis* (Philadelphia: Jewish Publication Society, 1989). A contrast in terms of environment and body, though, seems closer to the intention of the text.

[36] The ancestral figure does seem to be imagined as male in the second creation story, if only because of the pronouns, but one can still admire the care with which Phyllis Trible has reread this narrative, especially in her earlier study *God and the Rhetoric of Sexuality* (Philadelphia: Fortress, 1978) 72-143. Cassuto has had "daughters" as well as "sons."

together would define what we might call cultural being. Existence within a transmissible form of what can thus explicitly be called the covenant can then amount to the verbal aspect of the physical continuity effected by the "seed" being passed from father to son. As *haya* represents simple being, and *chaya* living being, so *zerah,* or "seed," might accordingly serve as a nickname for both halves of this, the third or individual degree of being, to the history of which the rest of Genesis is accordingly devoted.

But this third mode of existence, though indispensable for personal and therefore historical identity, would not yet be terminal. It is God, after all, who promises to make Abraham's name great (12:2) and in due course renames him (17:5). At the ford of the Jabbok, Jacob too is renamed by the one whose own Name he does *not* learn (32:25-31), though he finds himself able to name the place at least. The human individual is in the end dependent for his or her proper being on relation with Another whose identity remains (according to the final editor, if not one of his sources) hidden until the revelation to Moses on Sinai. This event is therefore placed, appropriately enough, in the next book on: Exodus is the "new" testament, we could almost say, of which Genesis is the "old." But through the patriarchal narratives too individual and therefore hereditable and expressible being is constantly shown as dependent on a God who alone makes it possible to exist at such a pitch at all. The height of human being must look to the infinity of divine being for its proper authentication. The survival of Noah and the birth of Isaac or his rescue from death, as well as Jacob's incomplete but premonitory encounter, thus testify in advance to what is at last openly disclosed with Moses: that is, a fourth degree of being, or the presence of the divine Other, which the Name names and the burning bush (which it seems fair to call the "tree of life" for a moment renewed) may be understood to embody.[37] Moses has revealed to him, that is, the Name of the one who began as the Namer, which would indeed conclude the sequence beginning with Genesis 1. To maintain what has become almost a series of rhymes, we might specify this fourth mode as being according to *ruach,* or spiritual identity, in the presence of which one therefore encounters the true cause for all the previous degrees of existence.

If such a trajectory might be traced from the first chapter of the first book of the principal text through the ante- or postdiluvian narratives and the various episodes of the patriarchal saga as far as the Mosaic moment, we would be in a

---

[37]Jon Levenson has observed in his attractive survey of the differences between *Sinai and Zion* (Minneapolis: Winston, 1985) that the burning bush, which combines such otherwise incompatibles as a tree with fire, is repeated in the menorah, which later enlightened tent and temple alike (20-21). A Christian could add that the same figure is repeated again every year as so many Christmas trees. Levenson's more recent *Creation and the Persistence of Evil* (San Francisco: Harper, 1988) emphasizes the "fragility" (and therefore, the same Christian could add, the sacramentality) of creation, which is always susceptible to redissolving into the sea of chaos.

position to realize that what we could still think of perhaps too narrowly as the creation story had better be read not only protologically but also eschatologically. We do not, that is, move away from an origin that was once upon a time closest to the divine center but on the contrary proceed from the circumference of the "physical" universe inward through ever-more-concentrated circles of being until we arrive, if not yet quite at the very core—for that, the fifth degree of being, is still very much ahead for us all, ancient and modern, Jew and Christian alike—at least as far as the presence of whoever can indeed be named by the Name. That much, the "nearness" of the End, *has* been revealed. It is possible, if not to know, at any rate to encounter—and therefore believe in—just this much.

Once again we find ourselves with indirect testimony to what we could fairly call a "singularity," which as such cannot help but remain beyond whatever might be known or even imagined, but must amount to what either of these should eventually mean, if meaning means anything at all. Difference accepted *is* unity, our first and easier reading proposed. The more extravagant detection of an eschatological trajectory all the way through to the heart of the typical text could prompt a similar proposition: that the circumference *is* the center; the origin *is* (means, implies, prophesies) the conclusion; or, to put the matter still more succinctly, that creation is already the body of Christ—on the scale, precisely, of the cosmos. What must be imagined as the act of creation would then be to the cosmic body as what must be defined as the incarnation is to the individual body—or what must be enacted in the Eucharist for the communal body. In that case creation would also be, whether as outlined in a single chapter or implied by the Torah as a whole, the best possible analogue to what we have found ourselves unable to formulate in rational terms as an entire fulfillment of the One within the context of cognition. The Bible would thus allow us (still within its own exceptional but also most typical vocabulary) to pass one step further along its own line than we can quite manage philosophically.

Yet the parallel with what has to remain transcendent to any rational reduction would also suggest that the corresponding point or circle could indeed be filled out by the same ideal "sphere" in faith if not yet quite in thought. Then we could also reverse the proposition just offered, still to the same general effect: the body of Christ on the scale of the cosmos would in Spirit and in truth be coincident with what the Bible portrays as creation, a "first person" version of which in cognitive terms would still have to remain the as yet unspecifiable meaning of the One. Along such a pair of parallel (or are they convergent?) lines it would then in theory be possible to reconcile Hebrew with Greek, imaginative with rational, verbal and mathematical—and so at last ancient theology with modern science. But the details of such an argument are clearly still to seek.

One might be tempted to continue following the motif of creation through so much of the biblical text as extends beyond the Mosaic moment at least as far, say, as the Book of Job. The end of that disturbing piece of wisdom would certainly supply yet another fascinating version of creation as the answer to a major question, in this case not of being but of justice. But if there is still something to add by way of example, we would presumably do better with a modern instance or two that might balance the Greek and Hebrew demonstrations of the rational and imaginative approaches respectively and, if not confirm, at least suggest the continuing relevance of their respective implications. They are as such, after all, quite literally old fashioned. One needs something more nearly contemporary, however minor or even parodic, if only to stimulate some better version of the kind of thinking or imagining, not to mention believing, that still remains to be done.

A decently amusing instance of the sort of thing one might come up with appeared the other year in the form of a long letter by Roger Archibald in the Harvard alumni magazine, exactly the journal for such a purpose. The topic of his communication was an atmospheric phenomenon known as the "green flash." This sometimes occurs at sea on a clear day at the moment when the last portion of the sun's disk disappears below the horizon. A film of green light moves in abruptly to outline the remaining edge. But this flash takes less than a second, and so has been considered unphotographable. It might accordingly stand as a type of what could be experienced but not really known—which would therefore remain dubious even for those who were all but sure they had actually caught sight of the event in question.

Archibald tells the story of an occasion on which he was in fact able to photograph the green flash. He happened (the circumstances seems very much part of the tale) to be on his way across the Pacific abroad a replica of Drake's *Golden Hind* when he observed the phenomenon on two successive evenings and determined to make a record of it on the third. His letter details the various technical decisions required and a solution he found for the problem of adjusting his body to the sway of the ship. Then came the crisis: "As the ship momentarily rested at the bottom of the swell, the last tiny extremity of the sun lost its bright orange color, seemed to turn clear for an instant, and then was overtaken by a bright green starting at the edges and working in toward the middle, all within less than a second. I responded... and took my picture." And there on a page of the magazine is indeed a reproduction of a color photograph, showing a narrow ellipse of yellow outlined in green on the horizon of a seascape.[38]

All this is splendid simply as a feat, and Archibald's tone of gentlemanly triumph is exactly right both for what was accomplished and the audience for his narrative of it. But the outline of the deed, as extravagant in its own latter-day Ivy League way as the first circumnavigations of the world, is so clear that it can also be read without difficulty as virtually an allegory of the ontological predicament rehearsed in it. A photograph is a "writing in light" in the form of an image that physically repeats just so much of its original. The radiation reflected from some scene is made to inscribe its chemical signature on a surface that may in turn be

---

[38] *Harvard Magazine* 86/5 (September/October 1983) 26-27. I learned more recently from a review by Terrence Rafferty in *New Yorker* (64/23 [25 July 1988] 77) that the "green flash" has also provided an occasion for a film by Eric Rohmer.

reproduced on paper for all to see. To "take" a photograph is then to render an experience comprehensible to just this extent. Archibald "proved" by his "experiment" that the green flash does indeed exist as a fact in our universe, which makes it at least one more object for the impersonal subject now shared by the discoverer with his social universe. Is not Harvard the university indeed? So far the exercise seems a species of tongue-in-cheek science.

But the phenomenon in question is at the same time a precipitation from and so a final clue to the boundary of the sun. It is therefore a last and all but invisible manifestation of that source of all our light. A photograph of such a thing would therefore find itself at the terminus of exactly that art—which is to say, of visibility as the type not just of cognition but of being in general, for without the sun there could be not only no photography but no photographer; no *Golden Hind,* original or reproduced; even no *Harvard Magazine.* The episode would accordingly enact the proposition that knowledge of any kind is of precisely the circumference of some otherwise all but unknowable sphere—which in this case would be represented not only by the sun, that primary body in our heavens, but also by the planet the uninterrupted horizon of which is called upon to bring about just this astronomical moment, and perhaps as well by the body of the exceptional individual himself, so carefully poised to coincide with both of these. This skill is his athletic version of a dialectic that could reach as far as the One in Plato, or of the successive divisions that dramatize the unity of creation in the first chapter of Genesis. The photograph which resulted then provides one more broken instance of the line that ideally repeats the circumference of all three natural bodies, that of the photographer, the earth, and finally the sun—though what we *see* reverses this order. The last of the series would then most easily represent what these three simultaneously signify and have in common—which must be the whole of creation indeed.

That the photograph can only "reproduce" this entirety at a succession of comic distances would presumably explain why nobody is meant to take the feat in question with full seriousness. For the sun is, we also know, too simple to do more than intimate finality, however enormous and far away. The body indeed would still have to be either well beyond or much nearer than the scope of this experiment. But the event could at any rate show why. Subject and object stare each other out of countenance and, in a quick spasm of triumph, exhibit their mutual likeness and limits. In the process they testify, at once ironically and cryptically, to whatever it is that transcends them both. Mr. Archibald had more in common than he needed to know with priests and philosophers before him, as well as with the more modern circumnavigator who evidently supplied his model. The discoverer, like the one discovered, is perhaps in the end always one person.

And had I not, I could also think, done something similar myself when, a summer following, I revisited Walden pond in an interval between other errands and, to pass that unexpected period of time, walked round this familiar body of water? When I got to the site of Thoreau's hut, there were already people studying the markers, and to avoid their puzzled talk I walked further up the slope to a level region I was free to imagine, perhaps mistakenly, could once have been occupied by the beanfield described in the best single chapter of that author's cosmology. Whatever the place may once have been, it had long since become an ordinary woods, covered with insignificant trees and crossed by a green road. I sat on a bank a while happily enough and then descended again to find a boy with a dog who was genuinely ignorant of what the granite fence posts, the cairn of stones, and the notice boards were in memory of. I exchanged some explanatory words with him, observing that he would probably read the book itself later in school, and when he did the monuments would make better sense to him. I could mention as well that he had come there to swim because of what the individual in question had once done and written, which explained why a state park had been set up. So many had arrived since that the path around the pond I was following had become badly eroded, and snow fences and signs had been erected since my last visit to keep visitors off the nearer shores. Then I went on myself to complete the circuit. I had only half an hour more to spend, and the coves were deep from that point on, so I had no time to lose. The path was lumpy, with exposed tree roots and embedded stones, and sloped steeply to the water. One had to watch one's feet. There was no opportunity for contemplation, or any indulgence of memory, though I could recall visits made to the further shore in a generation now past, couple by couple, love for love, loss upon loss.

But there was time at least to think that in walking around this pond, as too many others had already done, I was also rehearsing one more version of the argument I was beginning to compose for a book of my own that could not in the nature of the case turn into another Genesis or *Walden,* though it might after its own fashion become an equivalent for a letter in an alumni magazine, and to that extent a "Way of Truth" after all. Circumambulation, like circumnavigation, is yet another species of circumscription, which in turn is how any individual may do homage to the wholeness of the whole. Had not Nehemiah once done as much upon the newly rebuilt walls of Jerusalem—a gesture repeated more recently, I could learn from yet another newspaper story, by some Israeli and Palestinian activists who formed a "chain of peace" around the Old City.[39] The pond, Thoreau had written, was "God's drop," and so a sacrament of infinitude for him. Why else had he settled there? To walk around it, then, like fishing in it (as he had also done, and some boys were still doing), or measuring its depth with a line, was one more way to make sense of what as such had to surpass any of our terminologies, physical or mental, rational or imaginative, ancient or modern.[40] Meanwhile *Walden* had come to be for its day,

---

[39] The demonstration was reported in the *New York Times,* 31 December 1989, L:13.

[40] For a more immediate parallel to the instance provided, I could add Henry Adams, who I learn from the standard biography also walked around Walden to test, a letter reports, his recovery from a stroke in old age. See Ernest Samuels, *Henry Adams: The Major Phase* (Cambridge: Harvard University Press, 1964) 536. The *Education,* after all, might be claimed

as since in ours (for had I not taught this sufficiently canonical text many times?), a most thoroughgoing testimony to Walden, that pristine body of water. And the paths and the crowds, like the cairn and the posts and the boards, one of which even included a suitable quotation, were further repetitions of that initial response. He at least had known well enough that the present could only recapitulate the past and indeed understood his labor in the beanfield as one more instance of this necessary truth, and so already an anticipation of what he would in due course put down in words to celebrate another true, because altogether divine, work of art. And I could, it seemed, realize as much myself, however sketchily. Was I not also like him repeating earlier visits, as well as those later ones that already repeated these? My memories though were perhaps sadder than his. But that did not make an important difference. We had both been around the pond, and this was how.

Theological

But to indulge anecdotal instances, however authoritative or amusing, would still evade the question as this most truly appears in a modern form, where it continues to invite an intellectual rather than a technical or even an imaginative response. One wants to think the problem through, not just repeat a story. For some years now I have teased myself with the possibility of what I have called the "Jesus thought"; that is, an act of mind that would correspond to what has already been accomplished by the appointed individual in the context of history. We are still in need, it appears, of a Greek—and therefore a modern—equivalent of the crucifixion, that very Judaic counter-deed. Suitable approximations to what seems required are not easy to locate within the tradition. Paul, for one early instance, will clearly not supply what is wanted: to "make up what is lacking" in what had already become at once the typical and a final sacrifice is for him altogether an issue of the moral life, and so of the will rather than the intellect.

A better representation of the possibility through the several centuries since might conceivably be sought among the mystics. "Meister" Eckhart, perhaps the most prominent of these, would though be no help. His doctrine of *enpsychism,* as one might call it, by which the Father is perpetually begetting the Son in the core of the soul, borrows Christian language as an allegory for what one might better identify as a belatedly gnostic or prematurely Hegelian project. This would be an egotistic, not a cosmic, Christ.[41]

---

as one more latent model for the text now offered to my own reader.
[41]Such a conclusion would not suit such a latter-day disciple of Eckhart as Matthew Fox, whose *Coming of the Cosmic Christ* (San Francisco: Harper, 1988) mixes creativity as meditation, worship as play, "deep" ecumenism, environmentalism, child-centeredness, and feminism in a California casserole. The truth of mysticism generally may still be aesthesis, in which case this popular blend would amount to prophecy as comedy.

John of the Cross, on the other hand, could reasonably be read as meaning by the "union with God" that constitutes the goal of his quest an individual participation in the body of Christ on what we could legitimately call the cosmic scale: a "mystical body" indeed. The adaptation of the "Song of Songs" with which his *Ascent of Mount Carmel* begins and upon which all the prose works thereafter become an extended commentary would appear to imply as much: in this poem a young girl escapes her house at night for a rendezvous with her lover.[42] If intercourse with the Spouse is a proper image for what the soul seeks, this consummation must as in the dominical word on marriage be penultimate rather than absolutely terminal: one more parable, that is, for the Kingdom come. In any case, the union desired is arrived at, this authority teaches, by successive mortifications of "the senses" and "the spirit," as the soul learns to liberate itself from attachment to "creatures"—in our terms, bodies. The "dark night" of the several faculties requires a deliberate negation of any partial or mortal positive. The mystic would then be repeating the deconstruction effected by the original passion in terms of faith. An "abyss" of "silence" and "emptiness" becomes the way through to "everything." This recipe for fulfillment does read splendidly even to an outsider, but if no longer only or strictly ethical, as with Paul, the project is still clearly more practical than rational—pistic, we might call it, rather than epistemic. The relevant philosophical presumptions and consequences may be read out or in, as we have just ventured, but nothing of that kind is as such primary. We would still have to look about, that is, for what could fairly be called a Jesus *thought*.

And so far there has not been, as far as I know, anything of quite such a kind. An adequate version, after all, would have to be something more (or rather less) than even the most thoroughgoing dialectic, even if this endeavor did arrive at a rational equivalent for the cross, that most literal of terminal texts. It would have to be for knowledge what faith already is with respect to the works of the Law; a "Pauline" cognition then, as trans-Platonic as that is post-Judaic. "I through the Law died to the Law," says that authority in Galatians (2:19), "so that I might live in God." How might one die to the object (or its social or theological equivalents) through the object, so as to arrive at what must indeed be on the further side? For if "Christ is the end of the Law" (Rom. 10:4), then he should also be the fulfillment of thought as well, and therefore of the One to which any cognitive chaos may repeatedly be reduced. Such an intellectual eventuation, we have guessed already,

---

[42] I owe this interpretation of the connection between the poem and the prose texts to E. Allison Peer's familiar translation of the *Ascent of Mount Carmel* (Garden City NY: Doubleday, 1958). The language quoted is from this version. John of the Cross's employment of the Song of Songs for his purpose follows a monastic tradition that begins with Origen and was popularized by Bernard of Clairvaux. See R. P. Lawson's edition of *Origen: The Song of Songs, Commentary and Homilies* (Westminster: London, 1957) esp. 14-16, or Marina Warner, *Alone of All Her Sex* (New York: Knopf, 1976) 128-30.

would begin as the reduction of a reduction: a passage not just to the end of any line but all the way through the resultant point—a death, one could say (and this much *has* been said, unmetaphorically) of death indeed. It would have to be an *un*thought or *de*thinking: an annihilation of consciousness together with its object, and not by some mystical or Romantic abandonment, but by an absolutely appropriate completion. The mind would need to do away with itself by way of itself in a triumph of itself, as desire does in orgasm, say; or gestation in birth; or the imagination, we have also suggested, in community. Then consciousness would at last become conversion—*metanoia* in the most literal sense of that too-often-repeated word.

What should match the "Jesus thought" on the far side of cognition, we have agreed, would be namable ahead of time as creation, or what we could then call the body indeed on the scale of the cosmos. And this fulfillment, we have also seen, can be as elusive even to the imagination as the rational consummation that would most properly introduce it. But luckily (to speak profanely) we are not left without other modalities of the body that could serve in the meantime as types for what still remains only theoretically possible with respect to the universe at large. And of these the Eucharist must constantly remain the principal instance. If the crucifixion is the prototype of the necessary completion as this has already been brought about in the midst of human history, the Eucharist, which both anticipates and transcends this final deed, is surely the positive that most exactly balances that negative, for in the reproduction of this utterly eschatological parable we also share in the authorized instance of whatever could ever be meant by the resurrection—and therefore by creation as well. The Eucharist is the perennial sign that already announces, though in so apparently different a vocabulary, what in the cosmic context would indeed be revealed by a completion of the "Jesus thought," when and if that should ever be accomplished.

There is nothing else for the time being to think about, in that case, but just what this most central instance would continue to import for every other scale and context. The Eucharist is as much of the body proper as we have so far been able (most literally) to comprehend. It would accordingly provide our best clues to what the body indeed should amount to wherever else it may be looked for. And the implications of this most typical instance can indeed be traced here and there, as we have now been doing for some time. But a few of what might present themselves elsewhere as subordinate or corollary aspects of this model could seem especially relevant to the cosmic or most general possibility. We might add, for instance, to fill out these implications, that the Eucharist would suggest that space, which in our universe seems so important, is probably insignificant to creation, for it does not matter where we take part, whether in Jerusalem or on Concord Avenue. We could also claim that time does not matter either, though not in the mode of becoming indifferent, like space; rather it is disclosed that past and present together share in the same future. The Eucharist exhibits the fullness of time, not its absence or irrelevance. Eternity is evidently more rather than less "temporal" than we might have supposed. Time is not just a carnal weakness then but already a gift of the Holy Spirit.

We have observed too that the action as accomplished presumes a constant bias in favor of the concrete as opposed to the abstract. Jesus is clearly a materialist—at least as this identity might be contrasted with that of an idealist, or any other ideology that prefers the psychic to the "merely" sarkic of whatever kind. This disposition betrays itself as well in the anecdotes of the ministry. It sets him apart from the Pharisees as well as the influences out of Hellenism insofar as these were relevant at all. If we generalize this feature too, we are once again situated either before or after the act of cognition. For we can know only abstractions; or more exactly, it is the abstract alone that we are capable of knowing without qualification. But a concrete particular can never be completely understood. The fullness of its being is always escaping us. So its import too remains uncertain in proportion. The larger meaning of any existent is bound to be mysterious in the nature of the case.

And whatever else the Eucharist may be, it is obviously concrete. We cannot eat and drink abstractions. It would appear to follow that *to eon,* or the "thing in itself," or "Being," or whatever is eventually meant by any of these terms would also be what from this side we would still have to call concrete too, and not merely one or another idea, even in the mind of God. It is just this coincidence of character that would allow us to identify such a postcognitive possibility with the body indeed, and so fill out our appreciation of what seems implied by the central instance across the board. For all particulars, we could then remember, are already free to share in the graciousness of the cosmic body. We are free to suppose at least this much, though even the best inference from analogy would bring us no nearer than just so far. To realize the rest would still take faith—which within the eucharistic context can though be successfully acted out with our own bodies. Would it then always take a body to "know" the body? The possibility might be disconcerting to any philosopher, professional or occasional.

The Eucharist already presupposes, we have also observed, a disestablishment of objectivity, legal or cultic, and therefore the textual or rational. But it still involves an acceptance of polarity in its juxtaposition of the contrasting elements and their analogues in the individual and the community. At the same time it affirms that one pole of this repeated reproduction will always be of God, and so beyond the horizon of any authority in this world, while the other pole remains the very flesh of the flesh: that which is most elementary in our lives, and so by no means either elevated or advanced. The Eucharist presumes hierarchy, then, but not on any human scale, including the intellectual. Meanwhile it also accepts metaphoricity, quite without embarrassment. So likeness and difference too are wholly incorporated. The Eucharist is accordingly poetic but not allegorical, for its meaning continues to be produced as it occurs and cannot be predicted ahead of time. And finally the Eucharist reveals most dramatically that what has been provided is sure to be personal. This is *my* body, says Jesus, not just *the* body, though that is what we have been calling it. We may conclude that *the* body would have to belong to a person in other contexts too and on any scale: that all bodies, including the cosmic, are in proportion somehow personal. This implication can be disturbing too.

All these aspects or concomitants of the body as it is already most typically reproduced in the eucharistic action would seem to accumulate as an intuition that might then apply across the board. There is nothing, we might say, besides the body of Christ in any context or on any scale. One might put the implied proposition still more strongly: there *is* no body but the body. To employ the word *is* at all would in that case always evoke the presence of the body, or some intimation of it, though if this body is also personal, we had better not call it "it," except, of course, in such a critical text as this—which is to say, after a comparatively abstract manner of speaking. The presence of the body within the world as it goes on about its business (for we can use "it" for the world) would have to be immensely and indefinitely various. The results are sufficiently chaotic in virtually the technical sense, as when a stone falls into water and the resulting waves break on an already broken shore. We find ourselves within the chaos, we could say, that corresponds to *this* cosmos: a sea of parts and aspects, representations and parodies; alienated, anticipatory, even nostalgic. We must live as the disintegration of what we can still believe is at once already and ultimately composed. And if the proposition in question can indeed be entertained even from such a distance, then all our positives would sooner or later have some share in what we could formally call the risen body, as all negatives would in principle participate in the same body as crucified. There is no real presence, we might also say, but the real presence.[43] On either side of the relation, then, we could expect to take part. We would find ourselves repeating the central act in one style or another, parodically, partially, trivially, in ignorance or faith—if only because this is what there is to do anyway.

In that case the traditional collection of abstractions with which thinking ordinarily has to do would always harbor a further sense as reflections of the body in memory or hope. So being, presence, substance, essence, matter, nature, or even "the signified" could each serve to specify some manner or feature of the whole for this or that context. The link has sometimes been deliberate, as when the institutional church confirmed the term *substance* for the eucharistic presence. Neither *substance* nor *presence* would, to be sure, bring one quite as far as there still seems to go, but either could at least help us appreciate whatever is going on. Such expressions are not in the idiom of the original event, which as such remains

---

[43]The traditional expression has in fact been reemployed as a sufficiently polemical title by George Steiner for his *Real Presences* (Chicago: University of Chicago Press, 1989). Here too a latter-day postdeconstructionist would be endeavoring to recover intimations of "transcendence" from within the immediacies of aesthetic (in his case, chiefly musical) experience. One is sympathetic, though the results still seem neopagan, however Christian the metaphors.

"essentially" though not accidentally silent, but they can still serve as plausible generalizations from that. To object that they *are* only generalizations, and so linguistically and socially bound, as criticism has recently found it almost too easy to do, would then be in proportion to miss their indirect power to testify as well as explain. To be sure, difficulties have arisen whenever such abstractions have been allowed to define away the very particulars from which they in fact derive. But that consequence should be too familiar to scandalize anyone for long.

Abstraction is one way in which the body may project one or another aspect of its full being even in so inevitably disembodying a medium as thought. Another is what might be called premature totalization, as when this or that mortal species of bodiliness attracts a value proper only to the body indeed. An "ism" of any kind is apt to presuppose some such overinvestment in proportion to its attraction for "true" believers. Romanticism has focused on the vital privileges of the individual body, as if to reexperience these were already to enjoy the life of the whole. Positivism of any species excludes all bodies except the currently most irreducible instances of the cosmic body, whatever form these may take. Criticism has intermittently privileged the symbolic body, while sometimes denying that any such thing could exist. Eroticism treats the dual phase of the procreative body as if this were final, and so chiefly in the style of a fetish. Religiously speaking, all these would be instances of idolatry, which is to say, a mistaking of some body for the body. And this mistake in turn might be the product of an inability to take account of the true body's endless reproducibility—its motility, as it were, or disposition to modulate from one mode to another even within a single context.

Still another way in which indirect recognition might occur would be opposition or rivalry. Some theory of presence or substance or the person might appear that would in effect set itself against what had once been declared. In such a case (and the history of the West, we have observed, is virtually the sum of the major instances) the fact of rivalry might itself be concealed by a denial that any such warfare was going on. So Nietzsche, Heidegger, or Merleau-Ponty could all be read as in their analogous ways, aggressive or benign, in implicit polemic against Paul about whom the body belongs to, though the disciples of these contestants need not realize as much.[44] And on the more prominent psychic as opposed to the sarkic side, one version or other of what may be called a carnal *I am* has regularly placed itself over against its more or less obvious spiritual rival. So Descartes or Hegel or Emerson or Wallace Stevens, to mention another possible sequence of names, continue to remain typical precisely to the extent that their testimony in reverse to

---

[44]I am reminded of these connections by David Michael Levin's enthusiastic account of the "recovery" of the body by the three thinkers mentioned in his *Body's Recollection of Being: Phenomenological Psychology and the Deconstruction of Nihilism* (London: Routledge & Kegan Paul, 1985). As the subtitle indicates, Levin's survey is almost painfully up to date. But it does not occur to him even to mention Paul.

the person they more or less deliberately intend to replace is properly estimated. The subsequent critical demolition of precisely this multiple Antichrist has not proved as sensitive as it might have been to the agon out of which "the subject" it attacks has had to emerge, though this too might also be enlisted as one more species of testimony at still another remove. Derrida is not quite an evangelist, but he is certainly a hammer of heresy. Whether directly or indirectly, then, explicit counterpresences cannot help but reflect an implicit presence, as bodies the body—less innocently in most such cases, but all the more formidably, as too much history by now has shown.

An introductory formulation for any general conclusion to this argument would accordingly still need to be that there is nothing but the body. That formula could provide a topic sentence for any imaginable paragraph in support of or even in contradiction to what could otherwise be put down. For everything, positive or negative, that might seem expressive at all could in the end be understood, it is accordingly proposed, as some variation on this motif. There is nothing, *tout court,* might be one. Or, there is nothing but: facts, ideas, performances, lines of print, what have you. But all of these are, insofar as they are at all, still readable in the end as intimations of the whole, whether that is affirmed or denied. We do not really avoid what we are all the while being presented with, however hard we sometimes try.

What we are always free to do, then, is follow out whatever may be implied by the action that has placed us where we may indeed find ourselves. And perhaps our best clue here as well as our last is a necessity that is also a privilege. For to recognize the whole even from a distance is in proportion, as we have also seen, to reproduce it. That mode of apprehension is in fact one more manifestation of what could then be formulated as a corollary to the fundamental proposition that there is nothing but the body. The body there is nothing other than is bound to show itself always and everywhere as a reproduction of itself, which is already, we will also repeatedly be discovering, a succession of reproductions. Metamorphosis is not merely mythical or illusory or even subordinate but the norm. Being is revealed in the act of becoming, over and over—until we too are included within the change. This is what the body is up to: what proves it alive, before or after death. So it reproduces itself daily on the scale of the individual as each of us breathes, walks about, gazes at whatever attracts our attention, eats and drinks, sleeps—not to mention labors in some field or factory, though that may be no better than a desk. It reproduces itself on the scale of the couple as desire and the desirable from one generation to another. It reproduces itself imaginatively by such re-creations of itself in one medium or another as we are sometimes able to call works of art. It reproduces itself in thought as so many propositions, that is, in terms of ideas, which as such have to be abstracted from their respective bodies.

Metaphors, we have already observed, are implicit propositions; propositions, it is equally possible to appreciate, must also be metaphors, which repeatedly demonstrate the conversion of one body into another: A *is* B, we say, as if to proclaim the inevitable metamorphosis in verb and noun alike. What else would affirmation affirm? In all these ways the body does not cease to reproduce itself, even on the scale of a galaxy or a star—and, as far as we know yet, perhaps of the universe itself. That is what is going on, which is why, presumably, Jesus may be found doing it too. All parables are intertranslatable, we might therefore generalize from his case, because all are sooner or later parabolic of the same truth. The Kingdom is near precisely in this "mystery": the synonomy, that is, of its elements.

No wonder the Eucharist proves to be not out of the way but in our way: all too obvious indeed. It is in this respect, as in every other, absolutely typical. By way of just this action Jesus demonstrates what there is to believe in and therefore whatever may be desired or contemplated or taken for granted or hoped for: that which is, as philosophers before and after could say, and no mistake. In order to do as much, he has already had to step over, as it were, upon the other shore, from which to re-present the full truth of the matter to those of us who otherwise have to remain here in this world. Thus he embodies the body. This is *his* task. It follows that what he reveals need not be thought of as something absolutely unexampled. It is fairer, I would guess, to think of him as moving into coincidence with what had and has ever since always been the case. Creation, after all, is not new. But what his action also makes clear is that this creation is not static but active. Metamorphosis is the *is* of every other affirmation because it is already the copula for what we have just been calling the principal proposition: that there is nothing but the body. The body exists, that is, by turning into something else—which is still as much the body as ever, and so on, in *saecula saeculorum*. Reproduction reproduces.

Which would not mean, of course, that every instance even of the most complete or cosmic metamorphosis would need to be extraordinarily solemn or dignified. On the contrary, the memorable demonstrations may as ever be quite casual, though it can help if these too have some connection with the Eucharist. The other day, for instance, I buried a fish. A goldfish in the tank in the corner of the common room at the nursing home had died. The pale little body clung to an airpipe, mouth open, eyes blank. It seemed unsafe for the other fish to leave it there and unfair to the creature that had died to look for a trash can in the kitchen. So when we left after the communion service I reached inside and scooped it out. As I walked out to and sat in the car on our way back to campus, I held the limp chilly comma of flesh not so much in my hand as on my fingers. When we reached the bridge over a gorge on our drive up the hill, I asked my friend to slow down. It was unexpectedly easy to open the window on my side and fling the silvery body up over the railing of the bridge so it would fall, I hoped and believed, into the creek far below or at least on the rocks alongside. That was where it belonged. Why? It seemed to me that I didn't want some confusion of civilized practice to draw a line between what had once been alive and, so far as possible, wild, and the rest of the world. To throw this little body into the nearest approximation to unimprovable nature was then to perform an act of liberation after the fact at least. In death the goldfish might unite with the universe as a whole without any artificial barrier between, whether that was the glass wall of a tank or the skin of some green plastic bag. Decomposition would go forward uninterruptedly, while other creatures I could not predict might yet consume the remains. That would be the relevant metamorphosis in this case. Death is how the individual rejoins the cosmos, after all; it should, one could feel, be unqualified for oneself as well as those other creatures in which one has invested a certain quantity of imagination. I had turned off the noisy motor of their tank for our service often enough to give me at least that much interest in the fate of these fish. A singular body rejoins the whole: that seemed the point of the event.

And why else might such a gesture have seemed appropriate? Because, it also occurred to me, the flesh has an advantage over the rest of us to just this extent. Here was how our bodies could anticipate what we know we do not know. For we cannot otherwise get so far, even in prophecy—much less in thought, as we have just repeatedly observed, or even in imagination. Death and burial, then, in or out of quotation marks, might already constitute as good a parable of what there was still to do as we were ever likely to get. We are not yet quite so advanced in the Spirit as we have all got to be sooner or later in the flesh. So much is still ahead of us. In death the individual body can transcend itself while still remaining no more than itself. In which case the fate of the fish was perhaps already as good a figure as I was likely to find for the "Jesus thought" I had not yet been able to entertain in other terms. To be sure, it was cast in a language I could not translate either, though sooner or later we must each repeat what is being said. What will happen to us anyway could in that case amount to a sufficient version of the last possibility. This seemed a conclusion worth arriving at, at least for the time being.